St. Charles Theatre

SIXTH NIGHT OF

MISS CHARLOTTE

CUSHMAN

Who, in consequence of the rapturous applause bestowed upon her last Monday Evening by the largest audience of the season, will again appear as

MEG MERRILIES!

Wednesday Evenidg, Jan. 29th, 1851,

Will be performed, the Operatic Drama of

☞ GUY

MANNERING

Or, The Gipsy's Prophecy.

MEG MERRILIES,	MISS C. CUSHMAN
Col. Mannering,	Mr. J. M. Weston
Henry Bertram,	T. Bishop
Dirk Hatterick,	W. G. Jones
Dandie Dinmont,	DeBar
Gilbert Glossin,	Huntley
Bailey Mucklethrift,	Watson
Dominie Sampson,	H.S.Chapman
Gabriel,	M. Smith
Sebastian,	Uhl
Jock Jabos,	Fredericks
Barnes,	Geddes
Sergeant Macrae,	Everett
Franco	Miss Schoolcraft
Gipsies, Sailors, Soldiers, Gentlemen of the Company	
Lucy Bertram,	Mrs. W. G. Jones
Julia Mannering,	H. S. Chapman
Flora,	Shea
Mrs. McCandlish,	Russell
Gipsy Girl,	Miss Hill
Gipsies and Peasants,	Ladies of the Company

All the Original Music will be given, together with Introduced Songs, by Mr. T. Bishop.

To conclude with the interesting Drama in 2 acts, entitled the

MAID OF CROISSY!

Serjeant Austerlitz,	Mr. W. M. Leman
Walter,	Boswell
Conscripts, by the Gentlemen of the Company.	
Therese,	Mrs. Parker
Manette,	Chapman

Thursday—Seventh night of

MISS CHARLOTTE CUSHMAN,

When she will appear as

ROSALIND!

In Shakspeare's Comedy of

AS YOU LIKE IT.

LONDON ASSURANCE

Will be performed during the engagement of MISS CHARLOTTE CUSHMAN, who will appear (FOR ONE NIGHT ONLY,) in the character of

LADY GAY SPANKER,

As originally performed by her at the Park Theatre, on the first production of the Comedy in America.

Sunday Night next is assigned for the

Benefit of Mrs. Parker,

When a Very Attractive Entertainment will be announced.

PRICES OF ADMISSION:

Dress Circles, Private Boxes and Parquette	$1
Free Persons of Color in Parquette Boxes	75 cts
Upper or Third Tier	50 cts
Free Persons of Color in third tier right hand,	25 cts
Gallery	25 cts

THEATRE.

Mr. Field as Richard!

Mr. Sol Smith

As the Three Singles!!

THIS EVENING,

Friday, January 16, 1835,

Will be presented, (first time in two years) Shakspeare's Tragedy of

Richard the Third.

RICHARD,	Mr. J. M. FIELD.
EARL OF RICHMOND,	SPENCER,
KING HENRY VI.	SULLIVAN,
DUKE OF BUCKINGHAM,	RICE,
LORD STANLEY,	GAY,
CATESBY,	HUNT,
RATCLIFFE,	FLAGG,
LORD MAYOR,	SOL SMITH,
NORFOLK,	SULLIVAN,
TIRRELL,	SINCLAIR,
PRINCE OF WALES,	Master L. SMITH,
DUKE OF YORK,	M. SMITH.
QUEEN,	Mrs. SMITH,
LADY ANNE,	SULLIVAN,
DUCHESS OF YORK,	GAY,

To conclude with the eccentric Farce of

Three and Deuce,

OR,

Which is Which?

Pertinax Single,	Mr. SOL SMITH!
Peregrine Single,	SOL SMITH!!
Percival Single,	SOL SMITH!!!
Justice Touchit,	Mr. GAY,
Humphrey Grizzle,	HUNT,
Frank Woodbine,	SPENCER,
McFloggin,	SULLIVAN,
Renard,	FLAGG,
Tippy,	RICE,
Cramp,	JONES,
Emily,	Mrs. SMITH,
Phœbe,	GAY,
Taffline,	SULLIVAN,

☞ The public are respectfully informed that the justly celebrated Comedian,

Mr. H. J. FINN,

is engaged for FOUR NIGHTS. Due notice will be given of his arrival and first appearance.

☞ Doors open at 6, and the Curtain to rise a quarter before 7 o'clock, precisely.

☞ For the accommodation of the public, Tickets will be kept for sale at the two principal Hotels, besides at the Box Office of the Theatre.

☞ No person unconnected with the Theatre will be admitted behind the scenes, under any circumstances.

☞ Smoking positively prohibited, except in the Bar-Room.

☞ No postponement on any account; and to prevent any misunderstanding, no Song, Dance, or any other performance whatever will be given, which is not announced in the Bills, or incidental in the Play or Farce advertised.

THEATER
in the
ANTE BELLUM
SOUTH

1815-1861

by
JAMES H. DORMON, JR.

The University of
North Carolina Press
CHAPEL HILL

For Mahlon and his mother and
all of his grandparents

PREFACE

IN MANY WAYS THE PERIOD BETWEEN THE END OF THE WAR OF 1812 and the beginning of the American Civil War saw the high-water mark of American theater history. The number of playhouses devoted almost exclusively to legitimate drama has never since been exceeded, despite the multifold increase in population and the proliferation of urban communities since 1865. Public interest in plays and players has never since been greater. Some students of the American theater even contend that the mid-nineteenth century was the golden age of American stage artistry, at least if judged by the quality of the acting in the period.[1] The theater was the most important form of commercial entertainment available to the people of that remote time before the coming of electronic communications and organized athletics.

But the ante bellum period, in addition to marking a brilliant era of American stage history, also saw the American theater become

1. Arthur Hornblow writes: "It was a period of extraordinary brilliance that has never been equalled since. . . ." *A History of the Theatre in America From Its Beginnings to the Present Time* (Philadelphia: J. B. Lippincott Company, 1919), I, 299–300. See also John Ranken Towse, *Sixty Years of the Theater. An Old Critic's Memories* (New York: Funk and Wagnalls Company, 1916), pp. ix-x; Margaret G. Mayorga, *A Short History of the American Drama. Commentaries on Plays Prior to 1920* (New York: Dodd, Mead, and Company, 1932), p. 137.

[vii]

a truly national institution. North, South, East, and West, wherever an urban community existed, however small and primitive, a theater was almost certain to be found and actors and actresses certain to go. Yet the authors of general theater histories fail to treat the provincial theater of the period beyond brief observation that it existed. They then focus attention on the centers of theatrical activity in the Northeast, and there the focus remains, at least until the romantic story of the California stage demands telling.[2] Clearly, this approach, though understandable in view of space limitations, leads to a truncated picture of national theater history in the vital "middle period." A major distortion results from the neglect of the most important of the provinces—the so-called Old South. The primary purposes of the present study are to bring to light the details of theatrical development of the region and to evaluate the role of the South in the history of the nation's ante bellum theater.

Before anything meaningful may be said of Southern theater, however, it is necessary to establish what is to be meant by the "South" and what by "theater." Both terms are vague; both must be defined somewhat arbitrarily. "South" as used here refers to the group of states that ultimately constituted the Southern Confederacy plus the border states of Kentucky and Missouri. "Theater" refers to the acted drama of whatever literary merit, primarily English-language and primarily professional.

A word of justification on each count:

It might reasonably be asked why the South here includes Missouri and Kentucky but not Maryland. The answer lies in the structure of the theatrical circuits of the period. Baltimore, cultural center of Maryland, was from the colonial period to the Civil War tied to Philadelphia and Washington in the middle-state theatrical circuit. The managers and companies who were active in one city also played in and controlled the others.[3] Missouri, on the other hand, had as its

2. Among the standard theater histories treatment of Southern theatrical activity is fullest in Hornblow, *History of the Theatre*, and Mary Caroline Crawford, *The Romance of the American Theatre* (Boston: Little, Brown, and Company, 1913). Both studies are noticeably dated though generally sound.

3. See Thomas Clark Pollock, *The Philadelphia Theatre in the Eighteenth Century. Together with the Day Book of the Same Period* (Philadelphia: University of Pennsylvania Press, 1933), pp. 56–57; see also Reese Davis James, *Old Drury of Philadelphia. A History of the Philadelphia Stage 1800–1835 . . .* (Philadelphia: University of Pennsylvania Press, 1932), p. vii and *passim*; Oscar George Sonneck, *Early Opera in America* (New York: G. Schirmer, 1915), p. 166. Sonneck refers to Baltimore as "merely an operatic suburb of Philadelphia."

cultural metropolis St. Louis which, as will be seen, was tied to New Orleans and Mobile throughout the period as the northern terminus of a distinctly Southern, or more correctly Southwestern, circuit.

"Theater" as here defined is certain to give rise to questions. Is opera to be included? Minstrelsy? The circus? Vaudeville and variety entertainment? The answer in each of these cases would be a qualified no. Unless a given performance included a play (and circuses and variety shows frequently did) it would not qualify as theater for purposes of this study. Amateur and foreign-language theater receive some attention here but only of a secondary nature. The necessity of limiting the scope of the study is the only justification for slighting these important phases of theater history.

Another more fundamental question inevitably arises in discussing the subject of the theater in the South. Granting the overwhelmingly rural-agrarian character of Southern society, how could the theater, a profoundly urban institution, have existed at all? The effort to answer this poser involves recognizing the relativity of the urban concept. It is perfectly obvious that the Old South had towns; indeed the plantation-based economy required towns. Central points of exchange of goods and services were essential to an economy founded on the production and distribution of a staple commodity. Only a society in a truly frontier condition is without urban services. As the nineteenth century advanced and the South continued its evolution from frontier to a complex plantation-farm economy, the emergence of towns continued apace. Virtually every area of population concentration came by 1860 to be served by an essentially urban community.

The population of these towns was naturally small. But population figures are deceiving in this case. The towns provided certain goods and services to a great many who did not live in town but who had immediate access to town or who were transients. Both of these categories were large.[4] Urban services were available to a far greater proportion of the Southern population than is generally believed. Among the services provided by the towns were insurance, bank-

4. For example, the population of Macon, Georgia, was only 5,720 in 1850, but the population of Bibb County, which Macon served, was 12,699. See U. S. Department of State, *The Seventh Census of the United States: 1850* (Washington: Robert Armstrong, Public Printer, 1853), p. 366; James Dunwoody Brownson DeBow, *Statistical View of the United States . . . Being a Compendium of the Seventh Census* (Washington: A. O. P. Nicholson, Public Printer, 1854), p. 206. This was a typical case.

ing and credit facilities, medical, legal, and spiritual counsel, and all available forms of commercial amusement. Chief among the last group was the theater.

The organization of this study falls into two general divisions, each with its own special concern. The one is concerned with the origins and development of theater in the ante bellum South. Specific chapters treat the colonial and early national foundations, subregional development following 1815, and the compass of theatrical activity on the eve of the Civil War. The primary concern of this section is the development and ultimate extent of theatrical activity in the South. But in light of what has been said of urbanization, there is also an underlying purpose. To follow the development of theatrical activity necessitates following the continuing process of urbanization. Theatrical development may even be employed as a gauge of urban development. And the final survey of Southern theatrical conditions in the late 1850's reveals a substantially developed urban structure in the South.[5]

The second major concern of this study is the nature of the theater in the South. Attention is here directed to such questions as "What were performances like?" "What people attended the theater?" and "What plays and players did they see?" If the initial concern of this study is with what was largely theater history, the second is devoted primarily to social and intellectual history. It is possible to determine at least generally what plays were most popular in the Old South. An important part of this second section of the study is devoted to an analysis of these most popular plays and types of plays in an effort to ascertain what their popularity reveals about the region and the times.

The final chapter offers some conclusions, necessarily tentative and provisional, on the significance of theater in the ante bellum South. It should be noted here in the preface, anticipating the most important of these conclusions, that in no fundamental way did the theater in the South differ from that anywhere else in the country. There was no "Southern" theater. There was only that portion of American theater that had its development in the South.

5. It should be emphasized that "urban" as used here refers only to settled communities providing certain goods and services characteristic to cities or towns. It does not imply urbanity, cosmopolitanism, or even refinement, though elements of these qualities did exist in the urban South.

Sources for this study have been varied in nature and frequently ephemeral.[6] Contemporary newspapers were of great importance, particularly those of the theatrical centers of the four major sub-regions: New Orleans, Louisiana; St. Louis, Missouri; Richmond, Virginia; and Charleston, South Carolina. The *New York Spirit of the Times* (in its various incarnations) was invaluable, particularly in placing the theater of the South in national perspective. Manuscript correspondence of some of the Southern managers, notably Sol Smith, have been preserved and were indispensable, as were the original playbill files in several major repositories of American theatricana. Published diaries, memoirs, and travel accounts of actors, managers, and playgoers yielded much that was valuable.

But another type of source was important enough to rate special attention here: the laboriously compiled theatrical annals of various cities of the South. Naturally, these annals are of varying quality, but in form they are similar, consisting usually of a brief narrative account of the theatrical fortunes of the town in question, followed by a day-by-day record of every performance recorded in the contemporary press. I have not hesitated to cite the best of these chronicles on points of performance data. Their value to me cannot be overstated.

In the long course of researching and writing a work of this nature, one receives the assistance of many people (as many as possible). Acknowledgment of assistance received is a convention happily undertaken by most grateful scholars, certainly by this one. I would like first to add my name to that long list of fledgling historians who have expressed their boundless thanks to Professor Fletcher Melvin Green of The University of North Carolina at Chapel Hill, not only for his interest, encouragement, and assistance in the preparation of the project at hand, but for the measureless benefit they have derived from their association with him. I have no doubt that each of them felt the same gratitude that I now do. Among Professor Green's colleagues at The University of North Carolina at Chapel Hill, I would like to express my appreciation to Professors Frank W. Klingberg and Hugh T. Lefler for their aid

6. Chap. I is based almost entirely upon secondary sources. The story of the establishment of the American stage has often been told, most recently and most satisfactorily by Hugh Franklin Rankin in his *The Theater in Colonial America* (Chapel Hill: The University of North Carolina Press, 1965).

and comfort. I am also much indebted to Professors Paul T. Nolan and Amos E. Simpson of the University of Southwestern Louisiana for their valuable advice and assistance.

Pursuit of fugitive sources has necessitated great dependence on a number of librarians, more than there is space here to mention individually. Special thanks are due to Miss Helen D. Willard, curatrix of the Harvard Theater Collection, Harvard College Library; Mrs. Frances H. Stadler, archivist of the Missouri Historical Society; and the entire reference staff of the Louis Round Wilson Library, The University of North Carolina at Chapel Hill.

Finally, the value of a wife who combines the talents of a trustworthy research assistant, a constructive if argumentative critic, a hawk-eyed proofreader, and a slow-but-sure typist is virtually unlimited. I have such a wife. Thanks to her, too.

CONTENTS

ILLUSTRATIONS

Between pages 80 and 81

THEATER IN THE ANTE BELLUM SOUTH
1815–1861

CHAPTER I

THE COLONIAL
AND EARLY
NATIONAL
FOUNDATION

1.

IT IS DOUBTFUL WHETHER THE INCEPTION OF ANY SOCIAL INSTITUTION ever came less auspiciously than did that of the American theater. On August 27, 1665,[1] at Cowle's Tavern (near Pungoteague) in Accomac County, Virginia, three local citizens, by name Cornelius Watkinson, Philip Howard, and William Darby, presented a play. The tavern production was intended as a simple diversion, a break in the monotony of a long afternoon. It was called *Ye Bare and Ye Cubb*. There is no way of knowing how successful it was, but at least one person was not amused. On complaint of Edward Martin the entertainers were brought before the county court and ordered

1. A strong case may be made for dating the beginning of American theater in 1598 and placing it in what is now west Texas. On April 30, 1598, a play by Marcos Farfan de los Godos, a Spanish captain of the guard, was presented on the banks of the Rio Grande. The occasion was a religious ceremony in the camp of Conquistador Juan de Oñate, who had just taken formal possession of all of New Mexico. See Winifred Johnston, "Early Theatre in the Spanish Borderlands," *Mid-America*, XIII, n.s. II (Oct., 1930), 125–28.

to repeat the performance, in costume. The verdict of the court reflected Restoration tolerance; the three were found to be "not guilty of fault," and Martin was required to pay court costs.[2]

In all honesty, the *Ye Bare* production cannot be claimed to be of more than antiquarian interest. It led to no further theatrical activity, hence established no real theater tradition. Nor did the next recorded stage performance—the "pastoral colloquy" recited publicly by a group of William and Mary students in 1702.[3] The third performance, however, was of somewhat greater significance, if for no other reason than it marked the first appearance of a professional actor in the protohistory of the American stage. It is also significant that he appeared in Charleston, South Carolina, thereby opening the theater annals of that theatrically notable city.

Anthony Aston, a British actor-playwright, adventurer, and soldier of fortune, found himself in Charles-Town, South Carolina, in January, 1703. He had just returned from a military expedition, having accompanied Governor James Moore as a mercenary in the disastrous British-colonial sortie against St. Augustine.[4] Years later, in the autobiographical preface to his clever *Fool's Opera*, he recalled his Charleston experiences in an oft-quoted but ever-appealing passage: "Well; we arriv'd in *Charles-Town*, full of Lice, Shame, Poverty, Nakedness and Hunger:—I turn'd *Player* and Poet, and wrote one Play on the Subject of the Country. . . ."[5] Aston then went to Virginia, where he may have performed, and to New York, where he certainly did.[6] But though Aston may have introduced colonial Charlestonians to "theater" of sorts, he did not establish theater there. Nor did anyone else for years to come.

Following the Aston appearance fifteen years passed without producing another recorded theatrical event. Sparseness of popula-

2. Rankin, *Theater in Colonial America*, p. 11.

3. Oral Sumner Coad and Edwin Mims, *The American Stage*, Vol. XIV of Ralph Henry Gabriel, *et al.* (eds.), *The Pageant of America. A Pictorial History of the United States* (New Haven: Yale University Press, 1929), p. 11.

4. Rankin, *Theater in Colonial America*, p. 6; Sonneck, *Early Opera*, p. 7. Eola Willis clearly errs in dating the Aston appearance "about 1730"; *The Charleston Stage in the XVIII Century. With Social Settings of the Time* (Columbia, S. C.: The State Company, 1924), p. 5.

5. Anthony Aston, *The Fool's Opera; or, The Taste of the Age* (London: Printed for T. Payne at the Crown in Paternoster-Row, n.d. [*ca.* 1731], p. 20. No copy of the play has ever been discovered.

6. George Clinton Densmore Odell, *Annals of the New York Stage* (New York: Columbia University Press, 1927–1949), I, 7–8.

tion and scarcity of leisure rendered the North American colonies incapable of supporting commercial amusements of any form, even in those colonies where religious attitudes might have permitted such frivolity. But in 1716 the first American theatrical entrepreneur made an effort to gain profit by entertaining the public. In Williamsburg, Virginia, William Levingston undertook to build a theater.

The fact that Levingston was, among other things, a part-time operator of a dancing school indicates a certain cultural maturity in the old Virginia capital. In September of 1715, in order to expand the facilities of his school, Levingston purchased the services of indentured servants Charles and Mary Stagg.[7] The Staggs appear to have had some experience on the London stage, both as dancers and as actors. William Levingston decided to utilize that experience. In 1716 he released the Staggs from their indentures and contracted with them to operate the theater he was planning to build.[8]

The York County records reveal that Levingston agreed to build "at his own proper Costs & Charge . . . One good Substantiall house commodious for Acting such Plays as shall be thought fitt to be Acted there."[9] Following several delays, Levingston fulfilled his bargain. At some time between 1716 and 1721 the building, almost certainly America's first theater, was completed. By contrast with the rococo ornamentation so typical of later American playhouses, this one was a plain wooden building 86 feet long by 30 feet wide, probably painted red, with a shingled roof and five windows.[10]

Virtually nothing is known of the early productions in this playhouse.[11] Commercially it was a failure. A performance of Susanna Centlivre's *The Busy-Body* by a group of local amateurs in January, 1736, was recorded in the local press and was apparently well received, as were several other amateur productions. But Williamsburg was too small at this time to support a resident stock company, even when the General Assembly was in session. Prior to December 4,

7. Rankin, *Theater in Colonial America*, p. 12.
8. *Ibid.*; Robert Hunt Land, "The First Williamsburg Theatre," *The William and Mary Quarterly*, 3rd ser. V (July, 1948), 362.
9. Quoted in Rankin, *Theater in Colonial America*, p. 13.
10. *Ibid.*, p. 14. The precise date of the completion of this building has not been determined. Land contends that it was between Nov. 5, 1716, and May 29, 1721, "with the evidence pointing to its erection closer to the former than to the latter date"; "Williamsburg Theatre," p. 362.
11. Mary Johnston's sentimental romance *Audrey* deals imaginatively with its operation.

1745, the building was purchased by a group of local luminaries, and these "Gentleman Subscribers for the Play House" later donated the building to the town for public use.[12] But however short-lived the experiment, colonial America had had a real theater devoted to productions of legitimate drama.

Practically all of the sporadic theatrical activity recorded before 1732 had occurred in the Southern colonies, a fact that may or may not be of significance. The year 1732, however, saw a noteworthy event in the North. A real theater company performed for a season in New York, in a playhouse advertised as the "new Theatre."[13] The importance of this event to theater in the South lies in the fact that the company in New York, or part of it, may have been the one to appear in Charleston, South Carolina, in January, 1735,[14] play a brief season, and encourage construction of the first Dock Street Theater the following year.

The opening performance of the Charleston company, probably an amateur group though possibly in part professional, was advertised in the *South Carolina Gazette* of January 18, 1735. "On Friday the 24th instant, in the Court-Room," announced the *Gazette*, "will be attempted a Tragedy called 'The Orphan, or the Unhappy Marriage.'"[15] Tickets for the performance were soon to be made available at 40s. each, a price which indicates profit for someone even though the medium of exchange was depreciated South Carolina currency. If the intention of the promoters was to donate the proceeds to charity, a practice quite common later, no mention was made of such an intention in the press.

From all indications the play was well attended and popular. It was repeated the following Tuesday, and in all received four performances during this first Charleston "season." In addition, the local company brought out John Dryden's *The Spanish Fryar* for two performances, Colley Cibber's ballad opera *Flora, or Hob in the Well*, and a harlequinade, for a total of seven evenings' entertainment.[16]

12. Land, "Williamsburg Theatre," pp. 372–73. The civic-minded group included John Blair, Benjamin Harrison, Robert Tucker, George Braxton, Thomas Bray, Carter Burwell, and Beverly Randolph.

13. Rankin, *Theater in Colonial America*, p. 24.

14. Hornblow so contends; *History of the Theatre*, I, 50.

15. Quoted in Willis, *Charleston Stage*, p. 9. *The Orphan* is a Thomas Otway tragedy. Willis suggests that use of the court house indicates legal acceptance of the theater in South Carolina.

16. *Ibid.*, p. 16; Rankin, *Theater in Colonial America*, p. 26. It is generally accepted that the *Flora* production was the first operatic performance in the mainland colonies. See Sonneck, *Early Opera*, p. 12.

The final performance occurred late in March of 1735, by which time the impresario-apparent, one Charles Shepheard, had already solicited pledges to guarantee the appearance of the players for the enrichment of Charleston's next social season.[17]

So successful had been the initial efforts of the Charleston company that some unknown local entrepreneur, probably Shepheard again, saw potential profit in the ownership of a real theater. Public support was so strong that stock sales proved adequate to finance the playhouse. The *South Carolina Gazette* of January 31, 1736, was able to announce the proposed opening of the "new Theatre in Dock Street" for February 12. George Farquhar's ribald comedy *The Recruiting Officer* was selected as the opening production.

The original Dock Street Theater housed only this one performance. Immediately following the *Recruiting Officer* production Dock Street was renamed Queen Street, and the new theater became known as the Theater in Queen-Street. The house was divided into the conventional boxes, pit, and gallery, and six performances were presented during its first season of operations.[18] It then closed for the summer, reopening the following fall for five more performances. The close of the final performance of the fall season, 1736, marked the end of the theater in Charleston for another eighteen years.

After such auspicious beginnings, it might reasonably be wondered why the theater failed in Charleston as it had earlier in Williamsburg. The answer is not readily apparent, but it is significant that only six weeks prior to the final Charleston performance John Wesley had preached at St. Philip's Church.[19] The so-called Great Awakening had arrived in 1736. Public interest in the theater clearly ran counter to the ideals of the fervidly religious, and their new-found zeal proved too powerful a force to be countered. The theater in the mainland colonies, North and South, went into a temporary state of quiescence.

2.

As the great religious fervor waned the theater reappeared. The interlude gave the colonial towns time to grow, as much in cultural maturity as in population and area. Such growth was necessary if

17. Rankin, *Theater in Colonial America*, p. 27.
18. *Ibid.*, pp. 27–28.
19. *Ibid.*, p. 29. George Whitefield held forth in Charleston frequently in the years that followed.

the towns were ever to support professional theater. The next emergence of theatrical activity would begin the sustained, continuous history of the American stage. Two important touring companies, the Murray-Kean troupe and the notable Hallam Company, appeared almost simultaneously, offering theater of a quality never before available in America. Both companies centered their operations in the South.

The origin of the strolling company of Walter Murray and Thomas Kean is not clear, nor is the immediate background of its founders.[20] They appear to have been actor-managers of limited experience who organized a company of "comedians" of no experience, then set out to tour America. They tried their luck first in Philadelphia in August of 1749. Finding a pronounced anti-theater bias there, Murray and Kean took their raw troupe to New York, where they met with somewhat greater success.[21] But New York of 1750 was unable to support a full stock company for any sustained period. Late in the summer of 1751, Murray and the strolling "Comedians from New York" (as they were to become known) departed for Williamsburg, Virginia.[22]

An active movement was already underway to build a new playhouse in Williamsburg to receive the troupe. The *Virginia Gazette* of August 29, 1751, announced that permission had been obtained of Acting Governor Richard Lee to build the new theater. The *Gazette* further proposed that the house be built "by way of Subscription, each Subscriber advancing a Pistole [$3.80] to be entitled to a Box Ticket for the first night's Diversion."[23] There was sufficient enthusiasm for the project in and around Williamsburg to insure adequate financial support. The crude theater opened October 21, 1751, with a performance of *Richard III* by the Murray company.[24]

Little more is known of the first season in the new playhouse. Audiences proved limited, and financial difficulties soon necessitated further strolling by the Murray troupe. Virginia got her first the-

20. Theater historian Glenn Hughes follows Hornblow in asserting that they were English actors from the West Indies. Glenn Hughes, *A History of the American Theatre, 1700–1950* (New York: Samuel French, 1951), p. 12; Hornblow, *History of the Theatre*, I, 55.

21. Hughes, *American Theatre*, p. 12.

22. Rankin, *Theater in Colonial America*, p. 35. Thomas Kean had given up his share in the ownership of the company.

23. Quoted in Hornblow, *History of the Theatre*, I, 75–76; see also Hughes, *American Theatre*, p. 15.

24. Rankin, *Theater in Colonial America*, p. 37.

atrical tour, with Norfolk heading the tour itinerary. The company played there about a month. Then came Suffolk and Petersburg, followed by a return engagement in Williamsburg early in 1752. The comedians visited Hobb's Hole (Tappahannock) in the spring and arrived in Fredericksburg in time for the June Fair.[25] There the Virginia tour ended. Murray and Company departed for Maryland and none too soon, for competition was coming. The Hallams were on their way to Virginia.

Murray's Virginia tour was important in demonstrating that a strolling company could sustain itself in the towns of the South. But it was more important for what it promised than for what it fulfilled in making quality theater available to the colonials. The arrival of the Hallam company, or the "London Company of Comedians" marked the fulfilment of that promise. A consistent theater tradition in America commenced with the coming of the Hallams. Prior to 1752, theatrical activity north and south had been fitful and sporadic. Thereafter it was to be constant.

Theater historians almost uniformly agree that the Southern colonies were more receptive to the coming of theatrical entertainment than were the Northern or middle colonies. They cite the self-styled "aristocracy" of the South, a class which always endeavored to imitate the fashions of England, including fashionable amusements. They mention the absence of a strong Puritan (or puritanical) element, the existence of an established Anglican church in Virginia, and generally a more tolerant and hedonistic "Cavalier" spirit on the part of Southern colonists.[26] They argue that Virginia and Maryland were the only colonies that did not pass legislation prohibiting theaters.[27] They point to the Southern theatrical firsts: The first play performed in America; the first performance by college students; the first professional actor; and the first theater.[28] All of these points are matters of record. But whether they actually prove that the

25. *Ibid.*, pp. 38–40. George Washington saw the company perform in Fredericksburg.

26. See, for example, Coad and Mims, *American Stage*, p. 9; Hornblow, *History of the Theatre*, I, 24, 78; Montrose Jonas Moses, *Famous Actor-Families in America* (New York: Thomas Y. Crowell and Company, 1906), p. 7; Rankin, *Theater in Colonial America*, pp. 10, 25, 102.

27. Rankin, *Theater in Colonial America*, p. 7.

28. Susanne Ketchum Sherman, "Thomas Wade West, Theatrical Impressario, 1790–1799," *The William and Mary Quarterly*, 3rd ser. IX (Jan., 1952), 13.

South was more receptive to the theater is open to doubt. The choice of these arguments is selective; there are other considerations.

Prior to 1752, theatrical activity was too rare to form the basis for any general conclusions concerning acceptibility of the theater. By 1752, when such activity began to be more consistent, puritanical thinking had abated enough outside the South to permit theatrical development, notably in New York. Though Virginia and Maryland did not pass anti-theater legislation, North Carolina, South Carolina, and Georgia did do so. Organized religious opposition did exist in the South, and continued to exist, exerting a powerful negative influence on the theater throughout the nineteenth century. Finally, when the Hallam company first sought permission to perform in Virginia, it was denied. If there were distinct differences in attitude between the South and the other regions, they were differences only in degree, except perhaps in the Puritan bastions of the Northeast. Attitudes toward the theater and similar diversions tended to shift within each major section, frequently in direct proportion to the heat generated by visiting evangelist exhorters.

But when Lewis Hallam decided to attempt to recoup his family's sagging fortunes by means of a colonial theater tour, he believed that Virginia was likely to be more receptive to his efforts. Years after the arrival of the Hallams, Lewis Hallam, Jr., twelve years old at the time of the company's crossing, recalled that the decision to begin operations in Virginia rather than elsewhere was based primarily on the religious situation. The Anglicans were considered more liberal than the Puritans of New England or the Quakers of Pennsylvania. The Virginians were thought to be more fun-loving than the Dutch of New York.[29] Virginians were, after all, of "Cavalier" stock.

Early in May of 1752, the Hallam troupe departed from England aboard the "Charming Sally," bound for Yorktown, Virginia. The troupe was led by Lewis Hallam the elder, brother of William Hallam, the bankrupt manager of a minor playhouse in Goodman's

29. William Dunlap, *A History of the American Theatre and Anecdotes of the Principal Actors* (2nd ed.; New York: Burt Franklin, 1963), I, 12–13. The Dunlap *History* was originally published in 1832 and is something of a primary source of theatricana. Lewis Hallam, Jr., gave Dunlap a first-hand account of the decision forty years after the event, but there is no reason to doubt its general veracity.

Fields, London. Included in the company were Hallam's wife and three children and seven or eight other players, bound together in the venture by joint ownership of the troupe. All of the adults seem to have been experienced on the London stage, although the degree of excellence the company could claim is open to question.[30] Doubtless they were the best-organized, best-trained (they had rehearsed on the decks of the "Charming Sally"), and in all respects the most competent company yet to appear in colonial America.

On June 2, 1752, the Hallam company landed in Yorktown and immediately set out for Williamsburg. Their arrival in the Virginia capital was hailed by the local press. The *Virginia Gazette* of June 12, 1752, noted that the company was well equipped with "Scenes, Cloaths and Decorations . . . all entirely new, extremely rich, and finished in the highest Taste," to the end that "Ladies and Gentlemen may depend on being entertain'd in as polite a Manner as at the Theatres in London. . . ."[31] But the company did not open at once. They first needed permission of Lieutenant Governor Robert Dinwiddie.

The Virginia Council had been in session on June 13, 1752, when the subject of the players' arrival was brought to the attention of the Lieutenant Governor. Dinwiddie referred the question of whether the company should be permitted to perform to the Council for advice. The minutes of the Council reveal that "it was the advice of the Board that his Honour would not permit or suffer them to act or exhibit any plays or theatrical Entertainment in this Government."[32] Obviously the Murray company, in town shortly before the Hallams' arrival, had not behaved with much circumspection, thus further darkening the already none-too-bright reputation of strolling players.

Dinwiddie eventually lifted the ban, perhaps because the Hallams and their actors did behave well enough. The delay gave the company time to renovate the crude theater. The *Gazette* pointed out in August that "the Company lately from London have altered the

30. Barnard Hewitt contends, probably correctly, that none of the group had any reputation in England, that they were "close to the bottom of their profession"; *Theatre U.S.A. 1668 to 1957* (New York: McGraw-Hill Book Company, 1959), p. 14.

31. Quoted in Rankin, *Theater in Colonial America*, pp. 50–51.

32. Quoted in Fairfax Harrison, "Stage Plays Prohibited," *Virginia Magazine of History and Biography*, XXXI (July, 1923), 270–71.

Playhouse to a regular theater fit for the reception of Ladies and Gentlemen and [for] the execution of their own performances. . . ."[33] But despite Lewis Hallam's desire to begin performances immediately, it was not until September 15, 1752, that the house opened. Presumably, it took that long to convince the authorities that Virginians were imbued with the "Cavalier" spirit and longed for the theater.

The opening-night performance was *The Merchant of Venice*, followed by the farce *The Anatomist, or The Sham Doctor*.[34] As was then the custom, an "opening address" was spoken before the performance to commemorate the occasion. The address began:

> To this New World from fam'd Britannia's shore,
> Through boist'rous seas where foaming billows roar,
> The Muse, who Briton's charm'd for many an age,
> Now sends her servants forth to tread your stage. . . . [35]

The performance itself came off well. It was decidedly the best production America had seen and was viewed by "a numerous and polite audience," who responded with "great applause."[36] The Hallams' beginning was encouraging, no doubt the more so for the frustrations of past weeks.

The season inaugurated by this performance lasted some eleven months, during which time the playhouse was normally open three nights a week. Audiences were frequently large, for Williamsburg had by 1752–1753 developed that prime requisite of theater support: a large middle class with sufficient leisure to permit theater-going and sufficient motivation to attend plays.[37] The motivation was almost invariably desire for amusement, which Hallam provided by his choice of plays. He offered a variety of quality drama, but he always emphasized the entertainment factor. The repertoire of the

33. Hornblow, *History of the Theatre*, I, 80–81, quoting *Williamsburg Virginia Gazette*, Aug. 21, 1752.

34. Rankin, *Theater in Colonial America*, p. 54; Hornblow, *History of the Theatre*, I, 82.

35. Laurence Hutton (ed.), *Opening Addresses* (New York: The Dunlap Society, 1887), p. 1.

36. Rankin, *Theater in Colonial America*, p. 56, quoting *Williamsburg Virginia Gazette*, Sept. 22, 1752. Rankin contends that this performance "marked the inauguration of a more dignified drama in America and the beginning of the continuous history of the American theater."

37. Hornblow emphasizes the necessity for middle-class support in addition to that of the small "aristocracy." Hornblow, *History of the Theatre*, I, 39–40.

company featured the broad Restoration humor of George Farquhar's *The Constant Couple, The Beaux' Stratagem,* and *The Twin Rivals,* and William Congreve's *Love for Love,* and such eighteenth-century comedies of manners as Colley Cibber's *The Careless Husband* and Benjamin Hoadley's *The Suspicious Husband.* John Gay's *Beggar's Opera* was a favorite, as were such Shakespearean stand-bys as *Richard III, King Lear,* and *Romeo and Juliet.* Most of the popular farces of the day were offered as afterpieces.[38] Hallam seems never to have lost sight of the fact that his prime function was to entertain.

Late in 1753 the company left Virginia for the North. They bore with them a letter from Lieutenant Governor Dinwiddie attesting to their worth as players and as men.[39] They tried New York first and were successful, more so than in Virginia from the financial standpoint. Even Philadelphia, where they journeyed after leaving New York, afforded good support. The "London Company" had every reason to anticipate success when they departed from Philadelphia bound for Charleston, South Carolina, in the fall of 1754.

The *South Carolina Gazette* of October 3, 1754, announced the arrival of the company. "At the New Theatre on Monday next" read the announcement, "will be performed (By a Company of Comedians from London) A Tragedy called 'The Fair Penitent.'" The "New Theatre" had been built especially to receive the Hallam company. It contained boxes (including stage boxes), a pit, and a gallery. Seats were priced according to their location in the house, ranging from 20s. to 50s. each.[40] With such prices prevailing it is difficult to imagine how sufficient audiences were attracted to sustain the company. But the Charleston season of 1754 lasted until late December, when Hallam took his troupe to Jamaica for a winter season in the tropics.[41] The elder Lewis Hallam never returned to the mainland. He succumbed to yellow fever in Jamaica in 1756.

3.

Lewis Hallam's legacy included his company and his wife. Both were inherited by actor David Douglass—the next major figure in American theater history. Douglass had been performing in Jamaica

38. Rankin, *Theater in Colonial America*, pp. 56–57.
39. Hornblow, *History of the Theatre*, I, 88.
40. Quoted in Willis, *Charleston Stage*, p. 39. Willis surmises that the original Dock Street Theater was destroyed in the great fire of 1740.
41. Rankin, *Theater in Colonial America*, p. 72.

before the Hallams arrived in Virginia; indeed, his success in the islands had encouraged their American visit. He had also been briefly associated with the Hallam troupe in Jamaica. Shortly after her husband died, Mrs. Hallam became Mrs. Douglass. Douglass became manager of the Hallam company, with Jamaica as its high-spirited center of operations.

When David Douglass and company returned to the mainland colonies in the fall of 1758 they encountered one of the periodic resurgences of anti-theater sentiment that so bedeviled the early American managers. The touring company throughout its history was to find itself frequently opposed by evangelist preachers and revival meetings. When the Douglass company arrived in New York permission to perform was at first denied them. When it was finally granted it was only for a brief season.

Pennsylvania proved even less receptive when Douglass tried to play there in 1759. Though permission to open a theater was granted initially, the puritanical element pressured the General Assembly into passing "An Act for the More Effectual Suppressing of Lotteries and Plays," which fixed a fine of £500 for anyone attempting to perform a play.[42] Governor William Denny delayed the effective date of this law to January 1, 1760, proving himself on the side of the anti-puritanical forces. Douglass was able to play for a few months. But shortly after opening, the manager and the company became the targets of a violent attack by the press. Typical was the diatribe in the *Pennsylvania Gazette* of August 23, 1759, which described the activities at the "Play-House" as consisting of "Love Intrigues, blasphemous Passions, profane Discourses, lewd Descriptions, filthy Jests, and all the most extravagant Rant of wanton vile Profligate Persons, of both sexes, heating and inflaming one another with all the Wantonness of Address, the Immodesty of Motions, and Lewdness of Thought that Witt can invent. . . ."[43]

Doubtless this piece of inadvertent press-agentry attracted larger audiences than ever to the playhouse, but in January, 1760, the anti-theater law went into effect. The Douglass company departed for Maryland and a somewhat more friendly reception. On July 1, 1760, Douglass closed in Upper Marlboro, Maryland, and set out on his first Southern tour as manager of the London Company of Comedians.

42. *Ibid.*, p. 81. This law was disallowed Sept. 2, 1760.
43. Quoted in *ibid.*, p. 83.

The tour started with the towns of northern Virginia where the company played short engagements en route to Williamsburg, center of what was to become the "Virginia Circuit." Douglass recognized the advantage of spending the winter months in the South. He kept his company in Virginia from October, 1760, to May, 1761. Whenever business slacked in Williamsburg, manager Douglass could always take the troupe downriver to Norfolk, then to Suffolk, Petersburg, back to Williamsburg for a few weeks, then perhaps north to Fredericksburg for a "season."[44]

When summer came and Douglass was ready to return to the North he requested a letter of reference, or "character," of Virginia Governor Francis Fauquier. It was issued over the signatures of the Governor, Council, and nearly one hundred prominent Virginians. "The company of comedians under the direction of David Douglass," began the letter, dated June 11, 1761,

> has performed in this colony for near a twelvemonth; during which time they have made it their constant practice to behave with prudence and discretion in their private character, and to use their utmost endeavors to give general satisfaction in their public capacity. We have therefore thought proper to recommend them as a company whose behavior merits the favor of the public and who are capable of entertaining a sensible and polite audience.[45]

Armed with this strong recommendation, Douglass and his London Company of Comedians turned north toward difficult times in puritanical New England.[46]

The approach of winter in 1762 brought the company south again. They apparently spent about a year on this Southern tour, mostly in Virginia,[47] but fall of 1763 found them in Charleston performing under the name "The American Company of Comedians." "They come warmly recommended from the Northern Colonies," asserted the *South Carolina Gazette*, "where they have performed several years with great applause, and in their private capacities acquired

44. *Ibid.*, p. 90.
45. Quoted in *ibid.*, pp. 90–91.
46. It was in Newport, R. I., that Douglass found it necessary to perform Shakespeare in the guise of "moral dialogues."
47. Rankin has marshaled ample evidence that this was the case, contrary to the contention of Hornblow that the company was then in the West Indies. Rankin, *Theater in Colonial America*, p. 101; Hornblow, *History of the Theatre*, I, 118.

the best of Characters."[48] Douglass arranged for construction of yet another Charleston playhouse, this one on Queen Street, where the company performed successfully until May 10, 1764.[49] The American Company then departed for Barbados while manager Douglass journeyed to England to replace worn scenery and to add new talent to his stock company.

It was January of 1766 before Douglass returned to America. On January 17, he opened in Charleston with several new faces in his stock and excellent scenery, fashioned by the best scene technician in London—Nicholas Thomas Doll of Covent Garden.[50] The season that followed offered theater of better quality than ever before witnessed in America. Douglass and wife, Lewis Hallam, Jr., and Sarah Hallam were capable of performing most of the repertory leads admirably, and the stock was adequate if not brilliant. For three months the playhouse remained open, offering a variety of dramatic entertainment to small but delighted audiences. Still, when the company left for New York in April, 1766, it was not to return for several years.

The Douglass company's absence from the South gave rise to new strolling troupes which partially filled the void. Discouragingly little is known of these ephemeral strollers other than they existed. Only one of them left any substantial record. William Verling, a member of the American Company, set out on his own in 1767 with such actors as would join him in an independent venture. His makeshift troupe, known as the "Virginia Company of Comedians," seems to have opened in Norfolk, Virginia, late in 1767. By March, 1768, they were performing in Williamsburg in the "old Theatre, near the Capitol."[51] The approach of the June court brought crowds to Williamsburg, and it seems likely that Verling and company drew large audiences at least for a time. George Washington, always an enthusiastic playgoer, is known to have attended regularly.[52] But Verl-

48. Robert Adger Law, "News for Bibliographies," *The Nation*, XCVI (Feb. 27, 1913), 201, quoting (Charleston) *South Carolina Gazette*, Nov. 5, 1763.

49. Hughes, *American Theatre*, p. 35; Rankin, *Theater in Colonial America*, pp. 102–3.

50. Rankin, *Theater in Colonial America*, p. 103.

51. *Ibid.*, p. 142, quoting *Williamsburg Virginia Gazette*, March 17, 1768. This is the company that John Esten Cooke evidently confused with the Hallam troupe in his fictional account of early Virginia theater life, *The Virginia Comedians*. The novel is set in Williamsburg in 1768 but deals with the Hallams.

52. George Overcash Seilhamer, *History of the American Theatre* (Philadelphia: Globe Printing House, 1888–1891), I, 235. Rankin, *Theater in Colonial America*, p. 143.

ing obviously overestimated the capacity of Williamsburg to sustain a repertory company. When the troupe left for Alexandria, Virginia, they did so under cover of night to escape their creditors. Little more is known of the movements of the Virginia Comedians, but they toured the Old Dominion and even tried Maryland (as "the New American Company") before disbanding and vanishing into limbo.

Still less is known of a professional company performing in North Carolina at the same time Verling toured Virginia and Maryland. A "Mr. Mills" managed the company, and its leading man was Henry Giffard, who was held by Governor William Tryon to be "the best player on the American Stage."[53] Mills and company probably performed in Halifax, North Carolina, as a 1769 map shows a playhouse there, along with the gaol, court house, "Hampe House," and Tobacco House.[54]

David Douglass doubtless heard news of the Southern interlopers upon his domain. He and his American Company had been playing the New York-Philadelphia circuit since 1766. In June of 1770, once again under harassment by George Whitefield and the Philadelphia Puritans, and now by creditors as well, Douglass turned south. On June 14, 1770, the *Virginia Gazette* announced the arrival in Williamsburg of "Mr. Douglass, with his company of comedians" and the opening performance "the Beggar's Opera, and other entertainments."[55] The Williamsburg season lasted until mid-August, 1770, and was one of very few summer theater seasons ever offered in the Southern colonies. By late October, following a visit to Annapolis, Maryland, Douglass was back in Williamsburg for another season, a season which saw the first Virginia performance of *King Lear* (November 12, 1771).[56] Come summer, 1772, the troupe departed for the North and a more agreeable climate in which to pursue their vocation.

When Douglass returned south for the winter season of 1773, he again chose Charleston in which to commence operations. Arriving in mid-November, the manager learned that the new theater he had expected to find ready for occupancy had not been completed. The company had to wait until December 22, 1773, before opening. The

53. Rankin, *Theater in Colonial America*, p. 141, quoting William Tryon to the Bishop of London, June 15, 1768.
54. *Ibid.*, p. 218, n. 1.
55. *Ibid.*, p. 154, quoting *Williamsburg Virginia Gazette*, June 14, 1770.
56. *Ibid.*, p. 164.

impressive opening-night *mise-en-scène* apparently justified the delay. An account of the opening in the *New York Mercury* noted that the house was "elegantly furnished" and possibly "the most commodious on the continent." The evening's performance included Hugh Kelly's *A Word To the Wise* and the afterpiece *High Life Below Stairs*. Both "gave universal satisfaction" according to the *Mercury* account, as did the scenery ("new and well designed"), the costumes, the music, and "what had a very pleasing effect, the disposition of the lights. . . ." The audience manifested strong approval, expressing "the highest approbation of their entertainment."[57]

The Charleston season that followed this auspicious opening was perhaps the most brilliant in the colonial period. From December 22, 1773, to May 16, 1774, the company presented 118 performances for a total of 77 different plays. Included were 11 Shakespearean works, among them the first American production of *Julius Caesar* (April 20, 1774). Oliver Goldsmith was represented by *She Stoops to Conquer*, which had received its London premiere only months before the Charleston production. Douglass also staged all of the more popular works of William Congreve, John Dryden, George Farquhar, Colley Cibber, Richard Addison, Thomas Otway, and Sir John Vanbrugh. At least twenty musical plays, chiefly English ballad operas, were presented for the delighted Charlestonians. As one historian has written: "Nearly everything that then held the stage was produced at least once during [the] Charleston season of 1773-1774."[58]

The *South Carolina Gazette* at the close of the season had high praise for the company. "Warmly countenanced and Supported by the Publick," declared the *Gazette*, "the Manager and his Company were excited to the most strenuous Efforts to render their Entertainments worthy of so respectable a Patronage." The newspaper reported further that Douglass intended to journey to England for recruits, then to play seasons in New York and Philadelphia. The following winter the company planned to be back in Charleston "with a Theatrical Force hitherto unknown in America."[59] The group

57. *Ibid.*, p. 184, quoting *New York Mercury*, Feb. 21, 1774. The opening of this playhouse, the Church Street Theater, was considered important enough for the press of New York, Philadelphia, and Williamsburg to carry accounts. See Seilhamer, *American Theatre*, I, 329.

58. Crawford, *Romance of American Theatre*, p. 64. See also Willis, *Charleston Stage*, pp. 74–75; Sonneck, *Early Opera*, p. 50; Rankin, *Theater in Colonial America*, pp. 185–86.

59. Willis, *Charleston Stage*, p. 72, quoting (Charleston) *South Carolina Gazette*, May 30, 1774.

temporarily disbanded, each member going his separate way.

Douglass and company never returned to Charleston. On October 20, 1774, the Continental Congress, sitting in Philadelphia, passed a resolution that marked the effective end of American colonial theater. "We will," the Congress resolved, "in our several stations . . . discountenance and discourage every species of extravagance and dissipation, especially all horseracing, and all kinds of gaming, cockfighting, exhibitions of shews, plays, and other expensive diversions and entertainments. . . ."[60] The American Company left for Jamaica on February 2, 1775. A special prologue was spoken when they opened in the islands. It included the significant couplet

> The Muse alarm'd at the loud tempest's roar,
> Seeks an asylum on this peaceful shore. . . .[61]

Douglass had effected a strategic withdrawal in the face of troubled times. For five years theatrical activity in America was to remain at a standstill, save occasional amateur performances given as diversions for the troops of both combatants.

4.

Colonial America had seen the establishment of a strong though geographically limited theater tradition. In the South, the strongholds of the acted drama were, of course, Williamsburg and the Virginia Circuit, and Charleston, South Carolina. Despite the relative difference in population of these towns and the major Northern theater centers, New York and Philadelphia, toward the end of the colonial period the managers of the more important theatrical companies were touring the South each winter, offering seasons in such towns as could produce an audience. Even some of the smaller Southern towns had begun to build theaters, which were occasionally visited by strolling troupes. Amateur theater organizations were also becoming popular, and their productions provided recreation for participants and amusement for audiences.

It was only natural that new towns would develop as the population grew larger and the economy more complex; more people needed

60. Worthington Chauncey Ford, *et al.* (eds.), *Journals of the Continental Congress, 1774–1789* (Washington: Government Printing Office, 1904–1934), I, 78. The resolution was the eighth article of "The Association."

61. Quoted in Richardson Little Wright, *Revels in Jamaica, 1682–1838* (New York: Dodd, Mead, and Company, 1937), p. 63.

more services. Among the public buildings of the newly emergent towns there was frequently a theater. One Southern city of theatrical significance saw the genesis of its theater history even as the Revolution progressed. Savannah, Georgia, was fated to become a key city of the Southern circuit because of its proximity to Charleston. As was typical, the pioneer theater of Savannah began with performances by amateurs. As early as 1781 there had been amateur activity in the little Georgia port, when the royalist garrison then occupying the town presented several plays as charity benefits.[62] When the first professionals arrived in 1783, they were supported by local amateurs. And in 1785 the *Georgia Gazette* announced that "a respectable number of gentlemen have formed a Theatrical Society for the purpose of performing plays during the winter season. . . ." Any profits that resulted from the venture were "to be appropriated to publick utility," specifically to fence in the local cemetery. Dogs, it seems, had been digging up the shallow graves.[63]

There are indications that this amateur society was a manifestation of interest in the theater that had been generated by the appearance of Savannah's first professional actors. In October of 1783 two "dancing masters," James Oerling Godwin and an elusive "Mr. Kidd," arrived in Savannah. Both men had professional acting experience, chiefly in Philadelphia and Baltimore. By October 9 they had converted the public hall into a makeshift theater and were offering the first production of a projected "season," Nicholas Rowe's *The Fair Penitent* and the Garrick farce *Miss in Her Teens*.[64] Mrs. Godwin played the female leads, and the local amateurs, as mentioned earlier, assisted.

The short season that followed apparently proved lucrative enough to warrant repeating. Godwin and Kidd, while pursuing their careers as dancing masters, presented Savannah theatrical seasons in 1784, 1785, and 1786. By 1786 the ambitious entrepreneurs had decided to move their center of operations to Charleston, probably in an effort to concentrate their endeavors on theatrical productions in the larger city.[65] Theater had proved more lucrative than had dancing lessons in Georgia. Though Godwin and Kidd were not to return to Savan-

62. John Max Patrick, *Savannah's Pioneer Theater from Its Origins to 1810* (Athens: University of Georgia Press, 1953), pp. 2–3.
63. Wyoline Hester, "The Savannah Stage" (Master's thesis, Alabama Polytechnic Institute, 1930), p. 2, quoting *Savannah Georgia Gazette*, Nov. 10, 1785.
64. Andrew Sparks, "A History of the Theatre in Savannah, 1800–1836" (Master's thesis, University of Georgia, 1940), p. 2.
65. Patrick, *Pioneer Theater*, pp. 6–7.

nah, they had envisioned a Charleston-Savannah theater circuit. In time this circuit would enable managers of repertory companies to employ profitably their troupes for lengthy seasons in each of the two towns.

When Godwin and Kidd arrived in Charleston in 1786 they found that the city had been practically without theater since 1774. In 1785 a strolling company from Virginia headed by manager Dennis Ryan had presented a brief, successful season in "The Theater in the City Exchange,"[66] not a theater at all really, but a makeshift auditorium. Charleston had no theater, the Church Street house having been destroyed in the devastating fire of 1782.[67] Godwin, the more important of the co-managers, quickly moved to open a legitimate playhouse. He chose to locate at Louisburg outside the city limits of Charleston, presumably to avoid paying the £100 tax on commercial amusements demanded by the city. "Harmony Hall" in its location "without the city"[68] opened July 11, 1786. According to the *Charleston Columbian Herald*, the audience was "polite and numerous (though not overcrowded)," and the performance, apparently a lecture by Godwin with musical accompaniment, was acceptable in all respects.[69] There was no chance of a successful summer theater season in Charleston then or later. The heat, the diminished off-season population of the town, and the fear of fevers saw to that. Though several concerts were offered, the company of Godwin and Kidd had to wait until September 28, 1786, to open a regular season at Harmony Hall. This initial season lasted until late December.

On January 5, 1787, a second season commenced, this time without the services of Kidd. In his place was a local tyro, Christopher Charles McGrath, who was to have a long career on the American stage. The second season lasted until March 28, 1787, and though the company, only ten in number, was not of the highest caliber, the plays they presented were. Support of the theater was inadequate to draw Godwin back for a third season. Both he and McGrath departed for good to pursue their peripatetic careers elsewhere.[70]

As Godwin and Kidd were in the process of reintroducing the theater in Charleston, a new town was showing signs of becoming an important Southern theatrical center. In 1779, Richmond had suc-

66. Willis, *Charleston Stage*, pp. 89–90, quoting (Charleston) *South Carolina Gazette*, March 28, 1785.
67. *Ibid.*, p. 75.
68. *Ibid.*, p. 119, quoting *Charleston Evening Gazette*, Oct. 11, 1786.
69. *Ibid.*, p. 110, quoting *Charleston Columbian Herald*, July 13, 1786.
70. *Ibid.*, pp. 115, 126, 131–33, 143.

ceeded Williamsburg as the capital of Virginia. Its location at the
fall line of the James River made Richmond a likely spot for urban
development, and despite near-total destruction of the town by
Benedict Arnold in 1781, Richmond quickly developed following the
war. By 1785 the new capital was a flourishing town of some two
thousand people that claimed a subscription library among its public
institutions.[71] By 1785, too, Richmond had witnessed a full theater
season. Dennis Ryan and company had played there between June
and December, 1784, before audiences which included on occasion
young John Marshall.[72]

Perhaps credit for establishing theater in the burgeoning Virginia
capital, however, belongs to the well-known adventurer, pedagogue,
and promoter of academies, Alexander Quesnay. Quesnay was the
grandson of the great physiocrat François Quesnay. He was also a
Revolutionary War veteran who, during the early 1780's, devoted
himself to founding academies of languages and the arts in New
York, Baltimore, and Philadelphia. In 1786 he projected a similar
academy for Richmond, to be financed in part by presentation of
"balls, concerts, theatricals, and other public entertainments," as
well as a "pleasure garden."[73] The academy, which was actually little
more than a theater, was ready for occupancy by August, 1786. But
the students had to wait. The *Virginia Gazette* announced on August
30, 1786, that "as the Hall of the Academy will be for a short time
occupied by Messrs. Hallam and Henry, as a Theatre, during their
residence in this City, the Scholars shall be attended to as usual in
the . . . private House now occupied for that purpose."[74] Hallam was
of course Lewis Hallam, Jr. Henry was John Henry, actor and co-
manager of the old American Company, which had returned to North
America following the war. They were on their way to Richmond
from Baltimore.

The American Company was in 1786 still the strongest troupe
operating in America. The season which they commenced in Richmond, timed to coincide with the Richmond races, included pro-

71. Martin Staples Shockley, "The Richmond Theatre, 1780–1790," *Virginia
Magazine of History and Biography*, LX (July, 1952), 421–22.

72. *Ibid.*, p. 423; Susanne Ketchum Sherman, "Post-Revolutionary Theatre in
Virginia, 1784–1810" (Master's thesis, William and Mary College, 1950), p. 18.

73. Sherman, "Post-Revolutionary Theatre," p. 36, quoting *Richmond Virginia Gazette, or the American Advertiser*, May 8, 1786.

74. Shockley, "Richmond Theatre," p. 426, quoting *Richmond Virginia Gazette and Independent Chronicle*, Aug. 30, 1786. The "Scholars" were to have no
"communication with the Theatre—."

ductions of Shakespeare and eighteenth-century drama equal in quality to those presented in colonial times. And they were successful. Whereas Quesnay gave up his academy, leaving for France in December of 1786, the theater continued to operate.[75]

Lack of adequate population to support an academy of the type envisioned by Quesnay drove him out of Richmond. But the "New Theatre on Shockoe Hill," as the academy became known, continued to attract strolling companies throughout the remainder of the century.[76] In 1787 for example, five former members of the American Company along with the ubiquitous "Mr. Kidd" played a season in Richmond.[77] Again, in 1790 the experienced London co-managers Thomas Wade West and John Bignall opened the playhouse in Richmond with their touring company, renamed the "Virginia Company" for the occasion.

By 1791 West and Bignall had established a Richmond-Fredericksburg circuit and were presenting the most popular successes of the contemporary London stage in the remote Virginia towns. So effective was the British-American "cultural transfer" in the case of this provincial touring company that Richmond saw the American premier of several London successes.[78] When the Richmond theater burned to the ground in 1798, the people were so accustomed to their annual season that the Virginia Company had to perform in a "Temporary Theatre" in Market Hall.[79]

Nor did West and Bignall limit their Virginia operations to Richmond and Fredericksburg. In 1795 the company performed in Norfolk, in a new brick theater owned by West.[80] The following year

75. Rev. James Madison to Thomas Jefferson, Dec. 28, 1786, in "Letters of Rev. James Madison, President of the College of William and Mary, To Thomas Jefferson," *William and Mary Quarterly*, 2nd ser. V (April, 1925), 85. Madison wrote of having "just heard of Mons. Quesnay's Departure for France."

76. Sherman, "Post-Revolutionary Theatre," pp. 50, 53–54. This theater saw a different kind of drama when, during the debates of the Virginia Ratifying Convention of 1788, Patrick Henry used the stage to voice his opposition to ratification of the new constitution.

77. *Ibid.*, p. 58.

78. Sherman, "Thomas Wade West," p. 14; Sherman, "Post-Revolutionary Theatre," p. 90; Martin Staples Shockley, "First American Performances of English Plays in Richmond Before 1819," *The Journal of Southern History*, XIII (Feb., 1947), 93.

79. Sherman, "Post-Revolutionary Theatre," p. 214, quoting *Richmond Examiner*, Dec. 20, 1798.

80. Thomas B. Rowland, "Norfolk Theatres of the Olden Time," *The Lower Norfolk County Virginia Antiquary*, II (1898), 102. Bignall died in 1794, but his wife continued the partnership for a time.

West added Petersburg to the circuit, building a new playhouse there,[81] where during race week the theater was kept open nightly rather than the customary three evenings a week. Finally, in 1797 West built a theater in Alexandria, Virginia, and brought that town into his thriving circuit.[82] John Bignall could not have been serious when, in 1792, he wrote of the Virginia towns

> Too many Madisons in them are found
> Instead of fun, who study now the nation
> And talk of politics and reformation. . . .[83]

The Virginia Company of Thomas Wade West and John Bignall created a Virginia circuit in the 1790's, but their activity extended beyond Virginia. In 1793 the managers expanded operations to include the southernmost theatrical center in the United States, Charleston, South Carolina. Since the withdrawal of James Oerling Godwin in 1787, Harmony Hall in Charleston had been converted to other uses, and the city had no real theater. West and Bignall built one, or more correctly, led a move to have one built by public subscription. The building was quickly completed and opened on February 7, 1793, when the West and Bignall company performed John O'Keeffe's comic opera *The Highland Reel*.[84]

Recognizing the great importance of good public relations, the managers initiated a policy of offering an annual benefit performance for the local orphanage. The *Charleston City Gazette* of May 31, 1793, contained a letter from West and Bignall to the "Commissioners of the Orphan House" reporting on the proceeds of the first benefit. "We think it our duty to inform ye," wrote the managers, "the benefit for the noble and very laudable institution ye have with so much avidity espoused, amounts to 306 pounds, 13 s. 3 d., which sum we beg your convenient time to receive. . . ."[85] The charity benefit was to become a standard technique of nineteenth-century managers to improve the public image of the theater.

---

81. Edward A Wyatt, "Three Petersburg Theatres," *William and Mary College Quarterly Historical Magazine*, XXI (April, 1941), 88.

82. Sherman, "Post-Revolutionary Theater," p. 204. This theater, unlike most of the early American playhouses, lasted until 1871, when it was destroyed by fire.

83. Prologue recited by Bignall in Richmond in 1792, quoted in Seilhamer, *American Theatre*, III, 11.

84. Willis, *Charleston Stage*, p. 155.

85. *Ibid.*, p. 181, quoting *Charleston City Gazette*, May 31, 1793.

The successful Charleston benefit, together with the quality of the West and Bignall productions and the general personal deportment of the players, earned the company considerable support from the populace. A full-blown defense of the theater, probably a rebuttal to an unrecorded attack on the company, appeared in the *Gazette* of February 12, 1794. The article was headed "THE GOOD EFFECTS ARISING FROM A WELL-REGULATED THEATRE" and was signed "An Episcopalian." Among the good effects, the most important in the opinion of the correspondent was the entertainment afforded by the drama. "A pleasing comedy," he wrote, "dispels vapours, gloomy apprehensions, hypochondriac complaints, and especially revives the spirits after receiving many sharp duns during the day. . . ."[86] Episcopalian understood the true function of early American theater.

While the company of West and Bignall offered English-language drama and opera at the new playhouse, a French-language theater was opened in Harmony Hall in 1794. Successive seasons were long and colorful, giving Charleston a brilliant period in her theatrical annals. Customarily the two playhouses alternated performance nights, but during race week both theaters were open every night except Sunday. Led socially by the wealthy St. Cecelia Society, whose members supported the theater, Charlestonians adequately patronized both houses to keep them operating profitably.[87]

Good management was largely responsible for the success of the Charleston theaters. By 1799 Bignall and West were dead. Bignall had died in 1794; West was killed by a fall in his Alexandria, Virginia, playhouse in 1799. For nine years the energetic West had managed what was unquestionably the finest theatrical company in America and had proved the potential of relatively small towns to support a touring company in the South.

Following the death of West the company fell into the hands of his wife, Margaret Sully West, who curtailed operations somewhat. She cut both Alexandria and Charleston out of the circuit, though she did keep the company playing year-round in Petersburg, Norfolk, Fredericksburg, and Richmond.[88] One Charleston theater, the City, ceased operating as a playhouse and became the meeting hall for the

86. *Ibid.*, p. 199, quoting *Charleston City Gazette*, Feb. 12, 1794.
87. *Ibid.*, pp. 215, 250, 341. The playhouse of West and Bignall became known as the "Charleston Theatre," that of French proprietor John Joseph Leger Sollee was called the "City" or the "French Theatre."
88. Sherman, "Post-Revolutionary Theatre," pp. 216, 220–21.

South Carolina Lyceum. The other theater continued operations under several managers, falling ultimately into the hands of the former acting-manager of the French Theater, the talented French expatriate Alexander Placide. Placide maintained a stock company capable of performing both English and French productions and with this company moved into the position formerly occupied by West and Bignall—that of controlling the theatrical fortunes of Charleston and the entire Southern circuit.

5.

By the turn of the century, theater was a well-established form of commercial entertainment in the larger towns of the South. In 1803, for example, a Charleston resident signing himself "Thespis" was complaining in the *Courier* of the dull times between theater seasons. "It may be reckoned among the evils attending the severity of our Charleston summers," wrote Thespis, "that the public are for so many months deprived of the most rational, instructive and noble amusement which the genius of man has hitherto devised for the benefit and relaxation of a civilized society. It will be readily understood that I mean the exhibitions of the stage."[89] The sentiment expressed by Thespis was held by many townspeople and transients who were dependent upon the theater for such diversion as they were likely to find away from the gaming table, tavern, race track, and ballroom.

The theater continued its spread. Savannah, Georgia, became part of a near-permanent circuit with Charleston when in 1801 Alexander Placide expanded the scope of his operations by initiating an annual season in the Georgia port. The *Charleston Courier*, welcoming the Placide company home from Savannah in 1804, noted that their Georgia efforts had been well received. "Their houses were in general full," observed the *Courier*, "and the benefits were so profitable as to do great credit to the people of that town—to their taste and to their justice."[90] The Savannah seasons lasted five weeks or longer and

89. *Charleston Courier*, Nov. 7, 1803.
90. *Charleston Courier*, Feb. 1, 1804. The term "benefit" refers to a practice common in theater organizations throughout the nineteenth century whereby the often meager salaries of actors and actresses were bolstered. Once every season each member of a troupe was allowed the profits from a specified night's door receipts. The success of the benefit was an indication of an actor's popularity. The manager also took a benefit each season, usually on the closing night.

continued until 1812, when a religious resurgence and the War of 1812 temporarily halted theatrical activity there as elsewhere.[91]

The fugitive records of the strolling players, scarce though they are, indicate that there was some activity in the small Southern towns and villages in the late eighteenth century. Hallam and Henry's fine American Company of Comedians toured North Carolina in 1787, playing in Halifax, New Bern, Wilmington, Tarboro, and probably Fayetteville.[92] An offshoot of this company, the "Kenna Family," returned for a North Carolina tour in 1788 and performed in New Bern and Wilmington and possibly elsewhere.[93] The greater accessibility of Wilmington naturally attracted more strollers there than to the interior towns of North Carolina, but the more remote areas did get occasional theater, some of it first-rate. More frequent were the visits of strolling ventriloquists, singers, acrobats, magicians, rope dancers, sword swallowers, and other such intrepid entertainers of a subdramatic nature.[94]

There are examples of similar performers in the rural sections of South Carolina and Georgia prior to 1800. The *Augusta* (Georgia) *Chronicle* of November 26, 1796, advertised performances by the touring company of James Oerling Godwin[95] which took place in the court house. Columbia, South Carolina, saw at least one season in the eighteenth century when an offshoot from the Charleston company performed there for several nights in 1799.[96] No doubt there was more such activity. Just as the organized repertory company was an established fact in the towns of the Virginia Circuit and the Charleston-Savannah nexus, by 1810 the strollers had managed to perform in a remarkable number of rural villages in the South.

Since the Revolution the theater of the South, as well as that of the nation at large, had seen a steady advance, both in quantity and more particularly in quality. In 1792 Massachusetts repealed her law prohibiting the theater, thus opening Boston to rapid theatrical development.[97] The internationally renowned Park Theater in New

91. Patrick, *Pioneer Theater*, p. 44.
92. Archibald Henderson, "Strolling Players in Eighteenth Century North Carolina," *The Carolina Playbook*, XV (June, 1942), 43.
93. Sherman, "Post-Revolutionary Theatre," p. 66.
94. Henderson, "Strolling Players," p. 43.
95. Sonneck, *Early Opera*, p. 185.
96. *Ibid.*
97. Coad and Mims, *American Stage*, p. 39.

York was opened by William Dunlap in 1798.[98] Washington, D. C., got its first playhouse in 1800 when the capital was itself a mere village, thus beginning the long history of the National Theater.[99] Alexander Placide continually expanded his Southern operations, bringing both Richmond and Norfolk into his circuit by 1804. Despite occasional attacks by the puritanical, it seemed by 1810 that the American stage was on the verge of blossoming into an institution that would be as much a subject of national pride as other emerging American institutions. But in 1811, American theatrical development received a pronounced setback. On the night of December 26, 1811, the Richmond Theater caught fire in the middle of a performance. A crowded house had gathered to see the Placide company in a new play and afterpiece presented for Alexander Placide's benefit. One contemporary observer noted that "it was the fullest house this season," there being "not less than 600 present."[100] The fire started when a burning chandelier which provided stage lighting touched off some scenery stored over the stage. The fire quickly spread to the roof of the theater, a new pine roof with rosin still wet on it. Within minutes the wooden building was an inferno. The exits proved inadequate to accommodate the panic-stricken mob that fought to escape the blaze and the falling debris. Few escaped injury, and at least seventy-one people were dead, including Governor George William Smith, when the *Richmond Enquirer* account was published on December 31.[101]

Richmond and the entire nation were horrified by the tragedy. The *Petersburg Intelligencer* observed: "The public mind is estranged from everything save the horrible catastrophe at Richmond."[102] A mass funeral was held at the site of the fire on December 29, and a new church was built directly over the spot—the Monumental Church—which was completed and consecrated May 4, 1814.[103]

98. Hughes, *American Theatre*, p. 82.
99. William Burk Wood, *Personal Recollections of the Stage, Embracing Notices of Actors, Authors, and Auditors, During a Period of Forty Years* (Philadelphia: Henry Carey Baird, 1855), pp. 55–56.
100. John Shore to Samuel Webb, Dec. 30, 1811, in the Theater Collection, Valentine Museum, Richmond, Virginia.
101. *Richmond Enquirer*, Dec. 31, 1811. It was later established that seventy-six people had been killed, and scores were seriously injured.
102. *Petersburg Intelligencer*, Dec. 31, 1811.
103. William H. Gaines, Jr., "The Fatal Lamp, or Panic at the Play As Performed at the Theater in Richmond on the Night of December 21 [sic], 1811," *Virginia Cavalcade*, II (Summer, 1952), 4–8.

Predictably, the still powerful anti-theater forces used the Richmond fire as proof of God's wrathful opposition to plays and players. The attack of puritanical elements all over the country was renewed with added ferocity, and with unprecedented success. Not only was the theater attacked as an evil institution, but the players themselves were held somehow personally responsible for the disaster. The Placide company was banished from Richmond and was ostracized elsewhere.[104] Alexander Placide, who had lost a favorite daughter in the holocaust, died within a few months. The death of Placide and the powerful reaction against the stage following the Richmond fire temporarily ended theatrical activity in the South; the War of 1812 was to deliver the coup de grâce.

104. Edward Allen Cleaton, "Placide Players and Puritanism," *The Reviewer*, V (July, 1925), 95–96.

CHAPTER II

DEVELOPMENT

OF THE

SOUTHEASTERN CIRCUIT

1815-1825

1.

AMERICA CROSSED A WATERSHED IN 1815. THE PEACE OF GHENT MARKED the beginning of the national dynamic which characterized the postwar years, a dynamic that fed upon itself and generated the unflaggingly optimistic spirit with which the nation was imbued. Despite superficial economic dislocations and occasional manifestations of divisive sectional animosity, the United States for a decade or more after Ghent maintained its forward momentum.

It was only natural that the revival of the nation's spirit would bring with it the revival of her spirited social institutions. Once again Americans could seek entertainment unashamedly, and they did so in unprecedented numbers. The theater quickly recovered its prewar vigor. Before 1815 ended, the playhouses of Boston, New York, Philadelphia, Baltimore, and Charleston, the five theatrical centers of the Eastern seaboard, were back in full operation, and business was good.

Charleston had long been the cultural capital of the South and the most essentially urban of Southern towns. In 1815, as the leading port of egress for Southern rice and cotton,[1] Charleston was the major Southern commercial center. There was a decided connection between culture and commerce everywhere in ante bellum America. The vitality of the theatrical operations of a town reflected the vitality of its economy. The economy of Charleston was later to enter into a relative decline and so was her theater—almost in direct proportion. But in 1815 the South Carolina port was bustling and healthy.

The *Charleston City Gazette* of October 25, 1815, announced the long-awaited reopening of the theater. The announcement pointed up the economic foundations of local theater support. "From the rapid and prosperous increase of every kind of business," observed the *Gazette*, "and the great number of visitors who will spend the season in our city, we presume the enterprise and labor of the manager and the company will be richly rewarded."[2] Trade and transients were the dual cornerstones upon which rested the theatrical edifice of any town.

On November 1, 1815, the first postwar Charleston season opened with Thomas Holcroft's "celebrated Comedy of the ROAD TO RUIN" heading the evening's program.[3] The *Courier* advertisement of the performance indicated that no one had forgotten the Richmond fire of 1811. A committee appointed by the city council had investigated the theater and found "that the Outlets are sufficiently numerous and constructed in such a manner as to ensure the safety of the Citizens, in the event of fire, or any other alarm."[4]

The playhouse in which the 1815 season commenced was the "old" Charleston theater, opened by Thomas Wade West and John Bignall in 1793. It was typical in most respects of theaters of the early nineteenth century, possibly slightly larger than most relative to the city's population.[5] The inside of the auditorium measured 125 feet in length by 56 in width. At floor level was the pit, traditionally the domain of the groundlings but in this particular house the location of the very choicest seats. Good seats were also found in the first

1. *Niles' Weekly Register*, X (May 18, 1816), 194.
2. William Stanley Hoole, *The Ante-Bellum Charleston Theatre* (Tuscaloosa: University of Alabama Press, 1946), p. 11, quoting *Charleston City Gazette*, Oct. 25, 1815.
3. *Charleston Courier*, Nov. 1, 1815.
4. *Ibid.*
5. The aggregate population of Charleston remained fairly stable from 1810 to 1820 at about 24,700. See United States Department of the Interior, Census Office, *Report on the Social Statistics of Cities*, Pt. II, *The Southern and the Western States* (Washington: Government Printing Office, 1887), p. 95.

two tiers of boxes which formed a semicircle about the pit. The third tier or gallery was considered the resort of the lesser social classes, possibly even of the demimonde. Altogether 1,200 constituted a full house, though it is doubtful that the house was ever full. The stage traversed the width of the interior and was framed by an ornate, embellished proscenium. Reflecting the eighteenth-century construction of this playhouse, a semicircular apron projected from the stage well into the auditorium.[6]

An important alteration, one which tells much about the Charleston social structure, had been made on the theater prior to its opening. The *Courier* of November 2, 1815, declared, "due care has been taken to secure Ladies of character from the possibility of being improperly associated" while attending the theater. Not only was seating to be strictly segregated with the pit and first boxes reserved for "Ladies of respectability exclusively," but even the "avenues" leading to the upper-class seats were kept "completely distinct."[7] Prices of theater admission were sufficiently high to keep the lower ranks of society out altogether. Pit and box seats were $1.00, gallery seats $0.50. The effort to maintain an elitist theater later contributed to the decline of Charleston's theatrical fortunes.

An experienced and talented actor-manager, the British-born Joseph George Holman, headed the Charleston company of 1815. Holman had made his acting debut at Covent Garden in London and had been a member of the stock company at the Park, New York, before assuming management in Charleston. Covent Garden and the Park were two of the world's foremost theaters at the time. Holman secured as his leading comedian the popular Northern favorite Thomas Hilson, and the stock company was strong.[8]

From the outset of the season it was apparent that Charleston was ready for the theater's return. Audiences were large despite the playing schedule of six nights a week, and the season was long. It was not until summer that the playhouse closed its doors. In May, 1816, manager Holman took his troupe on the road, first to Savannah, Georgia, then to Virginia for a short tour.[9]

---

6. William Stanley Hoole, "Two Famous Theatres of the Old South," *The South Atlantic Quarterly*, XXXVI (July, 1937), 274, quoting *Charleston Gazette*, Aug. 14, 1792; *Charleston Courier*, Nov. 2, 1815. This theater operated until 1833. It was one of two important Charleston playhouses prior to 1860.

7. *Charleston Courier*, Nov. 2, 1815.

8. Hoole, *Charleston Theatre*, pp. 11–12.

9. *Ibid.*, p. 13, quoting *Charleston City Gazette*, May 21, 1816; *Richmond Enquirer*, May 11, 1816.

By June of 1816, Holman was en route to England to recruit new talent for his company. America had not yet begun to produce actors and actresses endemically, largely because of the stigma still attached to anything theatrical. But there were always players in Great Britain and Ireland willing to try their luck on the American stage. In Dublin, for example, Holman recruited a talented young actor named James Henry Caldwell for his troupe.[10] Caldwell was destined to create a theatrical empire in the South.

Manager Holman returned to Charleston with his new talent, reorganized and rehearsed his company, and opened the Charleston season of 1816–1817 on November 4.[11] Two nights later, the manager introduced Caldwell, his new romantic lead, to the Charleston public as the elegant Belcour in Richard Cumberland's *West Indian*.[12] Caldwell was a strikingly handsome man, with dark curly hair, expressive eyes, and fine physique. He immediately became a favorite in Charleston, especially with the ladies.[13]

Caldwell's quick success fed his innate ambition. Though he was still a young man, only twenty-four years old in 1817, he aspired to star status. By March of 1817 he was quarreling bitterly with Holman over benefits and other matters, and especially over the parts assigned him by the manager. Holman, arguing that Caldwell had misconstrued the verbal agreement between them, discharged the rebellious actor and publicly appealed for support from the Charleston theatergoers. His appeal was unsuccessful. When it became known that Holman refused to grant Caldwell's requests, a riot broke out in the theater that was quelled only by the appearance of the City Guard with muskets and fixed bayonets.[14] It is entirely possible, though not certain, that the dispute between actor and manager was settled finally by a duel on Sullivan's Island.[15] In any case, Holman relinquished his Charleston management shortly after the dispute, while Caldwell set out to seek his theatrical fortune.[16]

Management of the Charleston theater passed into the hands of

10. Paul Smith Hostetler, "James H. Caldwell: Theatre Manager" (Doctoral dissertation, Louisiana State University, 1964), p. I.

11. Hoole, *Charleston Theatre*, p. 80.

12. *Ibid.*, p. 80; Hostetler, "Caldwell," p. 3.

13. See the ultra-romantic portrait of the young Caldwell by John Wesley Jarvis, reproduced in Odell, *Annals*, III, facing p. 478.

14. Hostetler, "Caldwell," pp. 5–8.

15. *Ibid.*, p. 13; *New York Spirit of the Times*, Nov. 19, 1836.

16. Emmett Robinson (ed.), "Dr. [John Beaufain] Irving's Reminiscences of the Charleston Stage," *South Carolina Historical and Genealogical Magazine*, LI (July, 1951), 171. Holman died on Aug. 19, 1817.

Holman's brother-in-law and erstwhile musical director, the capable
Charles Gilfert. Gilfert realized that he had to regain the public
support alienated by his rash predecessor. In announcing the opening
of the 1817–1818 season in the *Courier,* the new manager was modest.
"The manager is well aware of the difficulties of the task upon which
he has entered," Gilfert wrote. "To present himself as the Caterer
for the mental gratification of the public, in so important a branch
of their amusements, is a truly arduous undertaking." But he solemn-
ly promised to exert his every effort to satisfy. On December 12,
1817, he opened with the Thomas Morton comedy *Speed the
Plough.*[17] Yet, despite all his efforts, the season was notably less
successful than the previous one.

It had long been the practice of Charleston managers to visit
Savannah, Georgia, when business grew slack at home. The Georgia
port, with a population of only 5,215 in 1810,[18] had never been able
to sustain a company for long periods, but the resident population,
when bolstered by the transients ever present in an active commercial
town, could usually supply audiences three nights a week for several
weeks. In November of 1818, manager Charles Gilfert took the
Charleston company to Savannah.[19]

In Savannah as elsewhere, theatrical activity had been relatively
scarce during the war and the years just before the war. In 1808,
when two female freaks appeared on exhibit, the *Savannah Republican* described the show as "a delightful and rational amusement
. . . ,"[20] an evaluation that indicates a dearth of commercial entertainment. The desire of the people of Savannah for theater was
manifest when, in 1818, they built a playhouse.

The new theater was ready for occupancy by December of 1818.
Charles Gilfert and the Charleston company, under contract with
the major Savannah theater promoters to perform two seasons annually, opened the house on December 3, with Andrew Cherry's
popular comedy *The Soldier's Daughter* and the farce *Raising the
Wind.*[21]

As was true of most of the frontier theaters, the Savannah Theater
was designed in the traditional manner. Though often only crude

17. *Charleston Courier,* Dec. 9, 1817.
18. U. S. Census Office, *Social Statistics,* p. 173.
19. Hoole, *Charleston Theatre,* p. 16.
20. Sparks, "Theatre in Savannah," p. 25, quoting *Savannah Republican,*
April 5, 1808.
21. *Ibid.,* p. 5, quoting *Columbia Museum and Savannah Daily Gazette,* Dec.
3, 1818. The theater was located on Bull Street at Chippewa Square.

wooden structures with benches for seats, the community playhouse was usually a source of pride; consequently it had to observe the conventions. The interior had to have a pit, boxes, a gallery, and elaborate decorations; otherwise it was not a theater at all. The Savannah Theater was capable of holding about one thousand people, but as was the case in Charleston it almost certainly never did so.

The *Savannah Georgian* of December 9, 1818, described the playhouse. Most impressive according to this account was the elaborately painted house curtain. The foreground of the curtain painting depicted the Muses cavorting with Shakespeare, Ben Jonson, and Colley Cibber. In the background, according to the *Georgian*, "Macbeth, in scarlet tartans, dimmed by a murky cloud, holds communion with the wierd sisters, whose horrid forms are partly hid by the darkness that enshrouds them."[22] The tone of the *Georgian* description of the playhouse interior was jocular; no doubt the painting was badly executed. But it does indicate what the local designers of the playhouse decor believed the proper concerns of a theater should be—Shakespeare, Jonson, the Muses.

The Savannah press from the outset of the season followed theatrical affairs closely. In addition to advertising all performances, the press carried theater news and features. A noteworthy example of the attention devoted to theater appeared in the *Georgian*, December 12, 1818, when the playhouse had been open just over a week. The feature was epistolary in form, a letter from a pseudonymous "Bill Driggers" to a friend, "Jim Ruffin on the Oconee mauling rails." It bears lengthy quotation, both for its content and its style. "Dear Mate," began "Driggers,"

> I arrived here about an hour by sun and started right off to the Theatre, the place whar the player folks cut thar didoes—and you may depend on it beats [*sic*] bob tail. Thar was a monstrous sight of people and mightly likely galls, with powerful elegant dry-goods on—but they had great homely bunnets on thar heads, that looks for all the world like a yellow-jacket's nest, and kept everybody from seeing.

Bill commented that he would prefer that the ladies leave their hats at home. Anyone that happened to get behind one, he suggested, "has no more chance for the worth of his dollar, than a stump tail bull in fly time. . . ." Audience behavior was not all it should have been. Driggers particularly resented the continual "cracking and

22. *Ibid.*, p. 7, quoting *Savannah Georgian*, Dec. 9, 1818.

chumping" of nuts, the sound of which he likened to "a drove of hogs in the oakey woods in acorn season." There was also music at the theater, in the form of "a heap of fiddlers" who performed some "clever jigs," but who declined Driggers' request for "Parched Corn" and "Possum up a gum tree," occasioning Bill's reflection that "these low country quality knows nothing about good music."

Driggers also commented on the decor of the house. "Thar was a powerful chance of durned elegant picters all in gold stuck about on the pews, and the up stars was proped up with iron posts with more gold about them then you ever hurn tell of. . . ." Nor did the act-drop escape his critical attention. He identified "Jack Spear" and "polly Kibber," observing that "polly" was a "mighty quere name for a man. . . ."

"Oh Jim," Driggers concluded his breathless account, "I wisht you could have seen all I did, your hart would have been split if it had been made of black gum. I have forgot half I seed, fir my hed whent round like a wagon wheel."[23] Such was an evening at the theater spent by Bill Driggers, very likely a tongue-in-cheek member of the *Georgian* staff with a good ear for dialect.

There was some opposition to the theater in Savannah, as in every other town of the South in this period. Perhaps the opposition was somewhat weaker in Savannah than in most towns. As John Max Patrick has pointed out, "Savannah was never a very puritanical city." But, again in a phrase of Patrick's, there was a "puritanical fringe" in all of the towns, Savannah included.[24]

A defense of the theater in the *Savannah Republican* of January 19, 1819, seems to have been in dialogue with opposition forces. The defense was based on the existence of a natural "passion for amusement"[25] existing in all normal humans which should not be frustrated. As the unknown defender argued, "passion for recreation cannot be smothered; it will burst out somewhere. . . ." The truly wise would keep the theater operating to provide a harmless outlet for this passion. Whether or not it was on the basis of this natural-law argument, the pro-theater forces clearly won out in Savannah. The first season by the Gilfert company was longer than any ever before.

The theater remained open throughout December and into Janu-

23. Hester, "The Savannah Stage," p. 57, quoting *Savannah Georgian*, Dec. 12, 1818. The "Driggers Letter" is an excellent example of early "frontier humor."
24. *Pioneer Theater*, p. 49.
25. Sparks, "Theatre in Savannah," pp. 92–93, quoting *Savannah Republican*, Jan. 19, 1819.

ary, 1819. But on January 21, the *Republican* printed an account of activities at the playhouse that might have indicated waning enthusiasm for the theatrical entertainment. "Every performance improves upon us," claimed the editor, in what looks suspiciously like an editorial puff. He continued, "last evening's performance . . . was superior to any we have witnessed; and we venture to say that no theater was ever more crowded, to witness the representation of 'The Stranger' [Kotzebue-Thompson]. . . . The last scene was a most touching piece of acting—it called forth tears and shouts of rapturous applause."[26]

On January 29, 1819, the season closed. The Gilfert company returned home to Charleston.[27] But on March 3, 1819, the manager announced that he was closing the Charleston theater to return to Savannah, where he was "under an obligation to the Citizens . . . to perform for a certain extent of season. . . ."[28]

Gilfert was also under an obligation, albeit self-imposed, to perform in Augusta, Georgia. Augusta had been since 1817 the third stop on his Southern circuit. The little town on the upper reaches of the Savannah River, incorporated the same year Gilfert introduced theater there, was at the time the most important inland community in Georgia. Even so, the population was tiny—under 2,500 in 1810[29]—and the potential for supporting a theater was quite limited. Gilfert and his successors recognized the limitations. The early managers played but brief seasons in Augusta. Still, the few weeks there usually proved profitable enough, sustaining the company while enthusiasm for theater was rekindled in Charleston and Savannah.[30] Augusta was thus a significant part of the Southern circuit from the beginning and continued to be significant throughout the ante bellum period.[31]

In 1819, this southernmost theater circuit on the East Coast included only Charleston, Savannah, and Augusta, no one of which could sustain a repertory company for a long period. Together, how-

26. *Ibid.*, p. 35, quoting *Savannah Republican*, Jan. 21, 1819. See below, pp. 261–64, for a detailed examination of this enormously popular play.

27. *Ibid.*, p. 35.

28. *Charleston Courier*, March 3, 1819.

29. U. S. Census Office, *Social Statistics*, p. 163.

30. Robinson, "Irving's Reminiscences," p. 171.

31. On the continuing importance of Augusta see, for example, *Charleston Courier*, Dec. 6, 1827; Holland Memorial [William Brown Maclay?], *Sketch of the Life of George Holland, The Veteran Comedian, with Dramatic Reminiscences, Anecdotes, &c.* (New York: T. H. Morrell, 1871), p. 40.

ever, considered as a unit, they could sustain a troupe at least part of each year. And the Southern hinterlands were soon to produce new towns. Each one would add to the circuit; each would permit more profitable operations for the primary company in the region and attract adventurous new troupes to that region.

2.

Manager Charles Gilfert could not wait for towns to develop in the Charleston-Savannah-Augusta area. He had a company to maintain, and it seemed in May of 1819, following a profitless season in Charleston, that expansion of his company's circuit was essential to survival.[32] He naturally thought of a fourth Southern town that had once supported a theater—Richmond, Virginia.

The Virginia capital had grown rapidly since 1794, when a canal was dug to bypass the falls in the James River near the town, facilitating river traffic.[33] By 1819 the aggregate population was about 12,000, more than double that of 1800.[34] When the state legislature was in season the large transient element added substantially to resident population. Richmond was accessible to the river, and her embryonic port served the entire central tidewater of Virginia. But since the great fire of 1811, there had been only the most ephemeral type of professional entertainment available to the people of Richmond.

By 1818 some were growing acutely dissatisfied with this dearth of entertainment. Samuel Mordecai, for example, wrote his wife in February of 1818 that "the people of Richmond are desperately in want of public amusements." To illustrate he told her of a group of shoddy strollers who had "advertised an entertainment of music, dancing, balancing and mathematical experiments at the Eagle [Hotel]." Bad as they were, he continued, "at least 400 persons were present and were so charitable as to applaud ten times where they hissed once." Mordecai had also sought diversion at a concert, where he was "so squeezed and stewed . . . that [he] did not enjoy it."[35]

32. *Charleston Courier*, May 12, 1819.
33. U. S. Census Office, *Social Statistics*, p. 80. This canal was the initial version of what later became the James River and Kanawha Canal, source of much of Richmond's later prosperity.
34. *Ibid.*, p. 79, gives the population in 1800 as 5,737; in 1820, 12,067.
35. Agnes M. Bondurant, *Poe's Richmond* (Richmond: Garrett & Massie, 1942), pp. 140–41, quoting Samuel Mordecai to Rachel Mordecai, Feb. 8, 1818. Mordecai described the "Mathematical experiments" as "the old slight of hand tricks with cards, cups and balls. . . ."

Other subdramatic forms of entertainment drew well in Richmond in 1818. The *Richmond Compiler* of March 9 advertised a variety program to be offered that evening at the Union Hotel. It featured a touring company called "The Wandering Minstrels" who sang songs and recited "pieces," all for an admittance fee of only $1.00 per person. The show was editorially recommended. The same *Compiler* also advertised the "NEW CIRCUS, RICHMOND," which was beginning its "LAST WEEK BUT FOUR" locally. The tent show included tightrope and slackwire performers, "Equestrian Exercises," and "Still Vaulting, By the Troop of Flying Phenomena."

In January of 1819 a touring theatrical company played in Richmond, the first since the fire. Its manager was James H. Caldwell, who had organized a strolling company shortly after leaving Charleston in 1817. Caldwell and company came to Richmond from Alexandria, Virginia, performed at Richmond in the circus arena, then continued on their tour.[36] Perhaps the Richmond "season" stimulated local enthusiasm for theater. Before the year was out a new playhouse had opened.

Like most playhouses built in the period, the Richmond Theater of 1819 was financed by public subscription. Shares of stock numbering 188 and valued at $200 each were offered for sale.[37] They were purchased by those interested in investing in the venture, either as a public-spirited act or as a commercial investment, usually the former. Almost uniformly the investors were of the highest social classes. Among the stockholders of the Richmond Theater, for example, were John Marshall; another eminent justice, William H. Cabell; Thomas Ritchie of the *Enquirer*; William Wirt; Virginia Attorney General John Robertson; Dr. Micajah Clark; James Rawlings, president of the Farmers' Bank of Virginia; and other social leaders. The lessee and manager of the theater was Charles Gilfert, who purchased twenty shares of stock.[38]

The new playhouse, completed by June of 1819, was located on the corner of H and Seventh streets. It was made of brick, "handsomely stuccoed," as the *Compiler* pointed out, with an interior designed in the conventional manner. The *Compiler* description fur-

36. Hostetler, "Caldwell," p. 19.
37. Martin Staples Shockley, "A History of the Theatre in Richmond, Virginia, 1819–1838" (Doctoral dissertation, University of North Carolina, 1938), p. 1.
38. *Ibid.*, p. 19. Samuel Mordecai was a member of the Executive Committee of the theater.

ther noted that the house was "built with sufficient doors, to let out a retiring crowd in a few moments, independently of the numerous windows, which are made on every side of it."[39] Memory of the fire was, of course, still strong in Richmond.

Early in June, 1819, the touring company of Charles Gilfert steamed up the James aboard the "Powhatan," having just played a brief season in Norfolk, Virginia. The company, essentially the same as when it had opened in Charleston in 1817, was twenty-seven strong. It included seventeen men, nine women, and a boy, most of whom were British imports. Leading the stock were the ever-popular comedian Thomas Hilson and Gilfert's talented wife, known to her public and by posterity only as "Mrs. Gilfert." Altogether it was a strong company, large and experienced, though probably not "the best Company in America" as claimed by the *Compiler*.[40] On June 11, 1819, they opened the new Richmond playhouse.[41]

The Gilfert company's first Richmond season offered much in the way of quality drama. Playing four, five, even six nights each week, Gilfert brought out, among many others, *Richard III*, *Hamlet*, and *The Merchant of Venice*, Richard Brinsley Sheridan's *School for Scandal* (with Hilson as Sir Peter Teazle), Thomas Otway's *Venice Preserved*, and Edward Moore's persuasive anti-gambling tract *The Gamester*.[42] Gilfert made a practice of alternating heavier and lighter plays, offering heavy tragedy or tragic melodrama one evening, comedy or romantic drama the next. Afterpieces were always performed, usually the stand-by farces of the day.

Company benefits began late in July, 1819, and the season closed August 4.[43] By October 11, 1819, Gilfert was back in Richmond for his second season. His troupe was about the same as before, and so was their repertoire. But the manager, despite generally good houses and the strong support of the upper elements of society, ran into financial difficulties almost immediately. Fundamentally, the problem was that Richmond, with a population of under six thousand whites, was not large enough to support the elaborate operation Gilfert managed. But there were other related factors.

In the first place, the regular theater-goers were frequently share-

39. *Richmond Compiler*, June 14, 1819.
40. *Ibid.*, June 10, 1819.
41. Shockley, "Richmond Theatre, 1819–1838," p. 16.
42. *Ibid.*, pp. 288–98.
43. *Ibid.*, p. 298.

holders in the playhouse, thus had free passes to all productions. There were nearly two hundred of them. As the *Mercantile Advertiser* pointed out somewhat later, there were "taste, wealth and inclination sufficient to support the Theatre" in Richmond, "but the circumstances of there being so many proprietor's tickets, has . . . made the management of the Theatre a losing business."[44] In 1822 the stockholders agreed to sell their rights of permanent free admission to the manager, but by then considerable damage had already been done.[45]

A second force militating against Gilfert's financial success was the continuing attack upon the theater by the local clergy. Most Richmond preachers agreed with the Reverend Rees Lloyd, who in 1815, in a published sermon entitled *The Richmond Alarm* (a reference to the "alarm" sounded by God in the form of the fire), had condemned "stage-plays" as "a moral, natural, spiritual and eternal evil. . . ."[46] The *Virginia Patriot* of October 28, 1819, editorially attacked the "frequency of pulpit animadversions" against the theater. "Notwithstanding the great utility of this institution," wrote the editor, "we daily hear it abused and ridiculed" by the clergy.[47] Whatever the extent preachers were able to influence their parishioners, to precisely that extent did Gilfert suffer at the box office. And he needed every possible paid admission to offset the effects of the "free list."

Finally, the Panic of 1819 and the depression that followed it further deprived the theater of financial support. Economic dislocation always struck commercial amusements first and hardest. To those affected by depression, retrenchment came easiest in the area of entertainment expenses. And even as Gilfert opened his second Richmond season, troubled times had arrived. On October 29, 1819, the *Richmond Compiler* commented on the lack of support tendered Gilfert by the public. "The Manager of the Theatre has made great and laudable exertions," observed the editor. Gilfert was deserving of much credit but was being recompensed for his efforts with little more than "windy thanks." The editor further pointed out that the

44. Martin Staples Shockley, "The Proprietors of Richmond's New Theatre of 1819," *The William and Mary College Quarterly Historical Magazine*, 2nd ser. XIX (July, 1939), 308, quoting *Richmond Mercantile Advertiser*, Sept. 19, 1821.
45. Shockley, "Richmond Theatre, 1819–1838," p. 25.
46. Quoted in *ibid.*, p. 36.
47. *Ibid.*, quoting *Richmond Virginia Patriot*, Oct. 28, 1819.

"unprecedented pressure of the times" was largely to blame. This pressure "deprived a number of . . . citizens of the means of attending public amusements," and "instilled into others a jealous caution of expense. . . ."

In view of the financial difficulties that beset Gilfert and company in Richmond, it is remarkable that they were able to operate at all. Yet by dividing their time between Richmond and Norfolk, the company was able to continue operating in Virginia until mid-January, 1820.[48] The manager felt things would be little better elsewhere, and he was correct. National financial crises tended to affect theatrical operations nationally. New York, Philadelphia, Baltimore, Charleston—all experienced trouble similar to that in Richmond. Yet all managed to keep their playhouses open at least a part of each year. Indeed, at times it seemed as though people were trying to escape their financial troubles in the theater. "Hard times! Hard times! is the universal cry," sounded the *Compiler* on December 10, 1822, "and yet Richmond at this time assumes more gaiety than we remember for many years back. . . . Look at the crowds that flocked to witness Booth's acting on Monday night last. . . ."

An appearance of Junius Brutus Booth was likely to draw an audience anywhere, but Richmond had a special affinity for the renowned tragedian. He had, after all, made his American debut there. On June 30, 1821, Booth landed in Norfolk, Virginia, following a flight from England with his young mistress Mary Ann Holmes. He chose Virginia over the more populous Northern cities because he hoped to escape recognition by his jealous colleagues, notably Edmund Kean, who were certain to be found in the theatrical centers[49] and (Booth thought) would use the knowledge of his illicit liaison against him professionally.

Seeking an engagement and finding no theater open in Norfolk, Booth continued upriver to Richmond, where on July 6, 1821, with the Gilfert company he made his auspicious appearance in *Richard III*. He continued to perform in Richmond until July 20, appearing

48. The veteran New York theater manager and playwright William Dunlap was in Norfolk in October and November of 1819 and saw the Gilfert company perform frequently. After each performance he recorded his impressions in his diary. The diary entries reveal that Dunlap was favorably impressed with the work of this provincial company. See Dorothy C. Barck (ed.), *Diary of William Dunlap, 1766–1839* (New York: New York Historical Society, 1930), II, 479–86.

49. Stanley Kimmel, *The Mad Booths of Maryland* (New York: The Bobbs-Merrill Company, 1940), pp. 31–32.

in every major role in his repertoire: Richard, Sir Edward Mortimer (in *The Iron Chest*, by George Colman the Younger), King Lear, Octavian (in *The Mountaineers*, by Colman the Younger), Sir Giles Overreach (in *A New Way to Pay Old Debts*, by Philip Massinger), and Bertram (in *Bertram*, or *The Castle of St. Aldobrand*, by Charles Robert Maturin).[50] Booth then left for a brief engagement in Petersburg. His means of departure anticipated his later eccentricity. He left Richmond on foot.[51]

Despite an occasional good house, economic pressure ultimately forced Charles Gilfert to give up his Richmond operation. When his fall season of 1823, which opened August 15, bogged down after only seventeen performances, he closed the theater and allowed his lease with the proprietors to lapse.[52] It was to be some time before a repertory company would again operate in Richmond on a regular basis. Indeed, following a brief appearance by James H. Caldwell's strolling company in 1824, the playhouse was closed altogether until 1827.[53] And it would be much longer before theater of the quality offered by Gilfert and company was made available in the Virginia capital.

The Virginia career of Charles Gilfert was by no means limited to Richmond. Lynchburg was also indebted to this harried pioneer for the introduction of professional theater. The piedmont Virginia town served as a western terminus of the James River tobacco traffic and as a tobacco processing center for much of the sparsely settled Virginia interior. Lynchburg had been incorporated in 1805, acquired its first court house in 1812, and its market in 1813.[54] In 1816 a sluice was opened on the river that made the town more accessible to river trade. By 1830, when census figures (however inaccurate) became available, the aggregate Lynchburg population totaled 4,630.[55] But once again, as a center of exchange serving a large rural area, the transient element was considerable at most times.

A community far removed from the coast and as isolated as Lynchburg was suffered even more from lack of diversion than the Eastern towns of the seaboard. Perhaps isolation explains the existence in Lynchburg of an amateur "Thespian Society" in 1818, one which

50. Shockley, "Richmond Theatre, 1819–1838," pp. 385–91.
51. Kimmel, *Mad Booths*, p. 32. Booth made his New York debut Oct. 5, 1821, at the Park Theater.
52. Shockley, "Richmond Theatre, 1819–1838," pp. 5–6.
53. *Ibid.*, pp. 6–7.
54. U. S. Census Office, *Social Statistics*, pp. 60–61.
55. *Ibid.*, p. 60.

apparently performed in a small frame theater.[56] The production of plays was an especially appropriate diversion for the people of small interior towns; amateur performances provided entertainment for both the performers and for the members of the audience, who came to see, and probably to ridicule, their friends. In 1820 a group of Lynchburg residents built a new brick theater to house their amateur society.[57] Interest in society performances was clearly high in the little Virginia tobacco town. And when people were interested in the activities of the local players, they were almost certain to be interested in the strolling professionals as well.

The existence of a theater building usually served to draw touring companies to a town. In August of 1822, "Brown's Company," an ephemeral itinerant troupe under "Mr. F. Brown," appeared in Lynchburg. The *Lynchburg Virginian* of September 6, 1822, noted their presence in town. "The theatre has been opened," read the announcement, "and our citizens have . . . greeted with unbounded applause, the performance of some of the best plays in the language, by the first regular company that have ever visited this place."[58] The admission price was $1.00 anywhere in the house.

Another observation in the *Virginian* tells much of theater audiences in a small southern town. "It is gratifying to observe the correct and attentive deportment of the audiance [*sic*]", noted the editor; ". . . but for a few trifling circumstances, such as making remarks, cracking nuts &c, in the midst of the most interesting scenes, we think everything [is] conducted as decorously as it can be in so large and general a company."[59] Audiences were large then, and socially mixed, and they enjoyed themselves at the theater.

Naturally the players were attacked in Lynchburg, as everywhere, by the "puritanical fringe." Yet one letter in the *Virginian* indicates that an occasional local youth actually joined the company professionally. After a typical attack upon the immorality of the stage,

56. Richard Hanna Hadley, "The Theatre in Lynchburg, Virginia, From Its Beginnings in 1822 to the Outbreak of the Civil War" (Doctoral dissertation, University of Michigan, 1942), pp. 17–18.

57. *Ibid.*, p. 19.

58. *Ibid.*, p. 22, quoting *Lynchburg Virginian*, Sept. 6, 1822. The *Virginian* statement that this was the first company to appear in Lynchburg must be accepted as accurate, though the *Richmond Compiler*, July 30, 1822, noted that the Gilfert company was "to open the Lynchburg Theatre, for a short season, in the course of 6 or 8 days." Presumably Gilbert failed to appear in Lynchburg.

59. Hadley, "Lynchburg Theatre," p. 36, quoting *Lynchburg Virginian*, Sept. 13, 1822.

"Plutarch," the correspondent, turned on the memorization of plays as having "a very dangerous tendency. . . ." Committing a play to memory might incline the impressionable toward "the despicable means of obtaining a livelihood by play acting, of which we have had several instances."[60] The editor of the *Virginian*, however, issued a staunch defense of the stage, suggesting that certain plays could promote morality and influence toward good rather than evil.

On September 28, 1822, the first Lynchburg season closed. It had run for six and a half weeks, during which the Brown Company had performed such favorites as *Richard III*, the David Garrick adaptation of *Taming of the Shrew* called *Catherine and Petruchio*, *Hamlet*, *Macbeth*, James Sheridan Knowles's *Virginius*, Edward Moore's *Gamester*, and many others. Upon the departure of the company, the *Virginian* observed: "The success which the company met with leaves no doubt that hereafter we shall be gratified with the same delightful and innocent amusement every year."[61]

For several years thereafter Lynchburg did enjoy annual theater seasons. In October of 1823 the touring company of Palmer Fisher and Samuel Drake, whose operations were centered in the West,[62] performed a season there. It lasted until December 5, 1823, drawing well the entire time.[63] By June or July of 1824 another group, the "Herbert Company," was in town operating the theater and receiving, according to the *Virginian*, "uniformly good encouragement. . . ."[64]

When the [George P.?] "Richardson" company played Lynchburg in April, 1828, they advertised performances nightly.[65] In an editorial recommending the troupe, the *Virginian* of April 7, 1828, indicated that the theater drew upon "country" people as well as town-dwellers for support. "Our country friends," wrote the editor, "who have . . . less frequently than ourselves, an opportunity of participating in such amusements, will not, in all probability see a

60. *Ibid.*, p. 39, quoting *Lynchburg Virginian*, Sept. 17, 1822.
61. *Ibid.*, p. 46, quoting *Lynchburg Virginian*, Oct. 1, 1822.
62. See below, chap. iii, for a discussion of Drake's Western operations.
63. Hadley, "Lynchburg Theatre," pp. 51, 62.
64. *Ibid.*, p. 74, quoting *Lynchburg Virginian*, Sept. 21, 1824. "Herbert" was probably either the veteran British comedian John Herbert or his son, both of whom seem to have been touring the area in 1824. In 1825 both were performing in the stock of the Chatham Theater, New York. See Odell, *Annals*, III, 160–61.
65. Hadley, "Lynchburg Theatre," p. 93, quoting *Lynchburg Virginian*, March 24, 1828.

better company than that now playing here."[66] Implicit in this statement is the suggestion that the rural folk should come to town expressly to attend the theater.

Following a long season offered by "Messrs. Cargill and Campbell" [probably Cabell] in 1829,[67] Lynchburg had no record of professional theater for fourteen years. Two factors seem primary in
explaining the decline. First, the fundamentalist churches came to
exert a strong influence over the community beginning about 1825.
Something of a local religious revival occurred, bringing with it a
more puritanical atmosphere. The Baptists organized a congregation
and opened a church in 1826, and the Presbyterians followed in
1827. Indeed, the theater itself was purchased by a group of free
Negroes for use as a church.[68] Whenever the puritanical element
grew strong enough in a town to influence public policy, the theater
was generally prohibited or at least severely limited. Such seems to
have been the case in Lynchburg.

Economic dislocation, as already noted, invariably affected theater
operations. Lynchburg experienced severe economic difficulties during the late 1820's and after. As early as 1828 the *Virginian* complained of "the hardness of the times. . . ."[69] By 1833 economic unrest
had worsened considerably; money was scarce and credit hard to
obtain. Then came the Panic of 1837 and the long years of depression. During all this time there was no monetary incentive for strolling
troupes to move upriver to Lynchburg.[70] But the amateurs were frequently active in the absence of the professionals.[71] And when the
population grew sufficiently to dilute the concentration of the fervidly religious, and when prosperity returned to the country, the
theater returned to Lynchburg to stay.

3.

The center of Virginia theatrical activity throughout the ante
bellum period was, of course, Richmond. Lynchburg was peripheral,

66. Quoted in *ibid.*, p. 95.
67. *Ibid.*, p. 109, quoting *Lynchburg Virginian*, Jan. 19, 1829. "Campbell" is
almost certainly a misprint for "Cabell," who was co-manager of a touring company with Cargill at this time.
68. *Ibid.*, pp. 137–39.
69. *Ibid.*, p. 95, quoting *Lynchburg Virginian*, April 7, 1828.
70. *Ibid.*, pp. 140–42, makes a strong case for the primacy of the economic
basis of the theatrical decline.
71. *Ibid.*, p. 86.

as were Norfolk, Petersburg, Fredericksburg, and Alexandria. The company based in Richmond was the most important in the Virginia area. It served these smaller towns, and lesser strolling concerns were of secondary significance. But the activities of the smaller, more ephemeral, companies were not insignificant. They served an important function in spreading the drama, and as such deserve attention.

One in particular, the Virginia strolling company of James Henry Caldwell, is of special interest. In 1818 Caldwell organized his troupe and promoted the construction of the Petersburg, Virginia, playhouse, which he undertook to manage.[72] By 1819 his company had played in Washington, Alexandria, Fredericksburg, and Richmond, and in each of these towns, save Richmond, Caldwell was recognized as the more or less permanent theater manager.[73] Even after his portentous move to New Orleans in 1819, Caldwell continued for a time to return annually to perform in his Virginia circuit and perhaps also to visit his wife. In 1819 he had married the wealthy Fredericksburg widow Maria Carter Wormeley, great-granddaughter of Robert "King" Carter.[74] Maria never went with him to New Orleans, even after 1824 when he abandoned the Virginia circuit altogether.

Many such peripatetic companies toured the Virginia area prior to 1830. But the extent of the operations of these troupes is impossible to determine. Indications are that they covered remarkable distances and performed in the tiniest of towns. The *Lynchburg Virginian* of May 25, 1827, for example, announced that the company of "White and Howard" were en route there. "We know nothing of this Company," admitted the *Virginian*, "but the papers of Woodstock, Winchester, and Charlottesville, through which places they have passed, speak well both of their professional talent and private deportment."[75] Again, the troupe of Palmer Fisher and Samuel Drake had arrived in Lynchburg in 1823 from Liberty [now Bedford], Vir-

72. [James Rees], "The Southern Stage, Actors and Authors," *Dramatic Mirror and Literary Companion*, I (Dec. 11, 1841), 140. Caldwell personally furnished much of the information used here by Rees.

73. *Richmond Compiler*, May 13, 1819.

74. Hostetler, "Caldwell," p. 22. According to tradition, Maria saw Caldwell perform in Fredericksburg shortly after her husband's death, found the actor-manager irresistible, and threw herself at him, scandalizing the staid Virginia gentry.

75. Hadley, "Lynchburg Theatre," p. 86, quoting *Lynchburg Virginian*, May 25, 1827.

ginia, where the people had formed a favorable impression "of the histrionic talent of a part of the corps. . . ."[76] The tenor of these observations from small villages seems to point to considerable familiarity with strolling companies.

Nor were the strollers limited in their hinterland activities to Virginia. North Carolina, whose want of a single large town made her a culturally backward state, saw occasional touring companies perform. The strollers in North Carolina, as was customary, gravitated to those towns that had amateur societies and playhouses available. There were several such towns. New Bern, for example, claimed an amateur group, one with a brick theater, as early as 1802.[77] The Raleigh Thespian Society built a playhouse in 1815.[78] In Wilmington an amateur society contracted with the trustees of Innes Academy for the use of the lower part of the academy building as a theater; Salisbury saw a society organized in 1813, and Fayetteville in 1814.[79] The Warrenton "Thalian Society" received the accolades of the *Semi-Weekly Standard* for providing a worthwhile leisure-time activity for the town's clerks and mechanics.[80]

The professional strollers who played in North Carolina played only brief stands. These itinerants were usually on their way elsewhere, most frequently to Charleston, South Carolina, and they performed in the North Carolina towns only to help finance the trip. Still, the arrival of the players stirred considerable interest in those towns.

James H. Caldwell played in Raleigh, North Carolina, in 1817 and in 1818. The *Raleigh Register* of April 25, 1817, contained an advertisement for "A Dramatic Olio from Shakespeare, Otway, and Morton."[81] The Raleigh Thespian Society assisted Caldwell in the production. In 1818 Caldwell the strolling player became Caldwell the manager. That year he took his new company to Raleigh for a

76. *Ibid.*, p. 53, quoting *Lynchburg Virginian*, Oct. 17, 1823.

77. Francis Asbury, *The Journal of the Rev. Francis Asbury, Bishop of the Methodist Episcopal Church, From August 7, 1771 to December 7, 1815* (New York: N. Bangs and T. Mason, 1821), III, 51. Bishop Asbury felt that the building would make a "most excellent church." He estimated the population of New Bern at 3,500–4,000.

78. Guion Griffis Johnson, *Ante-Bellum North Carolina. A Social History* (Chapel Hill: University of North Carolina Press, 1937), p. 175.

79. *Ibid.*, p. 177.

80. *Ibid.*, quoting *Warrenton Semi-Weekly Standard*, March 9, 1859.

81. Quoted in Donald J. Rulfs, "The Ante-Bellum Professional Theater in Raleigh," *The North Carolina Historical Review*, XXIX (July, 1952), 347.

stand in July. On July 17, during the "season," the *Register* observed: "The theatre continues to be numerously and fashionably attended. The Patronage afforded it (in proportion to the population of Raleigh) it is believed, has never been surpassed in America."[82] More typical of Raleigh theatrical activity, however, was the program advertised in the *Raleigh Minerva* of November 24, 1820. Under the head "THEATRICAL," the newspaper announced: "We learn that Mr. and Mrs. Russel, of the theatre, who are on their way from Petersburg to Charleston, purpose [sic], on their arrival here, to remain one day, and to offer a Theatrical entertainment."

Other North Carolina towns visited most frequently by strollers were Wilmington, Fayetteville, and New Bern. When the company of John Herbert appeared in Lynchburg, Virginia, in 1824, the manager was announced as "manager of the Raleigh, Wilmington, Fayetteville, and New Bern Theatres,"[83] an indication that for a time at least, these towns formed something of a regular circuit. In any case, the playhouses in all four towns attracted such touring companies, or parts of companies, as happened to be in the area.

However irregular the appearance of players in North Carolina, they appeared often enough to excite the wrath of the pure-in-heart. When the acrimonious traveler-observer Anne Royall found a theater operating in Fayetteville in 1828, she warned, "look out, Red Necks!"[84] She was aware of the affront to the religious fundamentalists afforded by the existence of that playhouse and was certain they would fight it. They did. A letter in the March 7, 1823, *Raleigh Register* was representative of their assault. Indulgence in theatrical entertainment, the writer contended, involved the "risque of giving nature a victory over conscience," at least to the weak of will. The correspondent related (with apparent relish) the details of a recent occurrence in support of his contention. A part of the audience in a theater of a nearby town had left the theater indignantly "on account of indecent exposure of person in a female!" "Perhaps it will be said," he continued, "that this argues a virtuous refinement, preva-

82. Quoted in *ibid.*, p. 347. Rulfs gives the 1820 population of Raleigh as 2,674.

83. Hadley, "Lynchburg Theatre," p. 69, quoting *Lynchburg Virginian*, Aug. 24, 1824.

84. Anne Royall, *Mrs. Royall's Southern Tour, or Second Series of the Black Book* (Washington: Privately published, 1830), I, 151. Mrs. Royall estimated the population of Fayetteville at about 3,800. In addition to a playhouse, she found a Masonic hall, a court house, three banks, and three churches.

lent among those who attend the Theatre in our day. Not so—for the number that retired, was unfortunately but small."[85] The fundamentalist attack on the theater was stronger in North Carolina than in most Southern states, especially after 1825.[86] This attack, combined with the relative sparseness of population, rendered North Carolina theatrically one of the least active states in the Union.

4.

The first quarter of the nineteenth century saw the development of a recognizable theatrical circuit on the South Atlantic seaboard where the larger towns were able to attract talented repertory companies who performed quality drama on a regular season basis. Richmond was the upper terminus of this circuit, Charleston the lower. Each of those cities had its immediate adjuncts—somewhat smaller towns whose proximity to the theatrical centers made them ideal for short seasons, seasons that could be employed to make the longer seasons in the centers less protracted and thus more profitable.

Smaller towns and those more remote from the cultural centers were dependent upon the activities of the numerous, ephemeral, itinerant companies for their professional theater. Yet a remarkable number of these little towns attracted strollers by building real theaters to house local amateur societies and by supporting those troupes that happened by. But there was no real consistency in support of theater anywhere in the period. The forces of religious opposition and economic dislocation militated constantly against the theater, frequently with success.

Still, the strolling troupes continued to try. When stopped in one town they pushed on to the next. They were resourceful, sometimes even dauntless, in the pursuit of their strange profession. And even as the strollers persisted in their efforts in the East, far to the West their more venturesome counterparts were taking the acted drama into remote regions.

85. Quoted in Johnson, *Ante-Bellum North Carolina*, p. 178.
86. *Ibid.*, p. 178.

CHAPTER III

THE WAY
WEST

1.

AMERICA'S "NATIONAL DYNAMIC" OF 1815 WAS NOWHERE MORE IN EVI-
dence than in the transmontane West. Freed from the onus of
separatism by the symbol of New Orleans and by the demise of
Federalist particularism, cleared of "decadent" foreign influence,
open to new settlement and attracting numberless new settlers, the
West of 1815 was burgeoning.

The Mississippi River system formed the nerve complex of the
nineteenth-century West. When in 1815 the "Enterprise" made the
first steam-powered voyage upstream from New Orleans, Louisiana,
to Louisville, Kentucky, that voyage marked the commencement of
a new age of Western development.[1] By 1817 river steamers were
in considerable use on the Western waterways, and the transportation revolution was underway. The *Lexington Kentucky Reporter*
voiced some implications of that revolution when it exclaimed: "Less
than a week from Kentucky to New Orleans! . . . One can now hear
preaching in Kentucky on Sunday and on the following Sunday
attend mass in New Orleans."[2] The steamboat in effect decreased the

1. Bernard Mayo, "Lexington: Frontier Metropolis," *Historiography and
Urbanization. Essays in American History in Honor of W. Stull Holt*, ed. Eric
F. Goldman (Baltimore: The Johns Hopkins Press, 1941), p. 54.
2. Quoted in *ibid*.

[51]

size of the vast Louisiana Purchase territory by connecting its budding commercial centers. With the advent of the steamboat all Western produce with access to a river port gained access to the world market. It was clear that the Mississippi Valley was on the verge of coming into its own.[3]

As the countless people who constituted the "Great Migration" poured in to settle in the Mississippi watershed, many sought out the centers of relative population concentration for their new homes. Existing towns grew larger and new towns emerged to serve an ever more complex economy. In 1815 there were four major population centers in the Southwest. At the mouth of the Mississippi was of course New Orleans, gateway to the great valley and to the world trade routes. Far upriver, at the confluence of the Mississippi and the Missouri, was St. Louis, in 1815 still a small trading settlement, but growing, and so located as to be assured of future greatness. Nashville served the rich Cumberland district of middle Tennessee. Up the Ohio was the Kentucky urban complex of Louisville, Lexington, and Frankfort, serving the bluegrass country. Louisville stood at the falls of the Ohio, where it had developed as a point of transshipment for river traffic. Lexington to the east served as trade center to the Kentucky interior and as jumping-off place for frontiersmen headed south or west. Between the larger towns was Frankfort, political capital of the state.

It was this Kentucky group, Lexington in particular, that had first emerged as significant urban centers in the transmontane West. And "urban" is not an inappropriate term to describe these Kentucky settlements of 1815. From their inception they were intended to serve urban functions.[4] Louisville and Lexington (as well as St. Louis) were laid out and partly settled even before the surrounding countryside was cleared for farming.[5] The settlements, initially designed for collective defense, became centers of trade, of commerce, and of communication. And of course, as Richard C. Wade has pointed out, they were "the focuses of cultural life" in the area.[6]

3. See, for example, "Resources and Improvements," *Niles' Weekly Register*, VI (Aug. 6, 1814), 393–95.

4. Richard C. Wade, *The Urban Frontier. The Rise of Western Cities, 1790–1830* (Cambridge: Harvard University Press, 1959), p. i. See also Everett Dick, *The Dixie Frontier. A Social History of the Southern Frontier from the First Transmontane Beginnings to the Civil War* (New York: Alfred A. Knopf, 1948), pp. 148–49.

5. Wade, *Urban Frontier*, p. i.

6. *Ibid.* See also Dick, *Dixie Frontier*, p. 342.

Moreover, the people of the rural sections viewed themselves as different from their settlement counterparts, and vice versa. Both groups were aware of their differences in values, interests, pace. In 1811 a farmer living in the country outside of Lexington expressed the differences in a dialogue between "Rusticus" and "Urbanus," published in the *Kentucky Reporter*. Urbanus spoke of the "rude, gross appearance" of Rusticus, observing: "how strong you smell of your ploughed ground and corn fields. How dismal, how gloomy your green woods." Rusticus' reply illustrated clearly the rural image of the urbanites. "What a fine smooth complexion you have, Urbanus," wrote Rusticus. He continued, "you look like a weed that has grown up in the shade. Can you walk your streets without inhaling the noxious fumes with which your town is pregnant?—Can you engage in calm contemplation when hammers are ringing in every direction ... [?]"[7] Such were the differences in city life and country life, even when the city in question had, in 1810, an aggregate population of but 4,326.[8]

Despite the deceptively small population, Lexington was in 1815 the most important urban community in the Mississippi Valley north of New Orleans and had, in fact, considerable pretensions to urbanity. Transylvania University was founded in 1798, evidencing the desire for cultural elevation on the part of the Athenians of the West.[9] Before 1800, Lexington was introduced to such essentially urban phenomena as a public library, a musical society, a jockey club, a drama society, and, most urbane of all, "free Nancy's" bawdy house.[10] By 1810 the Lexington economic complex included three nail factories, four paper mills, six powder mills, seven brick yards, five hat factories, thirteen rope-walks, five bagging factories, and seven distilleries.[11] The local newspaper, the *Kentucky Gazette*, had been operating since 1787. Well might visitor James McBride observe in 1810 "Lexington ... has been, and yet is, the seat of wealth and refinement of the western country."[12]

Some form of theater had existed in Lexington since 1790 when the *Gazette* announced a performance of a tragedy and a farce by a group of Transylvania students "in the presence of a very respect-

7. Wade, *Urban Frontier*, p. i, quoting *Lexington Kentucky Reporter*, July 2, 1811.
8. U. S. Census Office, *Social Statistics*, p. 117.
9. *Ibid.*, p. 118.
10. Wade, *Urban Frontier*, p. 21.
11. U. S. Census Office, *Social Statistics*, p. 118.
12. Quoted in Mayo, "Lexington," p. 31.

able audience. . . ."[13] In 1797 the *Gazette* advertised the opening of "A NEW EXHIBITION ROOM . . . adjoining Coleman's Tavern," with admission prices of 3*s*.9*d*. to the pit and 21*s*.3*d*. to the gallery.[14] By 1801 there was a building in town identified as a "Theatre," presumably a public hall used occasionally by wandering entertainers and for amateur performances.[15]

The beginning of a consistent theater tradition in Lexington, and in Louisville and Frankfort as well, came in 1806 with the arrival of an ambitious Baltimore entrepreneur by the name of Luke Usher. Usher, along with his son, a quondam professional actor named Noble Luke, initially established an umbrella factory in Lexington, an endeavor in which they did well. By 1808 they were able to expand their interests to include a brewery. The entire second floor of the brewery they outfitted as a theater—probably the first real playhouse in Kentucky.[16]

Luke Usher first used his brewery-theater primarily for amateur performances in which Noble Luke appeared periodically. Occasionally, however, a professional entertainer appeared there. For example, James Douglass, son of the redoubtable David Douglass (of the early Eastern theater), performed with amateur support in the Usher house in 1808.[17] Young Douglass was so encouraged by the support he received that he set out to recruit a real company to play in the Kentucky towns.

As time passed and the bluegrass community developed, visits of strolling players grew more frequent. The *Lexington Kentucky Reporter* of October 31, 1809, contained a "communication" recommending the local playhouse and noting that the building had been recently "fitted up in a very handsome style . . .",[18] an indication of financially successful operations. Additional boxes were added to

13. Lucile Naff Clay, "The Lexington Theater from 1800–1840" (Master's thesis, University of Kentucky, 1930), p. 3, quoting *Lexington Kentucky Gazette*, April 26, 1790.

14. Beryl Meek, "A Record of the Theatre in Lexington, Kentucky, From 1799–1850" (Master's thesis, State University of Iowa, 1930), p. 28, quoting *Lexington Kentucky Gazette*, June 3, 1797.

15. Clay, "Lexington Theater," p. 5.

16. John Jacob Weisert, "Beginnings of the Kentucky Theatre Circuit," *The Filson Club Historical Quarterly*, XXXIV (July, 1960), 267. The building was located on the southwest corner of Vine and Spring streets.

17. Meek, "Theatre in Lexington," p. 12.

18. Mabel Tyree Crum, "The History of the Lexington Theatre From the Beginning to 1860" (Doctoral dissertation, University of Kentucky, 1956), p. 25, quoting *Lexington Kentucky Reporter*, Oct. 31, 1809. The correspondent did, however, complain of an inadequate "orchestry."

the auditorium in July of 1810, and another noteworthy itinerant player, John Vos, appeared in a quasi-professional performance of the Kotzebue-Sheridan *Pizarro* on September 11, 1810.[19] Usher was gradually converting his playhouse into a business venture, and the venture was doing encouragingly well.

In 1810 truly professional theater reached Kentucky. First came a small strolling company, apparently a "commonwealth" operation, led by William Turner and his wife Sophia, who arrived from Cincinnati to join Luke Usher in Lexington.[20] Experienced strollers, the members of this troupe proceeded to offer seasonal performances in a Lexington-Frankfort circuit under the auspices of the Ushers. The "Turner Company" seem to have operated with some success until the War of 1812 interrupted theatrical activities everywhere.[21] But Turner and some of his troupe were to return after the war to continue their careers as itinerant Western actors.

Following close on the heels of the Turner corps came James Douglass, with his newly recruited "company of Theatrical performers from Montreal and Quebec."[22] The *Gazette* welcomed the return of the popular player. "It is with sincere pleasure we are at length able to congratulate the Lovers of the Drama and the fashionables of the town," announced the *Gazette*. "After an absence of eighteen months, Mr. D. has succeeded in accomplishing the objects of his [journey], and has engaged a company sufficiently large to form an establishment in the western country. The citizens of Lexington and Frankfort will be gratified during the present winter with their performances, which . . . will contribute much to dispel the gloom of the season."[23]

Western traveler John Melish was in Lexington in 1811 during the Douglass company's first season, and he attended the theater. His account of the experience recorded in his journal provides a succinct specimen of early drama criticism. "We went in a body to the theater," wrote Melish. "The performers acted very well but there was a deficiency of actresses, and one of the men had to play a

19. Meek, "Theatre in Lexington," p. 12, quoting *Lexington Kentucky Gazette*, Sept. 11, 1810.

20. Crum, "Lexington Theatre," p. 47. There were, of course, professional entertainers in Lexington prior to 1810, dealing in a variety of subdramatic fare. One notable such stroller was "Mr. Rannie," who appeared at Traveller's Hall in April of 1805. *Ibid.*, p. 10. See below, n. 75.

21. *Ibid.*, pp. 47, 76; Weisert, "Kentucky Circuit," p. 272.

22. Meek, "Theatre in Lexington," p. 57, quoting *Lexington Kentucky Gazette*, Dec. 18, 1810.

23. *Ibid.*

female character, which did not suit my taste at all."[24] He also noted
that the company was to perform in Louisville and Frankfort as well
as in Lexington. So even before the outbreak of the War of 1812
Kentucky had an incipient theatrical circuit. The three towns had
actual theaters, albeit of makeshift proportions. And the circuit had
an impresario—umbrella-maker Luke Usher, who with his theatrically inclined son Noble Luke owned or leased the playhouses.

Luke Usher was naturally concerned by the effects of war upon
his enterprises. But he knew that peace would likely bring a revival
of interest in theater-going. So in the fall of 1814 he sent his son to
Albany, New York, to recruit a strolling company to come west and
perform in the Kentucky playhouses. When Noble Luke Usher arrived in Albany he found the company of John Bernard performing
in the new Green Street Theater.[25] Bernard's stage manager at
the time was an experienced British actor-manager, Samuel Drake.
Usher approached Drake with his proposition; Drake was interested.

Samuel Drake was a likely candidate for Western theater management. A restless, ambitious, capable man, archetype of the strolling
player, he had readily available in his talented family the nucleus of
a small company. He had only to employ one or two non-relatives to
fill out his theatrical cadre. One of the outsiders whom Drake hired
was a green young actor, a minor member of John Bernard's stock
by the name of Noah Miller Ludlow.

The career of Noah Ludlow prior to his joining the new Drake
company was typical of an increasing number of stage-struck youths
of the period. But in view of his prominence in Southern theater
history, Ludlow's early career is worthy of special attention here. He
was born in New York City, July 3, 1795,[26] into a respectable middle-
class family of rather puritanical views. Despite an early proclivity
for dramatic literature, at age twelve Ludlow took a clerkship in a
retail shop in New York which he kept for three years. Dissatisfied,
he gave up retail trade and tried, successively, clerkships in a wholesale firm and a shipping agency. By the summer of 1813 Ludlow,
restless, romantic, lacking in business acumen, was thoroughly disenchanted with the countinghouse routine. When his father died in

24. John Melish, *Travels Through the United States of America in the Years
1806 & 1807, and 1809, 1810, & 1811*, 2 volumes (Philadelphia: privately published by the author, 1815), II, 186.
25. Hughes, *American Theatre*, p. 123.
26. Noah Miller Ludlow MS Diary, July 3, 1856, in Ludlow-Field-Maury
Collection, Missouri Historical Society.

the fall of 1813, the young man left home and struck out for Albany, intent on becoming an "independent *Mechanic*."[27]

Upon arriving in Albany, Ludlow apprenticed himself to a mechanic, a painter of coach and carriage ornamentation. But despite his sincere effort to learn the new craft, the eighteen-year-old Ludlow, freed from parental supervision for the first time, became fascinated with the activity at the Green Street playhouse. He sought out the company of the young actors connected with the Bernard troupe and with their encouragement tried an occasional small part as an unidentified amateur. To his delight he proved a success in these fledgling efforts. He had latent talent as an actor. Late in 1814 Noah Ludlow joined the Bernard troupe. However green, he was now a professional actor.[28]

When the offer came to join Samuel Drake in the Western circuit, Ludlow was quick to accept. He saw in the Western tour the possibility of quick professional advance and the certainty of adventure. Both prospects were realized fully.

Many years later Ludlow wrote a long, detailed account of his career on the stage. His narrative of the trek west with the Drake company is still a first-rate piece of frontier travel literature as well as a classic of American theatricana.[29] The heart of the company

27. "Heads of the People," *St. Louis Saturday Evening Post*, July 17, 1847, clipping in Ludlow-Field-Maury Collection, Missouri Historical Society. This article is a long biographical sketch of Ludlow. The copy in the Ludlow Collection contains his penciled corrections and annotations.

28. *Ibid.*

29. Noah Miller Ludlow, *Dramatic Life as I Found it: A Record of Personal Experience* (St. Louis: G. I. Jones and Company, 1880), pp. 5–86. The reliability of *Dramatic Life* as a primary source is open to question. Ludlow did not write his memoirs until the late 1870's, when he was an old man. Moreover, he was animated by several strong biases which led him into frequent inaccuracies. Most notable among these biases was his desire to prove that he had first introduced professional theater in the various towns of the Southwest. Clearly he cannot be accepted too literally on matters of detail, and rigorous internal criticism must be applied where Ludlow is utilized to establish fact or judgment. But in his behalf it should be stated that he wrote from elaborate diaries and day books as well as from his personal playbill file and his business records, all of which he assiduously preserved. In short, his memoir is something more than random recollections of an old man. For all its inaccuracies in specific detail, for all its ungenerous judgments of the activities of his pioneering peers, as Carson has pointed out, *Dramatic Life* "is well-nigh invaluable in the history of the American stage"; William Glascow Bruce Carson, *The Theatre on the Frontier. The Early Years of the St. Louis Stage* (Chicago: University of Chicago Press, 1932), p. 19. Rusk deems *Dramatic Life* "the most important account of the Western theatre written by a contemporary observer"; Ralph Leslie Rusk, *The Literature of the Middle Western Frontier* (New York: Columbia University Press, 1925), I, 364.

consisted of six Drakes: Samuel and his offspring Samuel, Jr., Alexander, James, Martha, and Julia. Ludlow and Frances Ann Denny (later Mrs. Alexander Drake, an actress reputedly of consummate talent) were the only other actors and, notably, the only Americans in the company. The Drakes were all British. Rounding out the force were Lewis, the stage carpenter, and his wife, and Joe Tracy, "man-of-all work."[30] In May, 1815, after sending Ludlow ahead to arrange for accommodations for the troupe on their initial stops, Samuel Drake set out for the West with company, costumes, scenery, and stage properties in tow.[31]

Drake's plan was to perform in towns on the way to Kentucky in order to defray the expenses of the trip. His capital was strictly limited. The company first headed due west overland from Albany with the ladies on horseback or in the equipment wagon and the men on foot. Their first stop was in Cooperstown, New York, where, according to Ludlow, James Fenimore Cooper attended the performances and encouraged the troupe to continue the venture.[32] Bearing northwest from Cooperstown, Drake and company played in Utica on the Mohawk River, then, continuing west, stopped briefly in Herkimer, Auburn, and Geneva, all in New York. They then struck south across the state to Olean near the Pennsylvania border. Throughout western New York they encountered wild country, no end of adventure, and some danger, as, for example, when Mrs. Lewis was treed by wolves.

At Olean Drake traded horses and wagon for a flat-bottomed "broadhorn," and the troupe proceeded down the Allegheny River to Pittsburgh. River travel was difficult. Taking a wrong fork on one occasion the player-pioneers came near plunging over a waterfall. They had to cordelle in spots and to carry the boat by hand over the shoals. Food was frequently scarce. When the company encountered rapids they had to transfer to ox-cart for several miles and then

30. Ludlow, *Dramatic Life*, p. 8. Julia Drake was, according to Ludlow, a beautiful and talented actress. She was mother of Julia Dean, perhaps the most universally popular of the Western stars. Indeed, much of the history of the theater in the South could be traced through the individual careers of this remarkable group.

31. *Ibid.*, pp. 7–8. The scenery included six different back-drops with corresponding "wings" or side-scenes, a painted curtain-proscenium (adjustable in size), an act-drop, and a green baize carpet. The whole could be set up or taken down and packed in two or three hours.

32. *Ibid.*, p. 9.

return to broadhorn. By mid-August, 1815, they reached Pittsburgh, where they commenced a lengthy season.[33]

In November, 1815, Drake closed in Pittsburgh, purchased another broadhorn, and started with his company down the Ohio River for Kentucky. The first stop in Kentucky was at Limestone (later Maysville) where Drake procured transportation overland to Frankfort where the legislature was in session. Ante bellum strolling managers generally sought out the state capitals when the legislatures were convened. In Frankfort Drake added some new members to his company. A group of actors had arrived in Kentucky at the invitation of Noble Luke Usher only to find that the younger Usher had died prior to their arrival. The newcomers, deprived of their employer, joined Drake's troupe.[34]

According to Ludlow, the first Frankfort season opened early in December, 1815, with *The Mountaineers,* a popular melodrama by George Colman the Younger, and the operatic farce *Poor Soldier.*[35] Drake had the best troupe yet to perform in Kentucky and the people seemed to appreciate the players' efforts. "On the evening succeeding our first performance," wrote Ludlow, ". . . the manager was called on by three gentlemen, who came . . . to express the great satisfaction the people of Frankfort felt in the Company he had brought to their city."[36] On, or "about," March 1, 1816, the Frankfort season closed. Ludlow recalled that the most respectable people attended the theater regularly and that the players were received in the best of Frankfort society.[37]

From Frankfort the troupe continued overland to Louisville. Samuel Drake had taken care to notify the people of Louisville that his company was coming. In a letter to the *Western Courier* of June 29, 1815, under an Albany, New York, dateline, Drake had addressed himself to "The Ladies and Gentlemen of Louisville and its vicinity. . . . " In the letter the manager announced his intention to establish "theatrical amusements on a respectable and permanent plan—where

33. *Ibid.,* pp. 10–44.

34. *Ibid.,* pp. 80–81. Among the new recruits were John Vaughn, who was employed as a leading man, and Tom Jefferson, a character actor and grandfather of the great comedian Joe Jefferson.

35. *Ibid.,* pp. 81–82.

36. *Ibid.*

37. *Ibid.,* p. 86. Ludlow was always acutely concerned with social acceptance. He recognized the low esteem in which theater people generally were held and fought throughout his career to improve their public image.

the eye shall revel in fancy's fairy bower, and the heart expand in scenes of luxurious delight."[38] Little wonder Ludlow found on arriving in Louisville that the people were "on the tip-top of expectation, and anxious for the opening of the season. . . ."[39]

On February 28, 1816, after renovating the interior of the playhouse, Drake opened the Louisville season. Until April 17, the *Western Courier* continued to run theater advertisements two or three days a week.[40] Ludlow recalled that the house was usually crowded, that the people enjoyed themselves, and that the season's-end benefits were well attended; all in a town of "not more than three thousand inhabitants. . . . " But the people, he remembered, were "prosperous, gay, and fond of theatrical amusements."[41]

By May 20, 1816, Drake and company were in Lexington, principal town of their incipient Kentucky circuit. Manager Drake published a "Card" in the *Lexington Kentucky Gazette* announcing his intentions. "MR. DRAKE," it read

> Late Director [stage manager] of the Boston and Albany Theatres, Respectfully informs the Ladies and Gentlemen of Lexington and of the State of Kentucky in general, that he intends to establish the Drama upon a firm and permanent plan . . . by which his company will visit the principal towns
>
> for a small period annually. . . . The selection of his pieces, [and] the regularity of his play, he trusts will prove to the public his industry to render the Theatre an entertainment of rational worth blended with instruction.[42]

The playhouse that the company used in Lexington was Luke Usher's brewery-theater. It was, according to Ludlow, the "poorest

38. John Jacob Weisert, *The Curtain Rose: A Checklist of Performances at Samuel Drake's City Theatre and Other Theatres at Louisville from the Beginnings to 1843* (Louisville: University of Louisville Press, 1958), p. 2, quoting *Louisville Western Courier*, June 29, 1815. It is noteworthy that Drake addressed his announcement to the people around Louisville as well as to the townspeople.

39. Ludlow, *Dramatic Life*, p. 88.

40. Weisert, *Curtain Rose*, p. 4.

41. Ludlow, *Dramatic Life*, p. 89. A Louisville amateur society had built the theater in which the Drake company performed, probably in 1808. It was located on the north side of Jefferson Street between Third and Fourth. See Benjamin Casseday, *The History of Louisville, From its Earliest Settlement Till the Year 1852* (Louisville: Hull and Brother, 1852), pp. 116–17.

42. Crum, "Lexington Theatre," p. 166, quoting *Lexington Kentucky Gazette*, May 20, 1816. Ludlow asserted that the season in Lexington commenced in mid-June, 1816. In reality it was mid-May. This error is typical of Ludlow's mistakes. He is frequently a bit off in his dates. But the contemporary sources uphold his general account to a remarkable degree.

specimen of a theatre."[43] It was no more than 30 feet wide. Canvas-covered benches without backrests served as seats. They were graduated in height from front to rear of the house in amphitheater fashion to increase visibility of the tiny stage. A sloping platform at one side of the auditorium provided access to the back benches. Directly behind the pit were several crude boxes. Scenery was rudimentary. Understandably, both beer and whiskey were readily available on the premises.[44] The first Lexington season continued successfully until the heat of summer rendered the poorly ventilated "theater" unbearable. Then manager Drake called for a summer vacation.

Ludlow took advantage of the break to organize what was known as a "gagging-scheme" or "gagging-spree." Recruiting a few of the more adventurous players from the Drake corps, Ludlow borrowed some old scenery and set off with his makeshift troupe (twelve strong) to perform in the surrounding towns and villages. Watering places were favorite stopping places for such itinerant groups, who found the residents of the spas congenial and appreciative of the diversion afforded by the players. Moreover, according to Ludlow, people from miles around gathered to see the performances.

Leaving Lexington, the troupe performed first at Harrodsburg Springs, a popular resort of Kentucky's elite. Ludlow failed to secure a hall for the performances, but at the request of the local concierge, the company performed in the hotel ballroom.[45] From there they journeyed to Danville, Kentucky, where they played seven or eight times in the court house. Paris, Kentucky, was the strollers' last stop. Again they used the hotel ballroom for the performances, which provided a welcome diversion for residents and visitors alike. Ludlow and his charges then returned to Lexington in time for the commencement of the fall season with Drake. It should be remembered that the manager of the peripatetic company was then only twenty-one years old. The experience was doubtless valuable to him.

Samuel Drake regrouped his forces in Lexington and opened the second season there on September 30, 1816, with the William Dimond tragedy *Adrian and Orilla* and the afterpiece *The Liar*.[46] In announcing the opening, Drake made a special appeal to the rural folk. He assured the "ladies and gentlemen residing in the country"

43. Ludlow, *Dramatic Life*, p. 90.
44. *Ibid.*
45. *Ibid.*, p. 91.
46. Crum, "Lexington Theatre," p. 173, quoting *Lexington Kentucky Gazette*, Sept. 30, 1816.

that they could "depend on the punctuality of every performance advertised, violent sickness only making an exception."[47] The season lasted until the latter part of November, 1816, when the company departed for Frankfort, where the Kentucky legislature was scheduled to meet in two weeks.[48]

Following a brief season in Frankfort, Drake and company visited Louisville, but by August 23, 1817, they were back in Lexington, their center of operations. The *Kentucky Gazette* announced the season's opening. Further renovations had been made on the auditorium, apparently in an effort to attract more ladies to the brewery-playhouse. "A *Coffee Room* in the rear of the Boxes will be provided," noted the *Gazette*, "as well as a side room with *confections* and other refreshments."[49] The ladies could hardly be expected to imbibe with the "gentlemen" at the playhouse. Male theater-goers of the period made frequent use of the bar facilities during the performances.

Several local appraisals of Drake and his company appeared in the press during the 1817 season in Lexington; all were favorable. The *Gazette* of November 15, 1817, for example, credited Drake with "skill," "ability," and "persevering industry." According to the correspondent, the manager had "snatched our theatre from obscurity and gained a complete sanction for the establishment."[50] A visitor from Philadelphia who attended the theater wrote the *Gazette* editor of his impressions. The play was a melodramatic adaptation of *Ali Baba and the Forty Thieves*, usually performed under the name *The Forty Thieves*. Despite the fact that the visitor had seen the popular piece frequently in Philadelphia and in Baltimore, he had "never been more gratified than with its performance on the Lexington boards." He praised the scenery as "particularly natural, appropriate and splendid. . . ." If the company was not uniformly good, at least the principals were. "Upon the whole," he concluded, "we will only give expression to the general sentiment of the public, when we say that the tout ensemble . . . reflect credit on the Theatricals of the West. . . ."[51] It is clear that the Drakes were a talented family. Al-

47. *Ibid.* Many people living only a few miles from town returned to their homes after the performance; hence the assurance of punctuality by the manager.

48. *Ibid.*, p. 180; Ludlow, *Dramatic Life*, p. 101.

49. Crum, "Lexington Theatre," p. 192, quoting *Lexington Kentucky Gazette*, Aug. 23, 1817.

50. Francis Garvin Davenport, *Ante-Bellum Kentucky. A Social History, 1800–1860* (Oxford, Ohio: The Mississippi Valley Press, 1943), p. 33, quoting *Lexington Kentucky Gazette*, Nov. 8, 1817.

51. Clay, "Lexington Theater," p. 33, quoting *Lexington Kentucky Gazette*, Oct. 18, 1817.

though their productions may have lacked sophistication in staging and stage mechanics, and though the secondary cast members were inexperienced and amateurish, there is no reason to doubt the over-all quality of the theater offered by the company of Samuel Drake.

By 1817 the Drake company was well established in the Kentucky circuit. For several years the company performed annual seasons, beginning in the fall in Lexington, traveling to Frankfort for the winter session of the legislature, then spending the spring in Louisville.[52] According to Benjamin Casseday, the early chronicler of Louisville, Drake established with his Western circuit "the golden era of the Drama in the West."[53]

2.

In the summer of 1817, prior to the opening of the Lexington season, Noah Ludlow, John Vaughn, and several other players withdrew from the Drake company. Ambitious and eager, the young rebels formed a company of their own on a commonwealth (i.e., profit-sharing) basis, then headed south across Kentucky. They played the villages along the way—Elizabethtown, Russellville, Hopkins-ville. The group was bound for Nashville, Tennessee, where, according to Ludlow, "it was said theatricals were wanted, and where there had not yet been a regular dramatic company."[54]

Nashville was in 1817 the commercial center of the Cumberland River traffic, serving interior Tennessee and southern Kentucky. The town dealt in agricultural commodities and furs, trading both north to Pittsburgh via the Ohio River and south to New Orleans on the Mississippi.[55] The precise resident population in 1817 is uncertain. It was well under 5,000.[56] But the transient element was large and the town was active and lively. Ludlow was likely correct in believing that "theatricals were wanted."

By July of 1817 the former Drake players had arrived in Nash-

52. Rusk, *Middle Western Frontier*, I, 370; Weisert, "Kentucky Circuit," p. 283; Meek, "Theatre in Lexington," pp. 110–16. Louisville became the center of their operations in 1818 when Drake purchased the theater there and renovated it completely. The shift in locus from Lexington to Louisville reflects the beginning of the shift in the relative importance of the two towns.

53. Casseday, *Louisville*, p. 116.

54. Ludlow, *Dramatic Life*, p. 107.

55. U. S. Census Office, *Social Statistics*, p. 152.

56. *Ibid.*, p. 151. The first population figures anywhere near reliable are for 1830, at which time the populace numbered 5,566.

ville[57] and found no playhouse available. Ludlow and company were forced to convert a deserted salthouse to their purpose. This they accomplished by building a platform for a stage, then placing plank benches, neatly covered with green baize, in rows along the salt-saturated floor. With the addition of their crude scenery and the inevitable act-drop, the "theater" was complete—makeshift, perhaps, but effective. Ludlow insisted that the house was acceptable to the people of Nashville, to whom such entertainment was only too rare. To the salthouse came all classes of local society, including the "very finest ladies of the city," all of whom were perfectly willing to "sit out a long five-act comedy or tragedy on a narrow board not more than ten inches wide, without any support for their backs. . . ." Moreover, they were delighted with the performances.[58]

For three weeks the company played in Nashville, opening the theater four or five nights a week. But their repertoire was limited and they soon ran out of material. Ludlow, now *de facto* manager of the company, closed temporarily while he sought new talent to expand the potential of the troupe. But he promised to return to Nashville by September 1, 1817.[59]

Ludlow went immediately to Cincinnati, the nearest town likely to have a few strolling actors about. He was in luck. William Turner, pre-empted in the Kentucky circuit by the arrival of Samuel Drake, was disbanding his company.[60] Ludlow hired several members of the Turner stock and set out again for Nashville in August of 1817.

Manager Ludlow was especially anxious to reach Nashville on this journey. His fiancée, a young widow named Mary Maury Squires, was waiting there for him. On September 1, 1817, shortly after his arrival, they were married.[61] Noah Ludlow gained more than a wife by this union. He also acquired the free services of a fledgling comedienne. Mary Ludlow joined the company before the commencement of the second Nashville season.

57. Douglas Lucas Hunt, "The Nashville Theatre, 1830–1840," *The Birmingham-Southern College Bulletin*, XXVIII (May, 1935), 3; Ludlow, *Dramatic Life*, p. 114.

58. Ludlow, *Dramatic Life*, p. 113.

59. *Ibid.*, pp. 114–15, 120.

60. *Ibid.*, p. 116. William Turner appealed to the courts in a breach-of-contract suit to force Luke Usher to continue leasing the theaters to the Turner company. But Usher won the suit when the court upheld his contract with Samuel Drake. See *Lexington Kentucky Reporter*, Oct. 18, 1815, and Crum, "Lexington Theatre," pp. 155–56. Turner, however, continued his career as strolling manager in the West for many years.

61. Ludlow, *Dramatic Life*, p. 118. Mary Maury Squires was the sister of Matthew Fontaine Maury, the notable oceanographer and climatologist.

Annette Nelson as the Mountain Sylph
Columbia University Press

Comedienne Fanny Fitzwilliam
Columbia University Press

Actress-playwright Anna Cora Mowatt
Columbia University Press

Popular romantic heroine Clara Fisher
Columbia University Press

Theatrical pioneer Sol Smith
Harvard Theatre Collection

Junius Brutus Booth and son Edwin
Columbia University Press

Noah Miller Ludlow
Columbia University Press

James H. Caldwell
Harvard Theatre Collection

Charles R. Thorne
Columbia University Press

Joseph M. Field
Columbia University Press

Julia Dean as Juliet
Columbia University Press

Junius Brutus Booth as Richard III
Columbia University Press

Character actor Ben De Bar
Harvard Theatre Collection

Actor-manager Thomas Placide
Harvard Theatre Collection

William H. Crisp
Harvard Theatre Collection

By mid-October local interest in the performances of the commonwealth troupe had waned. Ludlow decided to move on downriver. He had heard that New Orleans by now had sufficient "American" population to warrant attempting an English-language theater season there.[62] His only problem was persuading the other members of the company that they should make the effort. The possibility of yellow fever, a pestilence for which New Orleans was widely noted, was a strong deterrent. But Ludlow convinced them that the fever season was over, and most of the players agreed to join him. Having purchased a keelboat for $200, subdivided its cargo space into living compartments, and packed the scenery and costumes aboard, Ludlow and the "American Theatrical Commonwealth Company," late in October, 1817, started down the Cumberland River.[63]

None of the strolling players had any experience in riverboat operation. Manager Ludlow was elected "captain" of the unique craft, aptly christened "Noah's Ark." The members of the troupe—his wife, John Vaughn and wife, Thomas Morgan and wife, "Alex" Cummings and wife, and Henry Vaughn—served as crew. They encountered all the typical hazards of river navigation. While still on the Cumberland they ran aground crossing Harpeth Shoals. On reaching the Ohio River they had to contend with a maze of snags, sawyers, and sandbars. All the while they were on the Mississippi they were in fear of attack by river pirates, rumored to be about. Altogether, they were considerably relieved when, in mid-December, 1817, they sighted the river bluff on which stood the town of Natchez, Mississippi.[64]

Natchez was in 1817 the commercial capital of the new state of Mississippi. Located in the heart of an incredibly rich agricultural region, the town was the congregating point of all the planters of the area. On three sides of the town, extending outward thirty to forty miles in each direction, were the creek bottoms along which were located plantations large and small. The inhabitants of these plantations and of the smaller farms had ready access to town and

62. *Ibid.*, p. 120.
63. *Ibid.*, pp. 120–23. See also Philip Graham, *Showboats. The History of an American Institution* (Austin: University of Texas Press, 1951), p. 5. Graham surmises that the company performed occasionally on board the boat and thus credits Ludlow with operating the first known river showboat.
64. Joseph Miller Free, "Studies in American Theatre History: The Theatre of Southwestern Mississippi to 1840" (Doctoral dissertation, State University of Iowa, 1941), p. 67; Ludlow, *Dramatic Life*, p. 132. Ludlow incorrectly dated the Natchez landing "about" Nov. 10, 1817.

were frequently to be found there, transacting business on the exchange, reading newspapers in the coffee houses, or purchasing their supplies. Moreover, Natchez was the last sizable port before New Orleans. Riverboats bound north or south invariably provisioned there. As early as 1814, *Niles' Register* referred to Natchez as "the chief town and place of commerce . . ." of the Mississippi territory.[65]

The local population received Ludlow's strolling company with open arms. Natchez residents had long been interested in the theater, at least since 1806 when the first strolling player performed there.[66] In 1808 the Natchez Theatrical Association was formed, immediately outfitting an old Spanish hospital as a theater.[67] And sometime between September of 1812 and May 25, 1815, the amateurs built the first real playhouse in town. The theater was a crude frame affair, but it was equipped with a bar and even had a "green room" to which "none but the players and their attendants" were to be admitted.[68] It was this playhouse that Ludlow and company used upon their arrival in Natchez late in 1817.

The troupe made but a short visit in Natchez, for they were anxious to get on to New Orleans. But Ludlow recalled that the people of Natchez and its environs were enthusiastic over the performances, filling the theater "every night, at $1 a ticket, no half price."[69] And when time came for the company to depart a group of the town's more avid playgoers exacted a promise of Ludlow to return for another season in the spring. Selling their keelboat, the company departed Natchez in style, aboard a river steamer.

On January 7, 1818, the American Theatrical Commonwealth Company disembarked at New Orleans.[70] They found a city of some 25,000 people, representing a variety of races and nationalities, a city that was a curious combination of Creole sophistication and fron-

65. *Niles' Weekly Register*, VI (Aug. 6, 1814), 394. See also William B. Hamilton, "The Theater in the Old Southwest: The First Decade at Natchez," *American Literature*, XII (Jan., 1941), 473.

66. Hamilton, "Natchez," p. 471. See below, n. 75.

67. *Ibid.*; Joseph Miller Free, "The Ante-Bellum Theatre of the Old Natchez Region," *The Journal of Mississippi History*, V (Jan., 1943), 15.

68. Free, "Southwestern Mississippi," p. 38, quoting *Natchez Mississippi Republican*, Nov. 30, 1814.

69. Ludlow, *Dramatic Life*, p. 134.

70. *Ibid.*, p. 137; Nelle Kroger Smither, "A History of the English Theatre at New Orleans, 1806–1842," *Louisiana Historical Quarterly*, XXVIII (Jan., 1945), 97. Ludlow dated his New Orleans arrival Dec., 1817.

tier crudity.[71] New Orleans in 1818 was still dominated by the Creole influence, commercially and culturally. Though the "American" population had increased substantially between 1803 and 1815, the great influx of American immigrants and the development of a distinctly American sector was to come after 1817. Ludlow and company arrived in an essentially foreign city.

Prior to their arrival the professional theater available in New Orleans was almost exclusively French-language. Since October 4, 1792, when the first playhouse opened, the city had known French theater.[72] But in 1804, after having been temporarily closed by order of the city council, the theater reopened under a new director, Jean-Baptiste Fournier. Assisted by a group of excellent actors from Saint-Domingue led by Louis-Blaise Tabary, Fournier measurably improved the quality of the productions.[73] From 1804 on, the French theater was an important ingredient of New Orleans cultural life, offering quality productions of French classical drama and opera to responsive Creole audiences.

The introduction of English-language theater in New Orleans was a gradual process. Ludlow asserted that the opening performance of his commonwealth troupe was "the *first representation* by a *regularly organized company*" of an English-language play.[74] Even with the important qualifier "*regularly organized*," the old manager may have claimed too much for his company. The American Theatrical Commonwealth Company was preceded in New Orleans by at least three English-language companies whose organization could be termed "regular."

The first New Orleans performance of a play in English probably came on April 21, 1806. It was advertised by "Mr. Rannie" in the

71. U. S. Census Office, *Social Statistics*, p. 213.

72. René J. Le Gardeur, *The First New Orleans Theatre 1792–1803* (New Orleans: Leeward Books, 1963), p. 4. Le Gardeur has finally put to rest the hallowed tradition that the French theater in New Orleans was founded in 1791 by refugee actors from Cap-François in Saint-Domingue. The first theater was actually built by two brothers from Paris who had lived in New Orleans prior to 1791—Jean-Marie and Louis-Alexandre Henry. The former was a businessman who financed the theater, the latter a carpenter-contractor who built it. For the origin of the myth see Joseph Gabrièl de Baroncelli, *Le Théatre Francais à la Nouvelle Orleans* (New Orleans: Muller, 1906), *passim*.

73. Le Gardeur, *New Orleans Theatre*, pp. 38–40. Theaters were opened successively on St. Peter, St. Philip, and Orleans streets prior to 1817, when the most famous of the French theaters—the Théâtre d'Orléans—commenced operations under the able John Davis. See Smither, "New Orleans," p. 90.

74. *Dramatic Life*, p. 140.

Gazette and Commercial Bulletin as "a favorite comedy in three acts called Ducks & Green Pease or the New Castle Rider. . . ."[75] But there is some doubt whether the performance actually came off. If not, the first recorded English performance came on April 29, 1806, when Rannie presented "A Theatrical Entertainment in Three acts called *The Doctor's Courtship* and two acts of the pantomime of Don Juan," at "the new theatre in Mr. Moore's large building, Chartres Street."[76]

Rannie offered several more performances before departing New Orleans in mid-May, 1806. One of them was worthy of special note. It was a marine "spectacular" concerning Napoleon and Nelson entitled *The Battle of the Nile*, which was advertised to include scenes of "men sinking and swimming and Crokadiles molesting them and Whales, Sharks, Dolphins, Swords, and Flying Fish and mermaids swimming on the surface of the water."[77] Rannie was obviously an ambitious scenarist, but whether the production came off as advertised is doubtful. It is perhaps significant that he departed New Orleans immediately after this production and is not known to have returned.

A second English-language company appeared in New Orleans in April of 1811. A small, loosely organized troupe under the management of another elusive actor-manager, William Duff, performed sporadically for about a year in New Orleans, utilizing the St. Philip Street Theater as well as various halls and ballrooms for their performances. In addition to light drama, their offerings included such subdramatic fare as bird imitations, ventriloquism, acrobatics, and balancing acts. But though they in no sense composed a strong

75. Free, "Southwestern Mississippi," p. 21, quoting *New Orleans Gazette and Commercial Bulletin*, April 19, 1806. "Mr. Rannie" is one of the most interesting and elusive of the American theatrical pioneers. He is particularly difficult to follow since there were clearly two "Mr. Rannies," father and son, who performed in the same period and had similar repertoires. One or the other of them seems to have appeared in practically every town in the United States, England, Canada, and the West Indies. Almost certainly one of them introduced professional theater in Lexington, Kentucky, in April, 1805, and in Natchez, Mississippi, and in New Orleans in 1806. See Odell, *Annals*, II, 143, 209–10, 344.

76. Roger P. McCutcheon, "The First English Plays in New Orleans," *American Literature*, XI (May, 1939), 184, quoting *New Orleans Louisiana Gazette*, April 29, 1806. Smither, "New Orleans," p. 90, follows McCutcheon in claiming this production as the first English-language performance in New Orleans.

77. Smither, "New Orleans," p. 90, quoting *New Orleans Louisiana Gazette*, May 16, 1806.

theatrical corps, the Duff performers were professionals, and they were organized as a company.[78]

Amateur performances by the "Thespian Benevolent Society" provided the only English theater in New Orleans between 1812 and 1817. But in 1817, several months prior to Ludlow's arrival, "A. Cargill," a Kentucky itinerant manager, appeared in New Orleans and organized a semi-professional company—the "American Performers." Cargill did employ amateurs, but he charged admission and took personal benefits. In December he was joined by "Mr. Vos," doubtless John H. Vos, a professional stroller of some note. The makeshift company attempted some quality drama, including an *Othello*, and on December 15 the *Louisiana Courier* expressed approbation of the troupe in a notice of a pending *1 Henry IV* production.[79] So Cargill and company also preceded Ludlow in New Orleans, though ultimately the American Performers proved unable to compete with the Ludlow troupe and were partly absorbed by the Commonwealth Company in 1818.[80] In all there were at least twenty-two English-language productions, professional and amateur, prior to Ludlow's arrival.[81]

By 1817, however, there was evidence that the American population of New Orleans suffered from want of diversion, especially theater. The *Gazette* of March 27, 1817, for example, in announcing an amateur production observed: "From the few opportunities of rational amusement afforded to that portion of our fellow citizens who do not understand the French language, an English play is at all times a matter of interest."[82] Ludlow's advent in New Orleans was timely.

On January 10, 1818, the *Ami des Lois* carried the announcement of Ludlow's intention to open an English season at the St. Philip Street theater. The announcement assured the "patrons of the Drama" that every exertion would be made "to select such pieces as shall tend to render the amusement at the same time pleasing, moral, and instructive."[83] Having received permission to perform from the mayor

78. *Ibid.*, pp. 91–92; McCutcheon, "English Plays," p. 186.
79. Quoted in Smither, "New Orleans," pp. 94–95.
80. *Ibid.*, pp. 100–101.
81. McCutcheon, "English Plays," p. 197.
82. Quoted in Smither, "New Orleans," p. 93.
83. Quoted in John Smith Kendall, *The Golden Age of the New Orleans Theater* (Baton Rouge: Louisiana State University Press, 1952), p. 7.

of the city, the American Theatrical Commonwealth Company opened on January 13, 1818, with John Tobin's popular comedy *The Honey Moon* and the farce *Midnight Hour, or a War of Wits*.[84] Prices of admission were advertised as $1.00 for boxes and pit and "six bits for gallery."[85] Ludlow recalled that the theater was crowded for the opening and that though half the people were French, understanding but little of what they heard, "the performance went off with great applause."[86]

The season that followed offered a variety of popular attractions. Included were the likes of Matthew Gregory Lewis's Gothic melodrama *Castle Spectre*, Goldsmith's *She Stoops to Conquer*, John Home's sentimental "tragedy" *Douglas*, Thomas Morton's comedy melodrama *Speed the Plough*, *The Stranger* of Kotzebue-Dunlap, and several Shakespearean selections.[87] If Ludlow did not bring New Orleans her first English theater, he unquestionably brought the best yet available there.

On May 1, 1818, the season closed. Somewhat earlier a correspondent in the *Gazette* offered an evaluation of the company. "Now tho' the players here would not bear a comparison with those of London, New York, or Philadelphia," wrote the local critic, "yet they are respectable in many walks of the drama. . . . They have done tolerable justice to some of the best comedies in the English language. . . ."[88] The evaluation was probably judicious. Whether the season was a profitable venture is open to doubt. Ludlow claimed that it produced a net profit of $3,000 for the company, but the contemporary press accounts indicate a lack of public support.[89] In any case, the company made enough to sustain itself and to continue operations. Shortly after closing they started upriver aboard the steamer "New Orleans," bound for Natchez. They were under obligation to return there for a brief season.[90] But Ludlow and his corps left behind in New Orleans the beginning of an appetite for English

84. *Ibid.* Ludlow dated his New Orleans opening Dec. 24, 1817. See Ludlow, *Dramatic Life*, p. 138.

85. Smither, "New Orleans," p. 97, quoting *New Orleans Ami des Lois*, Jan. 10, 1818.

86. *Dramatic Life*, 139.

87. Smither, "New Orleans," p. 97.

88. *Ibid.*, p. 99, quoting *New Orleans Louisiana Gazette*, March 20, 1818.

89. *Dramatic Life*, p. 152. But cf. *New Orleans Louisiana Gazette*, March 20, 1818, which contended the company had not made enough to defray expenses.

90. Ludlow, *Dramatic Life*, p. 152.

theater. They had offered a worthwhile sample and laid the foundations for the next remarkable theatrical developments in the Crescent
City.

3.

In the middle of the Natchez season of 1818 Ludlow was taken
seriously ill. It was necessary for him to retire temporarily to recuper-
ate with his wife's family in Nashville. There he limited his theatrical
activity largely (though not exclusively) to managing the productions of the local amateur society.[91] But when in the fall of 1819
itinerant actor John Vos suggested that the two of them join forces
to form another touring company, Ludlow accepted with enthusiasm.
Particularly appealing was Vos's suggestion that they take the company first to St. Louis in the Missouri territory.[92]

St. Louis was an isolated village when the United States finally
secured the area in 1804. The aggregate population numbered about
1,100. There were but 180 houses there and only two American families.[93] Moreover, in 1804 St. Louis was the last outpost of civilization
in the American West. But there was civilization and even the rudi-
ments of culture in the village. A nucleus of literate, educated Euro-
peans, Canadians, and New Orleanians, largely officialdom and its
relations, had resided there practically since its founding. The existence of 2,000 to 3,000 books in the private libraries of the town in
1804 evidenced a certain refinement.[94] This refined element later
served to leaven the crudity of American frontiersmen and remained
the social nucleus about which the emergent mercantile-professional
element gathered.

But the isolation of St. Louis and its dearth of population long
deterred any touring entertainers considering a visit there. It was
probably not until 1814 that the first, one Eugene Leitensdorfer, ap-

91. *Ibid.*, pp. 166–67. The Nashville "Thespian Society" in 1818 numbered
among its members Sam Houston (secretary of the society), John H. Eaton, and
Ephraim H. Foster. Andrew Jackson and Judge Felix Grundy were honorary
members. See *Nashville Whig and Tennessee Advertiser*, Sept. 19, 1818.

92. "Heads of the People," *St. Louis Saturday Evening Post*, July 17, 1847,
clipping in Ludlow-Field-Maury collection, Missouri Historical Society; Ludlow,
Dramatic Life, p. 181.

93. U. S. Census Office, *Social Statistics*, p. 571. There were, however, numerous American farmers living in the immediate environs of the town, attracted
there by the liberal Spanish land policy. See Wade, *Urban Frontier*, p. 5.

94. Wade, *Urban Frontier*, p. 6.

peared. The *Missouri Gazette* announced his program under the topic head "Sporting." Leitensdorfer was to appear "in the house of Joseph Robidoux" to present a "Spectacle of Recreative Sports of Mathematicks and Phisick . . . ,"[95] i.e., card tricks and sleight-of-hand. The performer was to climax his act by eating live coals "with as much facility as our young gentlemen and ladies would [eat] sugar-plumbs. . . ." Not drama perhaps, but dramatic enough. And in view of the scarcity of such entertainment, Eugene Leitensdorfer probably drew a crowd in St. Louis.

On January 6, 1815, St. Louisans witnessed the first production by their new amateur society. The *Gazette* carried an account of the performance, probably the first English-language drama west of the Mississippi. The featured play was John Tobin's comedy *School for Authors*; the afterpiece was the farce *Budget of Blunders*.[96] "Much curiosity was excited," observed the *Gazette*, "and a great many attended to witness the *blunders*;—but all were pleased—all were surprised to see tacticians in a parcel of recruits." The amateurs, encouraged by their success, performed regular theater seasons in 1815, 1816, and 1817.[97] In 1818 the professionals arrived.

The first professional troupe recorded as performing in St. Louis was the strolling company of William Turner and his wife Sophia, old hands at the business. They arrived on January 3, 1818, and arranged to perform in the "old Theatre"—in reality the court house.[98] The St. Louis season lasted from mid-February to late July or early August, 1818, and a lengthy and revealing evaluation in the form of a communication to the *Gazette* assessed the Turners' efforts. "A Stranger" began his observations with an appreciative remark. "It is peculiarly gratifying," he wrote, "to find remote from an Atlantic city, an amusement so rational and refined as the theatre, supported by the taste and liberality of an enlightened public."[99] The correspondent then praised the decorum of the audience, in particular

95. *St. Louis Missouri Gazette,* Jan. 15, 1814. The *Gazette* had been publishing since July 12, 1808. See U. S. Census Office, *Social Statistics,* p. 571.

96. *St. Louis Missouri Gazette,* Feb. 4, 1815. The same number of the *Gazette* carried a "bulletin" on the Battle of New Orleans.

97. Carson, *St. Louis Stage,* p. 318. Carson lists verifiable performances of fifteen plays and farces over the three-year period.

98. *Ibid.,* p. 19, quoting Ann Hunt to Judge J. B. C. Lucas, Jan. 4, 1818. In addition to their Kentucky career, the Turners managed theaters in Pittsburgh and Cincinnati and played elsewhere in the United States and Canada. Sophia Turner probably performed at the Park Theater, New York. See Odell, *Annals,* II, 293–94.

99. *St. Louis Missouri Gazette,* Feb. 20, 1818.

"the silent and respectful attention it is accustomed to bestow on the performance," and the performers, notably Mrs. Turner. He concluded with the observation that the existence of a "well regulated theatre, so remote from the seaboard" surely meant "that the refinements of polished life are rapidly travelling towards the west. . . ." And the Stranger was correct. The Western theater represented a true cultural contact with the East and was one of very few social institutions to do so.

By February 26, 1820, Ludlow and Vos with their company, twelve strong, were aboard the "Missouri Packet" bound for St. Louis, and the *Enquirer* announced that "the *Theatre* in this place will open in the course of 8 or 10 days. . . ." It is noteworthy that the only other available diversion mentioned in the *Enquirer* was in an advertisement for "PORTER AND WHISKEY, superior to any hitherto known in this Territory. . . ."[100] At least Vos and Ludlow would have no competition.

When the troupe arrived they found that a primitive but nonetheless real playhouse was available to them, one built by public subscription and opened on February 1, 1819.[101] Still, Ludlow was not impressed with St. Louis in general. "I confess I felt a little discouraged when I landed," he wrote. "[It] was not any thing like as cleanly, or as well built as any of the towns of the West or South that I had previously visited."[102] Streets were unpaved and sidewalks rare. Main Street, on which the theater stood, ran parallel to the river and was the only street worthy of the name in the entire town.

Despite the discouraging prospects, on March 8, 1820, Ludlow and Vos advertised their opening performance—Suzanna Centlivre's somewhat ribald comedy *The Busy Body* and O'Keefe's musical farce *The Poor Soldier*.[103] The managers assured the public that "no piece will be allowed to appear that shall be in any way either indelicate or improper" and stated their determination "to offer a source of amusement that shall be at the same time rational, moral and entertaining."[104]

100. *St. Louis Enquirer*, Feb. 26, 1820.
101. *St. Louis Missouri Gazette*, Jan. 27, 1819. This playhouse, the first in St. Louis, fronted east on Main Street between Olive and Locust.
102. *Dramatic Life*, p. 183.
103. *St. Louis Enquirer*, March 8, 1820. Ludlow was mistaken on all counts in dating the opening in mid-December, 1819, and making the opening production *The Honey Moon; Dramatic Life*, p. 184.
104. *St. Louis Enquirer*, March 8, 1820.

For about three weeks attendance at the playhouse was good. Then, according to Ludlow, cold weather set in, during which "the ladies were unwilling to venture out; and men stayed away from the theater because there were but few ladies attending the performances."[105] No doubt attendance did fall off. But the decline was due to competition, not to the weather. On March 22, 1820, Samuel Drake and his "Company from Kentucky" opened in "Mr. Bennet's Ball Room."[106]

Drake's arrival bode ill for Ludlow and Vos. The Kentucky troupe was clearly superior to that from Tennessee—after all, the Kentuckians were for the most part experienced English actors and actresses. On March 25, 1820, the *Enquirer* announced: "A compromise has taken place between the two companies of comedians recently arrived in this place. The result has been, that part of the company from Tennessee has joined that from Kentucky; the whole to be under the management of *Mr. Drake.* The talents of the two companies being thus combined, the expectations of the citizens cannot be raised too high."[107] The Drake company absorbed that of Ludlow and Vos. Ludlow, who had begun his career with Samuel Drake in 1815 was once again in the employ of his old mentor.

The combined company presented a season of about eight weeks, during which they offered twenty-four evenings' entertainment.[108] Local response, at least that reflected in the press, was enthusiastic in support of the theater. "We have been much amused," wrote one correspondent in the *Enquirer,* "with the Theatrical exhibitions of Mr. Drake's company of commedians [*sic*] from Kentucky."[109] He then offered a detailed and generally favorable critique of the company, member by member. Another St. Louis critic was particularly impressed with the ladies of the troupe, at least with their physical attributes. "The females attached to the corps," he wrote, "are all young and respectable performers, and it is a query whether there is a stage in the United States that can boast of a constellation of female beauty superior to that of St. Louis."[110] A third correspondent,

105. *Dramatic Life,* p. 186.

106. Playbill, St. Louis Theater, March 22, 1820, in Playbill Collection, Missouri Historical Society.

107. See also, Ludlow, *Dramatic Life,* pp. 186–88. Ludlow insisted that the Drake company won out simply because Drake had the hotel ballroom, which was warmer.

108. Carson, *St. Louis Stage,* p. 52.

109. April 5, 1820.

110. *Ibid.,* March 25, 1820.

a "Citizen of St. Louis," contended that the "style of acting" of the Drake company "is admitted to be good by those who have seen the best theatres in Europe and America. . . ."[111] An overstatement perhaps, but an indication that the St. Louis public was impressed. When the company departed there was little doubt but that they atrical pioneering in the transmontane West. A number of the emer- would return. The 1820 season of the Drake-Ludlow company marked the beginning of a long tradition of quality theater on a season basis in St. Louis.

The period between 1815 and 1820 was an active period of the- gent towns were introduced to theater of a remarkable quality, considering their geographic insularity. Even more remarkable was the popular response elicited by the theater. There is every indica- tion that large segments of the populace of these culturally isolated towns, hungry for diversion, in some cases even for refinement, en- thusiastically welcomed the strolling players.

But despite the very considerable pioneering activities of the Drakes, Ludlow, Vos, the Turners, Douglass, and still other itinerant companies, and the favourable response of their public, no real South- western theater circuit had developed by 1820, except in the Ken tucky bluegrass towns. A true circuit had to await the coming of a manager with great scope of vision and ability equal to that vision, a man who could create local desire for theater in the smallest of towns, afford leadership in erecting playhouses, and provide quality professional companies on a season basis to perform in them. In 1820 precisely such a man appeared in New Orleans in the person of James H. Caldwell.

111. *Ibid.*, April 8, 1820.

CHAPTER IV

CALDWELL,
THE CRESCENT CITY

AND THE

MISSISSIPPI VALLEY
CIRCUIT
1820-1833

1.

JAMES HENRY CALDWELL WAS AN ENTREPRENEUR OF HEROIC PROPOR-tions, one of that breed just beginning to emerge in the first quarter of the nineteenth century whose activities would so profoundly influence the development of the nation. Typical of his kind, Caldwell hated limitation or circumscription in any of his operations, and by 1818 he had become aware of the innate limitations of his Virginia theatrical circuit. First, there was strong competition in Virginia, which to the somewhat avaricious manager was a condition to be avoided whenever possible. Then, economic dislocation reduced the ability of the towns in his circuit, towns already limited in size, to support the company and produce the kind of profit he sought. Consequently, in 1818, Caldwell began to conceive a grand design.[1]

Caldwell's plan in its inchoate form involved the shift of his center of operations from the East to the West—specifically, to the Mississippi Valley. The steady westward flow of population, the Great Migration, as it has come to be known, was apparent to Caldwell, and the population increase suggested a new market for theater. Equally apparent was the position of New Orleans as the logical center of a theatrical circuit in the valley. As he later observed, New Orleans was always the "emporium of the South and West."[2] Although the manager did not initially intend to give up his Eastern circuit altogether, he decided in 1819 to test New Orleans. If he was successful there he would make the Virginia operation an adjunct of his Western-based activity.[3]

The timing of Caldwell's decision was perfect. New Orleans by 1819 was ready for high-quality English-language theater offered on a regular periodic basis. By 1820 the population of the "old quarter" had jumped to 27,176.[4] But more significantly, the years between 1815 and 1820 saw the beginnings of the so-called Faubourg Ste. Marie (St. Mary Suburb), the "American Quarter" above Canal Street. The great development of this section was to come later; indeed, Caldwell was to contribute substantially to that development. But in 1820, as more and more Americans arrived in New Orleans, their tendency was to gravitate toward the American section of the city. Moreover, the *batture*, or dock area, was the most convenient landing place on the river at New Orleans. The Americans of the *batture* were beginning to syphon off trade from the older docks. And in view of the increase in steamer berthings at New Orleans, that trade was considerable.[5] The Crescent City was clearly the focal point of Mississippi Valley commerce. Her economy was booming. And as always, commerce tended to attract culture. It was

1. [Rees], "Southern Stage," I, 140. As has been noted, Rees received his information directly from Caldwell.
2. *Ibid.*, quoting an undated letter from Caldwell concerning the New Orleans operations.
3. But cf. *New York Spirit of the Times*, Nov. 19, 1836, which states that Caldwell went to New Orleans only after failing in his Virginia management.
4. U. S. Census Office, *Social Statistics*, p. 213.
5. *Ibid.*, p. 251. In 1821 at least 287 steamboats cleared the port of New Orleans.

the profit potential that drew James H. Caldwell to New Orleans in 1819.

Late in November (or early in December) 1819, the Caldwell troupe sailed from City Point on the James River in Virginia. Some of the members of the company were not happy about the trip. Fear of pestilence was strong, and with justification. Fifteen epidemics of yellow fever visited New Orleans between 1810 and 1837,[6] and cholera and smallpox epidemics were frequent and deadly. Still, most of the troupe stayed with the able manager when he proved determined to make the effort. Early in January, 1820, they arrived in New Orleans.[7] From that time until his first "retirement" in 1833, James H. Caldwell dominated theatrical affairs in the Mississippi Valley, with New Orleans as his base of operations.

Upon arriving in New Orleans Caldwell leased the St. Philip Street Theater, a French-language playhouse, for use by his American Company.[8] On January 7, 1820, the company opened with John Tobin's comedy *The Honey Moon* and the farce *Three and A Deuce*.[9]

But to the vexation of manager Caldwell, there was competition afield. Aaron J. Phillips and a small itinerant company were operating at the Orleans Street Theater, a better playhouse than the St. Philip. Such a situation was intolerable to Caldwell, especially since he had the advantage of a better troupe. Phillips' makeshift group could not compete with Caldwell's company of twenty-three experienced players, the largest and most versatile troupe yet to play in New Orleans.[10] On January 21, Caldwell granted his erstwhile competitor a benefit at the St. Philip and immediately thereafter absorbed his troupe intact into the American Company.[11]

The combined troupe was an important one in theater history of New Orleans as well as in that of the entire Mississippi Valley. Manager Caldwell, a talented light comedian and a passable actor in all lines, played leads in both comedy and tragedy. Second leads went usually to Jackson Gray, Joseph Hutton, and William Anderson.

6. *Ibid.*, p. 253; [Rees], "Southern Stage," I, 146.
7. Hostetler, "Caldwell," p. 25.
8. Clipping, *New Orleans Louisiana Gazette*, Jan. 17, 1820, reprinted in Coad and Mims, *American Stage*, p. 134.
9. Hostetler, "Caldwell," p. 30, quoting *New Orleans Louisiana Gazette*, Jan. 10, 1820.
10. Smither, "New Orleans," p. 106.
11. *Ibid.*, p. 105; Hostetler, "Caldwell," p. 33.

Mrs. William Anderson handled the female leads along with a Mrs. W. H. Williams. For leads in opera and musical farce there were Mrs. Jackson Gray and Arthur Keene, an Irish tenor popular in the East. Richard Russell and his spouse, both of whom later figured prominently in Southern theatrical annals, were also popular singing actors. The company had a varied repertoire most of which they were capable of performing adequately or better than adequately.[12]

Within a few weeks after opening the strength of public support enabled Caldwell to expand his New Orleans operation. He occupied both the French playhouses, alternating performance nights with the French companies and playing four or five nights a week. The most popular play offered by the American Company in the 1820 season was Mordecai Noah's patriotic comedy *She Would Be a Soldier, or The Plains of Chippewa*, performed four times to enthusiastic audiences. In praising the piece, "Wagstaff," in a letter to the *Gazette*, reflected the rampant nationalism of the period. "While our country can boast of such writers as Mr. Noah," observed Wagstaff, "we see no necessity for our importing British Literature and British plays 'by the bale and by the hogshead.'"[13] But American theater was largely an extension of British theater at the time, in repertoire as in personnel. The American cultural nationalists would have to wait many years for the production of endemic drama in any notable quantity.

The 1820 season lasted twelve weeks, closing with Caldwell's benefit on April 19. The manager pocketed a substantial profit, large enough to encourage him to continue his New Orleans effort. Before departing for Virginia and a summer-fall season on his old circuit, Caldwell took a three-year lease on the Orleans Street Theater, at $10,000 per annum.[14] Late in January, 1821, the American Company reappeared in New Orleans, opening its second season in the "American Theater, Orleans Street," on January 31, with Andrew Cherry's popular comedy *The Soldier's Daughter*.[15]

12. Smither, "New Orleans," p. 106.
13. *Ibid.*, p. 108, quoting *New Orleans Louisiana Gazette*, March 16, 1820.
14. *Ibid.*, pp. 109–10; Hostetler, "Caldwell," p. 36; [Rees], "Southern Stage," p. 146. The *New Orleans Louisiana Gazette*, March 29, 1820, estimated Caldwell's season profit at $6,540, basing the figure on attendance records.
15. Hostetler, "Caldwell," p. 40. One noteworthy addition to the stock company this season was Noah Ludlow, who, with his wife, joined the company in April of 1821.

Caldwell had a surprise in store for New Orleans during the 1821 season—one of the first "stars" to appear in the West. On March 23, the manager presented a production of *Macbeth* with the eminent tragedian Thomas Abthorpe Cooper in the title role.[16] Caldwell reasoned that curiosity if nothing else would bring out crowds to see the renowned actor and that people would pay more for the privilege. Hence for each of the Cooper performances, prices jumped from $1.00 to $1.50. The experiment was successful. Despite some anguished outcries over the price hike, crowds did turn out. Some even commended the manager for raising prices on the grounds that higher admission would, in the words of one aristocratic correspondent in the *Gazette*, "prevent the greasy Kentuckians and the rabble from leaning over the backs of the boxes to the great annoyance of the ladies."[17]

Caldwell later contended that the success of the Cooper engagement convinced him that he should build his own theater in New Orleans. The manager also dated the beginning of his real success from the Cooper engagement. "From that day," he wrote, "I have wielded the tinsel sceptre, and commanded to the South and West, every distinguished member of the profession. . . ."[18] For all the egotism of the assertion (modesty was not one of Caldwell's virtues) it was unquestionably correct. Though he may later have rued the day, Caldwell did introduce the "star system" in New Orleans.

It was during his third New Orleans season that Caldwell began to develop his plans to establish a Mississippi Valley circuit. In December of 1821, he announced his intention to open a theater in Natchez, Mississippi.[19] The Natchez project was delayed temporarily, but in March, 1822, Caldwell bought land on Camp Street in the Faubourg

16. Smither, "New Orleans," p. 111. Cooper was a successful British actor who made his American debut Dec. 9, 1796. Because of his penchant for travel he has been described as a "more or less itinerant star." He was the first great British actor to become an American citizen. See Coad and Mims, *American Stage*, p. 45. Tradition has it that he sometimes traveled from town to town in a covered wagon which he drove himself.

17. Hostetler, "Caldwell," p. 40, quoting *New Orleans Louisiana Gazette*, March 26, 1821.

18. [Rees], "Southern Stage," p. 146, quoting undated letter from Caldwell concerning his early career.

19. William Bryan Gates, "The Theatre in Natchez," *The Journal of Mississippi History*, III (April, 1941), 79, quoting *Natchez Mississippi Republican*, Dec. 21, 1821. Caldwell promised to provide Natchez with "the best Dramatic Talent of America, and . . . make a *regular season of two months every year*."

The "New" Charleston Theatre
The South Carolina Historical Society

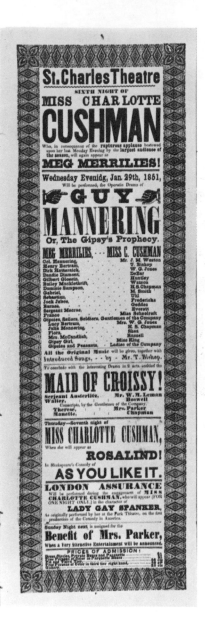

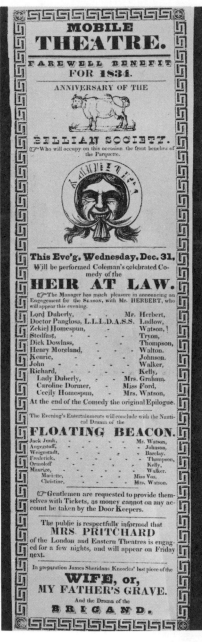

A historic performance at the St. Charles Theatre

Harvard Theatre Collection

A special benefit performance by the Ludlow Troupe, Mobile, 1834

Harvard Theatre Collection

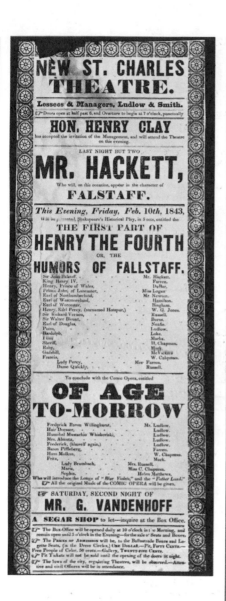

A playbill from the New St. Charles Theatre

Harvard Theatre Collection

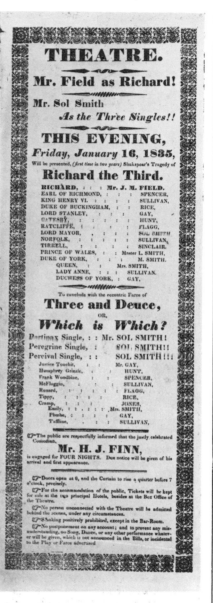

A performance by Sol Smith and Company, probably in Montgomery, Alabama, 1835

Harvard Theatre Collection

American Theatre,
ST. PHILIP STREET.

On Tuesday Evening, February 1st, 1820,
Will be acted the admired play (by request) of the

STRANGER.

[Translated from the German of Augustus Von Kotzebue.]

The Stranger	-	Mr. CALDWELL
Baron Steinfort		Hutton
Count Wintersen	-	Fielding
Francis	-	Carr
Solomon	-	Emberton
Peter	-	Russel
Tobias	-	Gray
Children	-	Miss Hutton &c.
Mrs. Haller	-	Mrs. Price
Countess Wintersen		Williams
Charlotte	-	Russel
Savoyards	-	Gray and Wheeler.

To which will be added for the first time in New-Orleans, the grand melo-dramatic spectacle of the

FORTY THIEVES.

With new Scenery, Dresses and Decorations.
The Scenery painted by Mr. Jones.

Ali Baba	-	Mr. ENTWISTLE
Ganem		Boyle
Cassim Baba	-	Fielding
Hassarac	-	Hutton
Selim		Price
1st Robber	-	Emberton
2d do.		Carr
Mustapha	-	Russel
Zaide	-	Mrs. Price
Cogia	-	Russel
Morgiana	-	Gray
Ardinello	-	William
Zelie	-	Hutton
Sylph	-	Wheeler
Goamer	-	Miss Hutton

The piece opens with the *View of a Lake*. Ardinelle [the fairy of the Lake] enters in a *beautiful shell car drawn by swans* attended by sylphs and Fairies Chaunt. Fairy of the glassey lake.

Scene 3 Represents a wild forest, on one side *a rude Cave*, where the Robbers deposit their treasury, and the other side *a large Tree*, in the back ground distant mountains.

A playbill from the American Theatre, New Orleans
Harvard Theatre Collection

Ste. Marie, and on May 29, 1822, he laid the cornerstone of the Camp
Street Theater. The subscription list he had opened to help finance
the project had provided sufficient capital to begin construction.[20]

To enrich his 1822 season, Caldwell brought in two stars. First
came Junius Brutus Booth, who commenced an engagement on
January 11, in *Richard III*.[21] In February Cooper returned to New
Orleans and continued to attract large audiences starring in such
productions as another *Richard III*, James Sheridan Knowles's
pseudo-tragedy *Virginius*, and the popular Beaumont and Fletcher
comedy *Rule a Wife and Have a Wife*.[22] In May, 1822, the company
benefits commenced, marking the close of another successful New
Orleans season. Once again Caldwell took his troupe to Virginia for
the summer.

Caldwell's New Orleans season of 1823 was the last for him in the
Orleans Street Theater. The Camp Street, or New American Theater,
was nearing completion. In May of 1823 Caldwell opened the new
house briefly in spite of its unfinished state in order to check for any
visual or auditory defects that might be corrected.[23] On January 1,
1824, the manager formally presented his finished playhouse to the
New Orleans public.[24]

Caldwell himself spoke the customary opening address in which
he recognized his audience as the "arbiters of wit" and invited their
support. The address, in reality a prize-winning dedicatory poem by
Thomas Wells of Boston, included a statement of the purpose of a
theater as well as an invocation of the muses:

> And, now, in scenic beauty drest, thou Dome—
> The shield of morals, and of Song the home—
> The nurse of Eloquence—the school of Taste . . .
> Hence be thy alters by the Muses graced.[25]

20. Hostetler, "Caldwell," p. 56; Ludlow, *Dramatic Life*, p. 238. Caldwell
sold shares of stock at $300 each. The buyer was entitled to free admission to
the house until, the certificates read, "the said amount shall be returned, which
is to be done on or before the first day of January, 1834."

21. Hostetler, "Caldwell," p. 54; Ludlow, *Dramatic Life*, p. 229.

22. Hostetler, "Caldwell," p. 54; Ludlow, *Dramatic Life*, pp. 232–34.

23. Clipping, *New Orleans Louisiana Gazette*, May 12, 1823, reprinted in
Coad and Mims, *American Stage*, p. 143; Hostetler, "Caldwell," p. 65; Smither,
"New Orleans," p. 121.

24. Hostetler, "Caldwell," p. 68; Ludlow, *Dramatic Life*, p. 249.

25. Laurence Hutton and William Carey (eds.), *Occasional Addresses* (New
York: The Dunlap Society, 1890), p. 19.

Following the address came the opening-night program—the Thomas Morton comedy *Town and Country* and the musical farce *Of Age Tomorrow.*[26]

The building itself, later described by a famous stroller of the period as "one of the prettiest of theatres,"[27] was designed in Greek revival style, built of brick and fronted by Doric columns. The interior, 60 by 160 feet in area, would seat 1,000. It contained pit, parquet circle (or parterre), three tiers of boxes, and gallery. A notable feature was the use of gas lighting both of the interior and the exterior of the house, including footlights and a chandelier. It was the first building west of the Alleghenies to be lighted with gas and the third theater in the country to be so equipped.[28] Several bars strategically located in the building dispensed refreshments. Altogether, the new Camp Street Theater was well designed, even elegant. It was for eleven years, until the opening of Caldwell's first St. Charles Theater, the finest playhouse in the South.

The Doric columns of the New American must have looked rather out of place on the Camp Street of 1824. Caldwell recalled that there were at the time only a few warehouses on the street in addition to the theater. The street itself was unpaved. "For several years," wrote the manager, "the public had to travel on gunwale side-walks, and ... carriages could not be used after a heavy rain. . . ."[29] But the Camp did not stand long in its splendid isolation. Led by Caldwell's new theater, other businesses soon appeared in the American sector of the old Creole city.

The opening of the Camp Street Theater marked a turning point in Caldwell's career. Though he made one more visit to his Virginia circuit in the summer of 1824, after that he concentrated his efforts in New Orleans and began to plan the next step in the formation of the circuit he envisioned in the West. Early in the summer of 1824 he took his troupe up the Mississippi for a season in Natchez, followed

26. Smither, "New Orleans," p. 123.

27. Joseph Leathley Cowell, *Thirty Years Passed Among the Players in England and America* (New York: Harper and Brothers, 1844), II, 95.

28. Smither, "New Orleans," p. 121; Hostetler, "Caldwell," p. 73. The lighting system in the Camp preceded by two years the introduction of gas lighting in New York.

29. Undated Caldwell letter in *New York Spirit of the Times*, Dec. 24, 1842. See also Ludlow, *Dramatic Life*, p. 248. The theater was located two blocks from the river front, between Gravier and Poydras streets.

by one in Nashville.[30] The sagacious manager wanted to sound out the prospects of expanding his operation. Although in 1824 he was not yet ready to expand, the trip upriver convinced him it should be done, as soon as he could further consolidate his position in New Orleans and build his investment capital.

Consolidation involved employing the best stock company at his disposal for the new New Orleans playhouse, and Caldwell managed to add some excellent new names to his company. Two in particular deserve mention. Jane Placide, the daughter of Alexander Placide, had the talent so striking in that remarkable family. She joined the American Company in 1823. By 1824, despite some adverse criticism in the local press,[31] the young actress (she was twenty years old) had become the leading lady in the company. With experience she became a markedly versatile actress-singer, capable of performing equally well in comedy, tragedy, or even opera. For ten years she was the local favorite in New Orleans, both of the audiences and, it seems, of manager Caldwell, too. His admiration for the vivacious actress was apparently unbounded.[32]

Tradition has it that the second noteworthy new member of the Caldwell stock in 1824 was also enamoured of Jane Placide. Young Edwin Forrest made his New Orleans debut on February 4, 1824, as Jaffier in Thomas Otway's *Venice Preserved*. Billed as "E. Forrest, from the Ohio and Kentucky Theatres,"[33] the green recruit made no particular impression on his New Orleans audiences. Whether Forrest actually challenged manager Caldwell to a duel when he proved unable to alienate Placide's affections for the manager, as is claimed by all the Forrest biographers (and denied by a recent biography

30. Hostetler, "Caldwell," pp. 66–67. At Nashville the Caldwell troupe performed in the "Cherry Street Theatre," built in 1820 by the Western managers Joshua Collins and William Jones. Ludlow called this crude structure "the Barn"; *Dramatic Life*, pp. 247–48.

31. For example, a critic in the *New Orleans Louisiana Gazette*, Jan. 17, 1823, observed of her performance of the Princess of Navarre in *John of Paris*: "Miss Placide . . . did not seem quite at home in mimicking the walk and gesture of royalty—the rolling motion which sets off a chambermaid does not become a queen." See Smither, "New Orleans," p. 118. But the *Gazette* of Jan. 6 found her the best thing in the company; *ibid.*, p. 117.

32. Her untimely death on May 16, 1835, cut off what might have been one of the most brilliant careers in American stage annals. See *New Orleans Bee*, May 18, 1835, for local reaction to the loss of this favorite.

33. Smither, "New Orleans," p. 123, quoting playbill, Camp Street Theatre, Feb. 4, 1824.

of Caldwell), is of no great consequence.[34] That Forrest improved as an actor under Caldwell's tutelage is significant. It is also noteworthy that Forrest's resignation after one season with Caldwell marked the end of the actor's apprenticeship. When he appeared in New Orleans five years later it was as a star with his then normal billing: "the greatest American tragedian."[35]

The 1826 season saw Caldwell enlarge his activities both in New Orleans and elsewhere in the Mississippi Valley. In New Orleans the manager began performing nightly (except Sunday) throughout the season, which in 1826 extended from January through May.[36] The company offered a wide variety of theater, ranging from Shakespeare's *1 Henry IV* to the William Moncrieff burletta *Tom and Jerry, or Life in London,* and including comedy, tragedy, melodrama, farce, and even opera. Von Weber's *Der Freischütz,* for example, was performed several times, though there are indications that the production was of dubious quality. Bernhard, Duke of Saxe-Weimar Eisenach, attended a *Freischütz* performance in March of 1826, recording his impressions in his travel journal. "The orchestra," wrote the Duke, "was very weak and badly filled, [and] hardly any of the performers could sing: I was told that the handsomest pieces of music are either abridged or entirely omitted."[37] There is no reason to doubt the validity of these criticisms. Indeed, it seems incredible that any repertory theater company would attempt a *Freischütz* production.

34. The Forrest biographers claim that the actor challenged the manager, then "posted" him as a coward and left the company when Caldwell declined the challenge. See William Rounseville Alger, *Life of Edwin Forrest, the American Tragedian* (Philadelphia: J. B. Lippincott and Company, 1877), I, 137; James Rees, *The Life of Edwin Forrest with Reminiscences and Personal Recollections* (Philadelphia: T. B. Peterson and Brothers, 1874), p. 84; Montrose Jonas Moses, *The Fabulous Forrest. The Record of an American Actor* (Boston: Little, Brown, and Company, 1929), p. 57; Richard Moody, *Edwin Forrest. First Star of the American Stage* (New York: Alfred A. Knopf, 1960), p. 46. Hostetler, "Caldwell," p. 91, denies the story as apocryphal. None of the Forrest biographers is able to document it adequately.

35. Smither, "New Orleans," p. 123, quoting playbill, Camp Street Theatre, April 10, 1829. Alger entitled his chapter on Forrest in New Orleans "Life in New Orleans—Critical Period of Experience." Alger, *Forrest,* I, 113. Rees wrote that with the Caldwell company "Forrest began to appreciate the value of true art"; *Forrest,* p. 80.

36. Smither, "New Orleans," pp. 379–83, lists the performances by date for the season.

37. *Travels Through North America, During the Years 1825 and 1826* (Philadelphia: Carey, Lea, and Carey, 1828), II, 81.

The denizens of the pit somewhat disturbed the aristocratic visitor's concentration at the performance. The pittites, he complained, "consisted of sailors and countrymen from Kentucky, who made themselves quite at home on the benches, and cracked nuts during the finest pieces of music. . . ."[38] The critical duke admitted, however, that the interior "decorations" were "tolerably good" and that the house itself was "arranged not untastefully."[39] In all, Caldwell's theater came off well in the estimation of this cultured German, and the public in general were also evidently pleased with the playhouse and the productions throughout the season, which did not close until May 26, 1826.

2.

Caldwell had a busy summer and fall in 1826. He opened new theaters and performed seasons in two new towns—Huntsville, Alabama, and Nashville, Tennessee. Before he could create a Southwestern circuit for his troupe, the manager had a thorny problem to solve. Fundamentally it was a logistical problem. He had to determine how to transport and sustain a large company from town to town, on a year-round basis, in a vast area where towns were uniformly small and widely separated from one another. Caldwell found a double-edged solution. First, the towns selected had to be carefully chosen for their accessibility as well as for their ability to sustain a theatrical company. This consideration dictated the selection of Nashville and Huntsville, which were close enough together to provide a possible nexus. Next, Caldwell determined he could either subdivide his company after the New Orleans season, so as to play two smaller towns simultaneously, or maintain his troupe intact while playing the larger towns. In small towns each part of the divided company would be smaller and require less to sustain it but would produce a yield equal to that of the entire corps playing together. Each subdivision of the company could be placed under an acting manager who would report directly to Caldwell. By opening new houses in Nashville and Huntsville in 1826, the far-sighted manager began to effect his design.

38. *Ibid.* The presence of sailors and Kentucky frontiersmen at an opera performance is an indication of the scarcity of commercial diversion.
39. *Ibid.*

Huntsville, Alabama, had been introduced to professional theater at least as early as 1819. Noah Ludlow visited the little Alabama village that year with a makeshift company he had organized in Nashville during his convalescence in 1818. The appearance in Nashville of strolling actors Alexander Cummings and his wife provided the impetus for Ludlow's sudden decision to tour again. But when he tried to recruit additional actors from the East to fill the new company, he found recruiting difficult. "The actors of the Eastern cities," wrote Ludlow, . . . "had no idea at that time what the West really was." Westerners, he continued, "were supposed by many to to be semi-barbarians; and to go to Kentucky or Tennessee was banishing yourself from civilization."[40] They simply would not come. As a result the company Ludlow and Cummings took to Huntsville in 1819 included only the co-managers, their wives, a fifteen-year-old orphan boy, two cabinet-makers who had never appeared before an audience, one tailor from Pittsburgh who had made only amateur appearances, and another tailor from Nashville, a former sailor with one leg.[41]

Arriving in Huntsville, then a town of well under two thousand inhabitants, the primitive troupe outfitted a room over a confectionary store as a playhouse. It was a room measuring "about sixty feet long by thirty feet wide," according to Ludlow, one used occasionally for dances.[42] There the troupe offered a season of about ten weeks, during which they made little profit beyond immediate expenses. But they did, it would seem, introduce theater in Huntsville, if what this company performed can be termed "theater." For the most part it included variety type entertainment and farces. Still, the company did attract audiences, audiences that principally came, according to Ludlow, not from the town proper, "but from two to five miles around in the adjacent country. . . ." They were, the manager recalled, "mostly planters, and men of wealth and leisure."[43]

Ludlow returned to Huntsville twice more before Caldwell's arrival in 1826. On both occasions, in 1822 and 1824, the peripatetic Ludlow took advantage of the summer break in New Orleans to lead strolling groups of makeshift proportions to the Alabama town. Despite the poor quality of the performances offered in Huntsville, Ludlow insisted they were sufficiently popular to encourage con-

40. *Dramatic Life*, p. 172.
41. *Ibid.*
42. *Ibid.*, p. 173.
43. *Ibid.*

struction of a real playhouse there. A group of prominent local residents decided in 1826 to build a theater by public subscription and to offer it for lease to Ludlow when completed—such at least was Ludlow's version of the story.[44]

But James H. Caldwell, unlike the impecunious Ludlow, had the means to invest personally in the theater building in Huntsville. And the New Orleans manager did so, insuring the completion of the enterprise and reserving the option to lease the house for use by his own company. Ludlow, who was from that time almost pathological in his conviction that Caldwell wanted to ruin him, could only fume and wait for revenge. On July 24, 1826, the Caldwell company opened the new Huntsville Theater.[45] The featured play was Caldwell's favorite opening-night vehicle, the entertaining John Tobin comedy *The Honey Moon*. For the afterpiece the company performed "the Operatical Farce called OF AGE TOMORROW."[46] Caldwell once again spoke the "Prize Address," a favorite technique of this manager (and many others) to stimulate public interest in his projects. The Huntsville address, employing hyperbole only slightly more outrageous than on most such occasions, concluded with a prayer that "circling halos" might "gleam" around the summit of "Drama's temple," and that "bursting visions" might "round its altar stream."

> May Fancy *here*, on waving pinions fly
> And pour her light from every star on high.
>
> .   .   .   .
> And here let knowledge, dignified and chaste,
> And truth and virtue, elegance and taste,
> Exclusive wit, amusive and refin'd,
> Unfold their splendor to the youthful mind.[47]

The first Huntsville season lasted until September 2, 1826, when Caldwell closed with his benefit, the younger Colman's *Managers in Distress*. Then the entire company set out north for Nashville. Caldwell had established Huntsville as part of his developing circuit, and he kept it on that circuit until his first retirement in 1833.[48] Such it was that a small isolated town in the wilds of north-central Alabama acquired a real theater in 1826, and an annual season performed

44. *Ibid.*, pp. 256–57.
45. Hostetler, "Caldwell," p. 103.
46. *Ibid.*, quoting *Huntsville Southern Advocate*, July 21, 1826.
47. Hutton and Carey, *Addresses*, p. 27.
48. Hostetler, "Caldwell," p. 106. Caldwell owned stock in the Huntsville Theater until 1843, when he finally terminated his theatrical enterprises.

by the strongest theatrical troupe in the South for several years thereafter.

Noah Ludlow had been active in Nashville theatrical affairs since 1817, when he took his first strolling troupe there. He had since then offered sporadic seasons and had appeared as a star with the strolling company of Joshua Collins and William Jones, after Collins and Jones had opened the Cherry Street "barn" in 1820.[49] In 1823, as noted above, Caldwell took his New Orleans company to Nashville to try a season. By 1826, the aggressive entrepreneur had a new playhouse under construction in the Tennessee city on the Cumberland.

In mid-September, 1826, Caldwell and company arrived in Nashville and opened a season in the Cherry Street playhouse pending completion of the new theater.[50] On October 9, 1826, according to the local press, Caldwell's latest "Dramatic Temple" opened "with the admirable comedy of the 'Soldier's Daughter,' and the farce of 'Turn Out.' "[51]

The theater was designed after the Camp in New Orleans, which it closely resembled. The opening night audience numbered some six hundred, and the first thing they were offered was Caldwell's recitation of the inevitable opening address. This time the manager called upon the audience to use carefully their power as arbiter of Nashville's theatrical fortunes:

> Foes to pretense, but friends to modest worth,
> 'Tis yours to draw the hidden talent forth,
> And while the sceptre of the mind you hold,
> Reject the tinsel—and refine the gold—.[52]

49. Ludlow, *Dramatic Life*, p. 204.

50. James Rees, *The Dramatic Authors of America* (Philadelphia: G. B. Zieber and Company, 1845), p. 66. This volume purports to be a series of biographical sketches of American playwrights. The Caldwell sketch was again based upon material furnished by the manager. Caldwell, a personal friend of Rees, qualified as a "dramatic author" on the basis of his dramatization of Bulwer's *Eugene Aram*.

51. Hunt, "Nashville Theatre," pp. 9–10, quoting *Nashville National Banner and Whig*, Oct. 11, 1826. The new theater was located on the corner of Union and Sumner (now Fifth Avenue) and was built on land purchased from Major William B. Lewis. Until 1850 it was utilized by all companies performing in Nashville.

52. Hutton (ed.), *Opening Addresses*, p. 57. Caldwell committed a strategic error in selecting this poem as the prize-winner. A Bostonian wrote it, and the Nashvillians resented its choice over the effort of second-place winner Isaac Clark of Tennessee. See Hostetler, "Caldwell," p. 108.

The press noted that the local people had "seldom" been offered "a performance better sustained throughout."[53] And the Nashville public lent good support to their new theater and to the interesting company operating there.

Occasionally a complaint of misbehavior in the audience reached the press. One lady objected to the men's custom of beating time to the music with walking sticks. "These gentry," she wrote, "keep up such a continual clatter with their sticks, during the performance of a musical piece, as quite to ruin the effect of the music, and to disgust everyone professing any taste for that art. . . ."[54] The practice was especially irritating when the men beat the rhythm *"out of all time"* with the music. But occasional complaints of this nature point up the strong local interest in the theater.

For two months and more the Caldwell company played in Nashville, waiting for cold weather to arrive and end the fever season in New Orleans. Finally, on December 23, 1826, the Nashville season closed and the troupe headed up the Cumberland. But there they ran into difficulties. The river proved too low for steamer traffic, and the Caldwell company had to resort to keelboat for transportation. Moreover, they ran into ice floes on the river, which slowed them even more. It was February 2, 1827, before they arrived in New Orleans to commence the winter season.[55]

The New Orleans season of 1827 closed on June 8. Manager Caldwell then took his troupe upriver to St. Louis to effect the next stage in his ever-widening Mississippi Valley operation. Since the departure of Samuel Drake's company in late spring of 1820, St. Louis had seen only sporadic and irregular professional theater seasons, and of course amateur productions. The city (and it was a city, having been incorporated as such in 1822)[56] was still somewhat remote from the main-traveled waterways, being too far north of the Ohio-Mississippi confluence. Still, the strolling companies did occasionally get there. Joshua Collins and William Jones, for example, presented a season of some seventeen weeks in late 1820 and early 1821, with a company that included the incredibly mobile Noah Ludlow.[57]

A local critic in the *St. Louis Gazette* offered an evaluation of the

53. Hunt, "Nashville Theatre," p. 10, quoting *Nashville National Banner and Whig*, Oct. 11, 1826.
54. *Ibid.*, p. 10, quoting *Nashville National Banner and Whig*, Nov. 8, 1826.
55. Hostetler, "Caldwell," p. 109; Smither, "New Orleans," p. 134.
56. U. S. Census Office, *Social Statistics*, p. 573.
57. Ludlow, *Dramatic Life*, p. 212; Carson, *St. Louis Stage*, p. 66.

Collins-Jones company at mid-season. Over the modest pseudonym "Omnes," the writer was generally favorable in his reaction to the troupe, singling out Ludlow and the leading lady, Mrs. Groshon, for special praise. But Omnes did have a revealing word of advice to the players in concluding. A "little caution," he advised, "is necessary with respect to the proper use of oaths, on the stage. . . ."[58] He then elaborated, admitting that "although it may please a few, to hear an old man calling his son 'a dam'd dog,' yet, I would advise the actor not to introduce it more than once in each sentence, as it is likely to pall upon the more respectable part of the audience."[59] The interpolation of extemporaneous matter into play texts, termed "gagging," was common in the period, and Omnes was only suggesting here that the players keep it relatively clean.

Theatrical activity in St. Louis slowed down considerably as a result of the depression of the early 1820's, which hit the Missouri city hard. There were, however, signs of returning prosperity in 1825. The *Missouri Republican* (successor to the *Gazette*) of July 4, 1825, asserted "business is thriving. . . ." And within a matter of weeks another strolling company arrived to play a brief season, a season that included a production of John Howard Payne's famous ballad opera *Clari*.[60] By fall of 1825 a new "theater" of sorts, another converted salthouse "fitted up in a style of neatness and elegance . . . ," was opened for the performance of the "St. Louis Thespian Theatrical Association."[61] The public was assured that no expense had been spared "to render it [the playhouse] comfortable and commodious."[62] It was in this playhouse, extensively remodeled and refurbished, that the Caldwell company opened its first St. Louis season in the summer of 1827.[63]

On June 21, 1827, the *Missouri Republican* printed Caldwell's announcement of his intention to bring theater to St. Louis on a regular season basis. The manager was, according to the announcement,

58. *St. Louis Missouri Gazette*, Jan. 10, 1821.
59. *Ibid.*
60. Carson, *St. Louis Stage*, pp. 80–81.
61. *St. Louis Missouri Republican*, Oct. 24, 1825. The members of the St. Louis Thespian Association were apparently as active as they were ambitious. They opened their 1825 season with *The Soldier's Daughter* (Andrew Cherry), and one week later performed Sheridan's *The Rivals*. See *ibid.*, Oct. 31, 1825.
62. *Ibid.*, Oct. 24, 1825.
63. Caldwell had leased the St. Louis Theater and dispatched his own carpenters and painters to renovate it early in May of 1827. See Smither, "New Orleans," p. 137.

"anxious to establish the Drama" in St. Louis "upon a liberal and respectable footing." To effect this intention Caldwell would "bring the whole of his establishment to St. Louis . . ."; he had "every confidence in the liberality of its citizens for an ample support." Finally, he promised, "Every novelty possible will be brought forward, and every exertion made to make the theater a fashionable and general resort." On June 26 the company arrived in St. Louis.[64]

The season offered by the Caldwell corps was not notably successful. Lack of comfort in the theater probably was to blame; the heat in the poorly ventilated playhouse was likely unbearable. Attendance remained low despite the efforts of a good company numbering seventeen to twenty members, an impressive reportory that included *Macbeth, Hamlet, Henry IV, School for Scandal,* and *Belle's Stratagem,* and the continuing encouragement of the local press.[65] Still, Caldwell retained St. Louis on his circuit until 1831, each summer dispatching his company or a part of it under one of his lieutenants to play a season. Though he might show little profit for the effort, Caldwell calculated that he would at least keep his company intact and ward off any possible interlopers.

At the end of the New Orleans season of 1828, manager Caldwell was ready to make his long-delayed move in Natchez, Mississippi, and to add yet another town to his theatrical empire. Natchez had experienced irregular theatrical fortunes since 1817 when Noah Ludlow's Commonwealth Company first offered real professional theater there. This same company, under Ludlow, John Vaughn, or (in 1820) William Jones, played annual seasons there until 1821, the five seasons totaling about seventy weeks of theater.[66]

Indications are that the public lent strong support. In January, 1819, the *Mississippi Republican* estimated the weekly theater receipts to be $700,[67] an overestimation surely, but a sign of crowded houses. "Celia" in the *Mississippi State Gazette* a month later mentioned the "brilliant and respectable audiences which every night crowd our theatre. . . ."[68] During the 1820 season, which opened on

64. *St. Louis Missouri Republican,* June 28, 1827.

65. See *ibid.,* July 12, 1827; Aug. 16, 1827. The usually critical Joe Cowell called this company "the best by far on the continent . . ."; *Thirty Years,* II, 95.

66. Free, "Natchez Region," p. 17.

67. Free, "Southwestern Mississippi," p. 99, quoting *Natchez Mississippi Republican,* Jan. 19, 1819.

68. *Ibid.,* pp. 99–100, quoting *Natchez Mississippi State Gazette,* Feb. 13, 1819.

January 4, the theater was extensively renovated, another sign of successful operations.

But the theater in Natchez was in trouble by 1820. Economic distress took its toll. Audiences dwindled, as the *Republican* observed, by virtue of "the distress felt by every class almost of our citizens. . . . "[69] Added to economic unrest in accounting for the Natchez decline was the inferior quality of Jones's company. A letter to the *Gazette* of March 25, 1820, pointed out: "It has long been a settled opinion among the best critics that an actor, in order to give effect to [a] part should study it. . . ."[70] Apparently there was an excessive reliance upon the prompter by many members of the troupe.

Despite the waning support, Jones offered some forty performances in the spring of 1820 and returned to open another season in November of that year, a season that extended, with some interruptions, well into March of 1821.[71] Again support was weak. When on October 13, 1821, the theater building on the bluff burned down,[72] a distinct period in Natchez theatrical history came to a close.

There was no real professional theater in Natchez from spring of 1821 to spring of 1823, when Caldwell made his exploratory visit there. The New Orleans manager outfitted the ballroom of Traveller's Hall, the town's largest hotel, and presented his company there under the acting management of Noah Ludlow. The season ran from April 19 to July 5, 1823, and was crowned by a star appearance of Thomas A. Cooper.[73] When Caldwell and Jane Placide joined the stock at mid-season, they proved popular attractions and further strengthened an already strong company. But the season was a financial failure. The ballroom-theater was simply too small to sustain a twenty-five-member company plus stars. Caldwell realized that Natchez would have to have a new playhouse in order to become a paying theater town.

Caldwell was not ready in 1823 to provide both the impetus and initial cash for construction of a new playhouse. For four years

69. *Ibid.*, p. 115, quoting *Natchez Mississippi Republican*, May 9, 1820.

70. Quoted in *ibid.*, p. 113. The same correspondent complained also of the accommodations in the playhouse, notably the oil used in lighting the house, which, observed the critic, "had somewhat of an unsavory smell with it."

71. *Ibid.*, p. 118.

72. *Ibid.*, pp. 126–27. The fire was apparently the work of an incendiary and was one of many theater burnings in the period. There is strong presumptive evidence that at least some, probably most, of these fires were the work of puritanical fanatics.

73. *Ibid.*, p. 151; Ludlow, *Dramatic Life*, p. 245.

Natchez was ill-served with theater, attracting only occasional circuses and exhibitions. In 1826, however, a group of prominent local
citizens began a project to build a playhouse by public subscription.
They sought and received Caldwell's support in the project.[74] On
April 30, 1828, the City Theater opened with the New Orleans company performing Tobin's *Honey Moon* and the farce *Of Age Tomorrow*.[75] This time the opening address, the work of an unknown
Natchezian, was spoken by a leading lady of the company, Mrs.
James S. Rowe. The burden of the dedicatory poem was directed
to the audience:

> To you we look, your care and patronage
> Will aid the struggle of our infant stage;
> Your gen'rous hands, our first, and firmest guard;
> Your tears, and smiles, our highest, best reward.[76]

One minor member of the company that opened the new theater
was a twenty-seven-year-old stroller named Solomon Franklin Smith,
a New Yorker by birth, a Westerner by extraction, who had joined
the Caldwell stock in 1827.[77] In his inimitable memoirs, Smith recalled what was to him the most memorable thing about the new
Natchez theater. The playhouse, it seems, was built on ground formerly occupied by a cemetery, and the dressing-rooms provided for
the players were located beneath the stage, well under ground. Smith
was taken aback upon entering the dressing area to find a quantity
of human bones "strewn about in every direction."[78] On opening
night, Sol recalled, "the lamplighter being a little 'pushed' for time

74. Free, "Southwestern Mississippi," p. 140; Hostetler, "Caldwell," p. 120.
Among the Natchez dignitaries involved in the theater project were: William B.
Griffith, a Princeton educated attorney and outstanding legal theorist; Dr.
Stephen Duncan, physician, planter, banker, litterateur, and owner of five
hundred slaves; Samuel Postlethwaite, wealthy merchant-banker and mayor of
Natchez in 1825; John A. Quitman, notable politician-soldier; John Routh, immensely wealthy cotton planter; and many others.
75. Free, "Southwestern Mississippi," p. 180; Hostetler, "Caldwell," p. 120.
The new theater was located at the east end of Main Street. It was built of
brick, with three arched entrances. The interior was 50 by 90 feet in area, accommodated about six hundred, and featured the traditional pit-boxes-gallery design.
76. Quoted in Free, "Southwestern Mississippi," p. 180.
77. Solomon Franklin Smith, *Theatrical Management in the West and South
for Thirty Years. Interspersed with Anecdotical Sketches: Autobiographically
Given* (New York: Harper and Brothers, 1868), p. 49.
78. *Ibid.*, p. 51. Smith's memoir, for all the outlandish exaggeration of some
of the "anecdotical sketches," is remarkably accurate in matters of fact concerning his important career.

... seized upon a SKULL, and, sticking two tallow candles in the eye-sockets, I found my dressing-room thus lighted." For the *Hamlet* production later in the season (the first *Hamlet* in Natchez), Smith, cast as First Grave-digger had "no difficulty in finding bones to 'play at loggats with.' "[79]

The 1828 season was well received and lasted until early July when the troupe departed for St. Louis. By late fall, having spent the summer period on tour in the valley circuit, they returned to Natchez for another season, a common practice for all touring troupes bound for New Orleans. But it was not the full New Orleans Company, and manager Caldwell was not along. The leaderless, abbreviated aggregation proved ragged, and the local press was quick in condemnation. Noteworthy was one letter in the *Southern Galaxy*. With but few exceptions, the critic contended, "we have never seen so much wretched playing in the same space of time as during the past week. . . ." The irate critic then proceeded to catalogue the weaknesses: continual prompting was required, characterizations were poorly conceived, pronunciation was a sort heard "only among negroes . . . ," gagging and byplay was excessive, and "more than all, some of the characters have made their appearance in a state of inebriation."[80] Natchez was not a town to allow shoddy performances to go unnoticed. Unlike many other Western towns, there were people about who had seen good theater.

Caldwell continued to offer regular seasons in Natchez for several years following the opening of the new playhouse there. Indeed, Natchez was throughout his career the most immediate adjunct of his New Orleans operations and as such had frequent opportunity to witness the foremost stars of the English-language theater. Such was at least the case after New Orleans became one of America's important theatrical centers; a development that was in 1828 on the verge of coming to pass.

3.

The American section of New Orleans experienced remarkable

79. *Ibid.*, pp. 51–52.
80. Free, "Southwestern Mississippi," p. 195, quoting *Natchez Southern Galaxy*, Nov. 13, 1828. Inebriated performers, like inebriated auditors, were common in the period.

growth between 1820 and 1830. Whereas the aggregate population of the old quarter increased by only some 2,500 people,[81] the "upper suburbs" of the city by 1830 claimed 9,513 residents, practically all American.[82] Moreover, the volume of trade increased 75 per cent over the decade, and most of that increase fell to the Faubourg Ste. Marie, or as it had come to be known, the "Second Municipality."[83] In short, the internal dynamic of the teeming New Orleans economy emanated from the Americans, and New Orleans was rapidly becoming an American-dominated city commercially.[84] The ever-aware James H. Caldwell fully comprehended the ramifications of the transformation. He chose the fall of 1828 to renovate his Camp Street Theater inside and out.

By December 19, 1828, the renovations were complete. According to the *Louisiana Advertiser,* the most impressive thing one encountered upon entering the revamped playhouse was the "majestic Proscenium." It was in the form of "an eliptic arch of thirty-eight feet span, supported by two Doric pilasters in imitation of Scarcolina marble, reoded in gold," with gilded bases and capitals. The "dome," or ceiling, was arabesque in design, with a blue background and a canopied center painted with clouds and "studded with silver stars," from which hung a "cut-glass chandelier nine feet in diameter." The front of each of the three tiers of boxes was elaborately decorated. For example, the first tier featured "wreaths of roses and flowers, supported by golden zephyrs. . . ." The "pit boxes" (those closest to the pit) were carpeted throughout and equipped with stuffed mahogany chairs and branched candelabrum. The entire house was, of course, "brilliantly illuminated with gas." Yet all of the elegance of the new decor was "eclipsed in the stage department." The scenery

81. U. S. Census Office, *Social Statistics,* p. 252.

82. U. S. Department of State, *Fifth Census, or, Enumeration of the Inhabitants of the United States. 1830* (Washington: Printed by Duff Green, 1832), p. 105.

83. *Ibid.* The *batture* above Canal Street, docking area of the American section, received most of the Western produce coming downriver for export; i.e., the cotton, tobacco, pork, beef, corn, flour, and Northern fabrics. The old quarter, whose merchants had always looked to France, Spain, and the West Indies for trade, dealt in such items as coffee, indigo, sugar, rice, fruit, and wines.

84. See Joseph G. Tregle, "Early New Orleans Society: A Reappraisal," *Journal of Southern History,* XVIII (Feb., 1952), 20–36. Tregle contends that the Americans by the mid-1830's dominated New Orleans socially and culturally as well as commercially.

was entirely new, with each painted backdrop covering "nearly 1000 square feet of canvas. . . ."[85]

It seems as though Caldwell was aware of the significance his New Orleans theater had taken on. In order to match the new physical splendor with productions worthy of their surroundings, the manager made several adjustments in his method of operation. First, he employed Junius Brutus Booth, universally acknowledged to be one of the great actors of the day, to serve as acting manager of the theater.[86] Then Caldwell strengthened the stock company Booth was to head. Jane Placide returned after an absence of nearly two years following a serious accident. Caldwell himself performed frequently. George Holland, the veteran comedian, was brought in as a permanent member of the stock. Sol Smith proved a local favorite in low comedy; his vocalist wife was equally popular in all singing parts.[87] The stars of the season were among the finest talents of the English-language stage. And the 1829 season at the Camp was nothing short of brilliant.

Booth appeared regularly in the leads of his repertoire from the beginning of the season, co-starring usually with Jane Placide. The stars came in rapid succession: Thomas A. Cooper, the Covent Garden tragedienne Mrs. John Sloman, Mrs. Alexander Drake—the "Siddons of the West,"[88] and finally Edwin Forrest, the pride of the American cultural nationalists. The result was a series of notable productions at the Camp, productions worthy of a city on the threshold of theatrical eminence.

The *New Orleans Louisiana Advertiser* of March 9, 1829, for example, announced a performance of Thomas Otway's tragedy *Venice Preserved* in which the principals were Cooper, Booth, and Mrs. Sloman. "Seldom has an audience in America," observed the *Advertiser*, "had a chance of witnessing so much histrionic excellence

85. Smither, "New Orleans," p. 144, quoting *New Orleans Louisiana Advertiser*, Dec. 19, 1828.

86. Kendall, *Golden Age*, p. 48.

87. See *New Orleans Argus*, April 17, 1828, on Smith's popularity. See also Playbill, Camp Street Theater, Dec. 18, 1828, Harvard Theater Collection, Harvard College Library.

88. According to John Howard Payne, it was the Duke of Saxe-Weimar who first referred to Fanny Drake as "The Siddons of the West." See Jane Elinor Jones, "A History of the Stage in Louisville, Kentucky, From Its Beginning to 1855" (Master's thesis, State University of Iowa, 1932), p. 35, quoting John Howard Payne to "Mrs. Winter," May 20, 1833.

concentrated on a single piece. . . ."[89] The observation could hardly be gainsaid. March 14 saw an *Othello* production with Booth as Othello, Cooper as Iago, Caldwell as Cassio, Mrs. Sloman as Desdemona, and Jane Placide as Emilia.[90] It is doubtful that a stronger cast could have been found anywhere in the world on a given night. Yet three days later practically the same cast presented another *Othello*, the only alteration being the replacement of Placide by Fanny Drake as Emilia.[91]

In April Forrest arrived, and the season continued unabated. On April 13, the American tragedian performed the title role in Knowles's *Virginius*, a role that Cooper had performed earlier in the season. A local drama critic, one of real perception, compared the performances in the *Advertiser*. He stated unreservedly of Forrest, "his Virginius is inferior to Cooper's," elaborating: "Mr. Forrest wants that *ensemble* which the more mature judgment of Mr. Cooper gives to his acting— the former sometimes produces more *éclat,* he is frequently more flashy, but the latter throughout emits more heat. . . ."[92] It was an acute evaluation.

On April 15, New Orleans saw still another *Othello*—that of Forrest. Booth played Iago.[93] Five days later Forrest performed Lear, with Booth as Edgar.[94] May 4 saw a *Richard III* with Forrest as Richard, Booth as King Henry, Caldwell as Richmond, and Jane Placide as the queen.[95] On May 8, Forrest made his final appearance of the season as Damon in John Banim's *Damon and Pythias* at a benefit for the Asylum for Destitute Orphan Boys.[96] Caldwell closed

89. Quoted in Hostetler, "Caldwell," p. 128.
90. Playbill, Camp Street Theater, March 14, 1829, Harvard Theater Collection, Harvard College Library. On March 6, another *Othello* had been performed with the male leads reversed—Cooper played Othello, Booth played Iago; *ibid.,* March 6, 1829.
91. *Ibid.,* March 17, 1829.
92. Smither, "New Orleans," p. 152, quoting *New Orleans Louisiana Advertiser,* April 15, 1829. It is noteworthy that of the three great tragedians to appear at the Camp in 1829, Cooper was past his prime, Booth was in his prime, and Forrest was yet to reach his prime.
93. Playbill, Camp Street Theater, April 15, 1829, Harvard Theater Collection, Harvard College Library.
94. *Ibid.,* April 20, 1829.
95. *Ibid.,* May 4, 1829.
96. Smither, "New Orleans," p. 153. According to the *New Orleans Louisiana Advertiser,* May 12, 1829, the orphanage, a favorite charity of manager Caldwell, received $1,300 from the benefit.

the 1829 season on May 22. It had been one of the finest yet to be presented in America. And from that season may be dated New Orleans' emergence as a noteworthy theatrical center.

The seasons that followed in New Orleans were only slightly less brilliant than that of 1829. The great stars continued to appear. Charles Kean, for example, played an engagement along with young Clara Fisher in 1831.[97] Important productions abounded.[98] Even the severe cholera epidemic of 1832 failed to stop Caldwell. On November 17, 1832, he announced the season's stars, among them Mary Ann Duff, Thomas Hilson, James Wallack, and Forrest again.[99] On December 5, 1832, the *Bee* observed that the Camp "at the present moment, not only presents a livelier appearance but holds out greater attractions than have ever, heretofore, been exhibited to our playgoing community. . . ." And the *Bee* was usually indifferent to English-language theater, being primarily an organ of the New Orleans Creole element.[100] The press in general staunchly supported Caldwell, frequently voicing his praise. The *Courier* of May 22, 1830, remarked on the "unremitting assiduity" with which Caldwell had "devoted his time and talents to amuse the public and contribute to the refinement of the age, and improve its taste. . . ." Caldwell had become something of a public figure in New Orleans.

Caldwell's business activities in the city were by no means limited to his theater operation. On March 1, 1833, the state legislature granted him an exclusive franchise for the manufacture and sale of illuminating gas in New Orleans.[101] He had already shown everyone the efficacy of gas lighting by introducing the exotic illuminating system in his theater. Now he had the opportunity to light the town and to pocket enormous profits for so doing. In order to finance the operation he formed the New Orleans Gas Light and Banking Company. But he realized that this was a full-time job, at least in its initial stages. Consequently he abandoned his theatrical career, ostensibly for good. On May 28, 1833, manager Caldwell took a farewell benefit

97. *New Orleans Louisiana Courier*, April 19, 1831.

98. For example, New Orleans saw the American premier of *Two Gentlemen of Verona* on Dec. 28, 1831. See Smither, "New Orleans," p. 176.

99. *New Orleans Bee*, Nov. 17, 1832. The cholera epidemic came in the wake of a yellow fever epidemic and destroyed one-sixth of the population. See U. S. Census Office, *Social Statistics*, p. 253.

100. Tregle, "New Orleans Society," p. 28. Tregle suggests, however, that in the early 1830's the *Bee* began to feature Caldwell's activities more prominently.

101. Hostetler, "Caldwell," p. 201.

and dramatically announced his retirement as manager of the **Camp** **Street Theater.** He then leased the Camp to his long-time associates Richard Russell and James Simon Rowe, former Camp stage **manager** and treasurer respectively.[102]

At the same time Caldwell disposed of his other theater interests up the valley. Russell and Rowe obtained leases on the Nashville theater and the magnificent playhouse in Cincinnati that Caldwell had opened on July 4, 1832.[103] He sold them his theater stock in Natchez outright.[104] For the rest, the manager simply allowed the operation of the theaters to fall to whoever wanted to try theater management. Actually Caldwell's efforts in the other towns upriver had proved disappointing to him. St. Louis had never lived up to his expectations. The seasons there by the New Orleans company (or a branch thereof) were plagued by lack of support, despite the frequent complaints in the press of the paucity of amusements available in St. Louis. The *Missouri Republican*, for example, in announcing an 1829 appearance of a second-rate troupe, noted: "The absence of every other species of amusement, if not the sterling merit of the company . . . is a sufficient inducement to bespeak a liberal patronage. . . ."[105] Yet Caldwell's forces drew poor audiences every season they performed in St. Louis from 1828 through 1832. A prime factor in accounting for the lack of success was the weather—the Caldwell system required summer seasons in St. Louis, and the poorly ventilated playhouse was uncomfortably warm in the summer.[106] Another factor was the prevalence of disease; people were afraid of congregating in public places.[107] Finally, the repertoire of the Caldwell troupe was apparently a bit too high-brow for the taste of the roughhewn Missourians. Typical was the complaint of the *St. Louis Beacon* of July 8, 1830: "Shakespeare's justly admired

102. *Ibid.*, p. 194. The lease was to run five years, beginning June 1, 1833. Russell and Rowe were to get all scenery and stage equipment for $5,000 and were to pay $12,000 per annum for the lease.

103. Paul Smith Hostetler, "Studies in Southern Theater History: I. The Influence of New Orleans on Early Nineteenth Century Theatre," *The Southern Speech Journal*, XXIX (Fall, 1963), 18. In 1831 and 1832 Caldwell had for a time played three companies simultaneously, in Louisville, Nashville, and Cincinnati.

104. Free, "Natchez Region," p. 21.

105. *St. Louis Missouri Republican*, June 2, 1829.

106. See Ludlow, *Dramatic Life*, p. 379. The *Missouri Republican*, Aug. 5, 1828, stated: "The season, we admit, is not propitious, and consequently, full houses cannot be expected. . . ."

107. Carson, *St. Louis Stage*, p. 134.

comedy of *Much Ado About Nothing* was performed last evening, to a not very numerous audience. . . ."[108] Caldwell was not too reluctant in giving up his operations in St. Louis upon his retirement in 1833.

In Louisville, Kentucky, Caldwell never did more than explore the possibilities of establishing regular theater seasons, and that not until 1831. Acting as agent, Ludlow took the Caldwell company to Louisville in July of 1831 for a short season in Samuel Drake's "City Theater."[109] In 1832, Caldwell rented the Drake playhouse, along with all scenery, for several months, again dispatching Ludlow there to perform.[110] The New Orleans manager was probably testing the feasibility of a Louisville-Cincinnati nexus, as he had another branch of the company playing simultaneously in Cincinnati.[111] If so, the possibility never materialized, though the two cities later developed close ties theatrically.

In 1833, then, James H. Caldwell precipitately bowed out of theater management. He felt his fortune lay in New Orleans, and for a while at least, in non-theatrical endeavors. He would soon return to his first interest, the production of top-quality drama, and on a grand scale. But by 1833 his accomplishments were already remarkable. Coming from Virginia in 1820 with a small touring company and but little capital, he had established the English-language theater in New Orleans and had then proceeded to make that city an American theatrical center. He had next extended his influence over the theater of the entire Mississippi Valley by stimulating interest in the theater, by motivating the construction of new playhouses and helping to finance them, by offering strong stock companies in worthwhile drama, and, by the success of these activities, attracting the biggest stars of the day to the Southwest. In effect, Caldwell created a vast American theatrical province. Though his personal operations up the valley were not always financially successful, the quality of his offerings demonstrated what good

108. Quoted in *ibid.*, p. 115. Ludlow complained of having to fall back on "spectacular pieces" and lurid melodrama to draw audiences in St. Louis; *Dramatic Life*, pp. 128–29.

109. Clipping, *Louisville Public Advertiser*, July 19, 1831, reprinted in Coad and Mims, *American Stage*, p. 150.

110. MS agreement between Samuel Drake and James Henry Caldwell, Sept. 18, 1831, in Ludlow-Field-Maury Collection, Missouri Historical Society.

111. James Henry Caldwell to Noah Miller Ludlow, Sept. 15, 1832, Sept. 26, 1832, Oct. 1, 1832, in Caldwell File, Harvard Theater Collection, Harvard College Library.

theater could be and should be. In addition to contributing to the increase in quantity of acted drama available in the region, his efforts lifted the standards of the theater in the Old South. And though his prime motives were unquestionably profit and power, one feels that the altruistic motive was a strong secondary force driving the man.

But though Caldwell dominated the theatrical developments of the period, he was by no means the only manager whose company played the Southwest at the time. Smaller companies and lesser managers toured constantly, performing both in the larger cities and in the hinterlands. Caldwell had competition in spite of all his efforts to avoid it. And the activities of his competitors are well worthy of consideration if the compass of Southern theatrical activity is to be accurately assayed.

CHAPTER V

SOME ITINERANT ACTIVITY

AND THE

FORMATION

OF A

PARTNERSHIP

1.

THE PERIOD BETWEEN THE MID-1820'S AND THE LATE 1830'S WAS THE heyday of the itinerant actor in the new West. It was a period of severe economic dislocation throughout the country, the effects of which were most patently apparent in the Eastern urban centers. Sensitive as they were to the slightest economic decline, the theaters there suffered acutely; manager after manager was forced to follow the example of Francis Courtney Wemyss in Philadelphia, who closed his playhouse in 1830 and advertised his situation in the local press as "starved out."[1]

1. Francis Courtney Wemyss, *Twenty-Six Years of the Life of an Actor and Manager.* . . . (New York: Burgess, Stringer, and Company, 1847, I, 148. Junius Brutus Booth wrote comedian George Holland describing conditions in New York in 1836. "There are four theatres in this city," Booth observed, "each endeavoring to ruin the others, by foul means as well as fair. Tragedians are in abundance. . . . [A] diversion to the South must be made—or to Jail. Three-fourths of the Great men and managers must go." Holland Memorial, *George Holland*, p. 34, quoting Junius Brutus Booth to George Holland, Dec. 24, 1836.

As a consequence the actors and actresses of the East, deprived of their means of livelihood, listened attentively to the rumors of successful theater operations west of the mountains and south of the Ohio River.[2] James Rees was doubtless correct when he wrote that the South of the period attracted actors like the fabled "El Dorado."[3] In an effort to escape the ruinous circumstances on the Eastern seaboard the players flocked West seeking greener fields, much the same as countless other hopeful migrants sought a bonanza, or at least a better life, on the frontier.

When the itinerants reached their destinations, usually towns on the Mississippi or Ohio rivers, they frequently found conditions little better than those they had fled. The towns populous enough to sustain a stock company were generally well provided with entertainment by one of the larger companies operating in the area, and economic conditions were little better in the West. Incessant touring was necessary for survival. The strolling companies proliferated, and visits by these troupes became familiar occurrences to the town-dwellers along the rivers. Even the small hamlets in remote sections of the interior attracted wandering bands of entertainers. They had to seek out towns that were in need of diversion, that were able to afford it, and that were not adequately served by the more established touring companies.

It would of course be impossible to trace all the movements of these myriad strolling troupes—their compass was broad. But an examination of the recorded appearances of the itinerants in one Western town, Lexington, Kentucky, for example, would serve to indicate the number of such companies operating and the nature of their activities. Although Lexington was originally one of the foremost theater towns of the new West, by 1820 it had declined significantly as a commercial center and consequently as a theatrical center. The commercial decline began with the introduction of the steamer and the opening of the direct water route from Pittsburgh to New Orleans via Louisville.[4] The corresponding theatrical decline

2. Typical was the claim of the *New York Spirit of the Times*, April 22, 1837, to the effect that there was a "universal desire throughout all the towns on the margin of the majestic Mississippi river to encourage the drama."

3. *Forrest*, p. 80. The strollers were sometimes motivated by other than monetary considerations. Joseph Jefferson, III, a great actor who began his career as an itinerant, once observed: "There is nothing a young actor enjoys more than itinerant theatricals. It is so grand to break loose from a big tyrant manager in the city and become a small tyrant manager in the country"; *The Autobiography of Joseph Jefferson* (New York: The Century Company, 1889), p. 111.

4. U. S. Census Office, *Social Statistics*, p. 118.

might be dated from 1820, when Samuel Drake dropped Lexington from his regular Kentucky circuit.[5]

Drake's absence after 1819 left a theatrical vacuum in Lexington that a lesser troupe was quick to fill. In 1820 the company of Joshua Collins and "Mr. Groshon" played a short season there, then returned in 1821 reincarnated as the Collins and Jones Company. William Jones, a notable early stroller, had replaced Groshon as co-manager.[6] For several years Collins and Jones included Lexington on their Western circuit, offering annual seasons in spite of generally poor returns. Frequent was the complaint of the local press that the theater audience of a given evening showed "a beggarly account of empty boxes. . . ."[7]

Nor did Collins and Jones have the benefit of a monopoly in distressed Lexington. Samuel Drake occasionally returned for a short season, as, for example, in September of 1823 when he engaged young Edwin Forrest as a minor member of his stock "for the season."[8] Again, in August of 1825 Drake and company returned to their old center of operations to try another season. Prices of admission for this season were advertised as "$1 Commonwealth, or 75 Cents, Specie . . . ,"[9] a sure indication that Lexington was experiencing currency problems. In 1828 Drake was back again to hinder the efforts of Collins and Jones, as he was once again in 1831, when his "Louisville Company" offered a season in "one of the large rooms in the Masonic Hall" which had been "fitted up as a Theatre."[10] In 1831 came still another interloper on the domain of Collins and Jones—J. Purdy Brown "with his company of Equestrian and Dramatic performers."[11] In 1832 Brown reappeared in Lexington, then

5. Crum, "Lexington Theatre," p. 220.

6. *Ibid.*

7. *Ibid.*, p. 231, quoting *Lexington Public Advertiser*, July 19, 1820.

8. *Ibid.*, p. 258, quoting *Lexington Kentucky Reporter*, Sept. 15, 1823. Forrest had begun his Western career with Collins and Jones in Pittsburgh in 1822. He had journeyed downriver with them by flatboat. See William Rouseville Alger, *Forrest*, I, 99–100.

9. Crum, "Lexington Theatre," p. 58, quoting *Lexington Kentucky Reporter*, Aug. 29, 1825.

10. *Ibid.*, p. 305, quoting *Lexington Kentucky Reporter*, Feb. 9, 1831. The old theater of Luke Usher had been sold at public auction in 1825.

11. Clay, "Lexington Theater," p. 69, quoting *Lexington Kentucky Reporter*, Oct. 5, 1831. "Equestrian performers" were trained horses (or their riders) who appeared in "equestrian drama," a popular precursor of horse opera. J. Purdy Brown, one of the best known of such equine managers, appeared with his troupe throughout the South and West.

again in 1834, this time with a company under management of "Brown and Cabell."

The prince of strolling managers, the Philadelphian John Sharp Potter, arrived in Lexington to offer a season in December of 1835, once again in the "large room" of the Masonic Hall.[12] The Drake company returned to Lexington in July of 1836, as did Potter and company. By 1837 Potter had joined forces with his former stage manager, Samuel Waters, forming the company of Potter and Waters, which offered a season in the Kentucky town. The strollers by this time had access to a real theater, or at least something approximating a theater, for a new playhouse had been opened during the summer of 1836.[13] Potter actually brought a "star" to Lexington this season, advertising him in the local press as "MR. SOL SMITH" of the Cincinnati, Louisville, Mobile, and St. Louis theaters. Sol chose one of his favorite roles, Mawworm in Isaac Bickerstaff's *The Hypocrite*, for his one-night starring engagement and closed the evening "with an original sermon."[14]

The next company to attempt Lexington was a truly ephemeral group under the management of "Ingersoll and Dyke."[15] They apparently toured widely in the South, leaving but little record of their activities. The same year, however, saw the appearance of a more significant group, that of the experienced actors James R. Scott and James Thorne, who promised upon opening that "nothing shall be wanting . . . to restore the stage to its original respectability in this city. . . ."[16] Scott and Thorne did achieve a measure of popularity probably unmatched in Lexington since the times of Samuel Drake's primacy. Finally, in 1839 appeared another troupe that left little record beyond the surnames of its co-managers—Bailey and Rogers.

12. Crum, "Lexington Theatre," p. 335, quoting *Lexington Kentucky Gazette*, Dec. 5, 1835. One old stroller described Potter as "the ubiquitous, the ever-persuasive, the always-promising John S. Potter. The man who built more theatres and opened more theatres, and closed more theatres . . . than any man in the union or out of it." Walter M. Leman, *Memories of an Old Actor* (San Francisco: A. Roman and Company, 1886), p. 240.

13. Meek, "Theatre in Lexington," p. 34. The new theater, one of makeshift proportions, was located on the corner of Main and Broad streets.

14. Crum, "Lexington Theatre," pp. 345–46, quoting *Lexington Observer and Reporter*, Aug. 24, 1836. *The Hypocrite* was Bickerstaff's popular adaptation of Molière's *Tartuffe*.

15. Meek, "Theatre in Lexington," p. 114, quoting *Lexington Kentucky Gazette*, June 28, 1838.

16. Crum, "Lexington Theatre," p. 360, quoting *Lexington Kentucky Gazette*, June 28, 1838.

Between 1820 and 1840 then, Lexington was visited with more or less regularity by at least nine different touring companies, and probably more. Some visited only once, some several times. Their activity considered together gave Lexington at least one theater season each year for nearly two decades despite her waning importance as a commercial center. Of perhaps greater significance is the consideration that each of these companies that left record of its activity in Lexington (and there were doubtless some that left no record) also played in other towns of the South. The same troupes toured year-round, playing at every opportunity. Virtually every town capable of providing an audience of any size could depend upon the occasional appearance of one of these companies, or one similar to them.

Nashville, Tennessee, to cite another example, had regular seasons offered by the Caldwell forces. But in addition Nashville witnessed the efforts of Noah Ludlow's various strolling troupes, of J. Purdy Brown and his horses, and of the curious Shakespearean stroller Charles Booth Parsons. Parsons was commended by the Nashville press in 1832 for performing Shakespeare more often than the other touring managers, most of whom tended to offer "pieces whose fantasy delights for a while, and leaves no solid impress upon the mind."[17] Other companies that left some record in Nashville included those of Jackson Gray and James S. Rowe, J. Warrell and Thomas M. Groves, John S. Potter, and C. C. Hodges, all of whom performed more than one season in the commercial capital of Tennessee.[18]

The less well-known strollers did more than just perform in the towns where theater was already an established institution. They frequently took the drama into virgin territory and built the playhouses that served to attract other companies. Ludlow, of course, claimed credit for introducing theater in practically every town in the Southwest, and some of his claims are credible. Warrell and

17. Hunt, "Nashville Theatre," pp. 39–40, quoting *Nashville National Banner and Daily Advertiser*, June 13, 1832. During this season Parsons and company performed *Othello, Hamlet, Merchant of Venice, Romeo and Juliet, Catherine and Petruchio, Richard III*, and *Macbeth*.

18. The 1839 season by the C. C. Hodges troupe lasted from Aug. 19 to Dec. 17. The featured attraction was the manager's wife, Annette Nelson [Hodges], a dancer noted primarily for the briefness of her costumes. Particularly revealing was her performance in *The Mountain Sylph*, a version of Taglioni's *La Sylphide* created especially for her. She performed the Sylph eight times during the long season. See Hunt, "Nashville Theatre," p. 79.

Groves announced in the *Spirit of the Times* in 1836 that they were building new theaters in Franklin, Tennessee, and Tuscumbia, Alabama.[19] In 1837 the *Spirit* carried the news that the same managers were opening still another playhouse in Memphis, Tennessee, an action made possible by "the rapid growth of this town, and the facilities of trade. . . ."[20] In Jackson, Mississippi, A. Cargill opened a theater in December of 1836 to take advantage of the sessions of the Mississippi legislature,[21] and in 1839 John S. Potter led a movement for a larger playhouse, which was duly built by public subscription and opened in the fall.[22] Potter also provided playhouses in Grand Gulf and Port Gibson, Mississippi, prior to 1840.[23] Scott and Thorne stimulated sufficient enthusiasm in Vicksburg, Mississippi, to warrant construction of a theater there in 1836, and by 1837 the *Spirit of the Times* correspondent in Vicksburg was crediting the co-managers with "the introduction and establishment of the drama in the state of Mississippi. . . ."[24] Such are but a few of the contributions of some lesser itinerant managers to theatrical development in the South.

By no means the least active of the strolling managers in the Old South was Sol Smith, who fortunately left an extensive record of his peripatetic operations. Close examination of one of the tours he led during his period of "journeywork" well illustrates the activity of a small itinerant company. Sol and his brother Lemuel, both members of the James H. Caldwell company during the winter of 1829, decided in February to leave the New Orleans troupe, as Sol wrote, "for the purpose of organizing a small strolling concern, intended to operate on the principal towns of Mississippi and West Tennessee. . . ."[25] Recruiting two or three more adventurous players

19. *New York Spirit of the Times*, Oct. 2, 1836.

20. *Ibid.*, April 22, 1837.

21. Edna H. McKee, "History of Theatrical Entertainment in Jackson, Mississippi, From August 1839 to April 1860" (Master's thesis, Florida State University, 1959), p. 11.

22. *Ibid.*, pp. 18–19. According to the *Jackson Mississippian*, Aug. 16, 1839, the new theater measured 60 by 140 feet, accommodated as many as twelve hundred people, and contained "a large and spacious saloon, two tiers of boxes, a pit and a gallery."

23. Kendall, *Golden Age*, p. 282.

24. May 27, 1837. The stock company of Scott and Thorne was strong for an itinerant troupe, numbering possibly up to thirty members. The *Spirit* correspondent declared that the managers "have brought us a company of which we are justly proud, and we trust that they feel the satisfaction and pride of having been rewarded for their liberal endeavors."

25. Smith, *Theatrical Management*, p. 57.

into their ranks, the Smith brothers and their wives set out upriver for Port Gibson, Mississippi, and the beginning of a tour.

Mid-February found the troupe in Port Gibson, where they were, according to Smith, "warmly greeted by the inhabitants."[26] After playing to enthusiastic audiences for several weeks, the strollers departed on the short overland trek to Vicksburg. There they leased a small playhouse that had been outfitted by a local amateur society and commenced a season that lasted some four weeks. Once more their efforts, Sol recalled, met with "unvaried success. . . ."[27] When the support in Vicksburg showed signs of waning the troupe again tried Port Gibson, too soon, it seems, for they met with little success on the return engagement. So, taking again to the river, they made for Memphis, Tennessee, at that time a small waterfront settlement at the mouth of Wolf Creek. There they performed, according to Smith, "in a room, fitted up for the occasion" in the home of a prominent local citizen,[28] commencing an eight-night stand on May 23, 1829. The *Memphis Advocate* declared that the band "regaled the citizens" with their efforts, the songs of Mrs. Sol Smith proving an unusually popular attraction.[29] So successful were the efforts of the group that they inspired the organization of a Memphis amateur society.

Upon leaving Memphis, Smith recalled, their " 'journey-work' commenced in reality." The troupe set out for the interior towns of Tennessee aboard "Common road wagons," heavy horse-drawn vans which "bore this small band of Thespians through the 'Western District,' if not in very great style, certainly in great safety, and at an extremely moderate pace." Their first stop was in Somerville, Tennessee, where, wrote Sol, "the inhabitants insisted on our giving an entertainment, which was attended by the whole village, the receipts amounting to $39." The program in Somerville included the Marie Kemble comedy *Day After The Wedding*, which they performed without scenery, and a variety of song and dance numbers, all well received. From Somerville the group continued overland to Bolivar,

26. *Ibid.*, p. 57; Free, "Southwestern Mississippi," pp. 245–46. The *Port Gibson Correspondent*, Feb. 14, 1829, confirmed Smith's account, declaring that the troupe was well patronized.

27. Smith, *Theatrical Management*, p. 57.

28. *Ibid.* According to Smith's records the gross receipts for eight nights were $319, or less than $40 per night.

29. Charles Clifford Ritter, "The Theatre in Memphis, Tennessee, From Its Beginning to 1859" (Doctoral dissertation, State University of Iowa, 1956), pp. 11–12, quoting *Memphis Advocate*, May (n.d.), 1829.

Tennessee, and opened in a room adapted for their purposes. The performances there, Sol recalled, "were fully attended, considering the size of the village. The people seemed to *come out of the woods . . . ,*" which in fact many of them did.[30] In a week and a half of performances the receipts of the company were $349, or almost $37 per night. At their normal admission price of $1 a head, children half price, Sol and his troupe must have attracted between twenty and thirty people to each performance.

From Bolivar the group journeyed all the way into central Tennessee to Columbia, a somewhat larger town, where they performed in the playhouse of the local amateur society with receipts averaging $60 a night. Leaving Columbia they headed due south, bound for Alabama. En route they stopped in Pulaski, Tennessee, where once again they performed in an amateur playhouse, a theater Smith remembered as being "about sixty feet long and thirty wide. No boxes—all pit." The house decor consisted of a curtain painting of "two ill-proportioned mermaids, or some other nondescript animals, blowing trumpets," and supporting a scroll inscribed with the words "THE WORLD IN MINIATURE."[31] In Jackson, Tennessee, the next stop, Sol presented his show in a log theater, played twelve nights, and grossed $480. Crossing into Alabama the troupe played first in Florence, using the garret of the town's principal hotel, which happened to be the largest room in the village. Seven nights of performances there brought $251 into the coffers of the company. At Tuscumbia, Alabama, they did not fare so well, drawing only $150 in six nights. In Huntsville, next stop on their itinerary, the troupe encountered difficulties with the forces of organized religion.

Fundamentalist preachers were as much a problem to strolling theatrical troupes in the Deep South as to those on the Eastern seaboard. During the eighteen nights that Smith and the corps performed in Huntsville they were in constant competition with the evangelists, who, according to Sol, "endeavored to make their hearers believe that all who visited the theatre would certainly be eternally roasted in the hottest sort of fires. . . ."[32] It seems that the preachers

30. Smith, *Theatrical Management*, pp. 57–58.

31. Solomon Franklin Smith, *The Theatrical Journey-Work and Anecdotal Recollections of Sol. Smith, Comedian, Attorney at Law, Etc., Etc.* (Philadelphia: B. Peterson, 1854), p. 61.

32. Smith, *Theatrical Management*, p. 60. The Huntsville stand opened Aug. 1, 1829. See Playbill, Huntsville Theater, Aug. 1, 1829, Harvard Theater Collection, Harvard College Library.

carried the day. Sol realized only an average of $50 per night in a town that could afford much more.

Following the season in Huntsville the group played their longest engagement of the tour in Tuscaloosa, then capital of the state. The season there ran from September 9, 1829, to January 8, 1830, and was hampered once more by the presence of the preachers.[33] To compete with the hell-fire sermons, the troupe offered on one occasion the didactic pantomime *Don Juan, or The Libertine Destroyed*. Sol recalled that the piece was performed "with all the 'accessories' of snakes spitting flames, fiends with torches, red fire and blue blazes in the last scene, which was represented in the bills of the day to be no other than the INFERNAL REGIONS, into which the amorous *Don* was cast without benefit of clergy."[34] Unfortunately for Smith the spectacular hell scene set the theater on fire, a development that the minions of piety did not fail to use in their continuing attack on the theater.

While in Tuscaloosa, Smith received an invitation to perform in Montgomery, where the citizens had just completed a "beautiful new theatre" for the use of a local amateur society.[35] Of course he accepted. On January 29, 1830, the *Montgomery Alabama Journal* announced the appearance of the Smith troupe in "the petit comedy of the LADY AND THE DEVIL," with the musical farce *No Song No Supper* and incidental songs, including a "Comic Song—'The Great Booby'" by Sol.[36] For two weeks the troupe offered similar productions in Montgomery, closing the short season there with a gross profit of $883 for their efforts.[37]

Next the company proceeded south to Selma, Alabama, "a very small Village," as Sol remembered it, where they played nine nights in a ballroom-theater to receipts averaging $70 a night. "The number of inhabitants," wrote Smith, "did not exceed 400, white, black, and children. Those who visited the theatre visited it *every* night."[38] Upon closing in Selma, the company journeyed down the Alabama

33. Smith, *Theatrical Management*, p. 60. The playbill collection of the Missouri Historical Society verifies Smith's account of the Tuscaloosa season.

34. Smith, *Theatrical Management*, p. 60.

35. *Ibid.*, p. 62; Henry W. Adams, *The Montgomery Theatre, 1822–1835* (Tuscaloosa: University of Alabama Press, 1955), p. 11, quoting *Montgomery Alabama Journal*, Jan. 15, 1830.

36. Quoted in Adams, *Montgomery Theatre*, p. 25.

37. Smith, *Theatrical Management*, p. 63.

38. *Ibid.*

River to Mobile, then took a ship for New Orleans and proceeded up-river to Natchez, Mississippi, where Smith had leased the Caldwell theater for a season.

On March 10, 1830, the little troupe opened in Natchez with Andrew Cherry's "popular comedy in 5 acts, called the SOLDIER's DAUGHTER," followed by the farce *Turn Out*, which featured a song by Sol intriguingly entitled "All in the Oyster Line."[39] On March 13 Smith announced that "the CITY's GUEST, HENRY CLAY, will attend the Theatre on this Evening,"[40] an event that no doubt bolstered the evening's receipts. Managers were always careful to advertise the anticipated presence of any celebrity likely to attract the interested and curious to the theater.

Finding profits in Natchez smaller than he had expected, Smith decided to send half the troupe to Port Gibson and to play both towns at once. But although the towns are fifty miles apart, Sol was determined to star in both of them. He found that he could make the ride from one to the other in five hours and arrive in time to prepare for the evening's performance. For nearly a month the manager-star traveled fifty miles a day on horseback and performed a strenuous routine every night. Sol recalled later that "*It almost killed me. . . .*"[41]

By April 23, 1830, the Natchez season had ended, and with it ended the tour. Sol settled with his well-traveled corps, pocketed $1,200 as his profit for the fourteen months of journeywork, then set out with his wife for Cincinnati. The rest of the troupe, whose enthusiasm for strolling was apparently undiminished, continued on under the banner of Lemuel Smith, directing their attention toward the interior towns of Louisiana. Smith and his wife could not resist the temptation to stop off and perform briefly in Vicksburg on their way to Cincinnati.[42] The 1829–1830 tour by the Smith company had taken them thousands of miles by water and by land in the most primitive of transportation facilities to the most remote towns of interior Tennessee and Alabama. And for all its storybook qualities it was typical of scores of other tours continually in progress in the period.

The most unique of the early strolling companies was that of William Chapman and his family, whose "Floating Theater" toured

39. Playbill, Natchez Theater, March 10, 1830, Playbill Collection, Missouri Historical Society.
40. *Ibid.*, March 13, 1830.
41. Smith, *Theatrical Management*, p. 64.
42. *Ibid.*

the river towns throughout the Mississippi and Ohio valleys between 1831 and 1847. Chapman was a talented British actor-manager who had played Covent Garden and even performed with Sarah Siddons in 1803. Having migrated to America in 1827, the adventurous Chapman designed his craft, had it constructed in Pittsburgh, and launched his career as a showboat manager in the summer of 1831. Chapman's floating playhouse was nothing more than a flatboat measuring 100 feet in length by 16 feet in width, with a shallow stage at the stern and wooden benches amidships. The company was composed of the members of the Chapman family: the elder Chapman and his wife Sarah, sons William, Jr., and George, daughters Caroline and Therese, William, Jr.'s, wife Phoebe, and grandson Harry. All the family were gifted, especially Caroline, whose acting received the acclaim of critics wherever she played throughout her long career.[43]

Chapman's mode of operation was to drift down the Ohio and Mississippi rivers, stopping at any likely landing for a one-night stand, then floating on downriver ultimately arriving in New Orleans. There the flatboat could be sold or scrapped, and the troupe could take a steamer back to Pittsburgh, where preparations were made to repeat the whole procedure the following year. Great profit was not the primary consideration of the elder Chapman. He was more concerned with the unified domestic arrangement the system permitted. But the showboat proved remunerative too. Wherever the troupe tied up and hoisted their green banner bearing the label "Floating Theater," they were sure to attract people living nearby to the performance. Even when the audience paid admission in farm produce, as was frequently the case, the manager could sell the chickens, beans, or whatever to steamboat stewards for cash, after withholding what was required for domestic consumption.[44] Few were the seasons that did not show a sizable profit for William Chapman and his family.

The Chapmans' prosperity permitted them in 1836 to substitute a fully equipped steamboat for the crude flatboat. "Chapman's Float-

43. Graham, *Showboats*, pp. 9–10; Tyrone Power, *Impressions of America During the Years 1833, 1834 and 1835* (Philadelphia: Carey, Lea, and Blanchard, 1836), II, 132–33.
44. "Falconbridge" [Jonathan Falconbridge Kelly], *Dan. Marble; A Biographical Sketch of that Famous and Diverting Humorist, with Reminiscences, Comicalities, Anecdotes, etc., etc.* (New York: Dewitt & Davenport, 1851), p. 107.

ing Theater" became "Chapman's Theatrical Steamboat," and the addition of steam power naturally widened the scope of the company's operations.[45] From Pittsburgh to New Orleans, and from New Orleans to Quincy, Illinois, the showboat provided theater of an excellent quality in all the towns on the water. The Chapman operation thus provided a remarkable instance of cultural transfer. The conventions and traditions established at Covent Garden by Mrs. Siddons and John Philip Kemble were carried to remote American frontier villages and were demonstrated for the pleasure of the Western folk in a repertory of English drama equal to that of most of the Eastern cities.

The success of the Chapmans naturally bred a myriad of imitators, though none were near the caliber of the original. Some of the derivative riverboat "theaters" were even operated by out-and-out mountebanks and thieves. As a result the reputation of showboats was blackened. Although several continued operation after the retirement of the Chapmans in 1847, it was not until the "Floating Circus Palace" of Gilbert R. Spaulding and Charles J. Rogers commenced operations in the 1850's that showboats again became popular and well supported.[46] But the day of the modern showboat of the "Cotton Blossom" variety did not come until after the Civil War.

The quality of the itinerant offerings varied widely. Depending on the composition of the troupe, it ranged from the very good theater of the Chapmans or the Drakes to the ludicrously bad, even dishonest efforts of the self-styled "entertainers" out to bilk a public hungry for entertainment. Huckleberry Finn's "Royal Nonesuch" troupe was more than a figment of Mark Twain's fertile imagination. "Nonesuch" companies existed; the frequent newspaper complaints of their activities attest to that.[47] But in spite of an occasional

45. Graham, *Showboats*, p. 18.

46. *Ibid.*, p. 29. Another showboat operating in the 1840's was the "Temple of the Muses," a converted man-of-war that featured a dress circle, parquet, and even private boxes. See Playbill, Temple of the Muses, April 2, 1845, Harvard Theater Collection, Harvard College Library.

47. See, for example, *Columbus* (Georgia) *Enquirer*, Oct. 20, 1832, for an account of a nefarious pair, Belcour and Howard, who posted bills, sold tickets, gave a "performance," then quickly skipped town. "We do not know," concluded the account, "that we should in this instance have held these gentlemen up to the gaze of the public had they not withall been so desperately mean as to defraud the poor Blackey, whom they had engaged to stick up their bills, of his hard earned pittance." William Osler Langley, "The Theatre in Columbus, Georgia, From 1828 to 1878" (Master's thesis, Alabama Polytechnic Institute, 1937), p. 19, quoting *Columbus Enquirer*, Oct. 20, 1832.

fraud, the arrival of the strollers generally was welcomed in the towns they played. And they unquestionably served a positive function in taking some form of diversion to settlements where diversion was all too scarce.

2.

Occasionally a rootless itinerant manager graduated to the ranks of the established circuit manager. Indeed, most of the established managers in the provinces began their careers as strollers—James H. Caldwell is an obvious case in point. In the mid-1830's two talented strollers were staking out circuits for themselves, focusing their activities in the emerging towns of the Alabama-Georgia interior. As new settlements developed and acquired sufficient population to support a theater, there were usually managers available to provide them with some sort of company. And during the "flush times" of the Deep South states the most active managers of the area were Noah Miller Ludlow and Solomon Franklin Smith. Each of them had been with Caldwell sporadically since arriving in the South. In fact, in 1831 they were in the Camp Street Company together. But each had also struck out on his own periodically, as has been noted above. Both aspired to independent management.

Ludlow had been operating for some time in southern Alabama, at least since 1824 when one of his makeshift companies first tried Mobile, the obvious town from which to develop a Deep South circuit. Mobile was the natural outlet for the enormous cotton crop made each year in the watershed of the Alabama and Tombigbee rivers. The bay community was also the port of entry for such commodities as were used by the planters and farmers of the rich Alabama interior. Moreover, like New Orleans with which she had close commercial ties, Mobile could claim a strong Creole heritage, and the cultural advantages that accompanied Creole cosmopolitanism. Though limited in population—the aggregate figure for 1830 was only 3,195—Mobile had a very substantial transient population, especially during the winter,[48] that must be considered in attempting to estimate the potential audience.

The first theatrical activity in Mobile for which there is positive record came in 1822, when city officials leased a large room in the old Spanish Royal Hospital for use as a theater, probably for ama-

48. U. S. Census Office, *Social Statistics*, p. 191.

teur productions.[49] Strollers visited the town in 1822 and 1823, performing brief engagements, and in 1824 the "City Ball Room" was outfitted as a theater by "Mr. Vaughan," probably Henry Vaughn, who promised in his opening announcement that he would make a "proper distinction in the prices of admission so that families can be accommodated, without being liable to be annoyed, or encroached upon by the crowd."[50] By 1824 a group of local citizens had initiated a movement to build a real theater by public subscription. On April 5, 1823, the cornerstone was laid for the new playhouse, and the *Commercial Register* predicted that if further stock was taken and paid up, "not more than six weeks will elapse before a building will rise up, both ornamental and creditable to the city."[51] The new house was contracted to Noah Ludlow, its principal stockholder, even before its completion.

At the close of the 1824 season in New Orleans, where Ludlow was a member of the Caldwell stock, the ambitious young actor recruited another commonwealth company to tour in Tennessee and Alabama. His plan was to end the tour in Mobile, where he would perform a winter season in the new theater. First the strollers tried Nashville where they met with little success. They proceeded next to Alabama, played five weeks in Huntsville, then tried a short season in Cahawba, where they performed, as Ludlow recalled, in a building "fitted up for dramatic purposes by a company of amateurs."[52] By Christmas Eve of 1824 the Ludlow troupe was in Mobile, commencing an engagement at the new playhouse with John Tobin's *Honey Moon* and the farce *The Liar*.[53]

The performances on opening night, Ludlow wrote, "were well received, and the people went away delighted with the idea of having theatrical amusements for the winter."[54] Public support continued throughout the season, and Ludlow, much encouraged, determined to make Mobile one leg of the Southern circuit he planned

49. Frances Margaret Bailey, "A History of the Stage in Mobile, Alabama From 1824–1850" (Master's thesis, State University of Iowa, 1934), p. 17. There is an unsubstantiated tradition that refugee actors from Saint Domingue played in Mobile in 1791 and 1792.
50. *Mobile Commercial Register*, Feb. 5, 1824.
51. April 7, 1823.
52. Ludlow, *Dramatic Life*, p. 258.
53. *Ibid.*, p. 263; Bailey, "Mobile Stage," p. 20. The playhouse stood on the corner of Royal and Theatre streets, measured 60 by 110 feet, and featured the traditional pit and boxes arrangement. It could accommodate six hundred to seven hundred people.
54. *Dramatic Life*, p. 263.

to establish, along with Nashville and Huntsville. James H. Caldwell blocked him in the latter towns, as has been seen, but Ludlow
at least had a monopoly in Mobile. For four consecutive years he
returned to the Alabama port to offer theater seasons. By recruiting
the strongest possible company and convincing the public that he
intended to provide quality theater, Ludlow consolidated his position in Mobile.

But no one town at that time could support a repertory theater
year-round. Ludlow's success as an independent manager depended
upon his ability to create a circuit. Having been pre-empted in Nashville and Huntsville by Caldwell, he turned to the Alabama interior.
First, in the summer of 1825, he tried Tuscaloosa, where his company was able to sustain itself for some twenty weeks, performing
in the hotel ballroom. Then Ludlow took the troupe to Montgomery,
a town of well under 1,500 residents, where the troupe performed
from mid-October to November 4, 1825.[55] Neither town proved adequate to do more than provide subsistence for the company. Though
there was an enthusiastic element of theater support in each case—
both towns had amateur societies of long standing—there was also
religious opposition to the theater and insufficient population as yet
to offer profits to a manager.[56] So both towns remained dependent
upon amateurs and itinerants for their theater, and Ludlow remained
dependent largely upon his Mobile operation for any profit he
showed at the end of each year.

The Mobile operations did, however, continue to improve. At
every opportunity the manager strengthened his stock and even
brought in an occasional star. According to Ludlow, Thomas A.
Cooper performed "his usual round of characters," i.e., Macbeth,
Virginius, Damon, Richard III, Hamlet, Rolla (in the Kotzebue-
Sheridan *Pizarro*) in the Mobile theater during the season of 1826–
1827.[57] And that season proved remunerative. By 1829 Ludlow was
advertising new talent recruited "at the North" and such coming at-

55. Adams, *Montgomery Theatre*, p. 14. Although the first river steamer had
reached Montgomery in 1821, the town was not served by a regular line until
later and remained relatively inaccessible. The overland route of commerce was
maintained from Charleston and Savannah. See U. S. Census Office, *Social
Statistics*, p. 200.

56. Ludlow, *Dramatic Life*, p. 268; Adams, *Montgomery Theatre*, p. 14;
Royall, *Southern Tour*, II, 184. Mrs. Royal wrote in 1829 that the "godly ones"
of Montgomery wanted to buy the "very handsome *Theatre*" for use as a church,
but the theater interest refused to sell.

57. *Dramatic Life*, pp. 288–89.

tractions as Cooper, Forrest, the John Slomans, "Little" Louisa Lane, and "probably several others of distinguished talent. . . ."[58]

But 1829 proved a disastrous year for Ludlow in Mobile. First came competition in the form of J. Purdy Brown and his "Equestrian Troupe," who commenced operations in a circus tent and proceeded to attract enthusiastic audiences.[59] The equestrians could usually outdraw legitimate drama in the South, and the appearance of the horses usually meant that the legitimate manager had to lower his standards or go broke. Ludlow answered the Brown threat by absorbing the horse troupe into his own company, then offering such "equestrian drama" as "El Hyder—With Horses."[60] For a while the combined company drew well, but then came disaster. On March 1, 1829, the Mobile theater burned to the ground, along with the full complement of scenery, props, and costumes—all uninsured.[61]

Ludlow immediately dispatched the company to Montgomery to play for their subsistence, while he remained in Mobile to arrange for a temporary playhouse in which to continue the season. He was successful. With the $2,000 that was immediately subscribed, the manager built a temporary structure that was complete and ready to open in just forty-two days.[62] Ludlow and Purdy Brown finished the season there. But during the summer of 1830 that theater too was destroyed by a fire.[63] Much against his inclinations, Ludlow was forced to rejoin the Caldwell stock in New Orleans for the season 1830–1831.[64] Mobile was left without theatrical entertainment until January of 1832. It is noteworthy that the year's hiatus was the only time Mobile was to have no annual theater season from 1824 to the coming of the Civil War.

Even as Ludlow was struggling to form a circuit in Tennessee and Alabama, Sol Smith, whose career closely parallels that of Ludlow, was attempting to form one of his own in Alabama and Georgia. It was Smith who reintroduced the drama in Mobile in January of 1832. Arriving from Tuscaloosa, where his latest strolling troupe had

58. *Mobile Commercial Register*, Jan. 7, 1829. The stock company was thirty-three strong and included young Thomas Dartmouth (later "Jim Crow") Rice. See Ludlow, *Dramatic Life*, p. 329.

59. *Mobile Commercial Register*, Feb. 20, 1829.

60. *Ibid.*, Feb. 23, 1829. *El Hyder* was a melodramatic spectacular by William Barrymore.

61. *Ibid.*, March 2, 1829.

62. Ludlow, *Dramatic Life*, pp. 335–36.

63. Bailey, "Mobile Stage," p. 25.

64. Joseph Patrick Roppolo, "A History of the American Stage in New Orleans, 1842–1845" (Master's thesis, Tulane University, 1948), pp. 4–5.

been playing to enthusiastic crowds,[65] Smith opened a small Mobile "theater," actually a room over a billiard parlor on Royal Street, "very commodiously fitted up," according to the *Mobile Commercial Register*, for the performance of plays.[66] Smith and company won immediate approval in Mobile. "Mr. Sol Smith, it has not been our good fortune to see, in his particular line of Drama until last night," noted the *Register* shortly after the season opened, "when a crowded house and a delighted audience gave ample assurance of the estimation in which he is . . . held."[67] On February 8, it was reported that the little playhouse had "crowded benches constantly" and that if "the accommodations could be enlarged, the support would enlarge also."[68] The local press lent strong support to the troupe. On February 10, the editor of the *Register* announced that "the Theatre is so prominent an item in our city's amusements, and withal so fashionable, that our duty, as well as inclination, prompt us occasionally to speak of it."[69] He then gave an account of the week's performances, praising each of them. There was, in short, every indication that Mobile was ready for theater on a regular season basis.

But the likable Smith was denied the honor of establishing seasonal theater in Mobile by the return of Purdy Brown and his inevitable horses. Brown had been at work on plans to open a new equestrian theater for some time. By March of 1832 his troupe was performing in their new "playhouse" on St. Emmanuel Street. Smith was forced to close his season on March 12 and leave Mobile with the best wishes of the press and people.[70] He was off for another tour, while the theatrical fortunes of Mobile were left in the hands of Brown and the trick riders. And though the *Commercial Register* frequently expressed a preference for the "small but excellent little company of Old Sol,"[71] Brown and his horses maintained their ascendancy

65. The *Tuscaloosa Intelligencer* had declared on Jan. 14, 1832: "We understand that *Old Sol, and his Company Dramatic*, will leave here in a few days for *Mobile*. The community here are certainly endebted to the members of the drama for many of their pleasantest sensations during the winter." *Mobile Commercial Register*, Jan. 23, 1832, quoting *Tuscaloosa Intelligencer*, Jan. 14, 1832.

66. Jan. 25, 1832.

67. *Ibid.*, Feb. 1, 1832.

68. *Ibid.*, Feb. 8, 1832.

69. *Ibid.*, Feb. 10, 1832.

70. *Ibid.*, March 13, 1832.

71. *Ibid.*, April 2, 1832. Sol was not universally popular, however, as was evidenced by a letter in the *Montgomery Alabama Journal* of March 13, 1832, which stated that the Smith company was "the most miserable of the miserable," and that "Sol himself should not be tolerated" save in the lowest of low comedy. Quoted in Adams, *Montgomery Theatre*, pp. 28–29.

(though not a monopoly) in Mobile until Brown's death in 1834.

From the time of his departure from Mobile in March of 1832, Smith toured incessantly, his route ranging from Augusta, Georgia, to Cincinnati, Ohio, and including most of the villages between. But by 1833 he was concentrating his operations more and more in a rough Georgia-Alabama circuit. He played the small interior towns of both states—Selma, Montgomery, Macon, Columbus, Milledgeville, Athens, Augusta. Sol introduced several of these towns to professional theater and frequently inspired the construction of playhouses. Columbus, Georgia, for example, built a temporary theater to receive the Smith troupe on their first visit, in May of 1832, and when the troupe appeared they "created a decided sensation" among the citizens.[72] Macon built another temporary theater for Smith. In Milledgeville the troupe found a theater already existing, albeit one that Sol compared unfavorably to the Augean stables. Thirty barrels of lime failed to remove all the odor, he recalled, but still the audiences were "large and fashionable."[73] Athens also built a playhouse for the use of the Georgia strollers. In other towns, smaller ones like Monticello and Madison, the company played wherever an audience could gather, and gather they did. Smith was popular in Georgia, as was the entire troupe. Typical was the comment of one Georgia newspaper editor, who wrote, "we doubt whether any company in the United States, enlivening our inland villages, combines as much talent for tragic and comic acting . . . as Old Sol's."[74]

Still, Mobile was the choice theater town in the Deep South cotton belt, and Smith quite naturally wanted to extend his operation to the Alabama port. He frequently received encouragement from individual Mobileans, notably the attorney-editor Thaddeus Sanford, who wrote to Smith describing conditions in Mobile in March of 1833. "Our city is overflowing with strangers," wrote Sanford. "The yankees are as thick as Musketoes.—every other man I meet presents a new

72. Smith, *Theatrical Management*, p. 78; Langley, "Theatre in Columbus," p. 6, quoting *Columbus Enquirer*, May 19, 1832. One of the Smith's widely quoted "Anecdotical Sketches" concerned a Columbus production of *Pizarro* in which the manager employed a group of drunken Creek Indians to play the Peruvians. Smith, *ibid.*, pp. 79–80. Smith owned the theater here and that in Macon outright. See Solomon Franklin Smith to Noah Miller Ludlow, Aug. 27, 1834, in Ludlow-Field-Maury Collection, Missouri Historical Society.

73. Smith, *Theatrical Management*, p. 80. Smith's brother Lemuel was murdered in a Milledgeville tavern argument during the 1832 season there.

74. Langley, "Theatre in Columbus," p. 20, quoting *Columbus Enquirer*, Feb. 9, 1833.

phiz. . . . They furnish the material for a *good* theatrical audience and a *good* company with a *good* house to play in would do a *good* business.—but all of these *goods* are *good* for nothing under existing auspices."[75]

But Mobile was well occupied by Brown as well as by an itinerant group under George Holland and could not possibly support another company.[76] For the time being Smith had to satisfy himself with his Georgia-Alabama circuit and await further developments in Mobile.

Meanwhile Noah Ludlow, who had never given up the idea of re-establishing himself in Mobile, was operating with his troupe in Louisville, Kentucky. He had built a temporary theater there in 1829, entering into competition with Samuel Drake, apparently envisioning a Mobile-Louisville nexus.[77] The Mobile fires had driven him back to Caldwell's stock in 1830, but only for one season. Then he had again set out on his own, playing in Louisville and touring widely. In 1834 he began operating in the Old Salt House playhouse in St. Louis, a town poorly served with theater during the two years preceding his arrival.[78] Ludlow saw real potential there and determined to include St. Louis on whatever circuit he eventually worked out. He even issued a proposal for a new theater, feeling certain that the stock would be quickly subscribed.[79]

But the death of J. Purdy Brown on June 7, 1834, created a theatrical void in Mobile, and the focus of Ludlow's attention quickly shifted to south Alabama.[80] Sol Smith was of course equally inter-

75. Thaddeus Sanford to Solomon Franklin Smith, March 2, 1833, in Smith Collection, Missouri Historical Society.

76. *Ibid.* Sanford wrote "Holland is here and . . . has rented the building on Royal Street . . . where he is giving recitations, playing and singing aided by his wife and [three others]," to houses of from $60 to $80 a night.

77. Ludlow, *Dramatic Life*, p. 340; Weisert, *Curtain Rose*, p. 20; Rusk, *Middle Western Frontier*, I, 405–6; clipping, *Louisville Public Advertiser*, Nov. 7, 1829, reprinted in Coad and Mims, *American Stage*, p. 145. Joe Cowell, a famous strolling comedian, described Ludlow's Louisville theater as "a cattle shed or stable . . . fitted up as a temporary stage." Of the company he observed: "Nothing I had ever seen in the way of theatricals could be likened to this deplorable party." Cowell, *Thirty Years*, p. 90. Cowell did, however, credit Ludlow with integrity and ability and even acknowledged that the manager did well with his poor material.

78. Carson, *St. Louis Stage*, p. 139.

79. Noah Miller Ludlow to Solomon Franklin Smith, Sept. 22, 1834, in Smith Collection, Missouri Historical Society.

80. *Mobile Commercial Register and Patriot*, June 7, 1834.

ested in Mobile, and his troupe was operating closer at hand. But apparently Sol knew of Ludlow's determination to re-enter Mobile. He further realized that the town could not support two companies. Consequently, early in September of 1834, Smith wrote Ludlow inquiring about the possibilities of a Ludlow-Smith partnership, with their combined companies operating in Mobile and elsewhere. Ludlow's reply expressed strong interest in the proposition. "I believe we could do as much or more, perhaps, for our means, than any other two men I know of in the profession," wrote Ludlow. "I will say to you frankly that I am much inclined towards the proposed connection."[81] He then suggested that the two meet in Mobile on November 1, 1834, to make further arrangements.

When Ludlow arrived in Mobile at the appointed time, he found that Smith had not arrived. Two weeks passed without word from Old Sol. So on November 13, 1834, Ludlow wrote Smith, who was in Milledgeville, announcing his intentions: Ludlow would take a lease on the erstwhile Purdy Brown's St. Emmanuel Street playhouse for the winter season, pay off some debts previously incurred in Mobile, and clear the way for the partnership for the following season.[82] The reason for Smith's absence later became the subject of considerable controversy between the two managers. Smith claimed that he was detained in Milledgeville with illness in his family and intended for Ludlow to take the lease in both their names.[83] Ludlow argued that Smith was engaged in a joint effort with George Holland in the Georgia circuit and simply let the Mobile engagement slip by default, planning to join Ludlow for the following season.[84] The Ludlow letter of November 13 seems to indicate that he did try to contact Smith but that he failed to hear from Sol and could not delay any longer. Very likely the whole matter was a simple misunderstanding, a failure of communication. In any case, Ludlow proceeded to lease the theater in his own name, as sole lessee, thereby cutting Smith out for the 1834–1835 season. Smith never forgave him. This contretemps provided the basis of discord between the two men that lay just beneath the surface of their personal relationship for the entire eighteen years of their partnership.

81. Noah Miller Ludlow to Solomon Franklin Smith, Sept. 22, 1834, in Smith Collection, Missouri Historical Society.
82. *Ibid.*, Nov. 13, 1834.
83. Smith, *Theatrical Management*, p. 116.
84. Ludlow, *Dramatic Life*, pp. 446–47.

On December 17 manager Ludlow opened the Mobile season with Tobin's evergreen comedy *The Honey Moon*.[85] The company was strong and Ludlow was determined to offer attractions he felt worthy of the town he so wanted to impress. Consequently, he brought in a succession of stars the likes of which Mobile had never seen: Mrs. Alexander Drake played her round of tragic heroines, George Handel Hill essayed all his inimitable "Yankee" roles, and Charles Webb and John Jay Adams portrayed the heroes of the traditional tragic drama.[86] The result was probably the best theater yet available in Mobile.

Toward the end of April, 1835, Ludlow closed the playhouse, packed his properties and scenery, and arranged for the departure of the troupe for St. Louis.[87] But before leaving Mobile he and Smith met to plan the details of their future partnership. It is likely they were spurred on in their determination to operate jointly by the knowledge that James H. Caldwell had come out of "retirement." On May 8, 1835, Caldwell laid the cornerstone of the splendid St. Charles Theater in New Orleans. Word was out that the manager was planning a more ambitious operation than ever before.[88] Both Ludlow and Smith were aware that in order to compete with Caldwell they would have to join their forces and resources. Caldwell had even written Smith on May 3, 1835, informing Sol that he was going to bid on the Mobile theater and that he knew Ludlow and Smith planned to do so also.[89] The letter was a lightly veiled threat that Caldwell was entering the lists against whomever aspired to operate in Mobile. It was ample incentive for Ludlow and Smith to patch up their personal differences and proceed with their partnership arrangements.

On June 2, 1835, the "Articles of Co-partnership" were completed and signed. The new firm was to be called "Ludlow and Smith," and the partners were to be equals, sharing both the assets and liabilities of the firm as well as the duties of management. The first season of the firm's operation would be in the fall of 1835, in Mobile, after

85. Playbill, Mobile Theater, Dec. 7, 1834, Harvard Theater Collection, Harvard College Library.
86. Bailey, "Mobile Stage," p. 72.
87. Ludlow, *Dramatic Life*, p. 434.
88. Hostetler, "Caldwell," p. 266.
89. James Henry Caldwell to Solomon Franklin Smith, May 3, 1835, in Smith Collection, Missouri Historical Society.

which the partners would operate in both Mobile and St. Louis.[90] Each partner was to contribute $250 immediately to provide the initial capital of the firm. The long-time strolling player-managers had at last settled down to the operation of a theatrical nexus of two towns soon to be theatrical centers of the Old South. And though Ludlow and Smith had no way of foreseeing it in 1835, prior to dissolution of the firm in 1853 they would come to dominate the theatrical fortunes of the entire Mississippi Valley.

In St. Louis, Ludlow continued his policy of offering a strong repertory company in support of celebrity actors and actresses. He opened in the Old Salt House Theater on July 3, 1835,[91] and immediately brought on the stars. In rapid sequence came "Mrs. Pritchard," a favorite melodramatic actress of the day, Sol Smith, who played a brief engagement en route to New York and a starring season at the Park Theater, Charles Kemble Mason, a ranking tragedian of the time, Eliza Riddle, long to be a favorite in the South and West, Mrs. Alexander Drake, and others.[92] The St. Louis summer-fall season of 1835 marked the beginning of an epoch in St. Louis stage annals. As if to commemorate the rise to theatrical distinction, Ludlow succeeded in securing some $15,000 in subscriptions toward the construction of a new St. Louis playhouse prior to his departure for Mobile.[93]

The Mobile season of 1835–1836, the first of a great many for the new partnership of Ludlow and Smith, opened on November 9, 1835, with the James Sheridan Knowles favorite *The Hunchback*. The Julia of the performance was Eliza Riddle, who had played the role in Philadelphia with Knowles himself in the male lead, in the American premiere of the immensely popular play shortly before.[94] During the off season a number of renovations had been made on the playhouse. Additional private boxes had been added in each of the theater's two tiers of boxes, and all boxes had been more elegantly

90. "Articles of Co-Partnership," Noah Miller Ludlow and Solomon Franklin Smith, June 2, 1835, in Smith Collection, Missouri Historical Society.

91. *St. Louis Missouri Republican,* July 2, 1835.

92. Carson, *St. Louis Stage,* pp. 144–56.

93. *St. Louis Missouri Republican,* Sept. 26, 1835. The *Republican* announced that construction was "to be commenced immediately." Ludlow and Smith's subscription books in the Missouri Historical Society reveal that many of the St. Louis social leaders were stock subscribers to the theater fund.

94. *Mobile Commercial Register and Patriot,* Nov. 7, 10, 1835.

furnished. A "new and very handsome drop scene" enhanced the interior decor of the auditorium.[95] Opening night was given full honors, including an opening address. Joseph M. Field, the author and a favorite member of the Ludlow stock, spoke the address, invoking the audience to behold the *"thrice* erected dome," a reference to the two Ludlow theaters destroyed by fire in 1829–1830.[96]

The policy of offering a strong stock company and first-rate stars that Ludlow had instituted the year before was continued this season, once again with success. The press and the public expressed continuing enthusiasm during the entire season, which lasted until mid-May when the summer heat forced the theater to close. Ludlow and Smith had reason to be pleased with their initial season. It resulted, Ludlow recalled, in a "considerable profit to the management."[97]

The company set out at once for St. Louis to open the summer season at the Old Salt House Theater. From June until late October of 1836 the old theater housed the performances of the talented company as well as enthusiastic audiences. By the end of the season the reputation of the Ludlow and Smith corps had reached New York City. The *Spirit of the Times* of October 2, 1836, declared that the co-partners were in St. Louis, "packing up for Mobile at the last accounts." "They have," continued the *Spirit*, "Miss Riddle, the Fields, Tom Placide, and several other clever people in the company, besides about all the stars in creation."[98] Established in their circuit and recognized as a new theatrical power by the chief organ of the American stage, Ludlow and Smith were well launched in their managerial career by the commencement of the Mobile season of 1836–1837.

It proved to be one of the best seasons ever offered there, and one of the last profitable seasons for several years. Two new members of the stock added strength to an already sound troupe. Vincent De

95. *Ibid.*, Nov. 10, 1835.
96. *Ibid.* Joseph M. Field was a British-born actor-manager-playwright whose career was centered in St. Louis and Mobile. He married Eliza Riddle in 1836, the year following Ludlow and Smith's Mobile opening, and the couple provided strong stock leads and second leads to stars for several years. Field died in Mobile in 1856. See William Winter, *Brief Chronicles* (New York: The Dunlap Society, 1889), I, 91.
97. *Dramatic Life*, p. 454.
98. "The Fields" referred to Joe and his brother Matthew C. Field, who later married Ludlow's daughter Cornelia. Tom Placide was, of course, Thomas Placide, talented son of Alexander Placide and brother of the even more talented Henry Placide.

Camp and Eliza Petrie, both young players with much talent, began their long Southern careers in Mobile that season, De Camp as stage manager and comedian, Petrie as the inevitable romantic heroine.[99] So strong was the company that, as Sol Smith wrote, even "pieces *without stars* were played in an admirable manner."[100] And there were stars too, including Mrs. Drake, the Northern comedian James S. Balls, and the renowned tragedian James W. Wallack. From the beginning of the season on November 9, 1836, the theater drew crowds nightly. In February, Charles Booth Parsons wrote Smith from Natchez: "I am glad to hear you are doing so well— every report that reaches me from Mobile is—Crowded Houses! Crowded Houses!!"[101] A Mobile correspondent of the *Spirit of the Times* wrote on March 13: "the house is filled every night, the managers having kept up a continual succession of novelty, perfectly irresistible. The company is decidedly a good one. . . ."[102] Among the "novelties" offered during the season was a portrayal of Andrew Jackson by Sol Smith in Charlotte Barnes's *Lafitte*, a performance that earned Sol the local nickname "Gineral."[103] Another great success was the production of the Rophino Lacy adaptation of Rossini's *Cinderella*. A *Spirit* correspondent wrote of that production: "I went to see it four times—(it was performed six, and to an average nightly receipt of Nine Hundred Dollars!) You will laugh when I tell you the scenery was better than that I saw at the Park but I do say it, and others agree with me. . . ."[104] The engagement of Annette Nelson drew enthusiastic audiences, consisting largely of young men in spite of (or perhaps because of) an editorial opinion that "she is no *actress* except in *form*."[105] The season was going better than the new managers could possibly have expected.

99. Smith, *Theatrical Management*, p. 123; Ludlow, *Dramatic Life*, p. 470.
100. *Theatrical Management*, p. 123.
101. Charles Booth Parsons to Solomon Franklin Smith, in Smith Collection, Missouri Historical Society.
102. *New York Spirit of the Times*, March 25, 1837.
103. Solomon Franklin Smith to Noah Miller Ludlow, March 26, 1837. Sol wrote that it was the "immense *likeness*" he bore to Jackson that "drew a great number to the house, who would not otherwise have gone to witness the trashy piece."
104. *New York Spirit of the Times*, March 25, 1837. The principals in the *Cinderella* production were Eliza Petrie, Joseph M. Field, Vincent De Camp, and Tom Placide—a strong cast.
105. Mary Morgan Duggar, "The Theatre in Mobile 1822–1860" (Master's thesis, University of Alabama, 1941), p. 70, quoting *Mobile Mercantile Advertiser*, April 28, 1837.

But the tides of theatrical fortune changed quickly. By April of 1837 there were signs of economic distress in Mobile. In May panic struck. By May 13 the local banks had suspended specie payment.[106] The effect of the pressure upon the public was typical as regarded commercial entertainment. As Smith wrote Ludlow, "The Theatre seems to be forgotten. All attention is absorbed by the *hard times*."[107] Even a visit by the governor of the state drew a house of only $283, a sure sign of a theatrical decline. Smith closed the theater to avoid further losses. And on that dismal note ended a season that had begun so brilliantly just six months before. For several years the effects of the depression following the Panic of 1837 were apparent in the troubles experienced by Ludlow and Smith and by all the other theater managers of the South and the nation.

Still, the theatrical structure of the new West had developed with notable rapidity since the coming of the Drakes and Ludlow in 1815. That development was made possible by the relative health of the Western economy. Economic conditions on the Eastern seaboard had not been so conducive to expansion of the theater. The sort of difficulty experienced by Ludlow and Smith in the closing days of their second Mobile season had long been plaguing the succession of managers who tried their luck in the urban centers of the South Atlantic states.

106. Solomon Franklin Smith to Noah Miller Ludlow, May 13, 1837, in Ludlow-Field-Maury Collection, Missouri Historical Society.
107. *Ibid.*, May 6, 1837.

CHAPTER VI

THE

EASTERN SEABOARD

YEARS OF DECLINE

1.

THE SURGE OF MIGRATION TO THE MISSISSIPPI VALLEY IN THE YEARS following 1815 was symptomatic of troubled times on the Atlantic seaboard, especially in the South. Between the mid-1820's and the mid-1840's the coastal states were in a near-continual economic decline. Beset by two major financial panics and their resultant depressions, deprived of an adequate circulating currency by a colonial status within the nation and by the vagaries of Jacksonian finance, physically undermined by a land-exploitative system of staple crop agriculture, the South Atlantic states languished in economic torpor.

As the economy of the Southeast lagged and as manpower resources were drained off by the irresistible pull of the frontier, the old urban centers of the region naturally lagged apace. New urban development all but ceased. The effects of such conditions upon the theater, an institution acutely sensitive to any decline in economic well-being, were baleful. In the former theater centers—Charleston and her adjuncts in the Southern circuit and Richmond to the north

—a long succession of short-term managers attempted operation of the playhouses and inevitably failed as season followed upon profit-less season. Activity in the hinterlands was limited to the efforts of the most ephemeral of strolling troupes. In all it was a dismal and continuing story of poor audiences resulting in a steady decline in the quality of theatrical offerings.

Charleston perhaps best exemplified the adversity of the times, if only because the South Carolina metropolis had relatively farther to fall. Population figures for Charleston are indicative of her eco-nomic decline. From 1820 to 1830 the aggregate increase was 5,509, from 24,780 to 30,289. But the next decade showed an actual popu-lation decline of 1,028.[1] Fewer people moved to Charleston; more left there—a phenomenon resulting largely from, as the *Courier* phrased it, "the dullness of the times and the almost entire annihila-tion of commercial prosperity. . . ." The same number of the *Courier* also carried news that was often to be repeated in years to come. In a report on theatrical affairs, the editor noted: "This season, un-fortunately for the *Thespian Corps*, has been one of anything but profit."[2]

The Charleston company in 1820 was, of course, still under man-agement of the able Charles Gilfert, who operated two circuits, one in the Charleston-Savannah area, the other in Virginia. He offered both areas quality drama, an excellent repertory company, and famous stars.[3] But Gilfert's financial success had never equaled his artistic success, and by the end of the 1820 season in Charleston he was in real trouble. In spite of appearances by Thomas A. Cooper and Henry Wallack, May of 1820 marked the close of another brief and profitless effort. Nor did the situation improve the following season, even though Junius Brutus Booth appeared in Charleston prior to his departure for New York.[4]

So bad had conditions become in the Queen City that in 1822

1. U. S. Census Office, *Social Statistics,* p. 95. The great fire of 1838, which destroyed some $3,000,000 in property, doubtless loomed large in the popula-tion decline.

2. *Charleston Courier,* May 12, 1819. The theater had been packed, however, on at least one occasion during the season. On April 28, 1819, President James Monroe, then touring the South, attended the theater to see Thomas Abthorpe Cooper perform Mark Antony in *Julius Caesar.* The appearance of the President attracted eighteen hundred people to the playhouse, the largest crowd ever assembled there. Hoole, *Charleston Theatre,* p. 17.

3. See above, chap. ii.

4. Hoole, *Charleston Theatre,* p. 19.

Manager Gilfert decided not to play Charleston at all but to continue operations throughout the fall and winter in Savannah. Frustrated by the absence of the accustomed addition to the winter social season, the local press could only complain of the "dearth of amusements in our city . . ." and bemoan the "absence of those sources of rational pleasure, which have heretofore at this season availed the people of Charleston. . . ."[5] But evidently Savannah too proved unremunerative to the hard-pressed Gilfert. On May 12, 1823, following the close of the long season, the manager altogether dropped Savannah from his Southeastern circuit.[6]

The stockholders or "proprietors" of the Charleston theater were aware that their investment was doomed to failure unless Gilfert could be persuaded to continue his Charleston operation. They were also aware that the manager had given up in Virginia in 1823 for want of profit and might well do the same in Charleston.[7] Consequently, the stockholders invested further in their playhouse by making improvements on the interior, including "an entirely new stage, with improved proscenium," new scenery, and a generally refurbished house decor.[8]

Gilfert did return to Charleston. On November 26, 1823, he opened the fall season in the renovated theater with a performance of Sheridan's *The Rivals*.[9] The season that followed proved somewhat more successful than its immediate predecessors. Evidence of success came, for example, on January 12, 1824, when star Vincent De Camp was "called out" at the end of a performance and in a curtain speech commended the Gilfert management and the audience support.[10] Gilfert gained further public approval when in February he gave three benefit performances for the local "Greek Fund."[11] The long season lasted until the end of May. It provided encouragement enough to bring the talented manager back for one more try in Charleston.

5. *Charleston Courier*, Feb. 8, 1823. On March 7, 1823, the *Courier* declared: "Few . . . are the opportunities of rational entertainment, which the public have been favored with in the present season. . . ."
6. Sparks, "Theatre in Savannah," p. 61.
7. See above, chap. ii. When Gilfert quit Virginia in the fall of 1823, he broke the theatrical connection between Richmond and Charleston. The two circuits were never reunited.
8. *Charleston Courier*, Nov. 26, 1823.
9. *Ibid.*
10. *Ibid.*, Jan. 14, 1824.
11. *Ibid.*, Feb. 2, 1824.

Charles Gilfert's final season must have been a bitter disappoint-
ment to the manager. In view of the relative success of the previous
season and the quality of his offerings, which included Booth and
William Augustus Conway in starring engagements, Gilfert might
well have anticipated success. But Charleston simply could not afford the type of theater the manager provided, and he would not
compromise with quality. The season failed. By February of 1825, the
long-suffering Gilfert had departed for Albany, New York, where,
as the sympathetic *Courier* declared, "better auspices and more
genial spirits are likely to await him."[12] The manager never saw
Charleston again. And it was many years before theater of the
quality he had provided was to be again available there. Indeed, the
decade following his departure saw a steady decline in Charleston's
theatrical fortunes.

Manager after manager tried his luck in the commercially troubled
city, none with any notable success. First came comedian Joe Cowell
in February of 1826. Cowell operated the theater in addition to a
"circus with equestrian department," alternating his shows nightly.[13]
But the circus proved popular whereas the theater was neglected,
and Joe Cowell failed to apply for a lease on the playhouse the following season.

Management of the theater during the two succeeding seasons was
attempted by a pair of prominent local figures: Dr. John Dyot and
Dr. John Beaufain Irving. Dyot employed actor Frederick Brown
as stage manager for the 1826–1827 season, but despite the appearance of such stars as Cooper and Thomas Sowerby Hamblin, the
season showed little profit.[14] Irving fared even worse in the winter
of 1827–1828. By December 8, 1827, the *Courier* was pleading for
better support of the theater, while communications in the press frequently complained of poor houses. One noteworthy letter revealed
another source of Charleston's theatrical ills. When an excellent
performance of Goldsmith's *She Stoops to Conquer* failed to draw
an audience, a local correspondent made some suggestions to the
management. "Above all," he concluded ". . . let the Manager positively forbid *politics* on [the] . . . stage: . . . Jackson and Adams
make up our breakfasts, dinners and suppers. For God's sake, let us

12. Feb. 28, 1825.
13. *Ibid.*, Feb. 23, 1826. The circus featured a "CAVALCADE BY SIX HORSES,"
tightrope performers, acrobats, "CORPUSCULAR MANOEUVRES," and a harlequinade.
14. Hoole, *Charleston Theatre*, p. 27.

be amused with something else when we 'go . . . to the play.' "[15] Along with economic unrest, political agitation was a sure means of reducing theater audiences in the period.

In February of 1828, Irving temporarily gave up the effort, renting the theater to the "Villalave Family" of acrobats and gymnasts.[16] When the manager took a benefit on April 26, 1828, the *Courier* urged the public to attend to help offset his "very considerable" losses.[17]

Nor did the next lessee of the ill-starred playhouse fare any better. John Jay Adams, a young and obviously American actor took a lease for 1828-1829 and despite the efforts of a strong stock company, failed to draw except on rare occasions. When Adams gave up in May of 1829, the *City Gazette* complained bitterly of the unappreciative Charleston public. "Adams has succeeded in giving to our boards a variety of splendour of exhibition," declared the editor, "and now he is about to leave us, not only without remuneration, but even impoverished."[18]

Adams returned in December of 1829 with the intention of trying once more, but his second attempt proved less lucrative than the first. His difficulties were compounded this time by the appearance of a rival show in "Apollo's Theatre" at "MR. LEGE'S LONG ROOM, QUEEN-ST."[19] On December 22, Adams abandoned the season rather than continue operating at a loss.[20] The theater fell into the hands of a local committee, a group of concerned citizens, who proved incapable of bettering the circumstances of the playhouse, even with the aggressive management and compelling programing of acting manager Thomas Faulkner.[21] Faulkner returned as sole manager in the fall of 1830, offering such stars as Forrest (his first Charleston

15. *Charleston Courier*, Dec. 4, 1827.

16. Hoole, *Charleston Theatre*, p. 28.

17. April 26, 1828.

18. Hoole, *Charleston Theatre*, p. 30, quoting *Charleston City Gazette*, May 8, 1829.

19. *Charleston Courier*, Dec. 19, 1829. The "Entertainment" at "Apollo's" consisted of "many incomprehensible experiments in Natural Philosophy, and apparent Necromancy; which for ingenuity and invention, surpasses any thing of the kind ever exhibited in this country."

20. *Ibid.*, Dec. 22, 1829.

21. An example of the lengths to which managers would go to attract an audience was the program for April 19, 1830. Following a performance of Charles Kemble's *Point of Honor, or The School for Soldiers,* a company of real soldiers from Fort Moultrie appeared in the "ceremony of shooting a deserter." *Charleston Courier*, April 19, 1830.

appearance), Cooper, and Mary Ann Duff, all to little avail. When the theater closed on April 4, 1831, Faulkner's Charleston career closed with it.[22]

The final two seasons at the old Charleston theater were spent under the management of the successful New York comedian Vincent De Camp. De Camp's first season opened January 31, 1832, with James Henry Hackett as Solomon Swap in *Jonathan in England*—an auspicious beginning.[23] Hackett was followed by the British tragedian Charles Kean (son of the great Edmund Kean), then Clara Fisher and Cooper. Nothing legitimate would draw. De Camp was forced to close after two months. In the fall of 1832 he tried again and failed again. On April 1, 1833, the final curtain dropped in the old Charleston theater. The proprietors, long burdened with the playhouse, sold it to the state for $12,000, to be used to house the Medical College of South Carolina.[24]

But despite the dreary succession of unprofitable seasons, Charleston's theater history had not reached its lowest ebb. Shortly after the sale of the old theater a member of De Camp's stock, W. R. Hart, announced that he would soon open the "Queen Street Theater."[25] This "playhouse" proved to be a barn-like, wooden structure utterly without the pretension so dear to the small group of regular Charleston playgoers who had supported the theater during the distressed times. The slow decline of the theater, in progress for a decade, came to an end, and Charleston precipitously descended into theatrical obscurity.

For several years the Queen Street Theater served as Charleston's only playhouse. The seasons offered there were sporadic and brief, usually planned to coincide with the social season in February and March. Manager Hart and his partner W. Hardy continued to offer an occasional star, but their stock was weak, their repertoire limited, and their playhouse altogether unsatisfactory. Support grew ever weaker, until finally, during the winter of 1836–1837, Charleston saw

22. *Ibid.*, April 4, 1831. The *Courier* declared, "we have reason to believe that the present season has not been a very profitable one to the manager. . . ."

23. Hoole, *Charleston Theatre*, p. 99. *Jonathan in England* was Hackett's own adaptation of George Colman's *Who Wants a Guinea* and one of the best-known "Yankee" plays of the period.

24. Hoole, *Charleston Theatre*, p. 33. The Irish comedian Tyrone Power observed in 1834 that the old theater had been converted into "a school of anatomy: so cutting up is still the order of the day; only the practice is no longer confined to poets, but extended to subjects generally." Power, *Impressions*, II, 61.

25. *Charleston Courier*, Sept. 9, 1833.

no drama at all. The closest things to theater available in the city that had for so long been the cultural capital of the South were ventriloquists, magicians, and acrobats.[26] James Rees, an early chronicler of the Southern stage, attempted in 1836 to account for the "lamentable picture of neglect" the Charleston theater presented. He could only conclude that "the spirit of the drama is not there."[27]

There were signs of a commercial recovery in Charleston in 1837. Both imports and exports increased considerably that year, especially the critical rice and cotton exports. Prices were also up on rice and cotton, and retail merchandise sales were substantially improved over preceding years.[28] Another indication of economic recovery was the $60,000 raised by public subscription for the construction of a new Charleston theater.[29] By mid-March of 1837, the "Charleston New Theatre Company," a corporation founded by a group of interested citizens, had begun construction on the playhouse.

On Friday, December 15, 1837, the "New Charleston Theater" was formally opened by lessee-manager William Abbott (sometimes spelled Abbot), formerly of the Haymarket Theater, London.[30] The opening night program consisted of Tobin's *Honey Moon* and the Charles Dibdin musical farce *The Waterman*. "After a long sleep, Rip Van Winkle like," declared the *Courier*, "the drama has again lifted her head among us under the most favorable auspices."[31] Charleston, it seemed, had experienced a theatrical renaissance.

The new theater was Greek revival in design. Its two-story facade consisted of a heavy arcade at street level, with a portico of four Ionic columns immediately above the vestibule. The interior featured

26. *Ibid.*, March 9, 10, 17, 1837; Hoole, *Charleston Theatre*, pp. 34, 37. The popular "Ravel Family" of gymnasts and pantomimists did open the theater briefly in March of 1837, but they did not perform plays.

27. [Rees], "Southern Stage," II, 84. Although this article was not published until 1842, the comments on Charleston were based on notes Rees had taken in 1836.

28. *Niles' Weekly Register*, LI (Sept. 17, 1836); *The Commercial Review of the South and West [De Bow's Review]* I (April, 1846), 333. See also John Glyndon Van Deusen, *Economic Bases of Disunion in South Carolina* (New York: Columbia University Press, 1928), p. 333.

29. William Stanley Hoole, "Charleston Theatres," *Southwest Review*, XXV (Jan., 1940), 196.

30. *Charleston Courier*, Dec. 18, 1837. Abbott had toured widely as a star in the United States. See William Abbott to Ludlow and Smith in Smith Collection, Missouri Historical Society. He also had the distinction of playing Romeo to Fanny Kemble's first Juliet at Covent Garden. See *New York Spirit of the Times*, June 3, 1843.

31. *Charleston Courier*, Dec. 18, 1837.

a "horseshoe" of three tiers of boxes, parquet or dress circle, and pit, altogether capable of seating twelve hundred. Four Ionic pilasters "of the richest order," along with an ornamental frieze, framed the proscenium opening. The inevitable dome was divided into twelve "compartments," each, according to the *Courier* description, "ornamented with arabesque and emblematic figures richly and beautifully executed in the brightest colors."[32] The house chandelier was soon to arrive. The large crowd that gathered for the grand opening found, in the opinion of the *Courier* editor, "one of the most beautiful and commodious theatres in the union. . . ."[33]

From the outset of the season it was clear that manager Abbott intended to offer the finest theater possible in Charleston. The stars abounded. Ellen Tree, the British tragedienne, led off the array and was followed in rapid succession by Thomas A. Cooper and his daughter, the rising young American actress Priscilla Cooper, the British tragedians John Vandenhoff and Charles Kemble Mason, James Hackett, and finally Junius Brutus Booth.[34] They played to crowded audiences. For the first time in many years the Charleston theater was producing a profit, and manager Abbott was credited with the success. "Abbott," reported the *New York Spirit of the Times*, "is much, and deservedly, lauded for the management of the theatre now under his auspices."[35]

The first season of the new theater was halted abruptly by the disastrous fire of April 28, 1838, a conflagration that destroyed one-third of the city.[36] But in spite of the physical and psychological effects of the great fire, Abbott opened the 1838–1839 season on schedule, in mid-December, 1838. Once more Charleston was offered the finest theater the manager could stage, as indeed was the case throughout his career. Perhaps the high point of that highly successful management came in his final Charleston season, in the winter of 1840–1841. Abbott brought in comedian Henry Placide, the ballet phenomenon Fanny Elssler, Edwin Forrest, and Tyrone Power—an impressive array of talent.

32. *Ibid.*
33. *Ibid.*, Dec. 14, 1837. See also the description of the theater in Robinson, "Irving's Reminiscences," LI, 201, and Hoole, "Two Famous Theatres," p. 276.
34. Hoole, *Charleston Theatre*, p. 105.
35. Jan. 13, 1838. The *Spirit* gave Abbott particular credit for banning the sale of alcohol in the playhouse, thus ending a practice "always felt to be a fertile source of noise and confusion."
36. *Charleston Courier*, April 30, May 1, 1838.

Placide was hailed upon his arrival as "a native of Charleston," and "withall one of the best actors living."[37] The public lent strong support to his engagement.[38] But if Placide proved a local favorite, Elssler was a sensation.

Fanny Elssler was one of that curious succession of foreign artists that created such turmoil in ante bellum America. They began arriving as early as 1829 when the French danseuse Céline Céleste made her much-heralded appearance, and the whole vogue climaxed with the Barnum-inspired visit of Jenny Lind in 1850. Elssler, next to Lind, created the greatest furor, especially in Charleston where the public seemed desperately anxious to prove their amenability to and familiarity with "high culture." The dancer, noted for her technical virtuosity as displayed in a small group of showpieces, had made her American debut in New York the previous May and had created havoc wherever she performed. Charleston proved no exception. The Charlestonians "leapt up at her," wrote Henry Wikoff in describing her tour in the *Spirit of the Times*. "In New York itself they never displayed greater enthusiasm. After the 'Cracovienne' [an especially showy showpiece] she was called out amidst the most deafening din. . . ."[39] And so it went for each of her four performances.

But for all the enthusiasm for Elssler, manager Abbott was losing money on the playhouse. Charleston was still incapable of sustaining a first-rate repertory theater. At the end of the artistically brilliant season of 1840–1841, Abbott gave up his lease, complaining of the lack of profit.[40] His successor, W. H. Latham, a British actor-musician and former member of the stock company, fared as badly as had Abbott. The 1841 season had been in progress only a short while when the complaints of poor support began to reach the press. A letter to the *Courier* headed "OUR THEATRE" was typical. Without better support, argued the writer, "in a very short time . . . we shall be without the only amusement now afforded us."[41] The letter closed with a fervent call for support of "the most intellectual and rational pastime civilization ever yet conferred." Support continued to be slight. On December 25, 1841, the *Dramatic Mirror and Literary Companion* told of the manager having to cancel a *Guy Mannering*

37. *Ibid.*, Dec. 7, 1840. Placide was born in Charleston in 1799.
38. *New York Spirit of the Times*, Dec. 19, 1840.
39. *Ibid.*, May 25, 1844.
40. *Charleston Courier*, March 15, 1841.
41. *Ibid.*, Dec. 16, 1841.

performance "for want of an audience." Latham gave up Charleston management early in 1842,[42] and the theatrical renaissance that seemed to prevail under Abbott proved an illusion.

It is clear that profound economic distress was the fundamental reason for the difficulties experienced by the Charleston theater managers. But there were also some non-economic factors that contributed to those difficulties. A contemporary observer, the dilettante actor Louis Fitzgerald Tasistro, noted several reasons for the Charleston theatrical decline. First, he mentioned programing for the theater. All too often, he contended, the public was offered plays of the "Satanic and alcoholic school of dramatic composition," i.e., gothic melodrama and sentimental domestic drama. The managers should instead have maintained high standards in selecting their programs.[43] Secondly, Tasistro argued that the long succession of managers lacked ability and usually were out to gain quick profits at the expense of quality productions. In the hands of a James H. Caldwell or Thomas S. Hamblin, he suggested, Charleston would fare well. Finally, and most notably, the actor blamed managerial coddling of the Charleston "aristocracy" for much of the trouble.

There were, Tasistro argued, two classes of theater-goers in Charleston: the "Mercantile," or business-professional class, which included the better-paid mechanics, and the "South Carolina Aristocrat," the large planters of the area.[44] The actor held the second category in rather low esteem, as is indicated by his description of the planter class. "They generally flock into Charleston about this period [February]," wrote Tasistro, "and may be distinguished from all the rest of mankind by their flowing locks, well oiled, brushed, and curled—fantastic, goatish beards, with whiskers and mustaches to match; all which forms their principal stock in trade. . . . Their propensity for aping European Continental manners renders them extremely obnoxious to the more sedate and sensible portion of the community. . . ."[45] Yet at the theater, Tasistro contended, "every species of *extra*-civility was lavished upon them, and the comfort of

42. *Charleston Courier*, Feb. 14, 1842.
43. Louis Fitzgerald Tasistro, *Random Shots and Southern Breezes, Containing Critical Remarks on the Southern States and Southern Institutions, with Semi-Serious Observations on Men and Manners* (New York: Harper and Brothers, 1842), II, 113–14. This contention is open to question. Presumably better plays would attract higher-quality audiences but not necessarily larger ones.
44. *Ibid.*, pp. 129–30.
45. *Ibid.*, p. 130.

everybody else was forgotten in the soul-engrossing desire to please and accommodate them."[46] Managerial neglect of the "most intelligent and influential portion of the community," the "Mercantile classes," resulted according to Tasistro, in lack of support by those classes.[47]

Doubtless the actor overstated his case—he was sincerely offended by the pretensions of the planters. But his underlying contention that the Charleston managers maintained strict attention to social distinctions was certainly valid, and their practice might well have resulted in reducing the potential Charleston theater audience. No manager of the period could afford to neglect, much less offend, *any* class of the public he served. If Charleston managers did indeed try to maintain an elitist theater, the effort surely affected their box-office receipts. It thus contributed to the decline that persisted for a time even after the rest of the nation began to recover from the stifling depression in the early 1840's.

Despite financial troubles and poor support however, after 1836 Charleston continued to have its annual theater season during which the playhouse was open five or six nights a week. When one manager gave up in disgust, there was always someone available to take his place. The Charleston stock companies, though no longer among the strongest in the country, were adequate to support the outstanding stars who regularly included Charleston in their Southern tours. At least from the standpoint of theater availability, Charleston remained an important theatrical center of the South, even during its days of decline.

2.

The course of events in Charleston between 1820 and the early 1840's was closely paralleled in the lesser towns of the Southeastern circuit, notably Savannah and Augusta, Georgia, and Columbia, South Carolina. Savannah was the largest and naturally the most active of the group and as always before, served as a "safety valve" for the Charleston managers. But the economy of the Georgia port was, of course, adversely affected by the general depression,[48] and

46. *Ibid.*
47. *Ibid.*, p. 131.
48. As was the case in Charleston, population figures for Savannah reflect the economic depression of the times. The aggregate increase in population was only 253 between 1820 and 1830. See U. S. Census Office, *Social Statistics*, p. 173. Savannah also experienced a disastrous fire in 1820, which destroyed some $4,000,000 in property.

Savannah also experienced a theatrical decline. As noted above, when Charles Gilfert closed his 1823 season in Savannah, the playhouse there remained closed save to amateurs for nearly five years.

By 1827, however, some of the residents were seeking to remedy the situation, and the press was calling for a theater season. "The circus has been well patronized," sounded the *Georgian* in February, "and we see no reason to doubt that an entertainment of an intellectual character, which has always met the particular favor of the Savannah public, would succeed for a few weeks."[49] In December of 1827 the call was answered. An evanescent strolling troupe under managers "Kent and Lamb" presented a short season in Savannah beginning on December 24, 1827.[50] Beginning with John Jay Adams in 1828, the Charleston managers once again began to play off seasons in the Georgia circuit. Adams and his successors even took their Charleston stars to Savannah on occasion. For example, Adams introduced Cooper and Clara Fisher to the Georgia port during his first winter season there.[51]

For a while it seemed as though Savannah could well afford a season or two each year. Support received by the touring companies there was initially substantial. But as economic conditions worsened, theater support waned. Vincent De Camp failed to draw with his company in 1832; the *Savannah Republican* complained of "the little encouragement which this gentleman [De Camp] has received since his last commencement. . . ."[52] "Our citizens have ever bourne the character for liberal encouragement of all amusements," declared the forgetful editor, obviously puzzled by the failure of De Camp's support. But despite the hard times, the Charleston managers continued to play in Savannah, and by the winter of 1834 there were signs of a theatrical recovery. The company of managers Hart and Hardy performed a comparatively successful season in Savannah commencing in December of that year.

The Charleston troupe was warmly welcomed by the press upon their arrival. The *Georgian* of December 8, 1834, expressed the hope that the players would be amply patronized so that the Savannah public might "receive in return, the satisfaction of whiling away the

49. Wyoline Hester, "The Savannah Stage," p. 79, quoting *Savannah Georgian*, Feb. 1, 1827.

50. Sparks, "Theatre in Savannah," p. 64.

51. *Ibid.*, pp. 67–69.

52. *Ibid.*, p. 77, quoting *Savannah Republican*, April 30, 1832.

tedium of many a monotonous winter evening."[53] When Henry J. Finn, a well-known comedian of the period, played a starring engagement in mid-December, he wrote his friend Sol Smith of a small boom in theater business "in these here parts."[54] And the season proved profitable for the co-managers. The following season was even better. Hart and Hardy kept the playhouse open from December 15 through February 4, 1836, performing thirty-three nights in all, in the finest season since the departure of Gilfert.[55] It should be recalled that Charleston at this time was all but unable to muster a theater audience.

Indeed, the actors and actresses who performed in Savannah during the 1830's and early 1840's were uniform in their praise of Savannah as a small but excellent theater town. Tyrone Power, for example, noted that he played to large audiences during his 1833 visit and that the theater-goers were "as merry and intelligent as heart could wish."[56] The playhouse itself he found to be "very well designed and well-built," though "a good deal the worse in consequence of neglect."[57] Priscilla Cooper had a fine time on her 1836 visit, both professionally and socially. "The last week I spent in Savannah was charming," she wrote shortly after leaving there. "I went to five parties and was a little of a d——d particular belle. My benefit was crowded, and three companies of soldiers, dressed in their uniforms, attended the theatre, entirely out of compliment to me. The pit was filled by them and ten boxes."[58] Following her benefit performance, the popular young actress was serenaded long into the night by military bands. Louis Fitzgerald Tasistro found Savannah audiences

53. *Ibid.*, p. 82, quoting *Savannah Georgian*, Dec. 8, 1834.

54. Henry J. Finn to Solomon Franklin Smith, Dec. 18, 1834, in Smith Collection, Missouri Historical Society. Finn's tour of the Southeastern theater towns took him successively to Charleston, Savannah, Augusta, Milledgeville, Macon, and Columbus prior to his arrival in Montgomery, where he starred with the Smith company. See Henry J. Finn to Solomon Franklin Smith, Oct. 10, Nov. 25, Dec. 18, 1834, and Jan. 11, 1835, in *ibid.*

55. Sparks, "Theatre in Savannah," pp. 142–46.

56. *Impressions*, II, 77.

57. *Ibid.* James Edward Murdoch, who visited Savannah in 1831, also observed that the playhouse was ill-kept but disagreed with Power as to the quality of its construction. See James Edward Murdoch, *The Stage, or Recollections of Actors and Acting from an Experience of Fifty Years* (Philadelphia: J. M. Stoddart and Company, 1880), p. 213.

58. Elizabeth Tyler Coleman, *Priscilla Cooper Tyler and the American Scene 1816–1889* (Tuscaloosa: University of Alabama Press, 1955), p. 57, quoting Priscilla Cooper to Mary Grace Cooper, Feb. 28, 1836.

superior to those of Charleston "both in character and numbers. . . ."[59]
The people of Savannah, Tasistro believed, "would generously re-
ward any actor . . . for his endeavors to entertain them."[60] So despite
the hard times, after 1833 a substantial number of Savannah residents
seem to have maintained interest in and enthusiasm for theatrical
entertainment.

Contrary to the general rule whereby the lesser towns of the Southeastern circuit served as secondary adjuncts to Charleston, during the
period from 1837 to 1841 the subordinate towns produced a manager
and a company that ultimately took over theater operations in
Charleston. The manager was the talented William C. Forbes, a
young American actor who had performed with Noah Ludlow in
Kentucky in 1832, then departed for New York to perform with the
stock company at the Bowery Theater in 1833.[61] By 1835 he had
become a leading tragedian with the Park Theater Company and had
appeared as a star at the Walnut Street Theater in Philadelphia.[62]
It was apparently early in 1836 that he undertook management on
his own with a company recruited in the East.

Forbes spent some time on tour with his company before eventually
choosing Savannah and Augusta, Georgia, as his centers of operations. The two towns were almost always operated in conjunction by
the managers of the time; their relative lack of population and their
proximity dictated such an arrangement.[63] Forbes quickly established
himself in the Georgia towns. In May of 1838 he offered a benefit
performance in Savannah for the Charleston fire sufferers.[64] A letter
from the Augusta correspondent to the *Dramatic Mirror* points up
the esteem in which the manager was held locally. The letter declared
that Forbes and company had been drawing crowds nightly for seven
weeks and had even presented a ten-night run of Dion Boucicault's
London Assurance. So strong was the company that they were able
to draw without stars. The theater under Forbes, the letter continued,

59. *Random Shots*, II, 190.
60. *Ibid.*, 168–69.
61. Ludlow, *Dramatic Life*, pp. 398–99; Odell, *Annals*, IV, 23.
62. Odell, *Annals*, IV, 23; Thomas Allston Brown, *History of the American
Stage* . . . (New York: Dick and Fitzgerald, 1870), p. 129. Brown contends
that Forbes made his New York debut at the Park on Aug. 10, 1835, Odell that
he was probably the "Forbes" who played at the Park in 1833.
63. U. S. Census Office, *Social Statistics*, p. 163. The population of Augusta in
1840 was 6,403. The town had been quickly rebuilt following a devastating fire
on April 3, 1829.
64. Hester, "The Savannah Stage," p. 100.

was "better managed, and more successful . . . than two thirds of the theatres in the country. . . ."[65]

Forbes's success in Georgia led him in December of 1842 to attempt management in Charleston, thereby establishing a regular circuit of the three towns.[66] This arrangement gave him the advantage a circuit always afforded; he could bring in more stars by offering them the incentive of successive engagements in each of his towns. Forbes's success in re-establishing a Southeastern circuit thus enhanced the quality of the theater in the area. In January of 1842 the *Savannah Georgian* stated with accuracy that Forbes offered the best theater available in Savannah "since the time of Gilfert."[67] The same evaluation would naturally hold true for all the towns on his circuit. Although the manager would never reap great profits in the depressed region, he did succeed in restoring some of the theatrical excellence that had prevailed in bygone years.

Prior to his move into Charleston, Forbes had attempted to take his company pioneering in near-virgin territory: the wilds of northeast Florida. The residents of Florida had been introduced to theater of a sort as early as 1821. On July 17 of that boom year, the day the Spanish and American flags were exchanged, Andrew Jackson Allen opened the "Jacksonian Commonwealth Theatre" in Pensacola.[68] Andrew J. Allen, sometimes known as "Dummy" Allen, presented a season of some fourteen weeks in the appropriately named theater, then returned in 1822 to offer a second season. Unfortunately for the manager, the Florida boom did not last. Allen's second season failed, and Florida saw no theater of any description for six years. In the winter of 1828–1829 an ephemeral strolling troupe presented a few performances in a makeshift playhouse, after which nothing was recorded in Florida until 1837. On August 5, 1837, the *Pensacola Gazette* announced that a theater had been "very prettily fitted up at The Florida House," and that for the past few days the local residents had been "entertained with the scenic representations of a

---

65. *Dramatic Mirror and Literary Companion*, Jan. 8, 1842. The dateline of the letter was Augusta, Dec. 28, 1841.

66. Hoole, *Charleston Theatre*, p. 45. In 1840 Forbes had brought Columbia, S. C., into his circuit, as a peripheral town. See *New York Spirit of the Times*, Dec. 12, 1840; *Charleston Courier*, Dec. 21, 1840.

67. Hester, "The Savannah Stage," p. 106, quoting *Savannah Georgian*, Jan. 31, 1842.

68. William G. Dodd, "Theatrical Entertainment in Early Florida," *The Florida Historical Quarterly*, XXV (Oct., 1946), 125.

dramatic corps made up from the Theatre of New Orleans and Mobile."[69] Clearly however, the visits of the strollers were sporadic indeed in sparsely populated Florida territory.

In 1839 a truly rootless theatrical wanderer named Emmanual Judah built a playhouse in Apalachicola and by late December had his primitive company operating there. Judah's plans came to naught, however, when his entire family, which constituted most of his company, drowned in a shipwreck off Dry Tortugas.[70] It was shortly after the Judah accident that Forbes set out upon his similarly ill-fated Florida effort.

Forbes directed his attention toward St. Augustine and the garrisons in northeast Florida that were the main United States fortifications against the Indians in the Second Seminole War. The company arrived in May of 1840 and began performances for the entertainment of the soldiers and other occupants of the forts. But on May 23, as part of the troupe was en route from St. Augustine to visit a nearby garrison, they were attacked by the Seminoles under Chief Coacoochee. Two of the actors were brutally butchered and part of the company wardrobe was stolen by the Indians.[71] Reports of the incident were widely circulated, especially among itinerant entertainers. Joseph Jefferson, then a young stroller, heard of the affair and later described it in his extensive memoir. Several of the guilty Indians were captured, Jefferson recalled, "and as they were robed and decked in the habiliments of *Othello, Hamlet,* and a host of other Shakespearean characters,—for Forbes was eminently legitimate,— their identity as the murderers was established, and they were hanged. . . ."[72] The murder of the players only served to bolster the widely held opinion that Florida was, in Jefferson's words, "a wilderness of chaparral inhabited only by jack-rabbits and hostile Indians,"

69. Quoted in *ibid.*, p. 138.

70. *Ibid.*, p. 151. Judah apparently envisioned a nexus between Apalachicola and Tallahassee and even performed in the latter town in 1840 before the accident.

71. *Ibid.*, p. 168; Jefferson, *Autobiography,* pp. 49–50.

72. Jefferson, *Autobiography,* p. 50. Jefferson's account of the expropriation of the costumes is corroborated by the record of an encounter between the elegantly arrayed Indians and a contingent of U. S. cavalry on March 5, 1841. See Theophilus Francis Rodenbough (ed.), *From Everglade to Cañon with the Second Dragoons, (Second United States Cavalry.) An Authentic Account of Service in Florida, Mexico, Virginia, and the Indian Country, Including the Personal Recollections of Prominent Officers* (New York: D. Van Nostrand, 1875), p. 55.

and only the most intrepid of strollers ventured into such forbidding surroundings after 1840.[73] Sparseness of population would likely have rendered their efforts profitless anyway. Thus Florida remained throughout the ante bellum period largely untouched by organized theater.

3.

As hard times plagued the efforts of a succession of managers in the towns of the South Carolina-Georgia circuit, similar economic conditions prevailed in Virginia, and with similar effects. As noted above, Charles Gilfert had been forced out of Richmond by lack of support as early as October of 1823, having lost heavily in the Virginia operation.[74] Following his withdrawal, Richmond saw one more season, that of James H. Caldwell in the summer and fall of 1824. Then the theater closed for three long years. The proprietors of the playhouse could find no manager willing to take the lease. And with the close of the Richmond theater came the close of all the Virginia theaters dependent upon Richmond for theater troupes. The Virginia circuit, in short, entered a state of theatrical torpor that corresponded with the general economic depression of the times.

The reopening of the Richmond theater came at the hands of a local figure, a former amateur actor named George P. Richardson. Having failed in business, Richardson sought his fortune on the stage in New York. But finding the competition strong, he returned to Richmond with a company of his own and on November 28, 1827, opened the "long-closed" theater for a season.[75] The company he offered was small and inferior, but the productions apparently met with some initial success. When Richardson took his end-of-season benefit, the *Whig* commended him for having "sustained the Richmond Theatre on a very respectable footing."[76]

Encouraged, Richardson returned to Richmond for his second season with a larger company and a more extensive repertoire, beginning operations on October 1, 1828. The season was a failure. It

73. Jefferson, *Autobiography*, p. 49. There are extant records of very few strolling troupes in Florida between 1840 and 1845, and none after 1845. See Dodd, "Early Florida," p. 124.
74. See above, chap. ii; Shockley, "Richmond Theatre, 1819–1838," p. 5.
75. *Richmond Whig*, Dec. 1, 1827.
76. March 22, 1828.

closed in March with salaries unpaid, benefits untendered, and the troupe quite naturally torn by dissension.[77] Richardson's managerial career was over and Richmond entered another period of depression similar to that experienced by Charleston. It was characterized by the attempt and failure of manager after short-term manager to maintain a repertory company offering regular theater seasons. As the *Whig* had observed in January of 1828, Richmond remained "notoriously an unfortunate scene of adventure for theatrical efforts. . . ."[78]

Most of the unsuccessful managers are so obscure that their surnames are all that is known of them. For the spring season of 1829 co-managers Flynn and Willis had the lease on the playhouse but could only remain open about one month. Next came the regime of Herbert and Parnell, respectively former stage manager and orchestra leader of the troupe. Their one season of co-management proved longer and somewhat more substantial, offering quite a number of stars and a total of ninety-one productions between October 3, 1829, and January 27, 1830. Perhaps the high spot of the season came when ex-Presidents Madison and Monroe attended the theater together, assuring a "bumper" benefit for star tragedian John Sloman.[79] All things considered, Herbert and Parnell fared decidedly better than was usual for Richmond managers of the period of decline.

They might have fared even better had competition not arrived at mid-season. On December 11, 1829, "The Amphitheatre" opened its doors, featuring J. Purdy Brown and his horses.[80] The presence of the state constitutional convention in Richmond kept the two playhouses in operation, possibly even profitable operation, at least until late January of 1830. But in the seasons that followed, the competition of two theaters in a town that was barely able to support one certainly proved harmful to both and contributed substantially to the managerial woes in Richmond.

---

77. *Ibid.*, March 10, 1829. Richardson and his stage manager quarreled bitterly over the matter of benefits, each publishing his version of the story in the local press. See *ibid.*, Feb. 19, March 10, 1829.

78. *Ibid.*, Jan. 12, 1828.

79. *Richmond Compiler*, Nov. 2, 1829.

80. Shockley, "Richmond Theatre, 1819–1838," p. 52. The Amphitheatre for some years also housed circus companies and other such subdramatic attractions. For example, the company of "Palmer and Harrington" in 1834 advertised an "unrivalled stud of Horses, of upwards of 30 in number" along with "Equestrian Rope Vaulting, Singing, Dancing, and Comic afterpieces"; *Richmond Whig*, Sept. 26, 1834.

Parnell returned as sole manager for two brief seasons in 1830 and 1831.[81] During the second he offered his major attraction—a star appearance by Edwin Forrest. On April 12, 1831, Governor John Floyd attended the theater to see the tragedian as Damon in John Banim's *Damon and Pythias.* Floyd was impressed with Forrest, calling him "an actor of the highest attainments." But the governor was not impressed with the theater or its operation. "This is the first time I have been at the theater in Richmond," he wrote in his diary. "It will, I think, be the last, as the house is dirty, noisy and ill arranged."[82] Floyd's comments reveal much about the state of the Richmond theater. It is also revealing that Forrest's appearance proved second in drawing power to that of Madame de Jick, a trained elephant who appeared ten times in something called *The Elephant of Siam.*[83]

Following the close of Parnell's 1831 season, Richmond saw five years of acute theatrical depression. Newspaper sources reveal only two performances in 1832, three in 1833, three in 1834, and finally, in the year of Richmond's theatrical nadir, none at all in 1835. It is clear that only the most ephemeral of strollers were playing Virginia, and those only sporadically.[84] By November of 1833 the stockholders of the playhouse had determined to sell the theater and, according to the *Whig,* "to bring the accounts of the company to a close."[85]

The stockholders failed to sell their playhouse. Instead it reopened under new management on December 7, 1836. But manager Henry W. Preston, a largely unsuccessful itinerant actor-manager, fared little better than had earlier managers. His two seasons in Richmond in the winter and spring of 1836–1837 ended in financial distress and a fight between Preston and star Tyrone Power, who objected to

81. The Company of E. C. Willard, manager of the Holliday Street Theater, Baltimore, played a Richmond engagement prior to the appearance of Parnell in 1830.

82. Charles H. Ambler (ed.), *The Life and Diary of John Floyd, Governor of Virginia, An Apostle of Secession, and the Father of the Oregon Country* (Richmond: Richmond Press, Inc., 1918), p. 137. The entry was for April 12, 1831.

83. Shockley, "Richmond Theatre, 1819–1838," p. 11. The *Compiler,* April 13, 1831, termed Madame de Jick "the greatest performer that ever trod the boards of the Richmond Theatre. . . ." On her opening night the pachydermal performance outdrew Forrest's benefit; *Compiler,* April 14, 1831.

84. The scarcity of advertising in the local press does not necessarily mean a total absence of theater. Rather it indicates that the strolling troupes that did appear were the underfinanced little groups that failed to advertise other than in their "bills of the day."

85. *Richmond Whig,* Nov. 1, 1833.

both company and manager.[86] Another star who played in Richmond in 1837 found the company deficient in both dramatic ability and in "respectability of character," indications of a weak company indeed.[87] It is further obvious that the playhouse was in a sadly dilapidated state. The *Whig* in 1836 had warned the proprietors that the condition of the building was conducive to fire and that "its taking fire would prove disastrous to adjacent property."[88] The combination of poor management, poor company, poor theater, and hard times provided less than ideal conditions for a theatrical renaissance in Richmond.

In the spring of 1838 the stockholders began to discuss the fate of their investment. They decided upon extensive renovation of the playhouse, in hopes of attracting an able company. On April 4, 1838, the *Compiler* reported the plans for rebuilding and the name of the first postrenovation manager, George Jones.[89] Jones was a British-born actor who had made his American debut at the Federal Street Theater, Boston, in 1828. In 1831 he first appeared in New York and by 1837 was starring along with his wife, Melinda, at the Bowery Theater. In short, he was a professional trouper of talent and experience.[90] In August of 1838 the *Spirit of the Times* reported that Jones was in Richmond supervising the completion of the new playhouse, already named "The Marshall" in honor of a former Virginia theater-lover, John Marshall.[91] On November 11, 1838, the playhouse was ready for its grand opening.

86. *Richmond Compiler*, April 12, 1837.

87. William Knight Northall (ed.), *Life and Recollections of Yankee Hill: Together With Anecdotes and Incidents of His Travels* (New York: W. F. Burgess, 1850), p. 78. Another star who played Richmond in 1837 is worthy of note—Priscilla Cooper. It was during her starring engagement that she met Robert Tyler, son of John Tyler. In Sept., 1839, they were married. Priscilla Tyler later presided over the White House as acting First Lady in the stead of the frequently ailing Mrs. John Tyler, and following the death of the President's wife. John Tyler's marriage to Julia Gardiner relieved Priscilla of her White House duties. See Coleman, *Priscilla Tyler*, pp. 66, 89.

88. *Richmond Whig*, April 1, 1836. The warning further pointed out that the theater was "believed to be marked for conflagration by incendiaries."

89. Jones had taken a ten-year lease on the new playhouse.

90. Odell, *Annals*, III, 522; IV, 233; Thomas Allston Brown, *A History of the New York Stage From the First Performance in 1732 to 1901* (New York: Dodd, Mead and Company, 1903), I, 107–8. In later years Jones gained considerable notoriety in New York as the spurious "Count Joannes." Brown, however, contends that the title was legitimate.

91. *New York Spirit of the Times*, Aug. 25, 1838.

For his opening-night program manager Jones selected the entertaining John Howard Payne comedy *Charles II, or the Merry Monarch*, and the farce *The Young Widow*.[92] So extensive were the renovations on the playhouse that the audience that gathered for the occasion found an essentially new theater. The dome, which measured 120 feet in circumference, was painted, according to the *Compiler* description, in "imitation of the Rafaelique style, after the manner of the pannels [*sic*] of the Roman Vatican." The two tiers of boxes were semicircularly arranged, thus "affording greater facilities to sound and view." All box seats were cushioned in crimson damask. Each of the ten columns supporting the boxes was designed "in the form of a Roman fasce. . . ." The stage was enlarged and featured a proscenium opening 32 by 32 feet in dimension. Most striking was the new drop curtain, designed by Jones himself, which included a painting of Shakespeare "rising triumphantly above the storm of fanaticism," and other similar scenes. Finally, throughout the lobbies of the house were "appropriate saloons for refreshments." There was in all, concluded the *Compiler*, "a sort [of] *parlor elegance* preserved throughout the interior."[93]

The local press also reviewed the opening-night performance. "Mr Jones' Stock Company," declared the *Compiler*, "is unexceptionally good. His orchestra is the best we have ever had. . . ."[94] So impressed was the audience that Jones was called out after the final curtain, persuaded to make a curtain speech, and received loud applause. The *Enquirer* editor concluded his account of the grand opening with a plea for support of the elegant new house. The local citizens, observed the editor, must now prove "whether they are prepared to support and [*sic*] elegant, improved, and moral Drama."[95] Then he issued a warning. "If this effort fails, we may bid adieu for years to this rational and racy entertainment. If they [the people of Richmond] will not support this Theatre, then they will support none." But the *Compiler* had no doubt whatever that the worthy new man-

92. *Richmond Enquirer*, Nov. 14, 1838. Prices of admission were advertised as: A "transferable" season ticket, $50.00; a non-transferable season ticket, $25.00; a large private box, $20.00 per performance; a small private box, $10.00 per performance; a single box seat, $1.00; an "Upper Circle" seat, $0.75; pit seats, $0.62 1/2; first gallery seats "(for Mulattoes)," $0.50; second gallery seats, $0.25. The second gallery was reserved for Negroes.

93. *Richmond Compiler*, Nov. 15, 1838.
94. *Ibid.*
95. *Richmond Enquirer*, Nov. 16, 1830.

ager would win "the cordial support of Richmond. . . ."[96] The editor described the new theater as a public boon. It would "afford a most salutary intellectual amusement; and improve the public taste of our city." In addition, "its effects in inviting visitors, and helping to amuse and enliven the time of sojourners, are of great advantage to us."[97] Jones began his regime with high hopes.

The manager's optimism was short-lived. Just as had been the case in Charleston when William Abbott opened the New Charleston Theater in December of 1837, Jones's initial support rapidly dwindled as the depression worsened in Virginia. Despite all Jones's efforts, despite all his reforms in the theater under his management,[98] and despite his determination to maintain the highest of standards in his productions, he could not operate profitably in Richmond. The season of 1840–1841 was his last in the Virginia capital. When the theater opened for a spring season in 1841, it was under the management of "Mr. Lambert," who proved to be just another unsuccessful short-term manager.[99] By January of 1843, traditionally mid-season for the Richmond theater, the playhouse was closed. The only entertainment available was at the Exchange Hotel Saloon, where a "GRAND EXHIBITION" was being held. On exhibit were a "REAL" Fijee Mermaid, an Ourang Outang, Major Stevens, a forty-inch dwarf ("the most accomplished and perfect dwarf in the world. . . ."), and a demonstration of "FANCY GLASS BLOWING," all for fifty cents, children half price.[100]

Somewhat later in the year the theater opened for one of its sporadic "seasons," and George Vandenhoff, the British tragedian, appeared there as a star for one performance. His co-star was James H. Hackett, who like Vandenoff was en route to New York. These internationally known actors shared half of the gross proceeds of the evening; the $60.00 gross gave each star $15.00. As Vandenhoff ob-

96. *Richmond Compiler*, Nov. 15, 1838.

97. *Ibid.* The *Compiler* editor employed here the typical arguments used by the theater supporters of the period to defend their position. Theater would instruct, amuse, and attract transients to the town in question.

98. See *New York Spirit of the Times*, Aug. 17, 1839, for Jones's account of his reforms in the Richmond theater. See also "Rules and Regulations of the Marshall and the Avon Theatres, Virginia," in Theater Collection, Valentine Museum, Richmond, Virginia.

99. *Richmond Compiler*, March 5, 1841.

100. *Richmond Enquirer*, Jan. 5, 1843.

served, "Hard times, those!"[101] But Richmond theater conditions grew worse before they grew better. A search of the *Compiler* files for 1844 reveals no theater advertisements at all. Circuses and strollers once again claimed Virginia as their domain.[102] The Marshall Theater had to await the coming of prosperity before reopening as a repertory theater with regular seasonal operation.

4.

With theatricals reduced to such a low estate in Richmond, it was not strange that conditions in the Virginia hinterlands were much worse. Throughout the long depression the strollers provided the only commercial theater available in most of the smaller towns, and their visits were irregular. Lynchburg, a town that had seen considerable itinerant activity in the days of Gilfert, left no records of professional theater at all. The Philadelphia companies, also troubled by hard times, visited Wheeling now and then.[103] Tyrone Power played Alexandria, Virginia, in 1835, on a sidetrip from Washington, but found little enthusiasm and a small turnout for his performances. When the actor inquired of a local resident why the theater was so poorly attended, the Alexandrian replied that it was because of the bank controversy. The theater building, according to Power, was "very pretty," having been built in times of prosperity when theater-goers were numerous. But, "now," continued the comedian, "trade having decayed, and money ceased to circulate, the blood has also grown stagnant amongst this once gay people: the fire is out and the drama's spirit fled."[104] Power fully appreciated the connection between commercial prosperity and theatrical success.

George Jones's efforts in Virginia management were not limited to

101. George Vandenhoff, *Leaves from an Actor's Note-Book; with Reminiscences and Chit-Chat of the Green-Room and the Stage, In England and America* (New York: D. Appleton and Company, 1860), p. 216. The actor added, however, "I have since played . . . in Richmond . . . to very fine houses; and have received there the kindest attentions. . . ."

102. *Richmond Compiler*, Jan. 23, 1844. This number of the *Compiler* advertises two circuses in Richmond at the same time—Raymond's Olympic and Hanes's Great Olympic.

103. See, for example, Playbill, Wheeling Theater, Jan. 18, 1834, Harvard Theater Collection, Harvard College Library, which advertises the company of Francis Courtney Wemyss in Wheeling.

104. *Impressions*, I, 152.

his unsuccessful Richmond operation. He was also involved in an unsuccessful Norfolk theater speculation. In 1839, shortly after the opening of the Marshall Theater, Jones opened the Avon Theater in Norfolk. The playhouse had been built by public subscription under Jones's supervision, but it failed immediately and was sold under a mechanic's lien. Later a group of civic-minded individuals bought the theater for use as a public auditorium, but as the *Charleston Courier* pointed out on the occasion of its destruction by fire, the theater "afforded them very little profit on their investment."[105] Theaters afforded but little profit anywhere in Virginia during the years of the great decline.

But if conditions in Virginia were bad, those in North Carolina were worse. Theatrical activity in the overwhelmingly rural "Valley of Humility" was exceedingly rare. Raleigh, Fayetteville, Wilmington, and New Bern saw occasional visits by itinerants, usually roving "troupes" of two or three "entertainers" who would offer a show in the local hotel or tavern. On one occasion, however, Henry W. Preston did attempt to establish a North Carolina theater circuit. In 1835 the ambitious stroller leased the "principal Theatres in the State,"[106] i.e., those of Raleigh, Wilmington, and New Bern. He then renovated the dilapidated Raleigh playhouse and presented a season of some six weeks, during which, according to the *Register*, the "Corps Dramatique" exhibited talents that could not "be surpassed by any stock company in the United States. . . ."[107] But Preston never returned to North Carolina. Instead he tried, and failed, in Charleston in 1836, then moved to Richmond and repeated the process, as noted above, in 1837. Raleigh saw only one more season prior to 1860. In 1840 an unidentified troupe performed in the capital, taking advantage of the state Whig convention then in session. After that the people of Raleigh were dependent upon the occasional strolling entertainers for commercial entertainment.[108] Fayetteville saw two seasons between 1835 and 1860, both by the Charleston company. The first came in 1835, the second in 1841, years in which managers Hart and Abbott respectively were desperately seeking

---

105. *Charleston Courier*, Feb. 19, 1850. The Avon Theater burned on Feb. 18, 1850.

106. *Raleigh Register*, Nov. 5, 1835.

107. *Ibid.* Cf. the estimate of the company's ability in *Richmond Compiler*, April 12, 1837.

108. Rulfs, "Theater in Raleigh," pp. 353–54.

subsistence for their troupes.[109] But no manager succeeded in establishing a North Carolina circuit, nor did one choose to include any North Carolina town on another circuit. Remote from the urban centers, the state remained theatrically dormant throughout most of the ante bellum period.[110]

So the depression that sapped the economy of the South Atlantic seaboard between 1820 and 1845 exacted its toll on the theater of the region. The playhouses were among the first institutions to suffer from hard times and among the last to recover. People long accustomed to depression need considerable time to readjust to prosperity, and theater-going represented an expense few could justify until they became convinced they could afford it. That took time. But by the mid-1840's, there was promise of theatrical recovery, and the "prosperity decade" of the 1850's saw the realization of that promise, at least in part.

109. Donald J. Rulfs, "The Ante-Bellum Professional Theater in Fayetteville," *The North Carolina Historical Review*, XXXI (April, 1954), 128–9.

110. Occasional itinerants, of course, did reach North Carolina. One notable stroller was Joseph Jefferson, who visited Wilmington in 1856. So in need of repair was the "dusty old rat-trap of a theater," commented Jefferson, that three days were required to ready it for the opening; *Autobiography*, p. 143. Had Jefferson returned to Wilmington just two years later he would have found better accommodations. The new City Hall erected in 1858 had one wing designed for use as a playhouse. "Thalian Hall" was officially opened on October 12, 1858. See Donald J. Rulfs, "The Professional Theater in Wilmington, 1858–1930," *The North Carolina Historical Review*, XXVIII (April, 1951), 121.

CHAPTER VII

THE
EASTERN SEABOARD
A PARTIAL RECOVERY

1.

THE PROCESS OF RECOVERY FROM THE CRIPPLING EFFECTS OF PANIC
and depression was long and far from constant in the states of the
South Atlantic seaboard. It was a process involving ups and downs,
advance and retreat, even as the 1840's closed and the 1850's commenced. Theater recovery came similarly where it came at all. In
the towns of the Southeast, the managers found nothing certain but
uncertainty. A good season was all too often followed by a mediocre
one. Still, the general trend was upward in theater operations as
in the entire economy. And as the 1850's progressed, conditions in
both spheres improved astonishingly.

But theater operations following the great depression were not
the same as they had been before that trauma. Throughout the
decade of the 1840's there was a preceptible trend toward localization of the theater in the largest and most populous of urban centers.
Itinerant dramatic companies, it seemed, were on the wane. Several conditions contributed to this tendency, the first being the depression itself. It should be emphasized that although the theatrical

decline was relatively more severe in the Southeast, the decline was in every sense national in scope. New York and Philadelphia theaters suffered acutely, as was noted earlier, and the troubled times lasted quite as long in the Northeastern cities as in those of the South.[1] One effect of the depression was to deprive actors of jobs (or of salaries) in the Northern theater centers,[2] which meant that even more of them necessarily undertook strolling operations or joined touring companies in the provinces. Most of them went west; but a significant number chose the towns of the Southeast when they set out in quest of livelihood. Thus the smaller towns of the South had frequent opportunities to host touring professionals. When conditions in the Northeast began to improve, however, as they did in the mid-1840's, the actors returned to their old companies and the provinces were deprived of all but a meager group of the poorest itinerant entertainers. Such was the situation in the Southeast at least until the late 1850's, when a revival of itinerant activity occurred in the emerging towns of the Deep South cotton belt.

But there were also non-economic reasons for the localization of the theater in the cities. Of profound significance in the South, for example, was the rise of the temperance movement. The anti-alcohol forces were especially strong in the rural areas of the Southern seaboard states, and temperance agitation operated strongly against the theater. The rise of the lyceum lecture system and the vogue of the concert also hurt theater operations in all but the largest of urban centers.[3] Religious orthodoxy continued to militate against

1. For contemporary accounts of the effects of the depression upon the theater in general, see Anon., *The Actor; or, A Peep Behind the Curtain. Being Passages in the Lives of Booth and Some of his Contemporaries* (New York: William H. Graham, 1846), p. 175; Northall, *Yankee Hill*, p. 92; Jefferson, *Autobiography*, p. 52. Jefferson wrote that in 1842 the country "had been in a chronic state of theatrical bankruptcy since the panic of 1837, and continued in it for many years." For depressed conditions in New York specifically, see for example, *New York Spirit of the Times*, Jan. 26, Nov. 9, 1839; Odell, *Annals*, IV, 440, 603, and *passim*. Conditions in Philadelphia are assessed by a theater musician in Edward Woolf to Solomon Franklin Smith, July 11, 1841, April 25, 1842, in Smith Collection, Missouri Historical Society. In the 1841 letter, Woolf wrote "theatrical business here in the East, is in a most awful condition."

2. Edward Woolf wrote Sol Smith in 1841: "There are but a few managers [in New York and Philadelphia] who pay salaries regularly; and those salaries are mostly on a reduced scale." Edward Woolf to Solomon Franklin Smith, July 11, 1841, in Smith Collection, Missouri Historical Society.

3. Northall, *Yankee Hill*, p. 92. Again, competition for the theater was not limited to the South. Precisely the same conditions prevailed in the Northeast. Edward Woolf wrote Sol Smith in 1842 that the Philadelphia theaters were suf-

the theater, especially in rural areas. And finally, the star system took a decided toll in small theatrical troupes.

The effects of the star system[4] have been long debated and are still debatable. Some contend that a theater offering the greatest individual talents of the time is to be preferred to one offering only the efforts of a mediocre repertory company. Others argue that the system necessarily decreases the availability of any theater by impoverishing managers of smaller playhouses, ultimately driving them out of business. Certainly the managers of the ante bellum period believed they were being ruined by the outrageous monetary demands of the stars and by the equally outrageous demands of the public, spoiled by star performances, for ever more and bigger stars.[5] There can be no doubt that the system did finish the career of many fledgling managers and thus reduced the number of active repertory companies considerably. But the system prevailed, and the necessity of providing stars in order to attract audiences meant that only the managers operating in large towns could hope to remain in business.

So it was a combination of circumstances that brought the virtual end of theatrical activity in all but the largest of Southern towns. The process was almost complete by the late 1840's. After that theater in the Southeast was limited almost exclusively to Richmond and such Virginia towns as the Richmond manager of moment chose to visit, to Charleston, South Carolina, and to the Georgia circuit, which came by the late 1850's to include Savannah, Augusta, Macon,

fering because of "nightly Concerts, Lectures, and Temperance meetings. . . ." Edward Woolf to Solomon Franklin Smith, April 25, 1842, in Smith Collection, Missouri Historical Society.

4. The term "star system" refers to that theatrical *modus operandum* whereby a famous actor or actress was engaged to perform a given number of nights supported by a local repertory company, in return for a share of the gross receipts for each performance.

5. See, for example, Hostetler, "Caldwell," p. 283, quoting James Henry Caldwell to Francis Courtney Wemyss, n.d.; Solomon Franklin Smith to Noah Miller Ludlow, July 20, 1836, in Ludlow-Field-Maury Collection, Missouri Historical Society; Ludlow MS diary, March 30, 1844, in Ludlow-Field-Maury Collection, Missouri Historical Society; James M. Bates [Manager, National Theater, Cincinnati, Ohio] to Solomon Franklin Smith, Sept. 12, 1846, in Smith Collection, Missouri Historical Society; Wood, *Personal Recollections*, pp. 391–92; Jefferson, *Autobiography*, p. 52. Naturally, the managers objected most vehemently to the exorbitant monetary demands of the stars, but they also objected to the secondary status the system imposed upon the stock company and the inability of mere repertory performances to attract audiences following the appearance of a star.

and Columbus. The other towns for the most part had to rely upon circuses, minstrels, menageries and camp meetings to provide commercial entertainment.

With an 1850 population of 27,570, Richmond was the second largest city in the Southeast,[6] quite large enough to sustain a repertory company throughout the winter social season, at least after the economic recovery. Following 1844, a year that saw no drama as such in Richmond, the Marshall Theater was open annually under one manager or another until the coming of the Civil War, and even beyond.[7]

The first manager to attempt a Richmond season after 1844 was the old itinerant, John Sharp Potter. In October of 1845 Potter opened the Marshall in conjunction with a Virginia circuit he envisioned for himself, a circuit including Lynchburg, Petersburg, and Norfolk. The company, according to the *New York Spirit of the Times*, was reputed to be "quite the best . . . which has ever appeared there."[8] Potter anticipated good support in Richmond, and indeed, despite the competition of "RAYMOND & WARING'S GRAND MENAGERIE," at the arena on Council Chamber Hill,[9] he seems to have been well patronized. The press was high in its praise of the productions generally, and Potter was able to offer stars of considerable renown. The dancer Julia Turnbull, for example, drew "crowded houses" with her "slender form and exquisite grace," winning applause "second only to Elssler."[10] The able tragedian George Jamieson was hailed as "second to no actor now on the American stage,"[11] and his appearance again won the encomiums of the press. In all, Potter seems to have done well in his initial season in Richmond, as he did when he returned for his 1846 effort. In the interim he played in Petersburg, Norfolk, and elsewhere.

6. DeBow, *Statistical View*, p. 378.

7. For Richmond's Confederate theater history see Iline Fife, "The Theatre During the Confederacy" (Doctoral dissertation, Louisiana State University, 1949), *passim*.

8. *New York Spirit of the Times*, Oct. 11, 1845. Potter arrived from Lynchburg, where he had just closed a brief season in the "NEW LYNCHBURG THEATRE. . . ." Hadley, "Lynchburg Theatre," pp. 154–55, quoting *Lynchburg Virginian*, Sept. 8, 1845.

9. *Richmond Whig and Public Advertiser*, Oct. 28, 1845. The menagerie featured an elephant and "A LARGE NUMIDIAN LION." Such traveling animal shows were common and popular in the period.

10. *Ibid.*, Nov. 14, 1845.

11. *Ibid.*, Dec. 30, 1845.

Potter's success in Richmond attracted a more prestigious manager, William Rufus Blake, for the season that began early in February, 1847. Blake was a Northern comedian of real merit who, following his American debut in 1824, had appeared prominently in the stock companies of several leading New York theaters. According to John Thomson Ford, a later Virginia manager, Blake brought "the golden period of the drama in Richmond. . . ."[12] The new company was strong, and its repertoire was strictly legitimate. "Great plays were given by great actors," recalled Ford, "who remained here [Richmond] all the season—and it was the fashion, and one might say the rage, to go to the theatre."[13] The stock leads were taken by Blake, George Jamieson, and Mrs. Coleman Pope, all first-rate talents by any standard. The stars manager Blake attracted were the likes of Forrest, Charles and Ellen Kean, and William Charles Macready.[14] Although Blake's regime was brief, lasting only from 1847 to 1849, it was one of the high points in Richmond theater history. At the close of the 1847 season, a correspondent in the *Enquirer* assessed Blake's initial effort. "This winter," he observed, "we have had by far the best Theatre that has been opened in Richmond for some years past, and we have been told by those who ought to know, that it is the best since 1812."[15]

But Richmond could not hold Blake. The lure of the theatrical metropolis was too strong, and he returned to New York to pursue his brilliant career. September of 1849 found the Marshall Theater under management of George W. Harvey, who offered his "original NIGHTINGALE ETHIOPIAN SERENADERS," featuring "MASTER FLOYD, the celebrated ETHIOPIAN ELLSLER."[16] Harvey and the minstrels held forth until early in 1850 before relinquishing the playhouse to the

12. Clipping, *Richmond Dispatch*, Sept. 29, 1891, in Theater Collection, Valentine Museum, Richmond, Virginia. The clipping contains a verbatim interview with the old manager.

13. *Ibid.* Among those Ford recalled as regular theater-goers during the Blake regime were John Moncure Daniel, editor of the *Examiner*, William Foushee Ritchie of the *Enquirer*, and James A. Cowardin, "a great lover of the dramatic art, then editor of the *Compiler.* . . ." Theater activities were, needless to say, well covered by the press.

14. Forrest and the Keans appeared in March of 1847. See *Richmond Whig and Public Advertiser*, March 2, 5, 9, 1847; *Richmond Enquirer*, March 4, 5, 1847. Macready arrived in Dec., 1848. Frederick Pollock (ed.), *Macready's Reminiscences, and Selections from His Diaries and Letters* (New York: Harper and Brothers, 1875), p. 585. On Jan. 4, 1849, the great British tragedian wrote in his diary: "Left Richmond with a most delightful recollection of all attaching to [his engagement]. . . ."

15. *Richmond Enquirer*, March 19, 1847.

16. *Richmond Whig and Public Advertiser*, Sept. 4, 1849.

more legitimate efforts of John Sefton and William H. Chippendale, who then presented, according to John T. Ford, "a memorable season."[17] That they presented only one season evidences a certain lack of patronage, as does the price reduction that the co-managers effected.[18]

By fall of 1850, the ubiquitous Potter was back, and the *Spirit of the Times* proclaimed his return: "*Potter*, . . . once more assumes the reins of management at Richmond, Va. . . . Actors of merit doubt whether to go to Potter or California."[19] The Richmond manager apparently won enough of the doubt-ridden actors to present an adequate season and even to attract an occasional star, as, for example, when "Yankee" comedian Joshua S. Silsbee made a Richmond appearance in January and February of 1851.[20] But Potter rarely played any one town more than a season or two, and Richmond proved no exception. He was replaced for the winter of 1851–1852 by James H. Taylor, a little-known provincial manager who maintained control in the Virginia capital for the next five years.[21]

For all his lack of fame, Manager Taylor offered substantial theater fare to his patrons and operated a well-regulated playhouse. Prior to his 1853 opening, he refurbished the theater, painting it inside and out and refinishing the interior "handsomely."[22] He then offered a fine season on a stock and star basis that lasted until mid-May, 1854. When star actress Eliza Logan appeared in January, she was impressed with his entire operation. "This is a perfect *model theatre*," she wrote her friend Sol Smith. "The company is excellent—well managed—theatre well furnished and every thing is in apple-pie order."[23] Miss Logan's evaluation indicates that another profitable season was in progress.

17. Clipping, *Richmond Dispatch*, Sept. 29, 1891, in Theater Collection, Valentine Museum, Richmond, Virginia.

18. *Richmond Whig and Public Advertiser*, Feb. 8, 1850. The new prices were: Boxes and center gallery, $0.50; pit and "Colored Gallery," $0.25; side gallery, $0.12 1/2.

19. *New York Spirit of the Times*, Oct. 19, 1850. The California boom attracted hundreds of actors and actresses from the East beginning in 1850. See Playbill, Marshall Theater, Oct. 17, 1851, Theater Collection, Valentine Museum, Richmond, Virginia.

20. *Richmond Whig and Public Advertiser*, Jan. 31, 1851.

21. Clipping, *Richmond Dispatch*, Sept. 29, 1891, in Theater Collection, Valentine Museum, Richmond, Virginia.

22. *Richmond Enquirer*, Oct. 7, 1853.

23. Eliza Logan to Solomon Franklin Smith, Jan. 26, 1854, in Smith Collection, Missouri Historical Society.

The emergence of Richmond from the slough of depression is further indicated by the richness of entertainment available there by winter of 1853–1854. Metropolitan Hall and Odd Fellows Hall, assembly halls available for commercial shows, were frequently open in competition with the playhouse, offering a wide range of "cultural" attractions. In October of 1853 the "CHINESE ARTISTES [*sic*]" held the boards at the Metropolitan, featuring the "DOUBLE JOINTED DWARF, CHIN GAN," and a "DECAPITATION SCENE, which must be seen to be appreciated." At the same time at Odd Fellows Hall the "FAKIR OF SIVA, and his burlesque Ethiopian, Operatic and Ballet Troupe" offered what must have been an unusual show.[24] At the other end of the cultural spectrum, the Italian Opera Company, featuring Rosa De Vries, appeared for an engagement in January of 1854, and Ole Bull and Adelina Patti, the ten-year-old "Musical Phenomenon," presented a series of concerts at Metropolitan Hall the same month.[25] All the while, it should be remembered, Taylor had the theater open six nights a week, except during the engagement of the opera troupe, when drama and opera alternated evenings.

The plethora of commercial entertainment continued unabated in the Virginia capital in the years that followed. In March of 1856, for example, in the final season of Taylor's management, the public had a wide choice of fare. On the evening of March 24 one might have attended the Marshall Theater or either one of the public halls. At the Metropolitan, Miss Clara Darling presented a reading of Longfellow's *Hiawatha* "in the FULL COSTUME OF AN INDIAN GIRL, With appropriate Forest Scenery, Indian Wigwams, and other illustrative decorations." Odd Fellows offered "MOVING DIORAMAS OF NAVAL BATTLES, PROCESSIONS, &c." Or, if one had been so inclined, he could have waited two days for the appearance of soprano Theresa Parodi, who was to hold forth at the Metropolitan along with Adelina Patti and pianist Maurice Strakosch.[26] The ability to

24. *Richmond Enquirer*, Oct. 28, 1853.
25. *Ibid.*, Jan. 10, 1854. The Italian Opera Company offered such vocal show-pieces as *Lucretia Borgia, Lucia, Norma,* and *Sonnambula*. The Bellini and Donizetti heroines were alway favorites of the coloratura sopranos and their audiences alike in a period when technical virtuosity was all that the majority of the public could possibly appreciate. In a typical critique of one *Lucia* production, a local Richmond critic observed "Madam Rose de Vries has a voice of great richness and power, and meledy [*sic*] gushes from her throat in an unbroken volume." *Ibid.*, Jan. 6, 1854.
26. *Ibid.*, March 24, 1856.

sustain such an abundance of commercial entertainment bespeaks flush times in Richmond.

In 1856 management of the theater fell to the hands of John Thomson Ford, an ex-minstrel impresario, and his associates George Kunkel and Thomas Moxley, also former minstrel men and provincial managers.[27] The Ford-Kunkel-Moxley triumvirate held the theater until the Civil War began. As none of them had at this time any significant experience with legitimate drama, they hired the rising young comedian Joseph Jefferson, then twenty-seven years old, to serve as stage manager. Jefferson, in addition to his directorial duties, also performed regularly with the stock company. The arrangement made for a strong troupe indeed. And during the first season they were called upon to support the star appearances of such giants as John Drew and Edwin Forrest. Jefferson later recalled that the season was "altogether quite a brilliant one. . . ."[28] Richmond was approaching the flood tide of her theatrical fortunes.

The seasons that followed provided still more stars of the first magnitude, and more notable productions—Maggie Mitchell, the phenomenally popular soubrette; Charlotte Cushman, the great American tragedienne; Barry Sullivan, the British tragedian; Joseph Jefferson, who had achieved theatrical pre-eminence since his one year of Richmond management; and a host of similar luminaries.[29] Among the numerous productions that might be singled out for special notice, one in particular demands mention. On January 6, 1860, Caroline Richings, "the American Prima Donna," appeared in "Mrs. Anna Cora Ritchie's great American Comedy of FASHION!"[30] The actress-playwright Anna Cora Mowatt, internationally renowned as the author of the satirical comedy *Fashion, or Life in New York*, had married William Foushee Ritchie on June 6, 1854. The couple made their home in Richmond, where Ritchie was editor-in-chief of

27. Clipping, *Richmond Dispatch*, Sept. 29, 1891, in Theater Collection, Valentine Museum, Richmond, Virginia. Ford later became Civil War manager of the theater in Washington, D. C., in which Lincoln was assassinated.

28. *Autobiography*, p. 157. Jefferson dated this season 1854, but is clearly in error. See *Richmond Enquirer*, Feb. 13, 1857; Playbill, Marshall Theater, Feb. 28, 1857, in Harvard Theater Collection, Harvard College Library; Playbill, Marshall Theater, May 1, 1857, Valentine Museum, Richmond, Virginia.

29. *Richmond Enquirer*, Nov. 10, 1857; Jan. 18, April 12, 1859; Dec. 7, 1860. Playbill, Marshall Theater, May 18, 1858, Valentine Museum, Richmond, Virginia. Jefferson chose one of his favorite roles for his benefit on Dec. 7, 1860—Asa Trenchard in Tom Taylor's *Our American Cousin*.

30. *Richmond Enquirer*, Jan. 6, 1860.

the *Enquirer*.[31] The local production of her best play created considerable enthusiasm, as Mrs. Ritchie was a leader in Richmond society.

On December 28, 1860, at mid-season, the *Enquirer* advertised the benefit performance of Emma Waller, who was to play the leads in Bulwer's *Lady of Lyons* and *The Stranger* of Kotzebue-Thompson, perhaps the most popular of the "domestic melodramas" so dear to the times.[32] The same *Enquirer* described the evacuation of Fort Moultrie by the United States forces under Captain Robert Anderson, and a "late dispatch" announced somewhat prematurely "The War Has Begun."[33] The ante bellum period was drawing to a close. As it did Richmond was at the height of her theatrical prosperity.

2.

Outside of Richmond, the Virginia town most frequently visited by theatrical companies was Lynchburg. In 1850 the aggregate population of this important tobacco processing town was 8,071,[34] not quite large enough to support professional theater on a regular season basis but sufficiently large to attract the Richmond company rather frequently. John S. Potter, for example, included Lynchburg in his plans for a Virginia circuit in 1845, declaring in his opening announcement there that "the Theatre is fitted up in good style, and is capable of accommodating over 500 persons." The ubiquitous manager further guaranteed that "the performance selected will be of sterling merit . . ." and that "order and regularity will be observed in every department. . . ."[35] The theater itself was a building constructed by the Universalists in 1842, then rented out for use as a playhouse whenever a troupe needed one, an arrangement that lasted until 1855 when two public halls opened. Theater companies appearing in Lynchburg after 1855 performed in either Dudley Hall or Masonic Hall, both of which were adequate for play production.[36] Such appearances had been rare, however, prior to the mid-1850's.

31. Eric Wollencott Barnes, *The Lady of Fashion. The Life and the Theatre of Anna Cora Mowatt* (New York: Charles Scribner's Sons, 1954), p. 337.
32. *Richmond Enquirer*, Dec. 28, 1860.
33. *Ibid.*
34. U. S. Department of State, *Seventh Census*, p. 258; DeBow, *Statistical View*, p. 320.
35. Hadley, "Theatre in Lynchburg," pp. 154–55, quoting *Lynchburg Virginian*, Sept. 8, 1845.
36. *Ibid.*, p. 146.

After that Lynchburg saw a regular theater season, in addition to frequent minor engagements, that kept the playhouses open throughout the fall and winter of each year. In August of 1858 George Kunkel extended the Richmond operation to Lynchburg, thus creating a regular circuit. Kunkel then renovated Dudley Hall to receive the troupe, which was, according to the *Virginian*, composed of nothing but "masters of the histrionic profession."[37] This company, often buttressed by top stars, visited Lynchburg on a regular season basis until just prior to the outbreak of war.[38]

Beyond the Richmond-Lynchburg nexus, theatrical affairs in Virginia were near-dormant between the mid-1840's and the mid-1850's. When in March of 1850 the theaters in both Petersburg and Norfolk burned within days of each other, the *Spirit of the Times* could observe accurately: "Quite as well—they were of no use to any body."[39] But as the boom decade of the 1850's advanced, there were indications of a theatrical rebirth in some of the lesser Virginia towns. In 1853, for example, two new playhouses were built in communities that had formerly supported the theater. First came Williamsburg, where interested citizens opened, according to the *Spirit*, a "neat little theatre."[40] Shortly thereafter the Petersburg theater, newly rebuilt, opened its doors as "Phoenix Hall."[41] In 1856 Wheeling witnessed a theater season under management of "D. Hanchett," during which John Edmond Owens played a star engagement.[42] In August of 1860, William H. Crisp, a key Southern manager in the later years of the ante bellum period, leased the playhouses in Portsmouth, Norfolk, and Petersburg for operation as a circuit.[43] But political agitation ruined the chances for a complete revival of the Virginia theater. In October of 1860, comedian George Holland reported from Norfolk that receipts were "shy, to a degree owing . . . to the great excitement caused by the coming election."[44] The agitation grew

37. *Ibid.*, pp. 218–19, quoting *Lynchburg Virginian*, Aug. 12, 1858.
38. *Richmond Enquirer*, Jan. 18, 1859.
39. *New York Spirit of the Times*, March 9, 1850.
40. *Ibid.*, Feb. 26, 1853.
41. Wyatt, "Three Petersburg Theatres," p. 106.
42. Playbill, Wheeling Theater, Oct. 11, 1856, Harvard Theater Collection, Harvard College Library.
43. *Wilkes' Spirit of the Times*, Aug. 25, 1860.
44. George Holland to Solomon Franklin Smith, Oct. 14, 1860, in Smith Collection, Missouri Historical Society. Holland added that the Norfolk residents "take me for a spy or something of that character—so I have kept in my miserable room all the time."

considerably worse as months passed. As a result the promising Virginia renaissance was realized only in part.

3.

Theatrical affairs in Charleston, South Carolina, proceeded quite like those in Richmond for the final fifteen years of the ante bellum period, with one major exception. Whereas Richmond was at theatrical flood tide at the close of the period, Charleston, acutely beset by political agitation, was in a state of theatrical quiescence when the war came. Moreover, there are indications that Charleston managers fared less well financially than did those of the Virginia capital throughout the period.[45] But though the Charleston audiences generally may have been somewhat smaller, the star offerings and the productions were of the highest quality.

From 1842 to 1847 Charleston's theatrical fortunes were in the hands of the able William C. Forbes, who had entered the South Carolina metropolis by way of his Georgia circuit. His position as circuit manager enabled Forbes to attract a succession of top stars to Charleston, and the brightest lights of the English-speaking stage performed in rapid succession there, supported by a small but able stock company. The annual seasons extended usually from mid-November until late April or early May. As always before they were designed to coincide with the winter social season when the transient population was largest.[46]

Forbes's second season in Charleston was especially brilliant and indicates the degree of excellence toward which the able manager always strove. He opened the theater on November 2, 1843, with Hannah Cowley's *Belle's Strategem* and continued to offer stock productions of quality drama until December 12, when the season's first star, the American tragedian John R. Scott, began an engagement. Scott was followed by James Hackett in late December, Wil-

45. The relatively greater financial success of the Richmond managers must be explained by other factors than comparative population. The population of Charleston had jumped to 42,985 by 1850, whereas Richmond numbered but 27,570. U. S. Department of State, *Seventh Census*, pp. 258, 339. The more meaningful figure for determining the potential theater audience, however, is the total free population of the respective counties served by the two towns. By this standard, Charleston County claimed a lesser advantage, outnumbering Henrico County only by 29,069 to 27,463. DeBow, *Statistical View*, pp. 302, 320.

46. Hoole, *Charleston Theatre*, pp. 116–26.

liam Charles Macready early in January, 1844, Edwin Forrest in mid-February, the elder Booth in late February, James W. Wallack in early March, the Seguin Opera Company in mid-March, and finally Joshua S. Silsbee, who closed the season on April 3, 1844.[47] Each of the stars offered the strongest items in his repertoire, so the productions were not only consistently legitimate but the finest of the legitimate.

The high spot of the season was no doubt the Macready appearance. The *Courier* welcomed the British star to Charleston, referring to him as "the greatest tragical genius now living,"[48] an evaluation that must have deeply offended Edwin Forrest who was due to arrive in Charleston immediately after his archrival. Macready chose *Hamlet* for his opening night effort and for his final benefit performance. In the interim he performed Macbeth, Richelieu, Werner (three times), Othello, Claude Melnotte in Bulwer's *Lady of Lyons*, and Virginius. Some time later Dr. John B. Irving recalled that Macready's reception "and the whole of his engagement, was the most triumphant I have ever seen in Charleston. He was fully appreciated—." Irving considered the appreciation evidenced by the Charlestonians "a sure indication of the correct judgment and classical refinement of the audience."[49] On January 20, after his great Charleston debut, the star moved to Savannah for an appearance.[50]

Another star whose engagement provoked considerable excitement in Charleston was Anna Cora Mowatt. In December of 1845, while on her first theatrical tour, the popular actress opened in the South Carolina port. Mrs. Mowatt was decidedly a curiosity in Victorian America—a lady of wealth and quality antecedents (she was born a New York Ogden) who went on the stage to try to recoup an ailing husband's fortunes. But she was well received by the Charlestonians. Her engagement, she later recalled, "was of long duration [December 4–30, 1845], and was followed by a succession of prosperous reengagements." She deemed Manager Forbes "able"

47. *Ibid.*, p. 118.

48. *Charleston Courier*, Jan. 8, 1844.

49. Robinson, "Irving's Reminiscences," LI, 204. The validity of Irving's judgment is open to question. It was typical of the period for audiences to accept a performer's greatness on the basis of hearsay and ballyhoo, viz., the Jenny Lind furor. But certainly the Charlestonians had ample opportunity to compare Macready's efforts with those of other fine actors.

50. Pollock, *Macready's Reminiscences*, p. 520. He returned to Charleston on Feb. 7, 1844.

and the Charleston audiences "warm." In fact, she became "very much attached" to both town and people during her successful first appearance.[51]

But Forbes's able management came to an abrupt end on March 6, 1847, at the close of an engagement of the Seguin Opera Company.[52] It is obvious that the manager's stalwart efforts to offer the best in theatrical fare were costly. Stars of the first rank usually demanded an even division of the gross proceeds each evening, after deductions of only $100.00 to $200.00 for the manager's expenses. Sometimes they also demanded, and received, a minimum guarantee. Managers thus frequently lost money on star appearances, even those that drew large audiences. Manager Forbes proved a financial failure in Charleston despite his aesthetic success. In the spring of 1847 he gave up.

Manager Forbes's withdrawal may have also been strategic. For the five years following his departure, Charleston had five different theater managers, all inferior to Forbes and all financially unsuccessful.[53] Productions declined both in number and in consequence, and audiences grew ever smaller. Although occasional stars still came, the Charleston theater had reached another period of decay. Robinson and Eldred actually converted the theater into an incidental adjunct of their circus operation at the rear of the playhouse.[54] On September 13, 1851, the *Spirit of the Times* wondered editorially "who is to have Charleston next season?" "That beautiful city," continued the *Spirit*, "has been ungraciously used, dramatically, of late years. Why don't some monied men take hold of the theatre there, put it in 'serviceable condition,' and engage a really good company and orchestra. It would yield well. The pottering managements of late years have depreciated the property—but it is to be regained by industry and vigor."

It was prosperity and political quietude that Charleston needed

51. Anna Cora Mowatt, *Autobiography of an Actress; or, Eight Years on the Stage* (Boston: Ticknor, Reed, and Fields, 1853), p. 248.

52. *Charleston Courier*, March 6, 1847; Robinson, "Irving's Reminiscences," pp. 28–29. The season had included appearances by James Wallack, Anna Cora Mowatt, Henry Placide, Edward Loomis Davenport, Edwin Forrest, Dan Marble, John Sloman, and the Seguin troupe. The Seguins were Arthur E. S. Seguin and his wife, who toured widely with a full opera company including orchestra and chorus, presenting first-rate operatic productions.

53. The managers were, in order of their appearance, Henry W. Preston, Alexander Robinson and G. N. Eldred, F. C. Adams, H. S. Smith, F. C. Adams again, and Joseph Jefferson and John Ellsler. See Hoole, *Charleston Theatre*, pp. 126–31.

54. *Ibid.*, p. 53.

to regain theatrical eminence. As the decade of the 1850's advanced, prosperity arrived,[55] and indeed, it seemed for a time that the long-overdue theatrical renaissance would arrive with it. The "prosperity decade" saw the coming of three different managers, John Sloman, who lasted but one year (1852–1853), John Sloan who remained in command for four years (1853–1857), and George F. Marchant, who was manager when the war broke out.[56] Each of these able men maintained high standards of theatrical excellence, bringing in star after star to perform with an ever stronger stock company. The first three years of Marchant's regime were perhaps the most prosperous in Charleston theater history. The manager catered to a wide variety of dramatic and musical tastes, offering a judicious mixture of heavy and light drama, farce, and opera. His stars were diversified in their specialties. The 1858–1859 season, for example, saw William E. Burton the comedian, James Edward Murdoch the tragedian and elocutionist, Maggie Mitchell the dancer-soubrette, the Ravel Family, gymnasts and pantomimists, Julia Dean, the tremendously popular romantic heroine,[57] the New Orleans English Opera Troupe, and Edwin Booth, then just beginning his career as a star tragedian.[58] Each star was a recognized talent in his particular line, and Marchant reaped substantial rewards for his sensible programing.

But though prosperity prevailed, political agitation worsened and by 1859 had begun to take its toll on theater receipts. The season of

55. That the 1850's were a time of increasing prosperity for Charleston and the South is generally acknowledged. But for some evidence in support of the contention, see *The Commercial Review of the South and West* [*DeBow's Review*], XIV (Feb., 1853), 184; (April, 1853), 405; XVII (Nov., 1854), 538–39; XIX (Oct., 1855), 460; XXIX (Oct., 1860), 526–27; George Rogers Taylor, "Wholesale Commodity Prices at Charleston, South Carolina, 1796–1861," *Journal of Economic and Business History*, supplement to IV (Aug., 1932), 851, 866; Van Deusen, *Economic Bases of Disunion*, pp. 180–81, 240, 333. The above sources treat wholesale and retail commodity prices, retail trade figures, import and export tonnages and values, banking capital, and railroad development. It should be noted, however, that although Charleston realized an economic advance during the "prosperity decade," these same sources clearly reveal that the South Carolina port fell ever further behind such Deep South ports as Mobile and New Orleans.

56. Hoole, *Charleston Theatre*, p. 60.

57. Julia Dean was a southern favorite throughout her career. She was especially popular in Charleston both before and after her 1855 marriage to Dr. Arthur Hayne, son of Robert Y. Hayne. During an 1853 engagement, a poetic effusion in the *Courier* represented the lovely Miss Dean as "THE UNION OF NATURE AND ART." *Charleston Courier*, Feb. 14, 1853.

58. Hoole, *Charleston Theatre*, p. 149.

1859–1860 saw the stock company reduced in size to some fifteen members.[59] Moreover, with the exception of Edwin Booth and Julia Dean, no notable stars appeared during the season. Marchant offered only the lightest of fare, presumably judging that escapist theater was called for in troubled times. Buckley's Burlesque Opera Troupe played a long engagement and was followed by Donetti and Wood's Trained Dogs and the Marsh Juvenile Comedians.[60] The theater can hardly be said to have been operating at all.

The crisis winter of 1860 effectively finished repertory theater in Charleston. Marchant gave up his stock company altogether. He brought in minstrels, opera companies, and specialty acts, but no legitimate theater. And frequently the playhouse was nearly empty for the opera productions. The *Courier* of November 23, 1860, observed that a *Barber of Seville* performance of the evening before had attracted only a small audience. "It is to be regretted," declared the *Courier*, "that the political excitement should interfere with the aesthetical tastes of our numerous Opera-lovers." "Independence Day" for South Carolina, December 20, 1860, found the Original George Christy Minstrels holding forth at the playhouse.[61] They had been performing while the secession convention sat.

Following the departure of the minstrels, performances at the Charleston theater were rare indeed and usually presented "for a patriotic military purpose,"[62] as was the amateur production of *Lady of Lyons*, offered early in March of 1861. The performance was timed to coincide with the arrival of General Pierre G. T. Beauregard, who was en route to Charleston to take command of the Confederate troops there. It was an exciting social event; Governor Francis Pickens was at the theater with his suite, as was most of Charleston society. At its conclusion there was a military band concert and a "patriotic address" by poet Paul Hamilton Hayne. The climax of the evening came when a local belle sang the "Marseillaise" while furiously waving the banner of the Sumter Guard.[63] But the theater history of ante bellum Charleston had ended.

59. *Ibid.*, p. 151.
60. *Ibid.* There was a noteworthy performance on April 2, 1860, when Edwin Booth played Romeo to Julia Dean's Juliet before a packed house. *Charleston Courier*, April 3, 1860.
61. *Charleston Courier*, Dec. 21, 1860.
62. *Ibid.*, March 1, 1861.
63. Emma Holmes MS Diary, March 4, 1861. Typescript, Southern Historical Collection, University of North Carolina.

4.

Since the times of William C. Forbes, the Charleston managers had made a practice of taking their companies regularly to Savannah, Georgia, along with practically every major star that appeared in Charleston. The Georgians could always be relied upon to patronize the efforts of the visiting performers. With a population of only 15,321 in 1850,[64] Savannah could not support a prolonged theatrical season, so the theater was rarely kept open more than three weeks at a time. But the visits were frequent. And occasionally a company other than the Charleston troupe presented a Savannah season, as for example when John S. Potter and his corps played there in 1844.[65] And Savannah continued to be a favorite stop for the stars. Anna Cora Mowatt visited the Georgia port in 1846 and wrote of the engagement: "It was one upon which I look back with unmingled pleasure." Not only were her audiences large, but at the close of the season "a committee of gentlemen, formed of the most distinguished residents, gave us a magnificent entertainment in token of their esteem."[66] It is clear that the people of Savannah truly enjoyed the visits of the players, and their pleasure was manifest in their enthusiasm. Stars such as Booth, Forrest, Macready, Charlotte Cushman, Julia Dean, Eliza Logan, Dan Marble, and many others justified that enthusiasm.[67]

In addition to enjoying the performances of the greatest actors of the day, Savannah also participated in the opera craze that struck the country in the 1840's and 1850's. Typical were the visits of the Seguin Company in March of 1843, March of 1847, and December of 1848.[68] On each engagement the company presented twelve to fourteen performances, offering all the popular favorites: *Sonnambula, Cenerentola, Fra Diavolo, Massaniello, La Gazza Ladra,* and other standards of the Auber-Rossini-Donizetti repertoire. There is no reason to doubt that these technically difficult operas were well

64. U. S. Department of State, *Seventh Census,* p. 366. The population of Chatham County, largely comprised of Savannah and its immediate environs, was 23,901. DeBow, *Statistical View,* p. 206.

65. Hester, "The Savannah Stage," p. 111.

66. Mowatt, *Autobiography,* p. 249.

67. Hester, "The Savannah Stage," pp. 112, 118, 124, 126–27, 130. All the stars mentioned appeared between 1844 and 1850.

68. *Ibid.,* pp. 108, 119, 123.

performed, and they drew enthusiastic audiences. In light of the constant touring activity of such companies as Seguins, the Italian Opera Company, and the New Orleans English Opera Company, the two decades before the Civil War must be considered a brilliant period in the history of opera in the South as in the nation.

In 1853 an important new theater manager, William H. Crisp, entered the scene in Savannah, by bringing the Georgia port into a circuit that included Augusta, Columbus, and Macon, Georgia, and Montgomery, Alabama. Crisp, a talented actor, was Irish by birth. He had made his American debut at the Park Theater on September 30, 1844,[69] after which he had toured the United States with Anna Cora Mowatt, playing opposite the actress in all her performances. No doubt it was on that tour that Crisp conceived the idea of establishing a Deep South circuit, and from the time of his arrival his long and successful career was identified with the South.[70]

Crisp initiated operations with a company recruited in the East, establishing a Savannah-Augusta nexus in which he was an immediate success. Eliza Logan, one of the first stars he attracted to Georgia, thought highly of the manager, as she revealed in a series of letters to her friend Sol Smith. She first wrote Smith from Richmond in January, 1854, telling of a recent "pleasant and profitable sojourne in Savannah, Ga." She then told of being "handsomely received and treated" by the local citizenry, or at least by "the best of them," who organized a complimentary benefit for her, "which yielded $514." Her Savannah admirers also presented her with "some handsome jewellery." But neither her "time or vanity" would permit her to tell more of the "furore" she caused. "You know," she added, "the Southerners are a wholesouled people." Manager Crisp, continued Miss Logan, "paid me $1000 for 11 nights services. Good for a small town—eh?"[71] Finally, she told Smith of Crisp's plans to expend some $5,000 on improvements in the Savannah Theater.

Even before completing the letter, the actress had made up her mind to return to Savannah following a Washington engagement. "I *think* after Washington I shall join Mr. Crisp again," she wrote.

69. Clipping, *New York Clipper*, Jan. 10, 1847, in Harvard Theater Collection, Harvard College Library.

70. *Ibid.*

71. Eliza Logan to Solomon Franklin Smith, Jan. 26, 1854, in Smith Collection, Missouri Historical Society. Her Savannah engagement had commenced on Dec. 29, 1853. Hester, "The Savannah Stage," p. 132.

"He has a pretty circuit. Augusta, Macon Ga., Columbus, Montgomery Ala., and Huntsville Ala. All of which he invites me to visit and assures me I will do well."[72] She was not inclined to return north in mid-winter. "I have no desire to meet the 'Ides of March' in Philadelphia or Boston while Southern winds are wooing me," she concluded. The success of her second Georgia visit equaled that of the first. "I had an agreeable engt. with Mr. Crisp," she wrote Smith on April 29, 1854, having performed in Savannah, Augusta, Macon, and Columbus. "He paid me nearly $2,000 for five weeks' performance," she related, "and I had $2,000 worth of diamonds, presented by the citizens."[73]

Of the towns in Crisp's Georgia circuit outside of Savannah and Augusta, perhaps Columbus was the most important, and the emergence of Columbus as a community able to sustain an annual theater season is worthy of note. Between 1840 and 1850 the population of Muscogee County, with Columbus as its urban center, grew dramatically.[74] Creek removal and the development of a key cotton-producing and processing area contributed to that growth, and the town began by the 1840's to attract occasional touring entertainers. For example, Harry Watkins, a notable itinerant, performed in Columbus in November of 1851.[75] The local amateur society, the "Histrionics," had been formed in 1851, and the *Enquirer* pointed out that the members of the society had "skilled themselves suf-

72. *Ibid.*

73. Eliza Logan to Solomon Franklin Smith, April 29, 1854, in Smith Collection, Missouri Historical Society. An account of the Logan engagement in Savannah in the *Savannah Morning News* bears out the actress's story of the jewelry—in part. "However gratified Miss Logan may be at her professional success," observed the *Morning News*, ". . . she must derive even a higher satisfaction from the many proofs of warm friendship and, personal esteem which she has received. This feeling for her so general among our citizens, was manifested on Friday evening by the presentation of a set of diamonds—bracelet, breast pin and earrings—valued at $500—a present from a number of her Savannah friends." Hester, "The Savannah Stage," p. 135, quoting *Savannah Morning News*, March 6, 1854.

74. Although the population of Columbus was only 5,942 in 1850, between 1840 and 1850 the population of Muscogee County jumped from 11,699 to 18,578, of which 10,422 were free. U. S. Department of State, *Seventh Census*, p. 366; DeBow, *Statistical View*, p. 212.

75. Maud Skinner and Otis Skinner (eds.), *One Man in His Time. The Adventures of H. Watkins, Strolling Player, 1845–1863 from His Journal* (Philadelphia: University of Pennsylvania Press, 1938), p. 113; Langley, "Theatre in Columbus," p. 44. Watkins and his troupe probably performed in the public hall that had opened on Jan. 8, 1851, and was available for rent to all traveling shows.

ficiently by long and arduous rehearsals, to meet the expectations of those who are judges of such performances."[76] The *Enquirer* also observed that the Histrionics deserved "the patronage of our citizens over strolling companies" because "we know their characters . . . ," a strong indication that some of the strollers were of questionable character.[77]

In 1854 William H. Crisp brought Columbus into his circuit, and the short seasons that he performed there, occasionally with a first-rate star, proved extremely popular. The *Enquirer* declared of the Eliza Logan engagement: "Her every appearance is greeted with a round of applause, and at the close of each successive play, she is called before the scenes by an enthusiastic audience."[78] Crisp found that he could always count on a few profitable weeks in Columbus, and even after he moved his center of operations to New Orleans in 1856, he continued to visit the Georgia town with his troupe.[79]

Crisp also initiated such theater as was available in Atlanta, Georgia, prior to the Civil War. With an 1850 population of only 2,572,[80] theatrical activity was, of course, limited. But in 1855, Crisp undertook a season with his troupe at Parr's Hall, a three-flight walk-up of very little pretension. Totally unsatisfied with such accommodations, Crisp entreated local residents to provide something better, and in February, 1855, the doors of Atlanta's first playhouse were opened. Actually the new "theater," the second floor of a brick warehouse, was little improvement over Parr's Hall. The first floor was used by the owner of the building for his grain and produce commission business. But the building served as a playhouse for Crisp and such entertainers as followed in his footsteps until Sherman put it to the torch in 1865.[81]

In 1856 Crisp gave up his Georgia circuit and began operating a New Orleans theater called "Crisp's Gaieties." New Orleans became his center of operations for a circuit that ultimately included Nash-

76. *Columbus Enquirer*, Dec. 23, 1851.

77. *Ibid.*, Dec. 30, 1851. The offerings of the Histrionics this season included a production of *Lamorah, or the Western Wild*, written especially for them by Caroline Lee Hentz, the Columbus novelist.

78. *Ibid.*, March 28, 1854.

79. Langley, "Theatre in Columbus," p. 69.

80. U. S. Department of State, *Seventh Census*, p. 366.

81. Meta Barker, "Some Highlights of the Old Atlanta Stage," *The Atlanta Historical Bulletin*, I (Jan., 1928), 33.

ville and Memphis, Tennessee.[82] But he had built well in Georgia, and his circuit was maintained until the outbreak of war. In September of 1856, for example, the *Spirit of the Times* assured the people of Savannah that Crisp's replacement there, the comedian Henry Grattan Plunkett, would "prove all they could wish."[83] By 1858 Charleston manager George F. Marchant was operating the circuit in his off seasons, and the summer of 1860 found W. M. Fleming operating a circuit that included Savannah, Macon, Augusta, Columbus, Atlanta, and Wilmington, North Carolina.[84] Thus the Georgia towns saw a real burgeoning of theatrical activity in the late 1850's, and if the productions that were offered could not come up to the caliber of the Crisp efforts, they were still popular.[85]

The theatrical activity in Columbus in 1860 is indicative of the extent of interest in the theater on the eve of war. During the summer a group of interested citizens formed a company to build a new theater, and by July 17 had already subscribed three-fourths of the $40,000 they needed.[86] Meanwhile the old playhouse sufficed for the troupes playing there, such as the Fleming Company, or the corps that arrived in October of 1860 under a little-known manager by the name of Canning. The leading tragedian in the Canning troupe was a talented young player from Maryland, scion of a great actor and a promising tragedian: John Wilkes Booth. The people of Columbus were sympathetic when they learned that Manager Canning had accidently shot Booth on October 15, 1860, thus preventing him from playing Hamlet for his benefit that night. They were relieved when the *Enquirer* assured them that the wound in the actor's thigh was "not severe."[87]

But in spite of the injury sustained by his leading man, and in spite of the heightening political agitation, manager Canning con-

82. Hester, "The Savannah Stage," p. 146; Ritter, "Theatre in Memphis," pp. 231–32.
83. *New York Spirit of the Times*, Sept. 6, 1856.
84. *Wilkes' Spirit of the Times*, Aug. 25, 1860.
85. The decline in quality is evidenced by the Fleming offering in Savannah on Dec. 29, 1860: *Ten Nights in a Bar Room*, "Bamboozling," dancing, and "the Southern Rights Picture." Hester, "The Savannah Stage," p. 170.
86. Langley, "Theatre in Columbus," p. 75. The new theater did not materialize until after the war, when it finally opened as Springer's Opera House.
87. *Columbus Enquirer*, Oct. 16, 1860. Cf. the account of the accident in the *Spirit of the Times*, Oct. 28, 1860, which declared that the wound was quite serious and would "undoubtedly disable him for some time."

tinued his Columbus season. So did the other managers playing the towns of interior Georgia and Alabama in the fall and winter of 1860. Indeed, the newly emerging towns of the Deep South cotton belt were faring better than most of the older towns of the seaboard states. Such entertainment as was provided by the theater was more in demand in the booming cotton towns. There was also relatively less political agitation and less organized religious opposition to the theater. But even more important was the proximity of the new towns to the Mississippi Valley; they had greater access to New Orleans and the other major valley theater towns. And in the last two decades of the ante bellum period New Orleans, along with its immediate theatrical adjuncts, had developed into one of the nation's leading theatrical centers.

CHAPTER VIII

LUDLOW

AND

SMITH

1.

THEATRICAL DEVELOPMENTS IN THE MISSISSIPPI VALLEY BETWEEN 1837
and 1853 centered, to a remarkable degree, around the activities of
Noah Ludlow and Sol Smith. Their epic struggle with James H.
Caldwell, their ultimate victory, their building of the key valley
circuit encompassing New Orleans, Mobile, and St. Louis—such was
the sequence of events that formed the core of Southwestern theater
history throughout the existence of their famous partnership. Despite
economic distress, burgeoning competition, even fire and plague, the
co-managers pressed on with their operation, building upon the
base laid by their archrival and creating by the time of their retirement in 1853 one of the nation's most important theater circuits. It
was this circuit that attracted all the great stars of the day as well as
the legion of fine stock actors who filled the ranks of the repertory
companies performing in the valley towns.

As was noted in Chapter V, Ludlow and Smith were by 1837 established in their Mobile-St. Louis nexus. But the key city in the Mississippi Valley was clearly New Orleans, booming port of egress for

the valley's commodities and fourth largest city in the Union.[1] Theatrically, New Orleans was considered, in the words of the *New York
Spirit of the Times,* "the emporium of the Southern stage, as is New
York of the Northern."[2] The manager controlling the Crescent City
would necessarily dominate the entire valley. And in 1835 James
H. Caldwell had returned to theater operation there,[3] with a project
more ambitious than any ever attempted in the South; he had opened
the splendid St. Charles Theater. Ludlow and Smith, who previously
had considered extending their operations to New Orleans,[4] were
at least temporarily frustrated in their design.

On November 30, 1835, Caldwell presented the St. Charles to an
eager New Orleans public.[5] The featured attraction of the grand
opening was Sheridan's *School for Scandal;*[6] the afterpiece was Isaac
Bickerstaff's farce, *The Spoiled Child.* For an interlude the large
house orchestra performed the overture to *Der Frieschütz.* Altogether it was a program that manifested the manager's determination
to dedicate his new playhouse to the legitimate.

The theater itself was elegant, as impressive a playhouse as could
be created with the considerable means available to the manager. He
fully intended that it be a true "Temple of the Drama," as it soon
became known. Ten Corinthian columns fronted the 130-foot expanse

1. The *New Orleans Bee,* Sept. 30, 1835, estimated the population of the
city as 60,000 permanent white residents and 15,000 to 20,000 Negro residents,
slave and free. The census returns for 1840 show an aggregate population of
102,193, including all suburbs. By 1850 this figure was up to 116,375. U. S.
Census Office, *Social Statistics,* p. 213. Transients were, of course, myriad and
provided an important element of theater support.

2. May 18, 1839. James Rees, who lived in New Orleans for eight years prior
to departing for Philadelphia, contended that "the drama in New Orleans has
always been better patronized than it is in any other city in the union." *Dramatic
Mirror and Literary Companion,* March 5, 1842.

3. See above, chap. v.

4. On the desire of Ludlow and Smith to open in New Orleans, see James
Henry Caldwell to Solomon Franklin Smith, Feb. 24, 1835, Smith Collection,
Missouri Historical Society. Caldwell advised Smith against opening in New
Orleans. "I feel," wrote the egocentric Caldwell, "a paramount call to take
charge of the Drama again in this City." On May 8, 1835, he laid the corner-
stone of the St. Charles.

5. *New Orleans Bee,* Dec. 1, 1835.

6. The cast of *School for Scandal* indicates the strength of the Caldwell stock:
Vincent De Camp as Sir Peter Teazle, John H. Barton as Charles Surface, Benedict De Bar as Sir Benjamin Backbite, Clara Fisher Maeder as Lady Teazle, and
Louisa Lane (later Mrs. John Drew) as Maria. Other important members of the
company were comedians Joe Cowell and George Holland, and the then novice
singer Charlotte Cushman.

of the St. Charles Street façade, supporting a portico one floor above the street. Around the portico was a balustrade adorned with statues of Apollo and the nine Muses. The top of the building stood 86 feet off street level, and the entire façade was finished in shining imitation marble.[7]

But impressive as was the exterior, the interior was even more so. The auditorium formed a slightly elongated semicircle about the stage. It was traditional in design, consisting of pit, parquet, boxes, and gallery—in all, five tiers of seats. The entire house was decorated in the rococo elegance so dear to the times. Each box was draped in crimson, blue, and yellow damask silk, "pleasantly intermingled," and every seat was fully padded and upholstered, including even those in the gallery. The "grand saloon" of the house, with its rich furnishings and statuary, was on the level of the first tier of boxes and was the "fashionable promenade" of the theater. It was, according to the *Philadelphia Evening Post*, "the *chef d'ouvre* of architechtural [sic] elegance."[8] The stage was huge, perhaps the largest in the country, measuring 90 by 96 feet. It was framed by gilded Corinthian columns which supported the entablature of the imitation marble proscenium arch. Fronting the proscenium was the heavy red moreen curtain. With the addition of the famous chandelier at the opening of the second season the house decor was complete.[9]

Public opinion was virtually unanimous that the whole was an imposing structure. Louis Fitzgerald Tasistro merely echoed general sentiment when he wrote, "it is the only theater in the United States

7. The most complete description of the theater appeared in the *Philadelphia Evening Post*, May 14, 1836, reprinted in the *New Orleans True American*, June 14, 1836. See also *New Orleans Bee*, April 7, 1835; Tasistro, *Random Shots*, I, 61. The theater stood on St. Charles Avenue between Gravier and Poydras.

8. *New Orleans True American*, June 14, 1836, quoting *Philadelphia Evening Post*, May 14, 1836. It is noteworthy that the gallery of the house had its entrance on the outside of the building, at the top of a long flight of stairs, and did not connect with the grand saloon at all.

9. Smither, "New Orleans," p. 218. The chandelier was 30 feet in diameter and weighed 4,500 pounds. Among the features of the St. Charles likely to be of special interest to the theater historian, the following might be mentioned: The orchestra pit extended the full width of the stage, was 14 feet deep and was capable of accommodating fifty musicians. The stage itself was flexible—lateral movement of the wings rendered it larger or smaller depending upon production requirements. Vast quantities of scenery were flown and a prototype of the cyclorama was available when needed, yet crude gas borders, not footlights, provided primary stage lighting. Backstage were located the twenty-six dressing rooms and two green rooms in addition to a painting room and ample storage space for props, wardrobe, and scenery.

which bears any evidence of a comprehensive and well-digested plan; the only one which, for extent, variety, and magnificence, is truly worthy of a large city. . . . Thespis never had a prouder temple dedicated to her than this."[10]

But for all the grandeur of his new theater, Caldwell still had competition in New Orleans. Richard Russell, lessee of the old Camp Street Theater, was operating successfully and continued to do so until his death in 1838.[11] Moreover, the French-language Orleans Street Theater was open nightly, and the ever-present circuses, magicians, acrobats, menageries, and other such showmen contended with the theater for the patronage of the Crescent City's pleasure-seekers. When in his first season at the St. Charles Caldwell determined to offer nothing but the purest of legitimate drama and grand opera, he fared rather badly. By April 23, 1836, the *Bee* reported that the "temple," along with the other theaters of the city, was "almost deserted."

For the second season at the St. Charles, manager Caldwell realized that he would have to diversify his programing in order to compete. Consequently, he offered melodrama, spectacular pieces, and other lesser dramatic forms in addition to Italian opera and legitimate drama.[12] In effect he chose to pander to the lower reaches of public taste in order to finance his ambitious projects. It is to his credit that he insisted upon presenting quality theater, even at the risk of financial loss, in addition to the more remunerative popular productions.

There is no doubt that the people of New Orleans appreciated the efforts of James H. Caldwell in establishing the new theater; it was the showplace of the city. On February 19, 1837, they got the oppor-

10. Tasistro, *Random Shots*, I, 61, 67. Tasistro also wrote of the "grandeur of effect arising from every part of the house. . . ." Francis Courtney Wemyss, theater manager and early chronicler of the American stage, declared that the St. Charles was "a Temple worthy of the drama in this land of liberty, a Theatre surpassing in elegance any thing of the same description in England, France, Naples, or Russia. . . ." Francis Courtney Wemyss, *Wemyss' Chronology of the American Stage, from 1752 to 1852* (New York: William Taylor and Company, 1852), p. 36. The *New York Spirit of the Times*, Oct. 21, 1837, complained that New York needed just one theater of the pretensions of the St. Charles rather than the existing "half a dozen or more brick bandboxes, by courtesy yclept theatres."

11. *New Orleans Picayune*, May 20, 1838. James Simon Rowe, the other Camp Street lessee, had died in Nashville in 1835.

12. *New Orleans Bee*, June 7, 1836.

tunity to demonstrate their esteem. On that night, the manager terminated his acting career in a farewell benefit. His operations were too diffuse and demanding to permit frequent appearances with his stock company. The *Picayune* covered the program. "MR. JAMES H. CALDWELL took his farewell benefit and leave of the stage last evening," declared the account, "and was greeted by one of the most brilliant, fashionable and the fullest house we have ever seen in our lives."[13] The occasion was "peculiarly grand" but also rather melancholy—"to see the founder of the drama in the South-West—the man who has done so much, who has appropriated thousands for its support—" take his leave of the stage. But this time the retirement was real. Thereafter Caldwell performed only on rare occasions for charity or other special benefits.

Of course Caldwell continued in theater operation. Following the death of Richard Russell on May 19, 1838, his competitive position in New Orleans measurably improved. The able entrepreneur quickly picked up the Camp Street lease and contracted with actor George Barrett to manage the old playhouse for him, but Caldwell maintained control over policy at the Camp. In effect he again had a monopoly of English-language theater in New Orleans.[14] He used his position to good effect. Both houses were operated with strong stock companies and occasional top stars, featuring standard repertory plays and ballad operas, and indeed, the Camp held its own with the grand St. Charles. The *Bee* of October 31, 1838, noted: "The St. Charles and Camp are striving with generous rivalry to outvie each other . . . but as yet, the little Camp excels its huge competitor."[15] It is doubtful that the wily manager was distressed by the strength of his "competitor."

In 1839 Caldwell closed the Camp as a theater and rented it to one James Forster for use as a public ballroom. But within a month the *Picayune* printed an allegation that "the Camp Street Theatre

13. *New Orleans Picayune*, Feb. 20, 1837.

14. Hostetler, "Caldwell," pp. 382–83.

15. Naturally Caldwell did not publicize his connection with the Camp, and both houses were provided with stars of about equal consequence. For example, in the winter of 1838–1839 the St. Charles offered Joseph M. Field, John R. Scott, Josephine Clifton, Henry J. Finn, Ellen Tree, J. B. Booth, Celeste, Forrest, and the Ravels, while the Camp featured Dan Marble, Forrest, Booth, Tree, Clifton, and Scott. The less prestigious Camp, however, also offered James Porter, the "Kentucky Giant," Miss Sutor, the "German Dwarf," and Major Stevens, the "American Dwarf."

Ball Room is the resort of improper and disorderly persons. . . ."[16]
On the recommendation of the Police Committee, the ballroom was
closed and used only occasionally thereafter for plays. During the
summer of 1840 it was converted into a Merchant's Exchange, and
in 1842 it burned to the ground.

The restoration of a theatrical monopoly placed the St. Charles
in an enviable position. Toward the end of the 1840 season, when the
depression had taken such heavy toll on theater operations nationally,
Caldwell was operating at a profit. As the *Picayune* observed, "the
only manager of any theatre of note in the country, that made money
during the past winter, was Mr. Caldwell. The St. Charles did a good
business all winter."[17] So by 1840 manager Caldwell was ensconced
in his grand playhouse, with a monopoly on English drama in the
Crescent City. Doubtless he felt secure.

2.

While Caldwell was consolidating his position in New Orleans,
theatrical affairs upriver in St. Louis were in the able hands of co-
partners Ludlow and Smith. They operated the St. Louis theater
during the summer and early fall of each year, spending the winter
with their troupe in Mobile.[18] From the outset of their partnership
the veteran actor-managers had been recognized nationally as a
theatrical concern of consequence. As early as 1837 the *New York
Spirit of the Times* had advised local actors and actresses not to be
in any hurry to join a New York company. "Sol. Smith, Esq., is daily
expected in town," announced the *Spirit* on one occasion, "to make
engagements with stars and clever people generally, for his theatres
at Mobile and St. Louis. Ludlow & Smith pay capital salaries. A
word to the wise, etc."[19] Provincial managers receiving such attention
from the metropolitan press were rare indeed.

In 1837 the co-managers further strengthened their position in St.
Louis by opening a new playhouse there—the first real theater west

16. *New Orleans Picayune*, Jan. 15, 1840. In June of 1840 Sol Smith referred
to the incident as "that 'Whorehouse Ball' business" and suggested that it cost
Caldwell his election as alderman. Solomon Franklin Smith to Noah Miller Ludlow, June 3, 1840, Smith Collection, Missouri Historical Society.
17. *New Orleans Picayune*, July 24, 1840.
18. Ludlow, *Dramatic Life*, pp. 511–12.
19. *New York Spirit of the Times*, June 24, 1837.

of the Mississippi River.[20] Like most theaters of the period, it was financed by public subscription[21] and constructed under the close supervision of the co-managers, who already had the lease on it. On July 3, 1837, the new playhouse, located on the southeast corner of Third and Olive streets, had its grand opening, with the perennial favorite, John Tobin's *Honey Moon*, as the opening-night attraction. St. Louis' own Joseph M. Field recited the inevitable dedicatory address, written for the occasion by Edward Johnson of Greensburg, Pennsylvania. Addressing "Thespis," the "goddess bless'd," Field dedicated "This, thy *first* temple in the far, far, West!"[22]

It is evident that the St. Louis populace was proud of their new theater. A local correspondent in the *Spirit* wrote shortly after its opening that "the most magnificent Theatre in the whole Mississippi Valley, (the St. Charles alone excepted), is now in operation in this city."[23] An outsider, the journeyman plasterer-stonemason Henry B. Miller, was also impressed with the playhouse. It was, declared Miller in his journal, "quite a respectable theatre; the building is about 150 feet by 80, with two tiers of boxes & gallery; the Pit . . . is fitted up in better stile [*sic*] than we mostly see in the Eastern cities. . . ."[24] He was particularly impressed with the fact that even in the pit every patron had a separate seat rather than mere benches. The house would hold, Miller believed, "from 12 to 1500 persons without much inconvenience." The interior, he continued, "presents quite a neat appearance; the principal ceiling is canvassed with paintings of the Muses. In the front part of the house on the 3d story (over the offices) is the Gentlemans Saloon; this is a very fine room; it extends the whole width of the building. . . ."[25]

20. Carson, *St. Louis Stage*, p. 180.

21. Ludlow and Smith Stock Subscription Books, 1835–1837, Missouri Historical Society. Among the subscribers were many of the leading citizens of the town, including Colonel Meriwether Lewis Clark, William Preston Clark, Colonel Charles Keemle, Augustin Kennerly, and others. Ludlow and Smith agreed to retire 10 per cent of the total subscription annually, so that in ten years they would own the building outright.

22. Hutton and Carey, *Addresses*, p. 67.

23. *New York Spirit of the Times*, July 22, 1837.

24. Thomas Maitland Marshall (ed.), "The Journal of Henry B. Miller," *Missouri Historical Society Collections*, III (1931), 254. Ludlow and Smith were obviously trying to remove the pit as a source of disturbance. The new type of seats plus the $1.00 admission price to the pit indicate an attempt to upgrade a traditionally unruly part of the house. See Playbill, St. Louis Theater, July 4, 1837, Harvard Theater Collection, Harvard College Library.

25. Marshall, "Miller Journal," p. 254.

Ludlow added two noteworthy items in his description of the new house. First, as it was designed for use as a summer theater, it "was constructed with a number of very large windows on each side. . . ."[26] And, in addition to the men's saloon described by Miller, there was also a "ladies' retiring-room . . . furnished with refreshments and conveniences suited to such visitors."[27] Both concessions were, however, closed before the end of the first season—the ladies' because no one frequented it; the men's because it was the source of considerable rowdyism and other turmoil.[28] Abolition of the saloon was a reform the partners carried out eventually in all of their theaters, no doubt considerably reducing disturbances so often caused by inebriates in the theaters of the period.

But what sort of town was St. Louis in 1837 when the new playhouse opened? The observant Henry Miller left a good description. Among the notable public buildings of the city were, in addition to the theater, a court house and jail, two "market houses," a convent, a college (St. Louis University), St. Louis Charity Hospital, eight churches, and two orphan asylums, one Catholic and one Protestant.[29] The National Hotel on the corner of Market and Third streets was the best in town, but there were three others of lesser quality.[30] The two "Public School houses" had been operating only a short while.

But in addition to the institutions of public service in the town, there were also scores of public institutions of a headier sort that clearly bespeak St. Louis' proximity to the frontier. Miller reported that by actual count there were 250 "houses" dispensing liquor by the drink, plus two distilleries and four breweries. "In addition to these," wrote Miller, "there are constantly at our Wharf about 20 Steam Boats, nearly all of which have Bars aboard."[31] Most of the pubs were also "Gambleing [*sic*] houses," many of which were "of the worst kind where Cardes, Dice, and Bagatelles" prevailed. On the outskirts of town were at least twenty "Ten Pin Alleys," all selling liquor and many of which continually had "a number of Black Legs

26. Ludlow, *Dramatic Life,* pp. 477–78.
27. *Ibid.,* p. 478.
28. The ability of Ludlow and Smith to close the saloon yet remain in business is an important indication of a maturing frontier theater.
29. Marshall, "Miller Journal," p. 250.
30. *Ibid.,* p. 253. The famous Planters' Hotel was then (1838) under construction.
31. *Ibid.,* p. 270.

prowling round. . . ." The various "sports" were "constantly played . . . particularly on Sabbath days, when most of the mechanics have some money to spend. . . ."[32]

The total population of St. Louis was given by the *Evening Gazette* in 1839 as 16,207, of which 13,500 were free.[33] But as was usually the case, it was in large measure the transients who supported the theater. "It is plain enough," Sol Smith wrote his partner, "that the receipts [of the theater] vary according to the *arrival* and *departure* of the boats—and it is not the citizens who support the Theatre when it is supported."[34] Still, the population including transients was large enough and, as the Miller account indicates, the populace sufficiently fun loving to support an annual summer-fall theater season. As Smith recalled, "our first season in the new theatre was moderately successful."[35]

It is certain that the St. Louis public was interested in theatrical affairs from the time their new house opened. On July 28, 1837, the *Missouri Republican* complained of the number of letters the editor had received dealing with the theater. "Gentlemen, just stand back and give us room!" sounded the *Republican*. "We have now on our table, nine communications on the subject of the Theatre, all sent to us within the two days last past. . . ."[36] When two favorite actresses of the company, Eliza Riddle and Eliza Petrie, took their benefits toward the end of the first season, they were both honored with gifts of jewelry by an admiring public. Miss Petrie, for example, was given "a full set of pearl diamond jewelry [*sic*] which were provided for the occasion by the young gentlemen of the city."[37]

The *Spirit of the Times* had occasion to speak of St. Louis theatrical affairs early in the second season of operations in the new theater. Ludlow and Smith, declared the *Spirit* in June of 1831, "seem determined to keep their beautiful theatre in the very front rank of the best establishments in the Union. Ellen Tree speaks in

32. *Ibid.*, p. 271.

33. Carson, *St. Louis Stage*, p. 264, quoting *St. Louis Daily Evening Gazette*, April 23, 1839.

34. Solomon Franklin Smith to Noah Miller Ludlow, March 24–26, 1838, Ludlow-Field-Maury Collection, Missouri Historical Society. Smith had a habit of writing a letter to his partner over a period of several days, hence the odd dating here cited.

35. Smith, *Theatrical Management*, p. 131

36. The letters were described as "a compound of eulogies, complaints, admirations and approvals. . . ."

37. *St. Louis Missouri Republican*, Oct. 25, 1837.

raptures of the handsome manner in which she was treated by the public and the managers—to say nothing of the three or four thousand *solid* reasons she has to be pleased with her visit."[38] By the end of the second season the *Missouri Republican* was calling upon the public to demonstrate "some expression of *marked respect*" for the "worthy managers." "As men of respectability," remarked the editor, "as attentive managers and as citizens, these gentlemen have claims upon this community." He called for a handsome end-of-season benefit for the partners. "Let us give them a *bumper*," the editor concluded his appeal, "one which will be flattering to their feelings and an honor to St. Louis—one which will awaken in them new incentives for future exertions."[39]

A good benefit would have been most welcome to Ludlow and Smith at that juncture. As 1840 approached, the effects of the Panic of 1837 began to be felt in St. Louis. As Ludlow recalled, the "money crisis which had commenced in the Eastern States a year or two before had now reached the West, and the people, becoming alarmed and panic-stricken, had been drawing tight their purse-strings."[40] But in addition to the encroaching depression, Ludlow and Smith had other problems. Their failure to close the St. Louis theater before December 11, 1839, indicated trouble at the other end of their theatrical nexus—in Mobile, Alabama.

3.

Since the beginning of their partnership on November 9, 1835, Ludlow and Smith had controlled the theatrical fortunes of Mobile, the booming Alabama port that served the entirety of the rich cotton land drained by the Alabama and Tombigbee rivers.[41] Each year, upon closing in St. Louis, usually about the time of the first frost (Mobile was of course a notorious fever town), one or both partners would take the company downriver to New Orleans and thence to

38. *New York Spirit of the Times*, June 16, 1838. Ellen Tree was a British actress of great renown and later the wife of Charles Kean, with whom she frequently performed. Her St. Louis engagement had commenced April 13, 1838, lasted fourteen nights, and paid her $2661.93. See Solomon Franklin Smith to Noah Miller Ludlow, April 21, 23, 1838, Ludlow-Field-Maury Collection, Missouri Historical Society.

39. Dec. 11, 1839.

40. Ludlow, *Dramatic Life*, pp. 529–30.

41. The aggregate population of Mobile more than quadrupled between 1830 and 1840, jumping from 3,194 to 12,672. U. S. Census Office, *Social Statistics*, p. 191.

the Alabama port to open the winter season. Their efforts in Mobile had again attracted the attention of New York; the *Spirit* commented on one occasion that the Mobile populace formed "the most liberal community [for the encouragement of] . . . the drama of, perhaps, any in the union."[42] But beginning in 1838 Ludlow and Smith experienced an almost incredible run of bad luck and were forced by circumstances to take steps that were to prove of major significance in the history of professional theater in the Mississippi Valley.

At three o'clock on the morning of November 21, 1838, the old St. Emmanuel Street Theater, which Ludlow and Smith had just recently opened for the season, burned to the ground, along with all scenery, costumes, and properties. As the *New Orleans True American* observed, "not even a wig [was] saved."[43] The partners were desperate. Their whole company was dependent upon them for their means of subsistence, as new season contracts would be difficult to secure so late in the year. Smith rushed to New Orleans to try to buy new supplies while Ludlow proceeded to rent a small theater on Government Street, built and abandoned the year before by Louis Ferry, an ephemeral strolling manager.[44]

Smith contacted Caldwell, offering to buy anything the New Orleans manager could spare, but as he might have expected, his rival refused to sell anything at all.[45] Fortunately for the hard-pressed Smith, the wardrobe of Richard Russell, who had died some six months before, was for sale, and despite its somewhat shabby condition, Smith bought it all. By December 1, 1838, just eleven days after the fire, the resourceful co-managers were again operating in Mobile.[46] On December 29, the *Spirit of the Times* announced that the "company of Messrs. Ludlow & Smith," which would "compare advantageously with any in the Union," was "now in the full tide of success."[47]

42. *New York Spirit of the Times*, Sept. 24, 1842.

43. Hostetler, "Caldwell," p. 444, quoting *New Orleans True American*, Nov. 23, 1838. The theater was not insured, not, as Ludlow pointed out, because of negligence, but because "none of the insurance offices in Mobile would take a risk on theatres, on any terms"; *Dramatic Life*, p. 508.

44. Ludlow, *Dramatic Life*, p. 508.

45. Solomon Franklin Smith to Noah Miller Ludlow, Nov. 24, 1838, Smith Collection, Missouri Historical Society; *New Orleans Picayune*, Nov. 30, 1838. Caldwell insisted he could spare nothing.

46. Ludlow, *Dramatic Life*, p. 508.

47. The *Spirit* also mentioned that work on a new theater for Mobile would commence the following March.

The Mobile season of 1838–1839 at the Government Street Theater must rank in excellence with any in the ante bellum period. On November 10, 1838, the theater opened with a program of three farces, and stock productions continued nightly (six nights a week) until the arrival of the first star, William C. Forbes, on November 5.[48] Following the Forbes engagement, the stars came in rapid succession; among them were the greatest talents of the English-speaking stage. December 11 brought Mary Vos Stuart, a former member of the Ludlow-Smith stock and a popular romantic actress. Next came Dan Marble, the Yankee comedian, who was followed by the noted tragedienne Josephine Clifton.

Presumably to attain balance in their programing the managers next brought in "Mr. Waterman's Stud of Horses" for an engagement that included all the favorite equestrian pieces. February of 1838 brought Ellen Tree back to Mobile for another of her great successes. But no sooner had she departed than Edwin Forrest arrived to open an engagement in *Othello*. On March 6, 1839, Forrest took his benefit; on March 7 Junius Brutus Booth opened with Massinger's *New Way to Pay Old Debts*. Booth performed nightly for over a week[49] and was followed by the young Irish comedian-violinist "Master" Joseph Burke; then came an acrobatic troupe calling themselves the Bedouin Arabs.[50] On April 8, the season climaxed with the appearance of "Madame" Céline Céleste, the French ballerina-actress, who added yet another American city to her long list of conquests. The colorful season did not end until May 3, 1839, when Governor Arthur Pendleton Bagby entertained General Sam Houston and suite at the theater, contributing substantially to the benefit of Vincent De Camp. Without a doubt, it was the finest theater season offered in Mobile in the ante bellum period.

The theater had become a prominent concomitant of the Mobile social season. On March 2, 1830, a group of the city's notables (along

48. Bailey, "Mobile Stage," p. 235. The discussion of this season is based on performance data provided in this study, pp. 235–51. See also Ludlow, *Dramatic Life*, pp. 509–10.

49. According to Ludlow, Booth "got into one of his insane or drunken frolics (call it which you please), and ruined the engagement." Ludlow, *Dramatic Life*, p. 509. The unstable Booth was always a potential liability to managers of the time.

50. Ludlow wrote that they "literally jumped into the good graces of the public . . ."; *Dramatic Life*, p. 510.

with a few interested outsiders) presented Ludlow and Smith with a signed subscription list pledging funds for the building of a new theater. "The undersigned," began the proposal, "are desirous of having a large and commodious Theatre in the City of Mobile. With the view of aiding in the erection of such a building, we, by this instrument bind ourselves . . . to loan unto Messrs. Ludlow and Smith, Managers of the present Theatre, the sum, or sums opposite to our names. . . ."[51] Leading off the list of signers was Edwin Forrest, who pledged $3,000 toward the new playhouse.[52]

The summer and fall of 1839, however, brought calamitous times, not only to Ludlow and Smith but to all of Mobile. The summer months saw one of the most severe yellow fever epidemics in the history of the fever-ridden port. And on October 7, 1839, a devastating fire swept the city, destroying fully one-third of its occupied area, including the Government Street playhouse in which Ludlow and Smith were about to open the fall season.[53] Smith, still in St. Louis with the company, was forced to continue operations there in spite of weather, which was growing ever colder.

The co-managers once again proved resilient. By New Year's Eve 1839, they had prepared a serviceable if makeshift playhouse to receive the troupe, and that night they opened the season.[54] But the troubles of the managers were by no means over in Mobile. In the first place, disaster and depression began taking a serious toll on theater revenues. Then, the new theater, the State Street or "Swamp" Theater, was located rather remote from the center of town; as Smith recalled it "away up in the 'Orange Grove,' among the cotton warehouses. . . ."[55] Finally, Ludlow and Smith confronted serious competition in Mobile. William Chapman, the famous showboat manager, offered a season of some six weeks at another makeshift playhouse, the "Alhambra," thus reducing the patronage of the co-

51. Proposal and Subscription List for the New Mobile Theatre, March 2, 1839, in Ludlow-Field-Maury Collection, Missouri Historical Society.

52. Other names on the list pledging amounts of $500 to $1,000 were Richard Corré, George Davis Jr., Jacob Baptist, and Joseph Bogereau, all leaders of Mobile society.

53. *New Orleans Bee*, Oct. 11, 1839. The fire was one of a series of conflagrations presumed to be the work of "abolition agents and their misguided and thoughtless tools." On Oct. 12, the *Bee* announced that "our esteemed fellow-citizen" James H. Caldwell had offered a benefit for the fire sufferers.

54. *Mobile Commercial Register and Patriot*, Dec. 31, 1839.

55. Smith, *Theatrical Management*, p. 144.

managers.[56] In January the *Commercial Register* observed: "Our citizens do not seem to be aware that there is a very agreeable entertainment at the New Theatre; corner of Magnolia and State Streets," and implored that the public "see the play tonight, where Messrs. Ludlow and Smith will be very happy to see you."[57] The plea was to no avail. On March 19 Smith entered in his diary, "we are nightly adding to our already heavy losses."[58] By March 28 they were forced to close the theater. So ended the season that Smith later recalled was "of all the seasons I ever had any thing to do with . . . the most unsuccessful. . . . The losses of the season's business," he added, "could not have been less than $1000 per week!"[59] The partnership had fallen on difficult times.

While Ludlow and Smith reeled from the successive blows of 1839 and 1840, their rival James H. Caldwell moved in to deal what he believed would be the finishing blow. Taking advantage of his rivals' adversities, Caldwell had managed to win local support in the construction and operation of the new Mobile theater. He acted quickly. On January 11, 1841, the new playhouse, the Royal Street Theater, opened for business, occupied by an adjunct of Caldwell's New Orleans stock under the acting management of Joe Cowell.[60] The *Advertiser and Chronicle* described Caldwell's projected *modus operandus*:

> In associating this establishment [the new Mobile theater] with the St. Charles Theatre, New Orleans, the Manager believes he meets the wishes of the public of Mobile, as it will

56. Tasistro, *Random Shots*, I, 224–25. Tasistro performed with Chapman at the Alhambra, which he described as "an oblong room, situated over a drinking establishment of that name, temporarily fitted up for dramatic representation." But he was well received in Mobile society and enjoyed his visit there.

57. *Mobile Commercial Register and Patriot*, Jan. 15, 1840.

58. Smith MS Diary, March 19, 1840, Smith Collection, Missouri Historical Society.

59. Smith, *Theatrical Management*, p. 146. Smith recalled as the low point in his career the night during this season that the company played a five-act tragedy to "the bare walls, two or three bar-keepers, a dozen deadheads, and one paying auditor," who, incidentally, did not understand a word of English. *Ibid.*, p. 147. Ludlow vehemently denies that the season's losses were this heavy. Ludlow, *Dramatic Life*, p. 517.

60. *Mobile Commercial Register and Patriot*, Jan. 12, 1841; Clipping, *Mobile Daily Advertiser and Chronicle*, Jan. 11, 1841, reprinted in Coad and Mims, *American Stage*, p. 161. The prize poetic address for the occasion was written by Matthew C. Field, within a month to become Ludlow's son-in-law.

in future enable him to make arrangements with distinguished Performers to appear in both Theatres; and the
prominent members of the respective establishments [stock
companies] will be afforded an opportunity during the season of exercising their various talents in the two cities.[61]

The aggressive Caldwell obviously believed that he had finally disposed of his irritating adversaries. He knew full well that two theaters could not operate profitably in Mobile and that in any
competition his capital advantage would force Ludlow and
Smith out.

The theater that Caldwell built for Mobile was a worthy sibling
of the great St. Charles, or so the description in the *Spirit of the
Times* would indicate. Fronted by Doric pilasters, the entrance consisted of five arched doorways leading to a vestibule, which in turn
opened into the pit and parquet of the house. The interior of the
auditorium was, like that of the St. Charles, semicircular rather than
elliptical in shape, and there were three tiers and the inevitable gallery surrounding the pit area. Two saloons served refreshments to
the playgoers, 1,878 of whom formed a capacity audience. Naturally
the entire house was "brilliantly lighted with gas. . . ." The "form
and size" of the playhouse, concluded the *Spirit* description, "makes
[*sic*] it one of the most suitable theatres in the Union for the perfect
enjoyment of a play."[62] The new house quickly became a popular
resort of Mobile society. "Our theatre continues to attract and please,"
declared the *Commercial Register* on November 11, 1841. "The dress
circle is better suited to receive our lovely belles and dames, our
dashing beaus and intelligent citizens, than that of any Theatre we
have seen in the South."[63] Caldwell, it seemed, had won Mobile.

But Ludlow and Smith were not ready to be counted out. To the
acute irritation of James H. Caldwell, they had opened the Swamp
Theater in February, 1841, quite prepared to do battle. Moreover,
they brought out big guns—most notably the phenomenally popular
singer-soubrette Fanny Fitzwilliam, who drew so well that Caldwell,

61. *Mobile Daily Advertiser and Chronicle*, Jan. 11, 1841, reprinted in Coad
and Mims, *American Stage*, p. 161.
62. *New York Spirit of the Times*, Jan. 30, 1841.
63. Tasistro agreed. Even in the "stormiest weather," he wrote, "the boxes
have been filled with the beauty and fashion of the Place. Mobile is decidedly
the most essentially theatrical town in the whole Southern Hemisphere"; *Random
Shots*, I, 251.

to offset her engagement, came out of retirement to perform some of his favorite roles.[64] He was well received, but Ludlow and Smith's brief Mobile season cut deeply into his profits.

The partners, however, failed to open their Mobile playhouse for the 1841–1842 season, nor did they return for the season that followed. Their attentions were diverted elsewhere. The Caldwell troupe appeared both seasons, first with a Caldwell-appointed acting manager, then under the auspices of two local impresarios, the more active of whom was publican Jules Dumas.[65] But during the summer of 1843 Ludlow negotiated an important contract with Caldwell. The firm of Ludlow and Smith leased his Royal Street Theater in Mobile.[66] On July 2, 1843, Sol Smith noted in his diary that he and his partner were "about returning to Mobile as managers of Caldwell's Theatre there, under a lease from him—Caldwell retired from management!!"[67]

4.

The struggle in Mobile between the firm of Ludlow and Smith and James H. Caldwell was only a skirmish; the main battle took place in New Orleans. In 1840, the co-managers had extended their operation to the Crescent City. Whether their decision to do so was motivated by Caldwell's move to break their effective monopoly in Mobile is the subject of some controversy—Caldwell's biographer denies that the New Orleans manager wanted to ruin his rivals despite the published contentions of both co-managers to the contrary.[68] A Smith diary entry for August 20, 1840, would seem to settle the matter and also to reveal something of Caldwell's nature: "Two years ago," wrote Smith,

64. Hostetler, "Caldwell," p. 490. Three roles were particularly identified with Caldwell throughout his career: Vapid in Frederick Reynolds's comedy *The Dramatist,* Belcour in *The West Indian* by Richard Cumberland, and Duke Aranza in Tobin's ever-popular *Honey Moon.*

65. Cowell, *Thirty Years,* p. 98. According to Cowell, Dumas the saloon-keeper regained most of the money from the actors that Dumas the manager paid them.

66. Ludlow MS Diary, July 8, 1843, Ludlow-Field-Maury Collection, Missouri Historical Society.

67. Smith MS Diary, July 2, 1843, Smith Collection, Missouri Historical Society.

68. Hostetler, "Caldwell," p. 452; Ludlow, *Dramatic Life,* p. 520; Smith, *Theatrical Management,* p. 154.

James H. Caldwell threatened to build a theatre in Mobile, unless we [Ludlow and Smith] permitted him to *control* our establishment. I very quickly told him we would submit to no control—and as for his building a Theatre in Mobile, he of course could do so as soon as he pleased; but that the very moment he made this attempt *we should establish ourselves in New Orleans!* This Spring he *did make the attempt, and we have a Theatre two-thirds finished in Poydras street, within a Stones throw of the St. Charles.*[69]

It is apparent that Caldwell, ever the rapacious entrepreneur, had been, as Ludlow contended, trying to force both Ludlow and Smith out of business since their paths had first crossed in 1824.[70]

Both partners contend in their memoirs that it was Caldwell's encroachment upon their Mobile domain that sent Smith to New Orleans in search of a theater in June of 1840. Two theaters could not possibly survive in competition in a town the size of Mobile, but perhaps in New Orleans they could. When Smith found a near-finished building on Poydras Street, designed as a stable and circus arena, he leased it at once from its owner, the construction firm of DuBois and Kendig.[71] With but a few alterations the large structure made a "tolerably commodious" playhouse.[72]

Ludlow and Smith opened their "New American Theater" on November 10, 1840. Its distinguishing feature was its "Grand Equestrian Circle"—a ring in front of the stage (and connected to it) in which the various horse dramas could be presented. It was a scheme that Ludlow felt would draw well, as in fact it did.[73] The pit of the theater surrounded the ring on three sides, and the ring itself had a convertible feature: it could be quickly floored over for additional seating capacity when the horses were not to perform.

69. Smith MS Diary, Aug. 20, 1840, Smith Collection, Missouri Historical Society. Smith had attempted to obtain the lease on Caldwell's Camp Street Theater in June of 1840, but Caldwell had chosen to convert the building into an exchange rather than lease it to an opposition manager. Solomon Franklin Smith to Noah Miller Ludlow, June 9, 1840, Smith Collection, Missouri Historical Society.

70. Ludlow, *Dramatic Life*, p. 520.

71. Smith, *Theatrical Management*, p. 154; Ludlow, *Dramatic Life*, pp. 522–23.

72. Smith, *Theatrical Management*, p. 154.

73. Ludlow, *Dramatic Life*, p. 524. Ludlow recalled that the equestrian corps employed under "equestrian director" John Robinson was led by two fine horses, one named Ludlow, the other Smith.

Choice seats were to be had in the three tiers of boxes that rose behind the pit.[74]

The opening-night audience was both large and enthusiastic. Ludlow later recalled: "I doubt if ever an audience went out of a theatre more pleased with what they had seen and heard."[75] In a month, the new theater was enjoying the enthusiastic support of the New Orleans public. "Not only the people," declared the *Picayune*, "but the press of the city, with a warmth and candor which is as creditable as it is scarce, have stepped forward yielding patronage and praise to the new establishment. . . ."[76] In January of 1841 the *Bee* commended "the hearty good will with which every member of the establishment undertakes the business of the stage."[77] The new managers also gained considerable praise for the absence of "unruly conduct" in their theater, even in the "upper parts of the house."[78] In short, Ludlow and Smith from the outset afforded Caldwell and the St. Charles real competition.

Indeed, it seems that with their fine stock, both human and equine, their well-ordered house, and their popular productions of horse opera and lighter drama, the new managers were outdrawing the old entrepreneur. When, in an effort to recoup some of his losses, Caldwell brought in the phenomenal Fanny Elssler in March of 1841, Ludlow and Smith successfully countered with the equally popular Fanny Fitzwilliam, who burlesqued Elssler in an outrageous burletta appropriately called *Foreign Airs and Native Graces*.[79] "Fanny Fitzwilliam . . . is cramming the American every night," wrote Smith to a friend, "and throwing from 900 to 1000 people into fits (of laughter), and causing them to forget the hard times, short crops, and every thing else of a disagreeable nature."[80] And though

74. For a complete description of the New American see *New Orleans Picayune*, Nov. 6, 1840. As was required by custom, the house was fronted by columns, in this case Doric, and featured a "grand saloon," other saloons (three), and an elaborately decorated interior. The interior design was by Antonio Mondelli, who also designed the St. Charles.

75. *Dramatic Life*, p. 532. The featured attraction of the evening was a stock production of *Honey Moon*.

76. *New Orleans Picayune*, Dec. 19, 1840.

77. *New Orleans Bee*, Jan. 18, 1841.

78. *New Orleans Picayune*, Jan. 19, 1841.

79. Ludlow, *Dramatic Life*, p. 536.

80. Smith, *Theatrical Management*, p. 155, quoting letter to Edward Woolf, Feb. 7, 1841.

Elssler drew crowds to the St. Charles, her guarantee of $1,000 a night left little profit for the hard-pressed Caldwell.[81]

So disastrous was the season for manager Caldwell that he was forced to sell his St. Charles property. Heavily in debt, he made the sale to the New Orleans Gas Light and Banking Company, with an option to repurchase it in three years. He then leased the property and used most of the proceeds from the sale to retire outstanding debts.[82] By contrast, Ludlow and Smith realized a net profit of $20,000 for the season.[83]

One key factor in explaining the failure of Caldwell and the success of his rivals was the popularity of the horses. When the equestrian corps returned to New Orleans following a brief stint in Mobile, the press welcomed them back. "The taste for this amendment [the ring show] is by no means weary," noted the *Picayune*, "and the skilful success of change kept up by the management is admirably in union with public feeling. Let the horses run as long as the people want them, and when business grows slack, slack the reins and trot out the drama again."[84] In order to compete, Caldwell felt it necessary to bring out the horses himself in the fall of 1841. Consequently he employed a troupe of equestrians to perform at the St. Charles. "Only to think," moaned the *Spirit of the Times*, "that the sacred boards of the *Temple*, which had been trodden by the Divine Fanny [Elssler] and which had been consecrated for the sole use of biped representatives of the 'legitimate,' should be desecrated by illegitimate quadrupeds."[85] Sol Smith, however, was delighted with the deflation of Caldwell's pretensions.[86]

The whole matter of the horses seemingly bespeaks a sudden decline in the theatrical taste of the Orleanians. Such in fact was not the case. As long as Caldwell had a theatrical monopoly in New Orleans, he could, within reason, offer what he pleased at the Temple, and the public had to accept it or do without. With the advent of

81. *Ibid.*
82. Hostetler, "Caldwell," p. 498–99. Caldwell never regained possession of the theater.
83. Ludlow, *Dramatic Life*, p. 543.
84. *New Orleans Picayune*, March 30, 1841.
85. *New York Spirit of the Times*, Nov. 6, 1841. The *Dramatic Mirror* had bemoaned the decision even earlier. *Dramatic Mirror and Literary Companion*, Aug. 14, 1841.
86. See Smith, *Theatrical Management*, p. 161.

Ludlow and Smith, however, offering light, escapist entertainment, the public acquired a choice and opted for horses. There was no sudden decline in taste; there had never been a general desire for art theater in New Orleans. Caldwell was forced to forego his standards in order to stay in business. There are obvious parallels in the history of the various entertainment media both before his time and after.

The degradation of the Temple was not to endure long. On March 13, 1842, the grand theater was completely gutted by fire.[87] Matthew C. Field, the *Picayune's* poet "Phazma," commemorated the loss felt by all theater people (and many non-theater people as well) with a verse:

> In silent eloquence the painful story
> Those broken walls and smouldering ruins tell—
> Closing in flame an envied reign of glory,
> How the great TEMPLE OF THE DRAMA fell![88]

The entire city had suffered a real loss in the destruction of the "Boast of the sunny south!—pride of the western land!"[89] Caldwell's company disbanded; several members received benefits at the New American in the next few weeks, though Caldwell imperiously refused a proffered benefit for himself.[90] The immediate reaction of the manager was determination to rebuild his showpiece theater "upon a scale quite commensurate with its former magnificence...."[91]

Ludlow and Smith closed the New American on May 24, 1842, and departed for their summer season in St. Louis. On May 27, the *Picayune* issued a plaintive cry for some form of amusement in New Orleans: "The American Theatre is closed—the St. Charles is burned down—" declared the editor. "What are we going to do for amusement? . . . We are dying for something. Will somebody send us along an organ grinder?"

But the summer brought no relief from the famine in commercial

87. *New Orleans Bee,* March 14, 1842.
88. "Phazma" [Matthew C. Field], "Burning of the St. Charles," *New Orleans Picayune,* March 23, 1842.
89. *Ibid.*
90. See Smith, *Theatrical Management,* p. 165, for the offer and the refusal. Although the New Orleans Gas Light and Banking Company was the real loser on the building (it was underinsured), Caldwell's personal losses in scenery and interior fittings have been estimated at $70,000. Hostetler, "Caldwell," p. 515.
91. *New Orleans Picayune,* March 17, 1842.

amusements. Instead, on July 30, 1842, the New American Theater was also consumed by fire, the victim of yet another incendiary. "Our other theatre is gone," sounded the *Picayune*, "and the Second Municipality is now without a home for the drama."[92] Ludlow and Smith, like Caldwell before them, suffered a total loss in the expensive scenery and properties stored in the theater. And like Caldwell, they were determined to rebuild as quickly as possible. They received the assurance of owners DuBois and Kendig that work on the rebuilding would commence immediately.[93]

But Ludlow and Smith were not to get the lease on the rebuilt playhouse. Caldwell had decided that he could open sooner and far more cheaply if he took the lease from DuBois and Kendig rather than rebuild the St. Charles. He also knew that Ludlow and Smith were in arrears on their rent due the owners. So, presenting himself as the better risk, he won the lease.[94] If, however, Caldwell thought he had at last driven Ludlow and Smith out (as he certainly wanted to do) he underestimated his adversaries. When Smith arrived in the Crescent City and found Caldwell in possession of the near-complete New American, he quickly moved to lease the old St. Charles property from the Gas Bank, at the same time borrowing sufficient capital to begin work on a New St. Charles Theater.[95] Having accomplished this maneuver, Smith addressed his diary, with obvious satisfaction: "As Caldwell has got our stand, it appears very proper we should take *his*."[96] Within a matter of days work on the new theater had begun.

On December 5, 1842, Caldwell opened the New American, a house about the size of the Park in New York, with an interior, according to the *Picayune*, "more elegant in design than the architecture of the building would seem to allow. . . ."[97] The opening-night

92. *Ibid.*, July 31, 1842.
93. Ludlow, *Dramatic Life*, p. 551.
94. The last season had been profitless for Ludlow and Smith in New Orleans, largely due to the depression. They had been temporarily unable to meet their lease note of $10,000 but were certainly good for the sum, as DuBois and Kendig surely were aware. Both Ludlow and Smith considered Caldwell's act dastardly. Ludlow, *Dramatic Life*, p. 553; Smith MS Diary, Nov. 26, 1842, Smith Collection, Missouri Historical Society.
95. Smith MS Diary, Oct. 28, 1842, Smith Collection, Missouri Historical Society; *New Orleans Picayune*, Oct. 29, 1842; *New Orleans Bee*, Oct. 29, 1842.
96. Smith MS Diary, Oct. 25, 1842, Smith Collection, Missouri Historical Society.
97. *New Orleans Picayune*, Dec. 4, 1842.

program—Thomas Morton's *Speed the Plough* and the farce *The Hundred Pound Note*—seemed to indicate that Caldwell once again envisioned a completely legitimate theater for New Orleans.[98] But from the outset his receipts were poor. He blamed it on the times, which were indeed hard on theater managers. Moreover, James H. Caldwell had suffered a series of financial setbacks in months past and no longer had the capital accumulation to absorb the losses.[99] He could not continue the season. On January 8, 1843, he announced his pending retirement from management.[100] One week later the effective founder of the English-language theater in New Orleans appeared as Vapid in *The Dramatist*, for his farewell benefit. His new theater reopened on a commonwealth basis, under joint operation by the members of the stock, but it quickly failed.

Four days after Caldwell's farewell to the stage, on January 18, 1843, Ludlow and Smith opened their New St. Charles Theater on an obviously triumphant note. It is easy to imagine the satisfaction Smith felt as he made his diary entry for the day, concluding with the exclamation, "The work is achieved!"[101] Equally satisfying to the partners must have been their reception by the public. "The throng was great," observed the *Picayune*, "and the house well filled, . . . with a large number of ladies."[102] The program included Tobin's *Honey Moon*, with Ludlow himself as Duke Aranza and Smith as Jacques, the Mock Duke.[103] Although the New St. Charles could not compare with the old in size and splendor, it was well launched as New Orleans' most popular playhouse. A week after the opening it proved a fashionable resort as well when Governor Alexandre Mouton entertained his family and suite there on the occasion of his inaugural.[104]

The conquest of Caldwell by Noah Ludlow and Sol Smith gave the co-managers uncontested dominance over theatrical affairs in

98. *Ibid.*, Dec. 6, 1842.

99. Hostetler, "Caldwell," pp. 547–48.

100. *New Orleans Picayune*, Jan. 8, 1843.

101. Smith MS Diary, Jan. 18, 1843, Smith Collection, Missouri Historical Society.

102. *New Orleans Picayune*, Jan. 19, 1843. The immediate success of Ludlow and Smith gives credence to Ludlow's assertion that the New Orleans public had sided with the co-managers in the struggle with Caldwell. Each side had taken to the press to present its version of the contretemps, Ludlow and Smith in the *Picayune* of Oct. 25, 1842; Caldwell in the *Picayune* of Oct. 26, 1842.

103. *New Orleans Picayune*, Jan. 19, 1843.

104. Ludlow MS Diary, Jan. 18, 1843, Ludlow-Field-Maury Collection, Missouri Historical Society.

New Orleans, Mobile, and St. Louis, thus over the entire Mississippi Valley. In July of 1843, when Smith visited New York to recruit for the following season, the "Things Theatrical" column in the *Spirit of the Times* announced his arrival. Ludlow and Smith, declared the *Spirit*,

> have now under their direction three of the largest and most beautiful theatres in this country, and they feel disposed to offer the most liberal terms to talented members of the profession. To any "stars" that may meditate revolving or shooting about in our theatrical firmament, we commend the advantages offered by these managers, assuring all who may be unacquainted with them that they will find them always liberal, fair, and *paying* managers, as well as gentlemen and princely good fellows.[105]

And the stars apparently heeded the advice of the *Spirit*. For the season 1843–1844, the co-managers offered Mr. and Mrs. John Brougham, Henry Placide, James W. Wallack, William Charles Macready, James H. Hackett, Edwin Forrest, Mary Vos Stuart, Dan Marble, and Joshua S. Silsbee, among others.[106] Ludlow and Smith had lost no time in proving themselves worthy of command of the largest and most important theatrical province in the United States.

For ten years the co-managers maintained their dominant position among Southern theater managers. With an expanded stock company they offered winter seasons concurrently in Mobile and New Orleans; the summer and early fall found them in St. Louis and on tour. Ludlow had established his home in Mobile, so the senior partner usually handled most of the business there while Smith, a St. Louis resident, ordinarily administered the company's Missouri activities. The partners shared managerial duties in New Orleans, though Smith was more often on hand there; Ludlow's activity in Mobile kept him in Alabama during most of the winter. In all cases their affairs were managed with a competence born of long experience.

But in the early years of their valley domination, the partners had a difficult time financially. The depression did not lift in the West until the mid-1840's, and of course the theaters suffered. Moreover, the managers always faced competition from the constantly increasing number of non-dramatic or subdramatic entertainment forms,

105. *New York Spirit of the Times,* July 8, 1843.
106. Roppolo, "American Stage in New Orleans," pp. 50–57.

most notably circuses and minstrel shows. And of course there were always competing theatrical troupes, ephemeral but only too often present. Ludlow's diary entry for April 7, 1844 revealed an end-of-season situation typical for the early 1840's: "Well another season of hard toil and little profit is over. This season has just about paid all expenses, and allowed myself & partner, about as much as paid our family expenses. We paid about $2000.00 in old debts & left about $1475.00 unpaid of this season."[107]

In Mobile the managers never did find the financial success they believed the theater capable of providing there. Indeed, Ludlow recalled that the season of 1844–1845 as being "disastrous to the management."[108] But despite financial disaster the season that followed saw another brilliant array of stars, including the elder Booth, Dan Marble, and James H. Hackett, and joint engagements by Henry and Thomas Placide, Anna Cora Mowatt and William H. Crisp, and Charles and Ellen Kean.[109] This season Ludlow and Smith realized a profit in Mobile, the first in several years.[110] Still, the seasons that followed produced but small returns, despite the continuing effort of the managers to provide theater of consistently high quality.

A major problem in Mobile, perhaps even more important than the depression, was the quantity of competition and the relatively smaller population of the Alabama port. In 1848, Ludlow was forced to close the season in early January "for want of patronage," according to the *Advertiser*. "Whether the Managers expect to open again this season . . . we have not heard." If not they could hardly be blamed. "On Thursday night last," the editor declared, ". . . there were just *eighteen* persons at the theatre. The same night there were over TWO THOUSAND at Spaulding's Circus."[111] The situation was not unusual. When Ludlow and Smith chose not to return for the Mobile season of 1848–1849, no one was surprised.

Following the withdrawal of the co-managers from Mobile, the Royal Street Theater was occupied by lesser troupes under [Wil-

107. Ludlow MS Diary, April 7, 1844, Ludlow-Field-Maury Collection, Missouri Historical Society. Ludlow referred here to the Mobile season of 1843–1844. He listed the total receipts for twenty weeks as $30,073. Of that amount, $8,608 was paid out to stars; expenses, he estimated, were $1,000 a week. The estimate of expenses was clearly too high and probably included capital outlays for scenery, repairs, and wardrobe.

108. Ludlow, *Dramatic Life*, p. 617.

109. *Mobile Register and Journal*, Dec. 5, 13, 1845; Jan. 15, 19, Feb. 2, 6, March 2, 23, April 4, 1846.

110. Ludlow, *Dramatic Life*, p. 641.

111. *Mobile Daily Advertiser and Chronicle*, Jan. 5, 1848.

liam?] Deering in 1848–1849 and Robert L. Place of New Orleans in 1849–1850, both of whom presented seasons that fared little better than had those of Ludlow and Smith. But in 1850 an able and aggressive new manager, Joseph M. Field, took over the Mobile playhouse and with the advantage of an economic boom returned the theater to successful operation. Field, long a member of Ludlow and Smith's stock, had risen to star rank prior to entering management. By January of 1853 he had become, in the words of the *Register*, "the very manager of all managers."[112] It was only fitting that Ludlow and Smith's protégé should take over in the city so long dominated by the partners and see to its return to theatrical success.

In St. Louis, Ludlow and Smith fared better financially than in Mobile, at least after the return of prosperity. Competition was very much in evidence there, but the population was able to sustain the theater in addition to other forms of entertainment.[113] Still, there were trying times for the managers in the early 1840's when the town was in the depths of depression. William G. B. Carson, historian of the St. Louis stage, appropriately entitled his monograph on theatrical affairs there from 1840 to 1844 *Managers in Distress*.[114] But the partners continued their operation, distressed or not, and offered annual seasons during which the playhouse was open six nights a week each summer and fall. They featured an able stock company and as many top stars as Ludlow or Smith could entice to the South.

Perhaps the lowest point in the financial history of the firm's St. Louis operation came in 1844. Despite starring appearances by the likes of Macready, Hackett, Forrest, and Henry Placide, the theater simply could not draw. A June diary entry by Ludlow indicates the despair so common to the times: "Mr. H. Placide played Secret Service & Double Bedded Room to $51—!! Where is the taste of the St. Louis audience?—Damme! if I think they ever had any—One of the best—indeed the *very best actor* in the United States playing to empty benches."[115] But by the end of the 1844 season the worst had passed. In 1845 the co-managers began to fare better in St. Louis.

112. *Mobile Daily Register*, Jan. 22, 1853.

113. The free population of St. Louis County had jumped by 1850 to 104,978. DeBow, *Statistical View*, p. 266.

114. William Glascow Bruce Carson, *Managers in Distress. The St. Louis Stage, 1840–1844* (St. Louis: St. Louis Historical Documents Foundation, 1949).

115. Ludlow MS Diary, June 27, 1844, Ludlow-Field-Maury Collection, Missouri Historical Society.

In fact, so successful were Ludlow and Smith's St. Louis seasons between 1845 and 1850 that their good fortune inspired the construction of a second theater there. John W. Bates, long-time proprietor of theaters in Cincinnati and Louisville, built a new playhouse and opened it on January 9, 1851.[116] Bates fared rather poorly in St. Louis, however. He was never personally popular, and when Ludlow and Smith opened the old theater in April of 1851, the public quickly deserted Bates for their old friends.[117]

But by 1850 the era of Ludlow and Smith was coming to a close in St. Louis. Long plagued by acrimonious personal differences, the partners were ready to give up theater management. During the summer season of 1851 they sold their scenery, sets, stage machinery, and wardrobe to "The St. Louis Dramatic Varieties Association" and took other steps to terminate their St. Louis operation.[118] Early in October they offered a benefit for the Orphan's Home, and following the performance, appropriately Tobin's *Honey Moon*, Smith appeared before the curtain with a farewell address. He reminded the audience of the quarter-century he had been appearing before them and their parents and of the stars he had offered and the entertainment and culture provided by the theater. Then he concluded: "It is my belief that the citizens of St. Louis will hereafter look back with pleasure on the happy hours they have spent in this house, and speak with pride of the companies which acted before them."[119] Very likely they did.

By fall of 1851, then, only New Orleans remained to the co-managers. Since emerging as proprietors of the St. Charles in 1843 they had had troubles similar to those in the other towns on the circuit, despite the size and importance of the Crescent City. Smith later termed the New Orleans season of 1844–1845 "the worst of all seasons I was ever concerned in (always excepting that of Mobile in

116. Margaret Blackburn, "The Stage in St. Louis, Missouri, after 1850" (Master's thesis, State University of Iowa, 1927), p. 8; Smith, *Theatrical Management*, p. 223; *Missouri Republican*, Oct. 14, 1850.

117. Richard C. Ludlow to Cornelia L. Field, Jan. 19, March 23, 1851, in Ludlow-Field-Maury Collection, Missouri Historical Society; Auguste Waldauer to Solomon Franklin Smith, April 7, 1851, in Smith Collection, Missouri Historical Society. Waldauer wrote "You have no possible Idee [*sic*] how people here *hate* old Bates the manager. [They would] rather hear speaking of the devil, than of him."

118. Charles P. Chouteau to Ludlow and Smith, July 24, 1851, Ludlow-Field-Maury Collection, Missouri Historical Society.

119. Smith, *Theatrical Management*, p. 224.

1839–40)...."[120] The roots of the problem were essentially the same in New Orleans as in the other towns: depression and competition meant financial hardship. But in New Orleans the competition of other theaters was more consistent and far greater than in Mobile or St. Louis. The New American Theater, under a succession of short-term managers,[121] was opened for a season every year and operated concurrently with the St. Charles.

When in 1845 the New American went bankrupt, Ludlow and Smith took the lease on it to remove it as a competitor,[122] and to good effect. The 1845–1846 season at the St. Charles was profitable. Ludlow and Smith offered strong repertory productions and such stars as Booth, the Keans, Marble, Henry Placide, Hackett, and Anna Cora Mowatt,[123] while sublessee S. P. Stickney at the American presented largely circus and equestrian entertainment. Smith remembered the season as "an improvement on all previous seasons in the new St. Charles. . . . The profits . . . were considerable."[124]

The coming of the war with Mexico coincided with the return of prosperity and both contributed to the continued success of theater operations in the Crescent City.[125] The season of 1846–1847, Smith recalled, "witnesses a continuation of the prosperity which had now become an assured fact. Business not only came up to a paying point, but went considerably beyond it."[126] So successful were the co-managers that they invested some $16,000 in renovating their play-

120. *Ibid.*, p. 189.

121. The New American managers were, in order, William Dinneford, former proprietor of the Bowery and Franklin theaters in New York (1843), Mrs. John Sefton, well-known actress and sometimes manageress (1843–1844), and Charles H. Mueller and Robert L. Place, New Orleanians who operated the theater as a partnership for one season (1844–1845).

122. Solomon Franklin Smith to William H. Chippendale, April 19, 1845, in Smith Collection, Missouri Historical Society.

123. Ludlow, *Dramatic Life*, p. 641; Joseph Patrick Roppolo, "A History of the English Language Theatre in New Orleans, 1845–1861" (Doctoral dissertation, Tulane University, 1950), pp. 133–36. *The* (London) *Theatrical Times*, June 27, 1846, reported that the Keans had just completed "their fiftieth night with Ludlow and Smith." "These fifty nights," continued the incredulous report, "have been occupied between New Orleans, Mobile, and St. Louis, and from them Mr. and Mrs. Kean have realized fifteen thousand dollars, being an average of three hundred dollars per night. This is truly great. . . ."

124. Smith, *Theatrical Management*, p. 199.

125. In March of 1847 Smith began the popular practice of reporting the latest war news from the stage of the St. Charles. See Smith MS Diary, March 20, 1847, Smith Collection, Missouri Historical Society.

126. Smith, *Theatrical Management*, p. 202.

house, remodeling the interior and replacing the benches of the parquet, dress circle, and second tier with "large and commodious cushioned chairs. . . ."[127] So complete was the economic recovery that even the return of the American Theater to operation on a stock-and-star repertory basis and the opening of still another playhouse did not adversely affect the co-partners.

The new theater was called the "Varieties"; it had its origins in 1848 with the formation of the "New Orleans Histrionic Association," an ostensibly non-commercial organization of prominent local men.[128] Within a few months of its founding there was a split in the society; part of the membership, dissatisfied with the administration of the organization, seceded to form another group calling themselves the New Orleans Variété Association. It was this latter group that formed the body of stockholders in the new Varieties Theater, on Gravier Street between Baronne and Carondelet, which opened under the management of Thomas Placide on December 8, 1849.[129] From the outset it was a success, and the Varieties, or "Placide's Varieties" as it became known, immediately joined the ranks of the major English-language playhouses in New Orleans.[130]

The existence of three English theaters, a French theater (open nightly), and a multitude of ephemeral playhouses qualified New Orleans as a major theater center of the United States.[131] The sheer quantity of theater available was truly amazing. When Jenny Lind appeared in New Orleans, for example, creating the sensation that followed her everywhere, she had substantial active competition. French opera was offered nightly at the Orleans Theater, Placide's Varieties presented light comedy and musical pieces every evening

127. Ludlow, *Dramatic Life*, p. 648.

128. Among them James H. Caldwell, who may well have been planning to re-enter the theater business.

129. Ludlow MS Diary, Dec. 8, 1849, Ludlow-Field-Maury Collection, Missouri Historical Society. The stockholders of the Varieties included such notables as Caldwell, *Picayune* editor Cuthbert Bullitt, banker James Robb, and the immensely wealthy planter Minor Kenner.

130. The Varieties was reincarnated following a fire in 1854 as the "Gaiety," then as "Crisp's Gaiety" when William H. Crisp took over its management in 1856. See above, chap. ix.

131. Roppolo, "Theatre in New Orleans," p. 216, lists twenty theaters operating in New Orleans between 1845 and 1861. Noteworthy were the Olympic Theatre, a summer playhouse used as a circus during the winter, Dan Rice's Amphitheatre, largely a ring-show, and the Pelican Theatre, a vaudeville house. See also John Gaisford, *The Drama in New Orleans* (New Orleans: J. B. Steel, 1849), pp. 14–15.

to crowded houses, the American Theater featured the tragedienne Charlotte Cushman in her major roles, and at the St. Charles a ballet troupe appeared on alternate nights with Lind.[132] It is extremely doubtful that such a plethora of entertainment could be found anywhere in the country outside of New York City.

Ludlow and Smith, who had been so instrumental in the rise of New Orleans as a theater center, offered their final season there, or anywhere, at the St. Charles in the winter of 1852–1853. The season, opening on November 6, 1852, was a great success throughout; financially it was probably the best the old managers had ever had.[133] But they had agreed to terminate their partnership at its conclusion. Having arranged to sell all their theater holdings to Benedict De Bar,[134] who was to take control of the St. Charles, Ludlow and Smith formally announced their intention to retire. On Saturday evening, April 30, 1853, after a farewell benefit for the co-managers attended by an overflow crowd at the St. Charles, the senior partner made an emotional diary entry. "Last night of the season," wrote Noah Ludlow, "and last of the partnership of Ludlow & Smith—THANK GOD!!"[135] The dissolution of the partnership marked the end of an era in the theater history of the South and West. The last of the original pioneer managers had left the stage, to take up new careers.

Ludlow and Smith, in the last ten years of their partnership, had come to dominate the theater history of the Mississippi Valley and had built reputations second to none in the United States. But they were by no means the only managers operating in the Southwest during the period of their dominance. Other managers had been active, both in the older theater towns of the region and in the newly emerging towns on the very periphery of the amorphous frontier. The theater remained in the vanguard of the advance of urban society, and before the war came some noteworthy developments had occurred, both in the Mississippi Valley and beyond.

132. *New Orleans Bee,* Feb. 12, 1851.
133. Noah Miller Ludlow to Solomon Franklin Smith, March 28, 1853, in Smith Collection, Missouri Historical Society.
134. *Ibid.,* April 23, 1853.
135. Ludlow MS Diary, April 30, 1853, Ludlow-Field-Maury Collection, Missouri Historical Society.

CHAPTER IX

SOUTHWESTERN DEVELOPMENTS TO 1860

THE WIDENING PALE

1.

IN THE CITIES OF THE SOUTHWEST BEYOND THE IMMEDIATE CONTROL OF Messrs. Ludlow and Smith, theatrical affairs between 1840 and 1860 continued in a pattern established since the beginning of Western urban development; the fortunes of the theaters rose and fell with the fortunes of the towns they served. Some of the older theater towns—most notably Lexington, Kentucky, and Natchez, Mississippi—declined in importance as commercial centers and experienced a consequent decline in their theater operations. More often the old towns continued to grow and prosper, and so did their playhouses (and the pocketbooks of their managers). Finally, as the frontiers receded, and as new urban centers emerged, they spawned new theaters and major theatrical developments. As a whole, growth far exceeded decline, and the "prosperity decade" of the 1850's saw theatrical affairs reach boom proportions.

At the upper extremity of the lower Mississippi Valley, Louisville, Kentucky, experienced vast commercial growth in the decades immediately prior to the Civil War. And as usual, theatrical expansion accompanied commercial expansion. Since the coming of Samuel Drake in 1815, Louisville had known annual theater seasons and frequently one or more afterseasons offered by the numerous touring companies en route north or south.[1] Beginning in 1830 the regular season had become quite long; the theater was usually kept open several months each year. And by 1840 the playhouse was operating practically on a year-round basis.[2] The Louisville population assured the continuation of an active theater, and the town's strategic location on the water route between Cincinnati and the South assured a steady population increase. Between 1830 and 1850 the aggregate figure quadrupled, and by 1860 Louisville claimed almost 70,000 inhabitants.[3] The transient population was, as in all important river towns, large.

The year 1843 was a turning point in Louisville theater history. On May 21 of that year the old City Theater burned down and the venerable Samuel Drake retired from theater management to a farm outside of town.[4] By then the old playhouse had fallen into disrepair. In fact, a Louisville correspondent of the *New York Spirit of the Times* had called for a new one as early as 1837, commenting that Drake's playhouse was "one of the dirtiest theatres that you ever saw" and that "six hundred fills it till you are almost suffocated."[5] Although the depression following 1837 hit Louisville hard,[6] delaying construction of a new playhouse, the 1843 fire created an entertainment vacuum that was certain to be filled quickly.

In June of 1844 the Louisville press began a campaign for a new theater. "The want of a neat, capacious, and respectably conducted theatre in this city," the *Morning Courier* editorially contended, "is

1. Weisert, *Curtain Rose, passim*, is a comprehensive annal of the Louisville stage prior to 1843.

2. In 1842, for example, the theater opened in early January, remained open until June, then closed until early August only to reopen until mid-December. *Ibid.*, pp. 143–46, 146–48.

3. U. S. Census Office, *Social Statistics*, p. 122. The figures are: 1830—10,341, 1840—21,210, 1850—43,194, 1860—68,033. The population of Jefferson County in 1850 was 59,831, of whom 48,920 were free. De Bow, *Statistical View*, p. 238.

4. Noah Miller Ludlow MS Diary, May 21, 1843, Ludlow-Field-Maury Collection, Missouri Historical Society; Weisert, *Curtain Rose*, p. 149. The old theater was intentionally fired, again likely at the hands of a rabid fundamentalist.

5. *New York Spirit of the Times*, March 11, 1837.

6. See Samuel Drake to Solomon Franklin Smith, Aug. 15, 1842, Smith Collection, Missouri Historical Society. Drake wrote: "The Louisville Theatre like all houses . . . has been much depressed. . . ."

severely felt and generally acknowledged."[7] The arguments in favor of a new playhouse centered upon the commercial benefits derived from the theater:

> The absense of a theatre in this city, is felt not only as creating a hiatus in the range of popular amusements, but as a serious injury to the business of the city. Pleasure tourists, with money in their pockets, (and there are many thousands of this class from the South, who visit our city in the summer season,) will not remain long in a place which is destitute of the highest order of public amusements. . . . [There] is little doubt in the minds of those who are best acquainted with the character and feelings of our floating population, that large numbers of business men as well as pleasure travellers, are diverted from Louisville to other places, solely from the want of the attraction presented by a large and respectable theatre.[8]

The press campaign was apparently effective. By August of 1844 some sort of temporary structure had been made available for theatrical purposes.[9] But it was early in 1846 before a real theater opened in Louisville. The new house was built under the auspices of Cincinnati manager John Bates, who intended to operate it in conjunction with his Ohio theater, probably under management of his son, James W. Bates. On February 3, 1846, the *Morning Courier* pronounced the house "the handsomest, the best arranged, the most beautifully decorated, and the neatest theatre in the west or south, or even in the United States."[10] On February 9, 1846, "Bates's Theater" opened with Julia Dean speaking the prize address, then starring in Douglas Jerrold's *Time Works Wonders*. For twenty years this playhouse reigned supreme in Louisville.[11]

7. Jones, "The Stage in Louisville," pp. 80–81, quoting *Louisville Morning Courier*, June 13, 1844.

8. *Ibid.*

9. Ludlow Diary, Aug. 6, 1844. Ludlow and Smith considered taking the lease on this playhouse.

10. Mary Martha Dietz, "A History of the Theatre in Louisville" (Master's Thesis, University of Louisville, 1921), p. 40, quoting *Louisville Morning Courier*.

11. John Jacob Weisert, *A Large and Fashionable Audience: A Checklist of Performances at the Louisville Theatre 1846 to 1866* (Louisville: University of Louisville Press, 1955), p. iii; Casseday, *Louisville*, pp. 116–17. The new theater, located on the southeast corner of Green and Forth streets, was capable of seating 1,200.

But Bates's Theater was not to be without competition of other playhouses. In February of 1851 "Mozart Hall," designed primarily as a concert hall, was opened to the public.[12] An early performer of note appearing there was Jenny Lind, whose three Louisville concerts filled the new house to overflowing shortly after its opening. But the hall was available for use by touring theatrical troupes, and plays were frequently offered there.[13] The addition of the Masonic Temple in 1857 gave Louisville a third public hall, also devoted to commercial amusements. But the great majority of legitimate theater was provided by Bates and his successors at his Louisville theater.

As the 1850's advanced, the success of the Louisville repertory company (under several different managements) continued unabated; even the economic disturbance of 1857 failed to dampen the enthusiasm of the local playgoers. On July 10, 1858, the *Spirit of the Times* announced the conclusion of a 43-week season that elicited "handsome and remunerative support from the citizens of Louisville." Even as the political turmoil immediately preceding the war grew louder and more agitated, there was no perceptible effect on theater operations. As a member of the company later recalled: "The usual list of stars appeared and the business was good in spite of the political excitement until the bombardment and capitulation of Ft. Sumter [*sic*]. . . ."[14] Only then did theatrical affairs decline. Louisville, one of the earliest theater towns of the Old South, also proved one of the most durable.

Such was not the case with Lexington, another early Kentucky theater center. As the town declined into relative commercial insignificance, its theater declined apace. Throughout the 1830's and 1840's, theatrical activity was minimal, limited to occasional strolling troupes that usually failed to draw, even when they of-

12. John Jacob Weisert, *Mozart Hall: 1851 to 1866. A Checklist of Attractions at a Minor Theatre of Louisville, Kentucky, Known Variously as Mozart Hall, Wood's Theatre, or The Academy of Music* (Louisville: University of Louisville Press, 1962), p. i. A semi-professional organization of German actors had begun operations in 1850 and were active for several years. See John Jacob Weisert, "Beginnings of German Theatricals in Louisville," *The Filson Club History Quarterly*, XXVI (Oct., 1952), *passim*.

13. Weisert, *Mozart Hall*, p. 1. The Lind concerts in Louisville were given April 7, 9, and 10, 1851.

14. Charles A. Krone, "Recollections of an Old Actor," *Missouri Historical Society Collections*, IV (1911), 431.

fered a strong stock company and first-rate stars. When, for example, in 1844 stars of the caliber of Augustus A. Addams, James H. Hackett, and Edwin Forrest visited the old "Athens of the West," they were largely ignored. The theater had not been open a month when the local press was forced to admit that "a continuance of neglect must necessarily close this most delightful resort for amusement."[15] As the 1850's progressed there was little if any improvement. By December of 1855 the *Kentucky Statesman* declared in disgust that a visiting troupe of actors was playing "to bare walls" while a touring monkey show and a "drunken band of bogus Negro minstrels . . . drew out the *fashionables* in a mass."[16]

There were signs of a theatrical revival in Lexington in 1857. Partly in response to public demand, a new playhouse, the "Lexington Varieties," was opened under the supervision of one William H. Hough on May 20, 1857.[17] The first season lasted over a month, operating with some success, but Hough absconded without paying his company and never returned to Lexington.[18] Another itinerant manager, the better-known [Samuel?] Benjamin Duffield, undertook operation of the Lexington playhouse in the fall of 1857, but despite strong management and the appearance of several top stars, he met with little success at the box office. On December 23, 1857, the *Observer and Reporter* declared: "We had hoped the theatre under judicious management would become a cherished institution—at all events for short seasons. This we now despair of."[19] Duffield's initial Lexington effort was also his last. He pursued his managerial career in Mobile the following season, and Lexington, cradle of the legitimate theater west of the Appalachians, ceased to be a theater town of the slightest consequence. Such drama as was presented there after 1857 was the work of the local amateurs.

Accounting for the demise of professional theater in a town formerly strong in support of the institution is a difficult matter. Population figures alone do not provide an answer; Lexington saw an increase in population between 1840 and 1860.[20] Often it was a

15. Crum, "Lexington Theatre," p. 392, quoting *Lexington Observer and Reporter*, May 4, 1844.

16. *Ibid.*, p. 488, quoting *Lexington Kentucky Statesman*, Dec. 7, 1855.

17. *Ibid.*, p. 532.

18. *Ibid.*, p. 537.

19. Quoted in *ibid.*, p. 545.

20. The population rose from 6,997 in 1840 to 9,321 in 1860. U. S. Census Office, *Social Statistics*, p. 117.

question of attitude, of environment, as well as of economic vitality and internal dynamic. And there is evidence that religious opposition in Lexington was militant and effective in creating an atmosphere decidedly unfavorable to theater operation. In 1846, for
example, a wandering artist, Alfred S. Waugh, observed: "The
people of this town are sadly preacher ridden, so much so indeed, that life is stript of its charms, there are no private parties,
no friendly interchanges of the courtesies of life. . . ."[21] Revivalism
was rampant at the time, Waugh noted, and the whole effect was
stultifying. Surely this factor, as well as the economic, contributed
to the decline and ultimate demise of professional theater in Lexington.[22] The same repressive fundamentalist mentality that had
cost the liberal Horace Holley his presidency of Transylvania University years before also cost the more frivolous Lexingtonians a
favorite pastime.

2.

If the two decades immediately preceding the outbreak of civil
war saw a steady decline of theater in the Kentucky interior, they
saw the emergence of two important theater towns in Tennessee:
Nashville on the Cumberland River, and Memphis on the Mississippi. Nashville was actually a comparatively old town by Western standards and according to her ablest chronicler was by the
decade of the 1830's becoming a "cultural oasis."[23] As noted above,
Ludlow was active there as early as 1817, and Nashville was a
regular stopping place for many itinerant troupes throughout the
1820's and 1830's. But the low quality of some of those strolling
companies damaged the reputation of the theater prior to 1839.
"Our theatre, for several years past, has been in bad repute owing to its former management," sounded the *Whig* in December of
1839.[24]

21. John Francis McDermott (ed.), *Travels in Search of the Elephant: The
Wanderings of Alfred S. Waugh, Artist, In Louisiana, Missouri, and Santa Fe,
in 1845–1846* (St. Louis: Missouri Historical Society, 1951), p. 86. The Thespian Society impressed Waugh, however; according to his account they performed "with great credit to themselves, and amusement to their friends."
22. A certain manifestation of religious opposition to the theater was the
"exorbitant tax" imposed upon theatrical troupes. Crum, "Lexington Theatre,"
p. 494, quoting *Lexington Kentucky Statesman*, Aug. 1, 1856.
23. Francis Garvin Davenport, "Culture Versus Frontier in Tennessee 1825–
1850," *Journal of Southern History*, V (Feb., 1939), 30.
24. Hunt, "Nashville Theatre," p. 73, quoting *Nashville Whig*, Dec. 2, 1839.

Things looked much brighter for the future of the theater in Nashville when a new manager, C. C. Hodges, appeared on the scene. "To a laudable enterprise," declared the *Whig*, "he adds all the requisites necessary to secure a well ordered house, and a respectable and, considering the patronage of the city, an efficient stock corps."[25] Although Hodges' Nashville management was short-lived, he might be said to have inaugurated the arrival of a new era of Nashville theater.

For several years however, the commercial center of the Cumberland Valley was left to the itinerants; no major troupe included Nashville on a regular circuit. Moreover, the depression affected theatrical affairs there as everywhere. When Joe Cowell performed in Nashville in 1842 with a troupe from the recently destroyed St. Charles Theater, he observed that the company "realized all we expected in that beautiful little city, *with the exception of money*."[26] Competition of circuses and the like also hurt theatrical operations in Nashville. Frequent were such comments as the following from the *Whig* of September 23, 1843: "the theater and the circus are both open, but the latter is the favorite resort. While hundreds nightly crowd the circus, the representatives of Thalia and Melpomene perform . . . before some thirty or forty listless listeners. . . ."[27] But the managers continued to try their luck in Nashville throughout the 1840's,[28] and by the time prosperity returned there was considerable local support for the drama. Indeed, by 1849 that support was sufficiently strong to warrant construction of a new playhouse.

The act passed by the Tennessee legislature incorporating the "Adelphi Theatre Company" clearly states the purpose of the proposed theater: "to erect in the city of Nashville an appropriate and handsome building for the legitimate drama, and by proper

25. *Ibid.* The 1840 population of Nashville was 6,929. By 1860 it had grown to 16,988. U. S. Census Office, *Social Statistics*, p. 151. The free population of Davidson County in 1850 was 24,707. DeBow, *Statistical View*, p. 302.

26. Cowell, *Thirty Years*, p. 302.

27. Quoted in Francis Garvin Davenport, *Cultural Life in Nashville on the Eve of the Civil War* (Chapel Hill: University of North Carolina Press, 1941), pp. 27–28.

28. One of those managers, J. A. J. Neafie, authorized Ludlow and Smith to contract star engagements for his Nashville theater—a common practice among the lesser managers of the time and one that points up the importance of the co-managers. See Solomon Franklin Smith to William H. Chippendale, May 10, 1845, Smith File, Harvard Theater Collection, Harvard College Library.

rules and regulations to elevate the character of the stage representations."[29] On July 1, 1850, the Adelphi Theater opened its first
season; its manager was John Greene, who had earlier brought
occasional touring troupes to Nashville. The first season, featuring a series of legitimate productions (in line with the act of in-
corporation), proved a great success.[30] The boom decade of the
1850's commenced auspiciously in Nashville theatrical affairs.

By 1851 theatrical affairs in Nashville had attracted the attention of the *New York Spirit of the Times,* and the Tennessee city
had its regular *Spirit* correspondent. One of his early letters reported the successful engagement of Julia Dean, who had closed
a Nashville engagement early in December, 1851. Her closing benefit, wrote the correspondent, attracted "the largest and most brilliant and fashionable audience which has ever assembled in our
city to greet any artiste, except Jenny Lind. . . ."[31] Greene's ability to attract stars combined with the growth of the town and the
quality of the new playhouse to lift Nashville into national theatrical prominence.

In 1856 the playhouse was renovated and opened under new
management, that of Joel Davis, who proved unable to maintain
the standard of quality established by his predecessor. "When will
our theatre manager learn," queried the *Whig* on one occasion,
"that the amusement seekers of Nashville can discriminate between
good acting and such ungainly and offensive antics and murder-
ing of the king's English as they have had the affrontery [sic] to offer
this season?"[32] In the winter of 1857 Davis was driven out by the
appearance of William H. Crisp, who expanded his already extensive domain by opening another playhouse, Crisp's Gaiety, in
Nashville.[33] The talented Crisp, with a company of over twenty
members, returned quality to Nashville theater productions and
initiated a period during which the public saw such stars as James
Edward Murdoch, Julia Dean, Eliza Logan, Charlotte Cushman,

29. Quoted in Davenport, *Cultural Life in Nashville,* p. 118.
30. *Ibid.,* pp. 119–20. The playhouse had the traditional pit and boxes, in this
case two tiers of the latter. The stage was reputedly among the largest in the
United States.
31. *New York Spirit of the Times,* Jan. 3, 1852. The letter was dated Nashville, Dec. 11, 1851.
32. Davenport, *Cultural Life in Nashville,* p. 133, quoting *Nashville Republican Banner and Whig,* Oct. 3, 1857.
33. *Ibid.,* pp. 134–35.

Edwin Booth, and other theatrical luminaries of the day.[34] During the summer of 1859 Crisp completely remodeled the interior of his playhouse, and the newly renovated theater continued to attract large and enthusiastic audiences until the very close of the ante bellum period.[35]

Nashville is an example of an old river town whose theatrical development was slow and steady, comparable to the growth of the town itself. Memphis, on the other hand, exemplified a town whose growth to prominence was sudden and whose theatrical developments, again, followed accordingly. The 1840 population of the bluff town has been estimated at 1,799 black and white.[36] That year it was incorporated as a city. But even as early as 1830 Memphis had boasted an amateur theatrical society and hosted barnstorming troupes, among them those of Sol Smith, Warrell and Groves, and Samuel Waters.[37] The frontier community had proved fertile soil for theatrical growth before. By 1838 "Hart's Saloon" was recognized as the local playhouse for all visiting entertainers and continued to be so employed until May of 1842, when a real theater opened.

The new playhouse was owned and operated by the ubiquitous John S. Potter, who had converted a livery stable into a theater and opened it on June 18, 1842, with, according to the *American Eagle*, "a full and efficient company. . . ."[38] The initial response of the press was favorable to the endeavor. "The boxes and parquette are roomy, airy, and commodious," observed the *Eagle*. "Each seat has a comfortable back, and the boxes form an admirable position for the assemblage of the youth, beauty and fashion of our city."[39]

The first playgoers, however, discovered several drawbacks, the most objectionable of which was the unsavory odor of the house.

34. *Ibid.*

35. Nashville was one Southern town (Richmond and New Orleans were others) that saw an active theater during the war. See O. G. Brockett, "Theatre in Nashville During the Civil War," *The Southern Speech Journal*, XXIII (Winter, 1957), *passim*.

36. Gerald Mortimer Capers, *The Biography of a River Town; Memphis: Its Heroic Age* (Chapel Hill: University of North Carolina Press, 1939), p. 79.

37. Ritter, "Theatre in Memphis," p. 16.

38. Wanda Luttrell, "The Theater of Memphis, Tennessee, From 1829 to 1860" (Master's thesis, Louisiana State University, 1951), p. 12, quoting *Memphis American Eagle*, June 18, 1842.

39. *Ibid.*, June 17, 1842.

The *Eagle* editor suggested that "a barrel of Cologne" might hide the distinctly horsy smell that was an inevitable reminder of the theater's original function,[40] but neither the horses nor the puritanical forces that immediately rose up against the playhouse deterred the resourceful Potter. He continued to perform periodic seasons in his Memphis theater for several years and attracted a surprising number of high-caliber stars as well.[41] It was not until a fire destroyed his stable-playhouse in the spring of 1847 that Potter was forced to give up his regular Memphis operation. For a while the strolling troupes that stopped in the bluff city were forced to perform in the tavern of the Exchange Hotel.[42]

A more ephemeral stroller opened the next Memphis theater. When in the spring of 1848 showboat manager Thomas Frederick Lennox, "Old Tom" to most, lost his vessel in a judgment for debts, he converted the old Universalist Church into a playhouse and began active management as a land-locked theater operator.[43] And he proved a great success. At the close of the winter season of 1849 the *Tri-Weekly Appeal* declared: "The enterprising, liberal and judicious Proprietor, Mr. Lennox, has established the fact that the drama can be, and will be sustained in Memphis under proper management."[44] But on October 15, 1849, Old Tom died of dropsy, and a series of managers of greater or lesser ability followed in rapid succession. There was, however, no letdown in local enthusiasm for the theater. In March of 1850, with the playhouse under the well-known comedian Henry Plunkett Grattan, the *Daily Eagle* observed that the theater was "enjoying the full tide of popularity," operating on a stock and star basis.[45]

Memphis proved a strong theater town throughout the 1850's. The swelling of her population and the polyglot nature of her citizenry, along with the innumerable transients in constant quest

40. *Ibid.*, July 22, 1842.
41. Ritter, "Theatre in Memphis," p. 41; Luttrell, "Theater of Memphis," pp. 15–16. Among the stars appearing under Potter's management were Augustus A. Addams, Dan Marble, Julia Dean, James H. Hackett, Charlotte Cushman, Junius Brutus Booth, Mary Duff, and Joshua S. Sillsbee.
42. Luttrell, "Theater of Memphis," p. 17.
43. *Ibid.*, pp. 20–21.
44. Ritter, "Theatre in Memphis," p. 78, quoting *Memphis Tri-Weekly Appeal*, March 20, 1849.
45. Luttrell, "Theater of Memphis," p. 33, quoting *Memphis Daily Eagle*, March 12, 1850.

of entertainment, assured success of the theater.[46] And under Grattan's successor Memphis began her rise to theatrical prominence. In October of 1851 the *Appeal* announced that the Memphis theater had been leased by James S. Charles, "late the enterprising manager of the American Theatre in New Orleans."[47] Charles, a prominent figure in several Southern towns during the last decade before the war, was a New Yorker by birth, an actor of some ability (though not of the first rank) who determined to attempt management in the South in hopes of attaining greater success than was likely in the Northeastern metropolis.

After an unsuccessful stint as a summer manager in New Orleans in 1851, Charles made his timely arrival in Memphis. The following year he was joined by actor David Ash as co-manager, and the partnership lasted until 1855 when Charles again made a bid for New Orleans management, leaving Ash as sole proprietor in Memphis. Their partnership proved profitable both to the managers and to the Memphis public, who were offered quality theater, and who reciprocated with enthusiastic support. When Eliza Logan appeared in Memphis late in 1854 she wrote Sol Smith of her impressions. "Oh! What an excellent theatrical place this is," exclaimed the young actress. "Last night—my benefit—They tell me they turned as many away as were admitted. People in from 9 miles distant obliged to return without seats."[48] Memphis's theatrical fortunes were on the rise.

In 1855 David Ash extended his operation to include Vicksburg, Mississippi, by opening a new playhouse there in which he could employ his stock during the off season in Memphis.[49] Ash thus created another important theatrical nexus of the Old South by operating two of the burgeoning river towns in tandem. But his

46. Between 1850 and 1860 the population of Memphis increased from 8,841 to 22,621. U. S. Census Office, *Social Statistics*, p. 140. Gerald Capers suggests that the large German population swelled the ranks of the local theater-goers. Capers, *Memphis*, p. 131.

47. Ritter, "Theatre in Memphis," p. 114, quoting *Memphis Appeal*, Oct. 27, 1851.

48. Eliza Logan to Solomon Franklin Smith, Nov. 4, 1854, Smith Collection, Missouri Historical Society. Miss Logan was not exaggerating the size of her audiences. The *Daily Appeal*, Nov. 1, 1854, declared of her performance that evening: "It is not worth while to advise everybody to go, we know more will be there than can get in; and in view of this fact we would advise the outsiders to show their respect by just poking their money under the door." Quoted in Luttrell, "Theater of Memphis," p. 42.

49. Ritter, "Theatre in Memphis," p. 174.

reign as manager of the theater in Memphis was destined to be brief. A local amateur society began a move for construction of a new playhouse by public subscription. By fall of 1857 the new house was ready for occupancy, and its lessee proved to be no less formidable an adversary than William H. Crisp. On October 19, 1857, the new Gaiety Theatre opened to the public.[50]

Ash was not able to compete with Crisp, who had the resources of three Gaiety theaters to draw upon for variety in his stock. Within a year the old Memphis theater was forced out of contention; from then until the outbreak of war it was used primarily for burlesque and minstrel shows. Still, when David Ash was killed in a pistol accident late in 1858, the *Appeal* obituary justly observed: "In his position as manager of the theatre, his name will always be associated with the rise of the drama in this city."[51] It had been David Ash who, along with James S. Charles, brought Memphis to a position of theatrical prominence and laid the foundation for the later success of Crisp's Gaiety.

On October 6, 1860, *Wilkes' Spirit of the Times* contained a letter from its Memphis correspondent giving the current theatrical news. The theater had opened on September 24, the correspondent noted, to a full house that included "all the old *habitues* of the theatre. . . ." The impressive orchestra was under the direction of Carlo Patti, talented brother of singer Adelina. The "auxiliaries" of the company were "both awkward and imperfect," as was usually the case at the beginning of a season, but they had time to improve. In general the situation was satisfactory. The correspondent concluded on a note of anticipation: "now that our beautiful theatre has inaugurated another season under such promising auspices, we may fairly predict an uninterrupted season of brilliant success." And he was correct. The season was not interrupted until April of 1861.

3.

Memphis was a case of a new emergence into urban prominence in the prewar decades. Natchez, Mississippi, provided another example of a declining urban center and good theater town. The mid-

50. Luttrell, "Theater of Memphis," p. 56. The new theater was located on Jefferson Street below Third. The leading figure in the move to have it built was James Wickersham, a prominent local attorney.

51. Ritter, "Theatre in Memphis," pp. 263–64, quoting *Memphis Appeal*, Dec. 24, 1858.

1830's brought the "flush times" of old Natchez; by 1840 there were signs of decay, at first attributed to the Panic of 1837, but actually of more complex origins. The devastating tornado of May 7, 1840, marked a distinct beginning of Natchez' rapid decline from which she never recovered. Thereafter the population of the once-booming river town dwindled steadily,[52] as Natchez waned in commercial significance.

Among the dozens of buildings destroyed by the 1840 tornado was James H. Caldwell's old Natchez Theater.[53] Since 1833 it had been in successful operation, first under Caldwell's lessees Richard Russell and James Simon Rowe, then, following Rowe's suicide in 1835, under Charles Booth Parsons and, briefly, John S. Potter. The repertory companies operating in Natchez generally had been strong —the *Free Trader* boasted in January of 1838 that there was "no question that at the present time the stock company of the Natchez Theatre is superior to any other in the Southern Country. . . ."[54] And of course practically all of the stars touring the South played Natchez, most notable among them Josephine Clifton, Mrs. Alexander Drake, Mary Duff, Clara Fisher Maeder, James H. Hackett, Tyrone Power, Ellen Tree, and James W. Wallack.[55]

And until 1837 the theater received solid support. "Our Business here has been uniformly good this season," manager Parsons wrote Sol Smith in February of 1837.[56] But by April of the same year, support had fallen off substantially as a result of economic dislocation, which, according to the local press, had "driven the dollars from the corners of every honest man's pockets. . . ."[57] Within a month the Natchez banks had suspended specie payment, a reflection of the precipitous decline in cotton prices that occurred that spring.

Although financial distress dealt the theater a severe blow in Natchez, the institution survived—at least for a while. Russell died

52. The aggregate population of Adams County in 1840 was 19,434. By 1850 it had fallen to 18,601 of whom 14,395 were slaves. DeBow, *Statistical View*, p. 260. The total population of Natchez proper in 1850 was only 4,434. U. S. Department of State, *Seventh Census*, p. 448.

53. Free, "Natchez Region," p. 26.

54. Free, "Southwestern Mississippi," p. 328, quoting *Natchez Mississippi Free Trader*, Jan. 31, 1838.

55. Free, "Southwestern Mississippi," p. 259.

56. Charles Booth Parsons to Solomon Franklin Smith, Feb. 26, 1837, Smith Collection, Missouri Historical Society.

57. Free, "Southwestern Mississippi," p. 316, quoting *Natchez Mississippi Free Trader*, April 11, 1837.

in May of 1838 and Parsons retired from the stage to take up the pulpit (he had long been torn between the two professions). Potter arrived quickly to take over in Natchez and even to lead an unsuccessful move to open a new playhouse.[58] The following season saw itinerant co-managers James M. Scott and James Thorne in command of the Natchez Theater, which they operated in conjunction with their Vicksburg playhouse. Prior to opening the 1838–1839 season, the co-managers announced that "every star who visits the South" would be engaged for both theaters, and that remarkable year of Southern tours brought the Elder Booth, Forrest, Ellen Tree, Dan Marble, Madame Céleste, Josephine Clifton, and the Ravels to the two Mississippi towns.[59] But despite the array of fine talent they provided, Scott and Thorne lost considerable money for the season.

The co-managers returned to open their Mississippi theaters for the following season, but financial pressure forced them to close earlier than was usual. Support failed completely. By April 4, 1840, both houses had closed. Then on May 7, the great tornado swept Natchez, killing over three hundred and leveling the playhouse.[60] It marked the end of an era in Natchez theater history. Scott returned to open a makeshift playhouse on Main Street in February of 1841,[61] but met with practically no success. The following year proved no better, despite the claim of the *Free Trader* in January of 1842 that "our little gem of a Theatre is in full play."[62] In reality, Natchez was no longer capable of supporting a full winter theater season as she had in bygone years. Following the 1842 effort of James M. Scott, the town saw no regular professional theater for eight years.

In 1850 John S. Potter offered a brief season in Natchez. "After

58. Playbill, Natchez Theater, March 24, 1838, Harvard Theater Collection, Harvard College Library. The bill included Potter's proposal for "A new and *Splendid* THEATRE" to be built "in a central part of the city of Natchez. . . ."

59. Free, "Southwestern Mississippi," p. 403. The two theaters were operated simultaneously, Thorne managing in Natchez, Scott in Vicksburg.

60. *Ibid.*, pp. 432–33.

61. Solomon Franklin Smith to Edward Woolf, Feb. 7, 1841, Smith Collection, Missouri Historical Society; William Ransom Hogan and Edwin Adams Davis (eds.), *William Johnson's Natchez. The Ante-Bellum Diary of a Free Negro* (Baton Rouge: Louisiana State University Press, 1951), p. 318. Smith wrote that the new theater was "altered from warehouse, or something of the kind."

62. Gates, "Theatre in Natchez," p. 119, quoting *Natchez Mississippi Free Trader*, Jan. 6, 1842.

an interregnum of years," exclaimed the *Free Trader*, "Natchez has, at length, got a Theatre, and a good one at that."[63] But the 1850 season proved only a flash in the pan. Potter succumbed to the beckoning lure of California and did not return. By 1855 the Natchezians were welcoming the prospects of a visit by a company of amateurs from Clinton, Louisiana. "It has been some time since we had legitimate drama in our midst," the *Free Trader* declared, "and we doubt not that the company will be well received."[64] Thus long before the war came Natchez had ceased to be a theater town of the slightest consequence, just as she had ceased to be an important commercial center of the Deep South.

4.

As the paths of commerce swerved away from towns like Lexington and Natchez in the mid-nineteenth century, the directions they assumed gave rise to new urban centers that were quick to attract theatrical pioneers. One notable commercial path to emerge following the depression of the early 1840's bore westward in the Deep South. As the cotton country extended its reach up the Red River Valley and into the "Black Waxy" of east Texas and down the Texas Gulf Coast, great quantities of new land came under cultivation, and subsistence farmers became commercial planters. And planters required urban services.

In point of chronology, the Texas coast probably deserves credit for the earliest noteworthy theatrical developments south of St. Louis and west of New Orleans. Houston was the center of a flurry of theatrical activity that began shortly after the establishment of the Republic of Texas, and though that initial flurry was short-lived, it illustrates well the process of theatrical pioneering constantly in effect during the ante bellum period. As early as 1837, [George?] L. Lyons, an ambitious New Orleans actor, attempted to open a theater in Houston, but the wreck of the sea-going steamer in which he was transporting his company ended the venture.[65] In June of 1838, however, the *New York Spirit of the Times* declared incredulously: "They are about establishing a Theatre in Texas. . . .

63. *Ibid.*, March 23, 1850.
64. *Ibid.*, Jan. 15, 1855.
65. William Ransom Hogan, "The Theater in the Republic of Texas," *Southwest Review*, XIX (July, 1934), 383.

The cities of all Europe bloom with the flower of the drama, but here it blooms, and flourishes in our very wilderness."[66] And by 1839, the *Houston Star* could announce that the "city" of 2,073 inhabitants claimed not one but two theaters, both "in successful operation."[67]

Houston was one of those frontier communities composed primarily of roughhewn adventurers and soldiers of fortune that had sprung up on all of the several American frontiers. Like most such communities, Houston had a theater before she had a church;[68] religious opposition to the theater was minute, and the desire for diversion was nearly insatiable. Such was the fertile soil upon which co-managers John Carlos, a Houston merchant, and Henry F. Corri, a lesser member of the St. Charles company, planted their theatrical enterprise in 1838. On June 11, 1838, Houston saw the first professional drama offered in Texas when the imported stock company of Carlos and Corri, eleven strong, presented Knowles's *The Hunchback*, as well as "*A New Texian Anthem*, Written expressly for the occasion by Mr. CORRI."[69]

Opening night found the new playhouse crowded to the limit, and if the account of the local press may be accepted, the performance was a great success. The company, declared the *Houston Telegraph and Texas Register*, "have exceeded the expectations of their most sanguine friends. It must be exceedingly gratifying to every true friend of the drama, to behold its infancy in our country attended by such favorable auspices."[70] The review of their initial effort must have pleased the members of the troupe, who were all theatrical aspirants from the lower ranks of several Southwestern companies, chiefly that of New Orleans. For several weeks they continued to attract sizable audiences to the little playhouse; indeed, so successful was the enterprise that co-manager Corri determined to

66. *New York Spirit of the Times,* June 9, 1838.

67. Edward Garland Fletcher, *The Beginnings of the Professional Theatre in Texas* (Austin: University of Texas Press, 1936), p. 10, quoting *Houston Morning Star,* April 19, 1839.

68. The *Houston Morning Star* commented June 18, 1839: "It is a source of much astonishment . . . that while we have a theatre, a court house, a jail, and even a capitol in Houston, we have not a single church." Quoted in Fletcher, *Theatre in Texas,* p. 23.

69. Playbill, Houston Theater, June 11, 1838, reproduced in Joseph Gallegly, *Footlights on the Border. The Galveston and Houston Stage Before 1900* (The Hague, Netherlands: Mouton and Company, 1962), frontispiece.

70. Fletcher, *Theatre in Texas,* p. 8, quoting *Houston Telegraph and Texas Register,* June 16, 1838.

disengage himself from his partner and commence the next "season" as an independent manager. In February of 1839 he was back in Houston with a new company, a much better one, capable of supporting such stars as William C. Forbes, Charlotte Barnes, and John R. Scott, all of whom performed in his makeshift playhouse.[71]

By the end of July, 1839, Corri had succeeded in driving his erstwhile partner out of contention: the *Morning Star* of July 31, 1839, advertised the sale of Carlos' "Theatrical Furniture" and an offer to rent his theater to the purchaser.[72] But Corri's victory was decidedly Pyrrhic. In driving his rival out of business, he went into debt. His audiences began to dwindle in size as the novelty of the playhouse waned. Moreover, admission prices of $2.00 to $3.00 a person, even in inflated currency, proved prohibitive to many.[73] Corri failed to recoup his losses the following season; if anything he went further into debt. The transfer of the seat of government from Houston to Austin in October of 1839 certainly did not help his situation. By July of 1840 after having played only sporadically throughout the season, the manager was forced to give up, and the first period of Texas theater history came to a close. The effort to bring repertory theater to the frontier village had failed as it was surely doomed to do, given the size of the populace. Thereafter, such drama as Houston saw was provided by itinerant troupes.[74]

Throughout Corri's Houston management, his troupe occasionally visited Galveston to try their luck, usually in support of some visiting star. The *Morning Star*, for example, declared in April of 1839 that actress Charlotte Barnes had departed Houston for Galveston "with the intention of playing a few nights on the island, previous to leaving for the United States."[75] By fall of 1845 there was an actual playhouse—probably a room over the Gothic Saloon—available for use of such intrepid strollers as wanted to try Galveston. One such itinerant, young Harry Watkins, performed there in November and December of 1845; that he fared poorly is indicated by his journal

71. Gallegly, *Galveston and Houston Stage*, p. 30.

72. Quoted in *ibid.*, p. 29.

73. Complaints about the exorbitant admission prices were common. On one occasion, for example, the *Morning Star* pointed out that $6.00 was a fair daily wage for artisans and wondered how working men were to afford the theater. Hogan, "Theater in Texas," p. 389, quoting *Houston Morning Star*, n.d.

74. Hogan, "Theater in Texas," p. 390.

75. Gallegly, *Galveston and Houston Stage*, p. 47, quoting *Houston Morning Star*, April 8, 1839.

entry to the effect that his "best performance of the season" brought but $8.00 in door receipts.[76] The following year another notable stroller, Joseph Jefferson, attempted a season in the gulf port, with about the same success.[77]

The outbreak of the Mexican War brought still other theatrical opportunists to Texas; they collected wherever sizable numbers of troops were gathered. For example, when the United States forces billeted at Corpus Christi in August of 1845, two "theaters," appropriately called the "Army" and the "Union," attracted crowded houses nightly, at least until the soldiers marched south. And when they did, the players followed, first to Brownsville and even into Mexico, where they played at the various army headquarters.[78] Joseph Jefferson recalled playing in Matamoros "to the most motley group that ever filled a theater,"[79] an assertion of doubtless validity.

Following the war, prosperity came to Texas, and with prosperity came an influx of population. As had been the case so often before, the new towns that cropped up attracted new theaters, usually originating with the efforts of the local drama society. Between 1840 and 1860, such organizations as the "Lone Star Histrionic Association" of Richmond, Texas, appeared in virtually all of the smaller communities as well as in Houston, Galveston, and Corpus Christi.[80] Again as before, the playhouses erected by the amateurs often served to attract strolling professionals, who appeared before small but nonetheless appreciative audiences. But rarely did the strollers venture too far beyond contact with one of the settlements. They always remembered the experience of William H. Crisp's unfortunate troupe with the Seminoles in Florida, and as Joseph Jefferson observed, the thought of a similar fate at the hands of the "warlike Comanches" served to deter all but the foolishly intrepid.[81]

Galveston and Houston remained the chief theater towns of Texas. Both maintained their playhouses and Galveston got a new one in 1854, built by public subscription. Though neither was large enough

76. Skinner, *Adventures of H. Watkins*, p. 7. The journal entry was dated Dec. 2, 1845.
77. Jefferson, *Autobiography*, p. 57.
78. Hogan, "Theater in Texas," pp. 391–92; Skinner, *Adventures of H. Watkins*, p. 20; Jefferson, *Autobiography*, p. 67.
79. Jefferson, *Autobiography*, p. 67.
80. Lota M. Spell, "The Theatre in Texas Before the Civil War," *The Texas Monthly*, V (April, 1930), 299–300.
81. Jefferson, *Autobiography*, p. 60.

to support a resident stock company for any sustained period, both saw periodic professional theater seasons right up to the outbreak of war.[82]

The westward movement of the theater was further apparent in the development of the Red River towns of Louisiana and east Texas, especially in the late 1850's. One manager was most clearly identified with those developments. James S. Charles, after quitting Memphis in 1855, centered his efforts on New Orleans and those Louisiana towns with access to the Red River. He seems first to have tried the south-central Louisiana town of Opelousas, where in 1856 he converted some available structure into a "theater," labeled it the "Opelousas Varieties," and opened in November with his touring company. The editor of the *Opelousas Courier* reflected the general pleasure elicited by the troupe when he wrote of the "truly handsome performance of every actor in their respective parts, and the good taste and refinement in the elegant little comedies they played and the really delightful music which come [*sic*] from their splendid voices."[83] Charles discovered that the residents of such towns, virtually starved for entertainment, were only too happy to support a touring company for two or three weeks. It was only natural that he should look northward to such rapidly developing river towns as Alexandria, Natchitoches, and Shreveport, Louisiana, and even beyond.

Shortly after leaving Opelousas, Charles opened in Alexandria, where, according to the *Opelousas Patriot*, "the house was well filled, and, judging from the demonstrations given, we should suppose that the Alexandrians were in ecstasies."[84] From there Charles took his troupe upriver to Shreveport, converted another building into the

82. Gallegly, *Galveston and Houston Stage*, pp. 53, 61, 74.

83. Oran Teague, "The Professional Theater in Rural Louisiana" (Master's thesis, Louisiana State University, 1949), p. 15, quoting *Opelousas Courier*, Nov. 1, 1856. One noteworthy member of this troupe was billed as "Mrs. Ada B. Menken," later to become internationally notorious as Ada Isaacs Menken. She began her stage career with the Charles company.

84. *Ibid.*, p. 23, quoting *Opelousas Patriot*, Jan. 10, 1857. Alexandria had in fact a long theater tradition by 1857. As early as 1821 there was an active amateur society, and on April 25, 1840, the *New York Spirit of the Times* declared: "At Alexandria, 'way up on [the] Red River,' the Theatre is Flourishing. . . ." In 1841 no less a star than Augustus A. Addams, accurately described as "a tragedian of considerable celebrity," performed a season at the "Rapides Theatre." Wallace Allison Gray, "An Historical Study of Professional Dramatic Activities in Alexandria, Louisiana, From the Beginning to 1920" (Master's thesis, Louisiana State University, 1948), p. 8, quoting *Alexandria Red River Whig*, Jan. 23, 1841. The various "floating theaters" made regular stops there.

"Gaiety" theater, and presented a successful season, commencing on February 21, 1857, and lasting seven weeks.[85] Thus by 1857 the manager had created a theatrical circuit, one that came to include Natchitoches, Louisiana, and Marshall, Texas, before the outbreak of the Civil War.[86] By December of 1859 the press of Baton Rouge was complaining that these smaller Red River communities had regular theater seasons, while the state capital had no playhouse at all. "The enterprising folks up in Alexandria, Natchitoches, and Shreveport," noted one local editor, "have their regular theatrical seasons, and the consequence is, they have cultivated a popular taste for the drama and song, greatly to the prejudice, too, of the interests of itinerant charlatans and mountebanks who infest the country and make fortunes out of the gullability [*sic*] of country society. Why is it that Baton Rouge cannot have the same advantages for amusements and entertainments?"[87] James S. Charles must be credited with a considerable portion of the success with which repertory theater was introduced in the rapidly developing Southwest.

But the Southwest was by no means unique in experiencing substantial theatrical development on the eve of war. For years a similar phenomenon had been in progress, for example in the rural communities of Missouri. Once again the amateurs had begun things, and prior to 1850 there were theatrical societies, frequently with playhouses, in such remote towns as Hannibal, Columbia, Jefferson City, Boonville, Lexington, Palmyra, Fayette, and as far west as St. Joseph and Kansas City.[88] During the 1850's, Savannah, Chillicothe, Springfield, and Ste. Genevieve joined the ranks of the the-

85. Teague, "Theater in Rural Louisiana," p. 24; Henry Carlton Lindsey, "The History of the Theatre in Shreveport, Louisiana, to 1900" (Master's thesis, Louisiana State University, 1951), p. 9.

86. Spell, "Theatre in Texas," p. 300.

87. Alban Fordesh Varnado, "A History of Theatrical Activity in Baton Rouge, Louisiana, 1819–1900" (Master's thesis, Louisiana State University, 1947), p. 23, quoting *Baton Rouge Daily Gazette and Comet*, Dec. 7, 1859. Baton Rouge had never proved able to sustain a repertory company and was visited only infrequently by the strollers en route to New Orleans. The absence of a theater was a frequent subject of complaint in the local press. *The Daily Gazette and Comet*, Nov. 19, 1858, even offered to exchange "three of our half dozen churches for a theatre."—an offer that suggests religious opposition as one source of the problem.

88. Elbert R. Bowen, *Theatrical Entertainments in Rural Missouri Before the Civil War* (Columbia: University of Missouri Press, 1959), p. 71. Columbia acquired a society as early as 1832, when the population was not over seven hundred. See also Louise Jean Rietz, "History of the Theatre of Kansas City, Missouri, From the Beginnings Until 1900" (Doctoral dissertation, State University of Iowa, 1939), p. 24.

ater towns.[89] By 1835 the professional strollers had begun to pene-
trate the interior of Missouri, and they continued their activity
throughout the period. For example, A. Cargill and his wife were
recorded in Jefferson City in June of 1835, where they were encouraged in their efforts by the local press.[90] Boonville hosted the touring
company of Alexander McKenzie and Joseph Jefferson (the elder Jefferson) in 1840, and they continued to tour rural Missouri throughout
the spring and summer.[91] When Alfred S. Waugh reached Independence in 1846 he found "the Brittingham family delighting the citizens with their vaudevilles."[92] The troupe, traveling in a pair of
canoes lashed together, performed "in an upper room of the Noland
House. . . ."[93] Even tiny Kansas City attracted professionals before
1860. In 1858 one D. S. Scott gave a series of performances in the
court house, and he was followed by other strollers.[94] In Missouri as
in Louisiana and Texas, the theater people began to appear as soon
as pioneer settlements emerged on the frontier.

To a limited degree the drama even penetrated the sparsely populated state of Arkansas before the war. The "Little Rock Thalian
Society" was organized in 1834 in order to, as the members declared
"afford amusement and recreation to ourselves, as well as to the
people of Little Rock generally. . . ."[95] On November 4, 1834, they
presented their first play, Andrew Cherry's *The Soldier's Daughter*.
By 1838 Little Rock had even hosted a season by professionals—
the strolling company of John S. Potter and Sam Waters—who performed in a warehouse. The *Gazette* found the ladies of the troupe
"pretty and interesting," and a "great attraction to the bucks [of]
our city."[96] In January of 1839 Waters opened a real "theater," a

89. Bowen, *Rural Missouri*, p. 72. Several of these towns also had German-
language amateur societies. See Elbert R. Bowen, "The German Theatre of Early
Rural Missouri," *Missouri Historical Review*, XLVI (Jan., 1952), 157.

90. Bowen, *Rural Missouri*, p. 46, quoting *Jefferson City Jeffersonian Republican*, June 13, 1835.

91. Bowen, *Rural Missouri*, p. 48.

92. McDermott, *Wanderings of Alfred S. Waugh*, p. 105.

93. *Ibid.*

94. Rietz, "Theatre of Kansas City," p. 16.

95. Denham Lee Wooten, "Annals of the Stage in Little Rock, Arkansas
1834–1890" (Master's Thesis, Columbia University, 1935), p. 2, quoting *Little
Rock Arkansas Gazette*, Sept. 27, 1834. Typically, all profits derived from the
productions were to be devoted to charity.

96. D. Allen Stokes, "The First Theatrical Season in Arkansas: Little Rock,
1838–1839," *The Arkansas Historical Quarterly*, XXIII (Summer, 1964), 169,
quoting *Little Rock Arkansas Gazette*, Dec. 5, 1838. Stokes gives the population
of Little Rock in 1838 as 1,431, of whom 309 were slaves. This estimate is prob-

converted coffee house that the enterprising manager outfitted with boxes and even a saloon.[97] On January 30 the *Gazette* advised all who could "raise a dollar and love good acting and handsome painting," to patronize Waters' establishment.[98] They would not regret it, continued the *Gazette*, "unless they stop too long in the Recess or the Saloon after the performance."

Following the withdrawal of Waters, professional activity in Little Rock was rare. Religious opposition as well as the tiny population kept the strollers out, and it was well into the 1850's before they began to visit Arkansas again. The amateurs, however, organized in Fort Smith, Camden, Helena, and Pine Bluff before 1860, and the *Little Rock Gazette* observed in 1858 that "histrionics seem . . . quite the rage."[99] The same year Little Rock got a new theater, leased to Nick Maroney of the "Memphis Theatrical Company," and began regular seasonal operation that lasted until the outbreak of war.[100]

5.

In St. Louis and New Orleans, the two major theater towns of the prewar period, developments following the 1853 retirement of Ludlow and Smith came rapidly as the population of both cities grew substantially and prosperity continued unabated.[101] In St. Louis the population explosion resulting in part from the California gold rush gave rise to two new playhouses, the "Peoples Theater" and the "Varieties," which were operating along with Bates's Theater before the end of 1852.[102] Moreover, 1853 saw the organization of the highly successful "Philodramatische Gesellschaft," which offered German-language drama for the benefit of the large German population.[103] In short, St. Louis experienced an entertainment boom equal to (or

---

ably too high; the aggregate figure for 1850 was only 1,967. U. S. Census Bureau, *Social Statistics*, p. 211.

97. Stokes, "First Theatrical Season," p. 172.

98. Quoted in *ibid.*, p. 174.

99. Quoted in Wooten, "Annals," p. 25.

100. *New York Spirit of the Times*, Oct. 23, 1860. John Huntley, an itinerant actor-manager who toured Arkansas with a tent show between 1858 and 1860, credited that state with "the hardest set of people, and [the] worst roads in the union," but he admitted that he made money there. John Huntley to Solomon Franklin Smith, Nov. 20, 1859, Smith Collection, Missouri Historical Society.

101. The population of St. Louis rose from 77,960 in 1850 to 160,773 in 1860; that of New Orleans from 116,375 to 168,675 in the same period. U. S. Census Office, *Social Statistics*, pp. 213, 567.

102. Krone, "Recollections," II, 39.

103. Alfred Henry Nolle, *The German Drama on the St. Louis Stage* (Philadelphia: University of Pennsylvania Press, 1917), p. 16.

even surpassing) the general commercial boom in the prosperity decade of the 1850's.

The Varieties Theater was largely the work of the St. Louis Dramatic Varieties Association, an organization formed following the retirement of Ludlow and Smith. The purpose of the association was, like that of its New Orleans counterpart, to establish a playhouse to serve as center of the membership's social activities.[104] Under management of Joseph M. Field, since 1850 manager of the Mobile Theater, the new theater opened on May 10, 1852.[105]

Field ran into trouble shortly after opening. The members of the Dramatic Varieties Association, a frankly elitist organization, received considerable special attention at the playhouse, a practice that was offensive to the democratic sensibilities of the majority of St. Louisans, who refused to support the theater. As a consequence the operation proved profitless. Field gave up its management in May of 1855 (he died the following year), and thereafter the Varieties was used more and more for grand balls and other such functions, though touring dramatic troupes and opera companies frequently used its facilities.[106]

The People's Theater—the very name suggests that it was created as the egalitarian opposite number of the Varieties—opened to the public on December 9, 1852, under a local impresario, "Doctor" George T. Collins.[107] Initially this theater also experienced troubles, largely managerial. A succession of short-term managers tried and failed in its operation before it fell into the hands of experienced actor George Wood in 1854. Under Wood's able management the People's Theater, later known as "Wood's Theater," flourished. With a seating capacity of over 2,500, the playhouse was the largest to that time in St. Louis. Its operation was practically year-round, with only a short break in August, and despite the lower admission prices charged, it afforded quality equal to the other St. Louis houses.[108]

If the caliber of the performers acting in a given playhouse was

104. MS "Articles of Association, St. Louis Dramatic Varieties Association," 1852, Missouri Historical Society. Sol Smith laid the cornerstone of the new theater.

105. Ludlow MS Diary, May 10, 1852, Missouri Historical Society.

106. *Ibid.*, May 19, 1855; Krone, "Recollections," II, 40, states that Field's trouble originated in a comment the manager supposedly made to the effect that he "did not care to have a man who wore a check shirt" in his theater.

107. Ludlow, *Dramatic Life*, p. 730; Blackburn, "St. Louis Stage," p. 18.

108. Ludlow, *Dramatic Life*, p. 730; Blackburn, "St. Louis Stage," p. 20. Prices of admission were dress circle—$0.50; Parquett—$0.25; gallery—$0.15. Negroes paid $0.25 for gallery seats.

any criteria for judging its excellence, Wood's would have to rank high. Prior to 1861 such luminaries as Edwin Forrest, Edwin Booth, Charlotte Cushman, Eliza Logan (who married manager Wood), Maggie Mitchell, and John E. Owens performed there.[109] Unquestionably Wood's popular playhouse, despite its late arrival and its relatively brief duration, must qualify as one of the more important theaters of the Old South.

Bates's Theater, or the "St. Louis Theater," as it was also called, was the third noteworthy playhouse that operated during the 1850's. When the death of his son in 1855 deprived him of his acting-manager, John Bates gave up operation of the theater, and in 1856 he sold it to Ben De Bar, owner-manager of the St. Charles. De Bar thus inherited the mantle of his long-time associates Ludlow and Smith as the most important theater manager in the South.[110] De Bar enlarged the St. Louis house substantially, and his more than able management made his St. Louis Theatre the most profitable of the houses operating there when the war broke out.[111] In fact, De Bar had forced the People's Theater out of business by late 1859. Thereafter it was occupied only sporadically by such entertainers as wished to rent it.

But other competition quickly appeared. By fall of 1860 there were no less than five entertainment halls open to the public in addition to the St. Louis Theater.[112] Judging by the sheer quantity of theatrical or quasi-theatrical entertainment available by late 1860, there can be little doubt that St. Louis was at the peak of her theatrical fortunes when the war came.

The same was true of New Orleans, long-time theatrical metropolis of the South. It would be a difficult task even to list the various assembly halls and amphitheaters in which drama or subdrama was offered in the last years before the war. Two real theaters dominated the scene—the St. Charles under Ben De Bar and the Varieties

109. Blackburn, "St. Louis Stage," Appendix D, n.p. This appendix lists star appearances as recorded in the contemporary press.

110. Solomon Franklin Smith to William H. Chippendale, Nov. 3, 1857, Smith File, Harvard Theater Collection, Harvard College Library. De Bar paid $45,000 for the Bates playhouse.

111. De Bar had his close friend Sol Smith as an ex officio advisor on hand in St. Louis at all times. It was a considerable advantage. See Benedict De Bar to Solomon Franklin Smith, Jan. 11, Feb. 8, 1860, Smith Collection, Missouri Historical Society.

112. They were Wyman's Hall, the St. Louis Opera House, Library Hall (a minstrel house), the Laclede Theater, and the Melodeon. See *Wilkes' Spirit of the Times*, Oct. 23, Dec. 18, 1860.

(or the Gaieties) under several noteworthy managements. The Old American Theater on Poydras Street, a significant playhouse in the early 1850's, was destroyed by fire in 1855 and was never rebuilt.[113]

When Benedict De Bar assumed control of the St. Charles, "Old Drury of New Orleans," in 1853, he inaugurated a new period in the long life of that storied theater. Before opening, De Bar made extensive renovations on the house. He did away with the pit altogether, replacing the old benches with comfortable seats and enlarging the whole interior.[114] Indeed, he frequently boasted that his playhouse was "the *largest* Theatre in America holding seated *3000* persons."[115]

In general, the new manager followed the managerial policies of his predecessors, Ludlow and Smith. Opening his playhouse early in November each year, he provided an adequate stock company (though perhaps in this respect he fell below the standards of the co-managers) to support a series of top stars, in plays ranging from the trivial to the finest in the language. The seasons lasted until April when De Bar and company departed to begin spring and summer touring. Year after year he offered the kind of variety in programing that New Orleanians had come to expect of the St. Charles,[116] and the combination of quality and variety assured the manager's success. Ben De Bar may be said to have dominated the active New Orleans theater scene throughout the period of his management there.

His competitor, the come-lately Varieties, opened its 1853 season again under Thomas Placide with one of the strongest stock companies in the country. Placide intended to operate without imported stars, relying on the merit of his repertory troupe to provide quality theater, and he succeeded, at least aesthetically. In April of 1854,

113. Ludlow MS Diary, April 20, 1855, Missouri Historical Society. It had not been well patronized for several years prior to its destruction. *New Orleans Picayune*, April 20, 1855. For a partial list of lesser New Orleans playhouses see below, chap. viii, n. 138. The 1850's also saw the high-water mark of German-language theater in New Orleans. See Arthur Henry Moehlenbrock, "The German Drama on the New Orleans Stage," *Louisiana Historical Quarterly*, XXVI (April, 1943), 374.

114. *New Orleans Picayune*, Oct. 30, Nov. 12, 1853.

115. Benedict De Bar to Thomas McKean, June 14, 1853, De Bar File, Harvard Theater Collection, Harvard College Library.

116. Roppolo, "Theatre in New Orleans," is an excellent chronicle of New Orleans theatrical affairs based on a careful investigation of contemporary newspaper sources. The author lists virtually every play, player, and playwright represented on the New Orleans stage during the period.

for example, toward the close of the season, the *Picayune* warmly commended the talented Placide for a series of Shakespearean revivals performed "in a style that few theatres, if any in this country can rival."[117]

The fall season of 1854 in New Orleans was interrupted by yet another devastating theater fire. On November 21, 1854, Placide's Varieties was completely destroyed;[118] manager Placide was forced to move his company to Mobile to complete the season. But his losses drove him temporarily out of management, and when the Varieties reopened in 1855 it was under the management of actor-playwright Dion Boucicault, who called it the "Gaiety." Boucicault promised a theater devoted to comedy, comic opera, ballet, burletta, and farce[119] and indeed for a time fulfilled this promise. But Boucicault's New Orleans managerial career was brief. By spring of 1856 he had given up the Gaiety in order to manage more closely the acting career of his talented wife, Agnes Robertson, and the theater came under control of William H. Crisp, who thereby extended his Southern theatrical domain to include the theatrical capital of the South.

Crisp returned the Gaiety to stock-and-star operation but met with little financial success. It would have been difficult for any manager to compete with De Bar on his own terms, when the St. Charles could offer the likes of Charlotte Cushman, James W. Wallack, Jr., James Henry Hackett, Henry Placide, and others of their caliber.[120] In mid-February of 1858, Crisp was forced out by financial pressure, and the theater was advertised for rent.

December of 1858 again found the Gaiety (which had reverted to its original name) under Tom Placide, who returned with a repertory company that the *Picayune* termed at the close of the season "one of the very best and most popular ever known in this city."[121] Nor was this local opinion without outside confirmation. The *Spirit of the Times* declared in November of 1858: "Mr. Placide's company is the strongest that has ever visited New Orleans, and it will compare favorably with the best that we have had here [New York] re-

117. *New Orleans Picayune*, April 7, 1854.
118. *Ibid.*, Nov. 22, 1854; Ludlow MS Diary, Missouri Historical Society, Nov. 21, 1854.
119. *New Orleans Picayune*, July 13, 1855.
120. Roppolo, "Theatre in New Orleans," p. 193.
121. *New Orleans Picayune*, May 22, 1859.

cently." It included such acknowledged talents as George Jordan, John E. Owens, John Sefton, George Holland, A. H. Davenport, and Sol Smith's talented and highly successful son, Marcus Smith. The *Spirit* concluded that "with the unlimited means, capacity, and experience which Mr. Placide has, it seems certain that the Orleanois will have the best theatre in the Union. . . ."[122]

But the *Spirit* also realized that "the nightly expenses of the Varieties will be more than those of any theatre in this city, without counting the item of rent."[123] Those "nightly expenses" spelled financial ruin for the artistically ambitious Placide. New Orleans could not support theater of this quality in addition to the star-studded St. Charles, and the majority of the theater-going public opted for the stars. Tom Placide did not return to the Varieties for the winter season of 1859–1860.

Instead, one of the leading members of the stock, John E. Owens, assumed management of the playhouse, having taken a four-year lease.[124] He brought New Orleans a great season at the Varieties. His company was good, and he buttressed it with several carefully chosen stars. Among the many highlights were an appearance of Henry and Thomas Placide as the Dromios in *Comedy of Errors*, the New Orleans premier of *Our American Cousin*, and Boucicault's dramatization of *Cricket on the Hearth*, in which Owens played Caleb Plummer for the first time.[125] Moreover, the manager tended to offer long runs of some of the favorite plays, thus breaking distinctly with the hallowed tradition of offering a different play every night. Owens' wife later recalled with obvious satisfaction: "The wealth, beauty and fashion congregated in New Orleans, this winter, was never exceeded in that notably gay city; the 'Varieties' nightly thronged with pleasure seekers. . . ."[126]

When the two New Orleans managers opened their playhouses in the fall of 1860, there was of course considerable political agitation in the wind, and to a degree the playhouses were bound to be adversely affected. On October 29, 1860, for example, William Lowndes Yancey spoke in the Crescent City, attracting a mighty crowd. The *Picayune* observed that the throng that gathered "to see the proces-

122. *New York Spirit of the Times*, Nov. 27, 1858.
123. *Ibid.*
124. Roppolo, "Theatre in New Orleans," p. 201; Mrs. John E. Owens [Mary C. Owens], *Memories of the Professional and Social Life of John E. Owens, By His Wife* (Baltimore: John Murphy and Company, 1892), p. 102.
125. Roppolo, "Theatre in New Orleans," p. 201; Owens, *Memories*, p. 105.
126. Owens, *Memories*, p. 102.

sion and hear the speech, and behold the speaker, had a somewhat malign effect upon the theatres. . . ."[127] But even the fiery Yancey could not close the theaters completely. As the *Picayune* noted, despite the speech, "both at the St. Charles and at the Academy [of Music, a vaudeville type theater] there were compensating houses, and gay ones too."[128] Still, as Ben De Bar wrote Sol Smith in mid-December: "Business here is very Bad[.] nothing thought of but arguments about Politics &c &c."[129]

There is reason to doubt, however, that the winter of 1860 saw any consistent decline in entertainment available in New Orleans as a result of political turmoil. Certainly none of the theaters found it necessary to close for lack of support. And a dispatch from the New Orleans correspondent of the *Charleston Courier* late in November would indicate great activity in the New Orleans entertainment sector. "Our amusement season is now fairly inaugurated," the letter began. The writer then proceeded to catalogue the operating playhouses—three theaters and a newly completed opera house. "Political affairs continue to interest us here," the letter concluded, but I do not find so much excitement existing with relation to the eixgencies [*sic*] of the present crisis as was to have been expected."[130] Even as late as January of 1861 the *Bee* could still report: "Notwithstanding the wars and rumors of wars, our places of amusement are most peaceful and prosperous."[131]

January 26, 1861, was secession day in Louisiana. While the secession convention, sitting in Baton Rouge, concluded the bitter debate and took the final series of ballots, excited throngs milled about waiting for news a hundred miles downriver in New Orleans. The social season was at its height there, and the various centers of commercial entertainment were doing an excellent business. The crowd, resident and transient, could choose among a variety of shows to occupy the time while awaiting word from the state capital.

For the music lovers in town, the Opera House was offering Adelina Patti as Leonora in an early New Orleans production of Verdi's *Il Trovatore*.[132] The featured attraction for the evening at the St. Charles was the enormously popular Maggie Mitchell in the

127. *New Orleans Picayune*, Oct. 30, 1860.
128. *Ibid*. The Varieties had not yet opened for the season.
129. Benedict De Bar to Solomon Franklin Smith, Dec. 13, 1860, Smith Collection, Missouri Historical Society.
130. Nov. 24, 1860.
131. *New Orleans Bee*, Jan. 21, 1861.
132. *New Orleans Bee*, Jan. 26, 1861.

American premier of *Fanchon the Cricket*, the Auguste Waldauer dramatization of George Sand's "La Petite Fadette."[133] Tom Taylor's *Our American Cousin* was scheduled to begin its seasonal run that night at the Varieties. For the less discriminating, the Academy of Music offered a noon matinee performance of "DAN RICE'S GREAT SHOW," that was to be repeated in the evening. It featured Rice's "Shakespearean Burlesques" and "The Terrific Ascension by Mons. Zanfretti."[134] Spalding and Rogers's Museum, which adjoined the Academy of Music, advertised "the most astonishing, wonderful and interesting phenomena ever witnessed, CHRISTINE MILLY, THE TWO-HEADED GIRL," the "SWISS BEARDED LADY," and "the Lilliputian Queen, MISS REED."[135] And finally, Vannuchi's Wax Museum offered "over 250 FIGURES, LIFE SIZE, representing many of the most celebrated subjects in history." One prominent such subject was "OLD JOHN BROWN AND HIS ASSOCIATE MURDERERS, of Harper's Ferry notoriety. . . ."[136]

A similar quantity and diversity of entertainment continued to obtain after the secession convention moved to New Orleans to sit as a constituent assembly. It was not until March that the playhouses began to close and the managers and troupes to withdraw for points north.[137] Shortly after their departure, all the theaters save the St. Charles opened under typically ephemeral summer managements. There were even some new "playhouses"—the "Southern Confederation Garden" for example, had opened in mid-April, just after the fall of Fort Sumter.[138] The transition from peace to war was made with little noticeable decline in commercial entertainment in the pleasure-loving old Crescent City.

But Ben De Bar and John E. Owens were gone, in both cases for the duration. With a few exceptions the members of their troupes followed them, in quest of more stable circumstances in which to pursue their trade. The withdrawal of the theatrical establishment from the key Southern theater town may be taken to symbolize the close of a remarkable era in the theater history not only of New Orleans, but of the South and the nation.

133. *Ibid.* Maggie Mitchell was to rise to fame in this role following its New York premier in 1862. See Odell, *Annals*, VII, 388.
134. *New Orleans Bee*, Jan. 26, 1861.
135. *Ibid.*
136. *Ibid.*
137. *New Orleans Delta*, April 7, 1861; Owens, *Memories*, p. 114.
138. Roppolo, "Theatre in New Orleans," p. 207.

CHAPTER X

THE AUDIENCES

COMPOSITION

AND

CHARACTER

1.

IN 1844, THE YEAR FOLLOWING THE DESTRUCTION OF BOTH PLAYHOUSES in Louisville, Kentucky, the editor of the *Louisville Morning Courier* began a campaign for the construction of a new theater. In the course of his editorial defense of the drama and a lengthy argument in favor of his project, he described a theater audience as "a sort of social exchange—a compendium of character and classes."[1] It was an apt phrase. Indeed, it would be difficult to conceive of a better description of the typical ante bellum theater audience. Financial necessity dictated that theater managers cater to all social classes. The degree to which the manager succeeded in attracting the support of a broad spectrum of society was often the determinant of success or failure. As a consequence, the theater audience of the Old South was usually a polymorphous assortment of diverse social and economic types.

Obviously the wealthy leaders of society in any locale formed the

1. Jones, "The Stage in Louisville," p. 81, quoting *Louisville Morning Courier,* June 13, 1844.

most important single element of theater support. As has been noted frequently in the preceding chapters, it was the social elite that underwrote the financing of new playhouses, and the continued support of that elite was necessary to the successful operation of any theater. Planters large and small, professional men residing in town, wealthy members of the financial and mercantile "establishment"— all were substantially represented in the audiences of a successful theater, especially when, as was so frequently the case, the theater formed an integral part of the social season.

Theater attendance by the socially eminent is to have been expected. Since the early eighteenth century the upper echelons of society traditionally had supported the theater as an aristocratic diversion, and in the South, where aristocratic pretensions were pronounced, the gentry quite naturally provided support for an institution that permitted them to partake of continental customs. But the ante bellum period was above all an age of rampant political democracy, the social overtones of which were as pervasive in the towns of the various Southern frontiers as in any other part of the nation. Such a situation would hardly permit the existence of a purely elitist commercial institution. The lower classes also attended the theater as a matter of course, and their attendance was one factor rendering the theater of the period unique in the history of the American stage.

Contemporary writers on theater affairs provide ample evidence that the playhouse was a popular resort of the democracy. Sol Smith observed that the "hardy mechanic, with his wife and children, . . . the apprentice, the clerk—these and others flocked to the theatre to enjoy an innocent recreation. . . ."[2] Both Noah Ludlow and Louis Fitzgerald Tasistro mentioned the prevalence of riverboat men in the theater audiences of the time and indicated that this pungent element of society formed an enthusiastic and highly vocal part of any audience.[3] Tyrone Power referred to the presence of "the wildest and rudest specimens of the Western population" as well as the fashionables in his New Orleans audiences.[4]

Moreover, the managers actively sought the patronage of the

2. Smith, *Theatrical Management,* p. 233.
3. Ludlow, *Dramatic Life,* pp. 237–38; Tasistro, *Random Shots,* I, 58. Ludlow recalled that the flatboat and keelboat men were easily recognized "by their linsey-woolsey clothing and blanket coats. . . ." The theater was "crowded full" of boatmen the night in 1822 that he introduced Samuel Woodworth's famous song "The Hunters of Kentucky" to New Orleans.
4. Power, *Impressions,* II, 111.

lower classes. When in 1836 Richard Russell, then manager of the Camp Street Theatre, published a broadside accusing James H. Caldwell of elitist pretensions, specifically of disparaging the riverboat men,[5] Caldwell replied with a broadside of his own.[6] The St. Charles, it declared, was in large measure dependent upon the boatmen for support. Caldwell referred to them as those "to whom I owe so much, and have received heretofore so much encouragement from," and as "the most liberal patrons" of his theater.[7] He also flatly denied that he had made any derogatory statement about them. He had to deny it. He literally could not afford to lose their patronage.

On another occasion Noah Ludlow found it necessary to publish a similar denial of a rumor that he had spoken "in disrespectful, and unbecoming words" of Mobile's mechanics.[8] "I have ever reckoned the mechanics among my firmest friends, and liberal supporters," declared the incensed manager. How could he have spoken disrespectfully of mechanics, he queried, when his father, brothers, and male in-laws were all mechanics? "*I shall always be happy to receive the patronage of the Mechanics,*" he concluded emphatically, "and [I] am myself a mechanic."[9] Ludlow realized full well that a boycott by the Mobile artisans might ruin him. The difficulties experienced by Joseph M. Field as a result of a similar indiscretion when he was managing the St. Louis Varieties have already been noted.[10]

In spite of occasional objections to the practice, Negroes, both slave and free, were a part of virtually every theater audience of the period.[11] Once again it was largely a matter of economics—Negroes

5. Richard Russell, Handbill, "To the Masters, Pilots, Engineers and Boatmen of the West," Dec. 10, 1836, Harvard Theater Collection, Harvard College Library. The manager signed his broadside simply "Dick Russell."

6. James Henry Caldwell, Handbill, "To the Masters, Pilots, Engineers, and Boatmen of the West," Dec., 1836, Harvard Theater Collection, Harvard College Library.

7. *Ibid.*

8. Playbill, Mobile Theater, Dec. 27, 1834, Harvard Theater Collection, Harvard College Library.

9. *Ibid.*

10. See above, chap. ix.

11. An exception to the general rule of Negro attendance at the theater was found in Charleston, South Carolina, where Negroes were admitted under some managers and not under others. It is clear that the practice was not popular with white Charlestonians. Early Charleston playbills usually stated flatly: "People of Colour cannot be admitted to any part of the House." See Playbill, Charleston Theater, Dec. 24, 1805, Harvard Theater Collection, Harvard College Library.

formed too substantial a percentage of the population for the managers to ignore them. The profit margin was much too small for that. As a consequence, every playhouse from the largest and grandest to the most rudimentary included a segregated section for the Negroes, usually a part of the third tier. And the playbills and newspaper advertisements almost uniformly included the admission price to their section, frequently along with the declaration that "slaves will not be admitted without exhibiting passes from their masters. . . ."[12]

As was the case with other classes of society, evidence of theater attendance by Negroes abounds in the sources of the period. A letter in the *Richmond Compiler* as early as November of 1819 complained that the theater was likely to work as a corrupting influence on slaves, not only because it took them from their work, but because of "the scenes which they witness, and the society with which they mix in the gallery."[13] Apparently the complaint bore no fruit, however. In December of 1827 another Richmond theater-goer suggested that the manager either raise gallery prices or "keep a police, who may check the overflowing of a riotous spirit among the coloured persons who nightly crowd there."[14] The British-American actor James Henry Stoddart recalled that in Mobile the "colored servants" of the family with whom he lived for a while in 1858 "were frequently invited to go to the theater, and they were never denied the privilege by their employers."[15] William Johnson, the remarkable free Negro "Barber of Natchez," left diary records of attending the playhouse himself and of permitting his slaves and free apprentices to do the same.[16] And Sol Smith wrote of having reserved the third tier of his St. Louis playhouse for Negroes and finding them in general "as honest and virtuous a set of auditors, male and female, as can be found in any

12. *New Orleans Bee*, Dec. 1, 1835. Prices of admission for slaves were usually $0.25 or $0.50. Free Negroes were frequently charged more, as for example, at the first St. Charles Theater, where they were charged $1.00. Box seats for the white population were almost uniformly $1.00, except for the engagements of very special stars.

13. *Richmond Compiler*, Nov. 10, 1819.

14. *Richmond Whig*, Dec. 19, 1827.

15. *Recollections of a Player* (New York: The Century Company, 1902), p. 113. The euphemistic use of the terms "servants" and "employers" is misleading, but Stoddard clearly was referring to slaves and their masters.

16. William Ransom Hogan and Edwin Adams Davis (eds.), *William Johnson's Natchez. The Ante-Bellum Diary of a Free Negro* (Baton Rouge: Louisiana State University Press, 1951), pp. 114, 162.

community. . . ."[17] Negro attendance at the theater was normal and for the most part accepted.

Thus the typical audience was likely to include representatives of the entire range of the social spectrum, from lordly planter to plantation slave. But this is not to say that they mixed on a thoroughly egalitarian basis in the theater. The South had too strong a sense of place for that. If seldom tacitly admitted at the time, Southern society was stratified, and to a notable degree that stratification was maintained in the theater audiences. In a sense, stratification was the natural result of theater construction, which was designed to maintain social differentiation, and of ticket prices, which were graduated toward the same effect. As the *New Orleans Bee* approvingly observed of the St. Charles, there was a "convenient place for every respectable citizen according to his rank and means."[18]

Once again it was largely a matter of necessity for the managers to maintain social distinctions in their playhouses. If they were to retain the support of the wealthy elite, they had to offer a section in effect reserved for that elite, at least by prices high enough to be prohibitive to other classes. Otherwise, the most important element of their support would refuse to patronize the playhouse, to the ruin of the manager. Tasistro observed the desire for social stratification on his 1840 Southern tour. "To suppose," he noted, ". . . that the people of refinement in America have not as keen and as morbid an appetite for social distinctions as they have under the most aristocratic forms of government, is to suppose *that* which every-day experience proves to be preposterous and false."[19] Naturally his frame of reference was the theater.

When a manager failed to accommodate the upper class properly, there was frequently a reaction in the press. The editor of the *Natchez Free Trader* suggested in 1839 that a new playhouse would attract hundreds of "fashionable ladies and families" by removing them from contact with the pit and the gallery. He observed that under circumstances then prevailing "the dress circle of the boxes is but a hair's breadth removed from the pit, and the boxes are only benches, endorsed in the rear by the multitudinous gatherings of free . . . [Negroes]." Such a situation insisted the editor "is not an inducement calculated to weigh in the minds of the ultra refined or

17. Smith, *Theatrical Management*, p. 209.
18. Nov. 8, 1835.
19. *Random Shots*, I, 63.

luxurious."[20] His complaint was a common one, especially in the smaller towns, where the theater facilities were limited and proper distinctions difficult to maintain. But insofar as they were able, period managers segregated their lower-class patrons from the upper classes, and the Negroes from the whites.

In some areas, most notably in New Orleans and Mobile, the Negroes themselves were segregated, with mulattoes sitting apart from the other Negroes. Ludlow and Smith maintained a quadroon section in their theaters. One early Mobile playbill, for example, contained a special notice "TO THE QUADROONS OF MOBILE." In it, Manager Ludlow announced that "in compliance with their wishes," part of the third tier of boxes had been "partitioned off, and fitted up for them expressly." Admission prices were raised from $0.50 to $0.75 for such seats, which were equipped with locks and keys to keep out any possible interlopers.[21] The Marshall Theater in Richmond, Virginia, also provided separate facilities "for mulattoes" from the time of its initial opening.[22]

A final class of society that customarily frequented the theaters and were also in fact segregated, at least in part, were the traditional inhabitants of the third tier—the local strumpets. Since the Restoration, prostitutes had been accustomed to plying their trade in the third tier of the theaters, and the tradition had carried over into the nineteenth century. In 1826 the Duke of Saxe-Weimar Eisenach observed that the "upper gallery" of the American Theater, New Orleans, was devoted exclusively to "the mob and women of the street. . . ."[23] A decade later they were still operating there. The *Bee* noted that the Camp Theater, "like all others has its roost for 'ladies of a certain class'" as well as "its dramshop for drunkards

20. Free, "Southwestern Mississippi," p. 427, quoting *Natchez Free Trader*, Feb. 7, 1838. There were occasional suggestions that the pit should be abolished altogether. P. T. Barnum wrote Sol Smith in 1850: "I do most heartily detest seeing a set of ragged dirty chaps located right under the eyes & noses of respectable ladies & gents. as is generally the case where there is a *pit*." Phineas Taylor Barnum to Solomon Franklin Smith, Dec. 26, 1850, Smith Collection, Missouri Historical Society.

21. Playbill, Mobile Theater, Jan. 31, 1835, Harvard Theater Collection, Harvard College Library. Crisp's Gaiety in New Orleans also maintained "Quadroon Private Boxes" in addition to the "Colored Gallery." Playbill, Crisp's Gaiety, Feb. 16, 1857, Harvard Theater Collection, Harvard College Library. Ludlow insisted that the quadroons "would not condescend to mix with those that had purely negro blood. . . ." Ludlow, *Dramatic Life*, p. 256.

22. *Richmond Enquirer*, Nov. 14, 1838.

23. Saxe-Weimar, *Travels*, II, 82.

and smokers. . . ."[24] Indeed, so prevalent was the demimonde in the theaters of the day that Charles Booth Parsons, whose acting career was almost exclusively Southern, declared that the third tier was commonly called the "brothel quarter."[25] Moreover, Parsons contended, managers were aware that this quarter attracted customers to the playhouse, and as a consequence "a few of the *elite* of the frail sisterhood are [frequently] placed upon the 'free list,' in order to induce their regular attendance."[26] Despite the efforts of such managers as Ludlow and Smith to put an end to the situation, the third tier remained a convenient place of assignation throughout the period.[27]

2.

Given the motley array of citizens that constituted the typical theater audience of the period, it is not surprising that audience behavior tended frequently toward the indecorous, indeed on occasion toward the riotous. But there were other considerations that also conduced to the state of general disorder so common to the playhouses of the time. In the first place, despite the numerous statements to the contrary in the contemporary press, the vast majority of the playgoers went to the theater seeking pleasure, pure and simple, not intellectual stimulation or moral uplift. And the pleasure derived from the play and ancillary entertainment was almost always heightened by eating, drinking, and general conviviality at the playhouse. The theater provided a place for people to meet, to chat,

24. *New Orleans Bee*, Dec. 8, 1835. The *Bee* pointed out, however, that Caldwell's St. Charles Theater had no such "abiding place for the libidinous and disorderly. . . ."

25. [Charles Booth Parsons], *The Pulpit and the Stage; or, The Two Itinerancies. An Historic, Biographic, Philosophic Miscellany. By One Who Knows* (Nashville: Southern Methodist Publishing House, 1860), p. 65.

26. *Ibid.* It should be noted that Parsons wrote his account of his stage experiences after having taken up the pulpit, and his moralistic strictures against the theater may well have been colored by the fervor common to the convert. He found the female inhabitants of the dress circle, or "undress circle" as he termed it, little better than the prostitutes. The dress circle, he insisted, was "the nursery of vice" while the third tier was "the market place of its sale." *Ibid.*, p. 73.

27. Both Ludlow and Smith claimed to have abolished the evil by banishing "women notoriously of the *pave*" from their theaters. Ludlow's admission of the difficulty of effecting the reform, however, casts a doubt upon its absolute effectiveness. Ludlow, *Dramatic Life*, p. 478; Smith, *Theatrical Management*, p. 209.

gossip and joke, to see and to be seen, and in short to have a pleasant time.[28] It was in every sense a social institution. But a possibly unfortunate concomitant of the general informality that prevailed was the lack of decorum commonly exhibited by the inhabitants of every section of the playhouse, dress circle to gallery.

Certain qualifications are necessary, however, before any further meaningful generalization about audience behavior may be made. Although disturbances of one kind or another were common in all playhouses, the intensity of the disorder was often related to the size of the theater operation involved, the size of the community it served, and its distance from the frontier. Obviously, there was a greater potential for organized chaos in the playhouse of a small frontier community than in an old and established urban center with a long theater tradition. Charleston and New Orleans, for example, saw relatively less audience disturbance than did Houston in 1839.[29]

With these qualifications in mind, it is possible to state with considerable accuracy that varying degrees of audience uproar was the prevalent condition in the theaters of the South. The disturbances ranged from mere nuisance factors to pandemonium, riot, and murder, and the extreme forms of disturbance were not rare. All too common was the headline in the *New Orleans Picayune* that read: "Another Disgraceful Scene at the Theatre."[30] The Mobile Theater witnessed one murder, at least one riot, one accidental shooting, and a near-fatal stabbing all between 1835 and 1837.[31] Another Mobile riot in 1848 left the theater, according to an observer, "de-

28. Tasistro perceptively observed that many went to the theater "to show themselves, or to meet with their friends, or to escape from . . . ennui, or because they have nothing else to do. . . ." Tasistro, *Random Shots*, I, 65.

29. Joseph M. Field implied a somewhat less exaggerated distinction in writing of the St. Charles Theater. "The audience is certainly cold," he observed, "too dam'd genteel by half, especially after the hallooing of the Mobilians—." Joseph M. Field to Solomon Franklin Smith, June 7, 1836, Smith Collection, Missouri Historical Society.

30. *New Orleans Picayune*, Feb. 13, 1855. The article gave an account of a group of young blades who sat close to the stage so that they could turn their opera glasses on the audience to watch the goings-on there.

31. Power, *Impressions*, II, 138–39; Playbill, Mobile Theater, Feb. 10, 1835, Harvard Theater Collection, Harvard College Library; Solomon Franklin Smith to Noah Miller Ludlow, April 9, 1837, Ludlow-Field-Maury Collection, Missouri Historical Society. Smith wrote his partner of the stabbing affray: "I have no doubt that our business will suffer seriously from the affair."

faced and damaged materially. . . ."[32] A correspondent of the *New York Spirit of the Times* passing through Columbus, Georgia, attended the theater there and witnessed a not untypical situation. When quiet was requested of the vociferous audience in the midst of a prolonged cheer for the evening's star, some individuals complied. But others, according to the account in the *Spirit*, "continued uproariously, until one *quiet* individual strikes one of the noisy kind. Then, *then* 'our Southern chivalry' . . . was off: pistols popped, bowies came out, and one enthusiastic bounced on the stage, remarking that 'he should be most happy to meet any of the audience after the performance.' "[33] Outlandish and possibly prejudiced as the account sounds, it was probably not greatly exaggerated.

But although the larger towns experienced the extreme forms of audience disturbance to a lesser degree, they were by no means free of the problem. Joseph M. Field, for example, described a "row" at the Louisville theater in 1836 in which a part of the audience attempted to throw one actor into the pit.[34] William Charles Macready walked out on a *Hamlet* performance in St. Louis in 1844 because of "the continued vulgar speeches, ejaculations, and laughs of some ruffians in the second tier. . . ."[35] A riot occurred at the St. Charles Theater when an opera troupe failed to present the final scene of Rossini's *Semiramide* in 1837, almost resulting in the destruction of the famous chandelier.[36] Perhaps the most revealing commentary of all on the matter of audience disturbance is Sol Smith's laconic comment to his partner in an 1840 letter describing an evening's activity at the American Theater, New Orleans. "Hamlet just closing," wrote Sol. "Noisy house—several sent to Calaboose."[37]

32. Charles J. B. Fisher to Noah Miller Ludlow, April 26, 1848, Ludlow File, Harvard Theater Collection, Harvard College Library. Fisher, treasurer of the playhouse, described the scene as one of "more rioting and ill conduct . . . than I ever met, or heard of."

33. *New York Spirit of the Times*, Dec. 18, 1858.

34. Joseph M. Field to Solomon Franklin Smith, Oct. 11, 1836, Smith Collection, Missouri Historical Society. Field concluded that the reputation of the theater "for rows" was "fully sustained" by this affair.

35. William Toynbee (ed.), *The Diaries of William Charles Macready 1833–1851* (New York: G. P. Putnam's Sons, 1912), II, 269.

36. *New Orleans Picayune*, May 23, 1837. "The house," declared the *Picayune* account, ". . . presented more the appearance of a brothel, in the midst of a row, than a respectable resort for amusement."

37. Solomon Franklin Smith to Noah Miller Ludlow, Dec. 11, 1840, Smith Collection, Missouri Historical Society.

Far more common than these extreme forms of disorder was the general prevalence of lesser disturbance—what might be called the "chronic nuisances." This element of disturbance was noted by a *Spirit* correspondent who attended the St. Charles in 1846 to see the Placide brothers in *Comedy of Errors.* "The people in the gallery" he wrote, "wouldn't quiet it, but kept throwing peanuts on the people in the pit, and the buz buz, and hum hum, of small and large talk went all over the house.[38] It is easy to imagine the irritation of that small portion of the audience who had come to witness what must have been one of the most interesting productions of the season.

The presence of refreshments in the playhouses was always a source of disorder. The drunks invariably contributed to the rowdyism and general turmoil and must have been obnoxious indeed, especially when those in the gallery "emptied their overcharged stomachs in the dress circle," as the *Nashville Daily News* insisted was a not uncommon occurrence.[39] But an even more persistent and all-pervading annoyance was the constant cracking and consuming of nuts. Virtually every playhouse had to contend with the nut-eaters, despite frequent editorial campaigns condemning the breed. Most prominent of these campaigns was that of the *Picayune,* which finally admitted, in January of 1860, that it was a failure. Peanuts, at least, admitted the editor, apparently had become by custom and usage "an indefeasible franchise" and "an absolutely necessary adjunct to the pleasure of listening to a play." And at least peanuts were soft-shelled and thus limited in crack volume. But to his horror he discovered that "people are now cracking and eating . . . the English Walnut, the Spanish Pistachio, the Yankee Shagbark, the Kentucky Hickory and the Texas Pecan. . . . " Yet the editor tolerantly accepted even these noisy exotics, pointing out that "nut crackers" were an "indispensable accompaniment of the now almost universal lorgnette."[40]

Still another source of disturbance was the phenomenon of audience participation, which took various forms. Playgoers frequently

38. *New York Spirit of the Times,* March 7, 1846. The disorder in the house was compounded by the arrival of Henry Clay, who entered his box to the accompaniment of "three loud cheers."

39. Davenport, *Cultural Life in Nashville,* p. 144, quoting *Nashville Daily News,* Sept. 8, 1859.

40. *New Orleans Picayune,* Jan. 12, 1860.

competed with the players in impromptu performances in the audience and occasionally even intruded upon the stage itself. "There was a full and lively house at the Theatre last night," observed the *St. Louis New Era* in 1844. "The acting on the stage was good, and the cavorting in the pit, boxes and galleries was extremely interesting. A new performer called Peg-leg, showed off in the gallery with great applause. The managers ought to obtain his services permanently."[41] On an earlier occasion, the *People's Organ* had reported another typical form of audience participation that occurred during a performance of *Romeo and Juliet* in Ludlow and Smith's St. Louis theater. When the Juliet of the evening uttered the famous "Romeo, Romeo, wherefore art thou Romeo?" a wag in the gallery "set the house in a roar by answering 'Because, ma'am, Old Sol thought it would be a *strong cast* and draw a good house.'"[42] It is noteworthy that there was no editorial attack on the interjection. Such occurrences were common and generally accepted if not approved.

There is considerable evidence that some incidents involving audience participation resulted from the curious phenomenon of an auditor's becoming so involved in the plot of the play that make-believe became reality for him.[43] The results were sometimes ludicrous. Joseph Jefferson recalled a performance of Bulwer's *Lady of Lyons* in backwoods Mississippi when the audience "became excited over the trials of the hero and heroine, . . . talked freely among themselves, and, at times, to the actors."[44] One of the rural playgoers, who had apparently completely transcended reality, warned the villain of the melodrama to leave the heroine alone "if he knew what was best for him."[45]

But such incidents were not limited to the gullible rurals. They were common enough in the cities as well. A case in point was that of one Viocca Barra in New Orleans, who became so outraged with the activities of the villainous priest in the ballet *Esmeralda* that he could not contain his fury. As the *Picayune* reported it, "Barra shouted loud and long, and as he could not be prevented from

41. Carson, *Managers in Distress*, p. 260, quoting *St. Louis New Era*, June 4, 1844.

42. *Ibid.*, p. 201, quoting *St. Louis People's Organ*, Oct. 12, 1842.

43. Constance Rourke notes this phenomenon in her *American Humor. A Study of the National Character* (New York: Harcourt, Brace and Company, 1931), pp. 96–97.

44. Jefferson, *Autobiography*, p. 56.

45. *Ibid.*

threatening the priest with vengeance, he was removed to the Calaboose."[46] In the cities as in the country, audiences were in large
measure unsophisticated and eager to be entertained, therefore subject to total identification with stage performances.

In view of the all-too-frequent audience disturbances of the
period, it was only natural that the managers were forced to battle
continually for quiet and decorum in their playhouses. The com-
monest method of attempting to suppress rowdyism was simply to
hire private police to patrol the house, ejecting or arresting anyone
creating a disturbance. Most theater advertisements contained such
statements as that in the *Richmond Whig* in 1833, which assured
the public that "a strong police is engaged to preserve strict order
and decorum."[47] That the presence of police was not altogether effective, however, is evidenced by the continuing necessity of advertising
the presence of police at the theater.[48] Ludlow's contention that the
hiring of six men to police his Mobile theater resulted in "quiet and
order" is simply untrue.[49] Mobile audiences were if anything somewhat worse behaved than in most towns of the period. The effectiveness of the police in controlling boisterous audiences was always
strictly limited, largely because most people believed that any
member of the audience had the right to behave pretty much as he
pleased in the theater, so long as he did no actual bodily harm to
anyone else. After all, he had paid for his ticket[50] and could respond
to the performance as he saw fit.

Perhaps the most effective restraint upon the natural ebullition
of the playgoers was provided not by police or house rules but by
a show of disfavor on the part of the other members of the audience.
James H. Caldwell realized this at least as early as 1841, when he
issued his statement on police policy for his Mobile playhouse. First
he stated his primary reason for employing police at all. "As no public
establishment can succeed unless patronized by ladies," declared the
able manager, "and as ladies cannot possibly countenance a place of
public entertainment where the other sex are disorderly, it is the

46. *New Orleans Picayune,* June 3, 1852.
47. *Richmond Whig,* Jan. 3, 1833.
48. See, for example, *Richmond Compiler,* Dec. 9, 1836; Jan. 1, 1838.
49. *Dramatic Life,* p. 429.
50. A notable example of this common attitude was the case of the man
arrested for "rude and unseemly conduct" and striking a police officer in the
Varieties Theater, New Orleans. In acquitting the defendant, the local judge
ruled that "the dollar you paid at the door" entitled any individual to react as
he pleased to the performance. *New Orleans Daily Delta,* March 4, 1853.

intention of the Manager to make every effort in his power to maintain that decorum in the theatre which is observed in the drawing room."[51] As a consequence, Caldwell would as a matter of course maintain a police force to remove disturbers of the peace and to insure the equanimity of the ladies. But, he insisted, the use of police was never the best way to maintain peace, for "a police officer in attempting to remove an obnoxious individual necessarily occasions some disturbances—friends will sometimes interfere, and occasionally violent altercations ensue."[52] The best approach to the problem of noisy auditors, Caldwell believed, was for the audience itself to discourage disturbances. "The most effectual checks and severest rebukes" he had ever seen were those tendered by "the audiences themselves, who have without moving from their seats simply directed their attention to the place from whence the noise proceeded, and by a general burst of disapprobation, brought the offender to a due sense of decorum."[53]

Doubtless Manager Caldwell was correct in his assertion. But before an audience would quell a disturbance it had to be sufficiently engrossed in the performance to resent the disturbance. Which meant that the performance had to be good, or at least good enough to hold the interest of the audience. Otherwise the disturbance might prove more entertaining than the play. In short, audience behavior frequently depended on the quality of the performance, a circumstance that necessitates a brief digression at this point in order to note some pertinent factors relating to the productions themselves.

3.

The basic unit of theatrical organization was at that time the "stock company," or "repertory company," as the more modern term has it. Such a company was composed of a group of professional actors and actresses of widely varying skill and experience, each hired to perform whatever characters the manager assigned, which were usually

51. Playbill, Mobile Theater, Jan. 25, 1841, Harvard Theater Collection, Harvard College Library.

52. *Ibid.*

53. *Ibid.* Actor George Vandenhoff recalled a case in which an audience effectively quelled a nuisance at the St. Charles in New Orleans. When a boisterous auditor interrupted the performance with his antics, he was quickly "seized, raised off his feet, and literally passed through the air, from hand to hand, across the parquet, till he was outside the door. . . . The whole was the work of about ten seconds. . . ." Vandenhoff, *Leaves from an Actor's Note-Book*, p. 212.

only those fitting the "type" he was chosen to fill. For example, in listing his company roster in 1824, Noah Ludlow included the type description for each member. Heading the list was, of course, "N. M. Ludlow, manager, and genteel comedian. . . ." Then came

> A. M. Wilson, leading tragedian; Jackson Gray, first old men and some low comedy; George W. Frethy, low comedy; William L. Forrest, second tragedy; Samuel P. Jones, Heavy tragedy; Edwin A. Caldwell, second comedy; William Riddle, second old men and sedate fathers; Mrs. M. L. Riddle, romp and juvenile comedy; Mrs. Ludlow, soubrettes and best old women; Mrs. Mongin, second chambermaids; Mrs. Noke, general utility.[54]

With such a company, the manager could cast whatever plays he saw fit, rehearse them, and so build the repertoire of his troupe. The quality of the performances would depend upon a variety of factors, the most obvious being the ability of the individual performers themselves. In actual practice the companies, as has been noted, ranged from excellent to ludicrously bad, depending upon the manager's budget and his judgment. But other factors frequently militated against high-quality stock productions.

Most important of these secondary factors was the necessity of presenting a different program every night. Under such a schedule there was seldom adequate time for the actor to study and perfect a role and never adequate rehearsal time. As Matthew C. Field noted, for a salary of $12.00 a week in 1836 he was expected to perform in the feature attraction and the afterpiece every night, rehearse daily, and study new material frequently amounting to "*Seventeen Lengths* a day."[55] Little wonder that actors were so often unprepared, prompters so busy, and performances ragged.

When the star system became established, the situation worsened. Not only did managers have less capital to hire quality companies,

54. Ludlow, *Dramatic Life*, p. 256.

55. William Glascow Bruce Carson (ed.), "The Diary of Mat Field. St. Louis, April 2–May 16, 1839," *Bulletin of the Missouri Historical Society*, V (January, 1939), 99. One "length" was the equivalent of 42 standard lines of text, so the hard-pressed Matt was expected to memorize 714 lines a day in addition to rehearsals and performances. Two other notable accounts of the difficulties of stock actors in the period are Charlotte M. Martin (ed.), *The Stage Reminiscences of Mrs.* [Anne Hartley] *Gilbert* (New York: Charles Scribner's Sons, 1901), pp. 29–34; and Douglas Taylor (ed.), *Autobiography of Clara Fisher Maeder* (New York: The Dunlap Society, 1897), pp. 26–27.

they felt that quality companies were unnecessary luxuries. After all, the people came out to see stars, not the familiar faces of stock actors. But in addition to a general decline in the over-all quality of the repertory company, the star system also made the life of the stock actor even more difficult. Each star had his own personal repertoire and naturally insisted upon performing from it. Consequently the stock companies had to prepare themselves to support the star in his favorite roles, sometimes on extremely short notice. Despite the efforts of the managers to enforce the "rules" requiring each actor to be prepared for each performance at the risk of a fine or pay cut,[56] seldom was a troupe able to get through a new production in support of a star without considerable help from the prompter or the star himself. Improvisation or "gagging" was also common.

Another factor contributing to shoddy performances was the requirement that each player furnish his own costumes. Considering the meager salaries and limited leisure time at the disposal of actresses and actors of the day, the wonder is not that costumes were sometimes inadequate, but that there were any costumes at all. Again, though the rules frequently contained fines for improper costuming— Ludlow and Smith imposed a fine of $1.00 to $5.00 for appearing on stage "without the proper requisites of boots, tights, collars, gloves, fleshings, caps and feathers, or other articles required to be furnished by the performer. . . ."[57]—players often appeared improperly costumed, sometimes absurdly so. Matthew C. Field wrote Ludlow of a St. Louis performance of Knowles's *Virginius* in which a lady of the company played a slave girl "dressed in a shining silk frock, tight modern sleeves, [and] hair slicked up a la Paris. . . ."[58] Such cases were not uncommon. And obviously such costuming had

56. See "Rules and Regulations of the Theatres under the Direction of Ludlow and Smith," Ludlow-Field-Maury Collection, Missouri Historical Society. This printed list of rules, forty-seven in number, covered all aspects of company activity and behavior, along with penalties for infractions. Article 14, for example, states: "Any performer not ready in a Character, having had the usual time allowed for study, and receiving due notice of its representation, shall forfeit a week's salary." See also "Rules and Regulations of the Marshall and the Avon [Norfolk] Theatres, Virginia, and all others under the Management of George Jones, or His Deputy," Theater Collection, Valentine Museum, Richmond. Period actor Charles A. Krone asserts that the penalties were "seldom if ever enforced. . . ." Krone, "Recollections," III, 229.

57. "Rules of Theaters under Ludlow and Smith," Art. 18. Art. 38 required the players to provide full costumes.

58. Matthew C. Field to Noah Miller Ludlow, Feb. 2, 1838, Smith Collection, Missouri Historical Society.

an adverse effect on the entire production. Who could blame an audience for becoming somewhat indecorous when confronted with such a spectacle?

Considering all these factors, it is not surprising that stock productions, and more especially stock support of star performances, were often rather unprofessional. The Duke of Saxe-Weimar noted that in a Louisville production in 1826 "most of the actors were dressed very badly, had not committed their parts, and played in a vulgar style. One actor was so intoxicated, that he was hardly able to keep his legs."⁵⁹ The Duke might well have been describing numberless other productions of the ante bellum period.

In mentioning the intoxicated actor, Saxe-Weimar touched upon a problem that plagued every theater manager of the day and turned many a production to shambles. The hypermoralistic Charles Booth Parsons observed, probably with more than a grain of truth, that "there are very few of the [acting] profession, either male or female, who do not drink more or less during their performances, in order to stimulate their feelings."⁶⁰ In an age of hard drinking, theater people were notoriously hard drinkers. The stories of the elder Booth's prodigious feats with the bottle are legendary, and managers who hoped to get the great actor on stage sober were forced to take drastic expedients.⁶¹ The letterbooks of Ludlow and Smith are filled with notifications of dismissal for, as one letter phrased it, "having appeared on the Stage (several times) in a State of *inebriety.* . . ."⁶² There was nothing atypical about the performance at the Camp Street Theater described in the travel account of British author Thomas Hamilton. The company, he wrote, "was altogether wretched. I saw Damon and Pythias represented to a full house. Damon was so drunk that he could scarcely stand, and Pythias displayed his

59. Saxe-Weimar, *Travels,* II, 133.
60. *Pulpit and Stage,* p. 200.
61. On one occasion, for example, Ludlow and Smith kept Booth out riding the entire day before a scheduled performance in spite of a driving rain that gave the actor a severe cold. Skinner, *Adventures of H. Watkins,* p. 46.
62. Ludlow and Smith to "Mr. Radcliffe," Oct. 14, 1836, Ludlow and Smith MS Letterbook, Missouri Historical Society. Also typical was the notation beneath this letter that read: "Withdrawn, on Mr. Radcliffe's apologizing and promising amendment." See also Ludlow and Smith to "Mr. Manley," June 17, 1836; Ludlow and Smith to "Mr. H. H. Hamill," Oct. 16, 1840; Ludlow and Smith to Augustus A. Addams, June 30, 1843; Ludlow and Smith to Junius Brutus Booth, June 23, 1846.

friendship in assisting him off the stage."[63] Hamilton did not see fit to return to the theater in New Orleans.

The audiences, then, were not infrequently subjected to performances by actors and actresses who were inadequately prepared and forced to improvise to cover lapses in memory and who were on occasion noticeably intoxicated as well. Little wonder that hisses, groans, and stamping of feet were common and other signs of disapprobation bordered on the unruly or even the violent. Little wonder that when one auditor became indecorous the others in the audience often joined him rather than turning him out. The rowdyism of the playgoers was, in short, frequently justified.

Quite often there was a verbal exchange between an offending actor and his audience. If an actor was hissed or pelted he would drop his character and descend to the footlights either to berate the audience or to beg their pardon. If he chose the latter course, he was frequently forgiven. But if he complained, he usually provoked more ridicule than ever. Such was the case of the unfortunate Claudius in a Charleston production of *Hamlet* in 1842. Tasistro noted that when he met his demise at the hands of the melancholy Dane, "the pit set up such tremendous shouts of joy that the remainder of the play passed off in mere dumb-show."[64] Such was also the case in a St. Louis production of Stone's *Metamora*, in which, according to Ludlow, "the house literally screamed with delight" when an offending player died at the hands of the noble Redman.[65] These little contretemps were common indeed in the playhouses of the period and were accepted as a normal part of the theater experience.

But this is not to say that *all* audiences were boisterous and unruly. Quite often, as Caldwell contended, those who were enjoying the performance would insist upon at least relative quiet. Superior performances and particularly engrossing plays more often than not received respectful attention. In commenting on an 1844 production of John Howard Payne's melodrama *Therese, or the Orphan of Geneva*, the *St. Louis New Era* admitted that the local theater was "by no means distinguished for . . . quiet propriety" but pointed out

63. [Thomas Hamilton], *Men and Manners in America* (London: T. Cadell, Strand, 1833), II, 209.
64. *Random Shots*, II, 191.
65. Noah Miller Ludlow to Solomon Franklin Smith, May 9, 1839, Smith Collection, Missouri Historical Society.

that on this occasion the "stillness" of the audience "proved the popularity of the writer," and of the production.[66] For all the other considerations, people in the last analysis went to the theater to see a
play, and ordinarily they comported themselves at least well enough
that the play might go on without undue interference from the
auditorium.

If the theater-goers of the period were vociferous in their condemnation of inadequacies, they were equally enthusiastic in their
expressions of approval, even of adulation. The *Lynchburg Virginian*
suggested as early as 1829 that perhaps the audience should curtail
its expressions of appreciation, especially when the applause took the
form of banging with canes ("bludgeons") instead of the more traditional signs of approbation. "Discriminating applause is just," concluded the *Virginian*, "but there are some persons who seem to think
it a duty to applaud at the conclusion of every sentence."[67] It is only
natural that playgoers would respond as enthusiastically in approval
of what they liked as they did in censure of what offended them.
Indeed, they enjoyed applauding. It was another means of participating in the theater experience.

The chief recipients of the applause were the stars, male and
female. Popular favorites of the stage commanded the same kind
of adulation Americans have always bestowed upon professional
entertainers of the commercial media, and for the same reasons. The
stars were romantic, beautiful, talented, and faintly mysterious. Their
lives were exciting, or so most believed, probably somewhat less than
virtuous, and available to be shared vicariously by the hyper-
romantic but essentially Victorian public.[68] And from metropolitan
center to rural community, the stars were lionized, idolized, and
applauded.

In the South it was the actresses who received the greatest adulation, no doubt because the majority of theater-goers were male.[69]
Julia Dean, perhaps the most widely idolized of the star actresses,

66. Carson, *Managers in Distress*, p. 260, quoting *St. Louis New Era*, Oct.
10, 1844.
67. Hadley, "Lynchburg Theatre," p. 113, quoting *Lynchburg Virginian*, Feb.
9, 1829.
68. An obvious case in point was the national interest stimulated by the
scandalous Edwin Forrest divorce proceedings that commenced in 1849. See
Moody, *Forrest*, pp. 299–327.
69. Another important reason for the popular adulation of certain actresses
was their identification with a group of favorite heroines of the day, among
them Pauline Deschappelles in Bulwer's *Lady of Lyons*, Mrs. Haller in Kotzebue's *The Stranger*, and Julia in Knowles's *The Hunchback*. See below, chap. xi.

was so much in demand that tickets to her performances were frequently auctioned off, as they had been for the Jenny Lind concerts.[70] Eliza Logan, another Western actress to acquire an ardent following, and whose competition with Dean excited continual interest, was almost as popular. Typical was the report of the *Nashville Republican Banner and Whig* that observed of her local reception: "it seemed as if the audience, in the wildness and phrensy of their delight, would pull down the very walls of the theatre."[71] On one occasion in New Orleans, Fanny Fitzwilliam was nearly smothered by the floral tribute that descended on her from the auditorium. It included an enormous bouquet of magnolias from the Negroes in the gallery.[72] In St. Louis, British actress Ellen Tree was greeted upon her initial entrance with, in the words of the *Gazette*, "such yells and whoops as enliven the wigwams of the Pawnees and Pottawatamies."[73]

Gifts of money and jewelry like those bestowed upon the "two Elizas" in St. Louis in 1837 were not uncommon.[74] Actor-diarist Charles Roehr Pope, for example, recorded a similar honor that was bestowed upon the popular actress Avonia Jones in New Orleans when, in 1858, the mayor of the city crowned her with a "wreath of rose and orange blossoms," then "presented her with a magnificent diamond bracelet from the young men of Orleans, admirers of her genius and beauty."[75] Eliza Logan and Julia Dean were honored with such gifts countless times by the "young men" of virtually every Southern theater town.

Actors as well as actresses were lionized by the public. Edwin Booth, for example, was called out by an audience at the St. Charles in 1857 and was "almost buried with big and little bunches of flowers, which were showered upon him from the parquette, the dress circle, the private boxes and the third tier. . . ." "From one of the proscenium

70. See, for example, *St. Louis Missouri Republican*, Sept. 22, 1850, which reports that box tickets for her performance of Mrs. Haller brought premiums of up to $9.00 each.
71. Davenport, *Cultural Life in Nashville*, p. 121, quoting *Nashville Republican Banner and Whig*, April 10, 1858.
72. *Tallis's Dramatic Magazine and General Theatrical and Musical Review*, I (Nov., 1850), 4.
73. Carson, *St. Louis Stage*, p. 274, quoting *St. Louis Missouri Gazette*, April 25, 1839.
74. See above, chap. viii.
75. J. Alan Hammack (ed.), "An American Actor's Diary—1858," *Educational Theatre Journal*, VII (Dec., 1955), 326. Manager William B. Wood contended in his memoirs that such gifts were frequently "prepared and paid for by the 'grateful recipients'" for the publicity value. Wood, *Personal Recollections*, p. 261. In many cases, however, the gifts were genuine.

boxes," the account continued, "he was crowned, by fair hand, with a floral wreath, bearing his name." After the "thunders of applause" subsided he was permitted to "stagger off the stage, under his burden of bouquets" but was immediately called back to be presented with a "thunderbolt," a small purse full of money.[76] Even this early in his career, it is clear that Booth had become a figure of great celebrity, at least in the Crescent City.

But perhaps even more revealing of the attitude of the Southern public toward star performers was the reception given Joseph M. Field in the town of Wetumpka, Alabama, in 1835. Field, just beginning his acting career, had taken an adjunct of Sol Smith's roving troupe to play for a few nights in the little Alabama town. Of course, he was not a star at this time, but he was the manager and leading man of a group of strolling players and as such received a cordial reception by the local social elite. After a few days in town manager Field wrote to Smith in Columbus, Georgia. "[What] do you think," he exclaimed to his friend. "They have been giving *me a Dinner*. A darling affair I tell ye and the first ever given in Wetumpka— . . . We had a delightful time. I was toasted and then I *spoke*. And then I got quite enough wine to play Lear upon—And then I got along so so."[77] So the adulation of leading players was not limited to the urban centers. The people of Wetumpka and of countless towns like Wetumpka paid homage to their favorites too.

There remains but to determine, if possible, whether the theater audiences of the Old South differed in any material way from those of other parts of the nation. And such sources as are available would seem to indicate that they did not. In all their numerous accounts of audience behavior, none of the theatrical memoirs of the period draws the slightest distinction between (or among) the sections. If the accounts of Washington Irving's *Salmagundi* papers and of Mrs. Trollope's *Domestic Manners* are to be accepted, Southern theater audiences had no premium on exuberance or indecorum.[78] Frontier

76. *New Orleans Picayune*, March 21, 1857.
77. Joseph M. Field to Solomon Franklin Smith, April 24, 1835, Smith Collection, Missouri Historical Society.
78. See Frances Trollope, *Domestic Manners of the Americans*, ed. Donald Smalley (New York: Vintage Books, 1960), pp. 133–35, for her famous account of the theater in Cincinnati in 1828; see [Washington Irving], *Salmagundi; or, The Whim-Whams and Opinions of Launcelot Langstaff, Esq., And Others* (New York: G. P. Putnam and Company, 1857), *passim*, for accounts of the New York stage in the early nineteenth century.

theater was frontier theater, whether it was on a Southern frontier or one in the Northwest. As for the cities, all the conditions that influenced Southern audience behavior prevailed in the Northeast— social admixture, plentiful refreshments, audience participation, and the star system. And they operated to the same general effect. Moreover, in the North as in the South, people went to the theater to enjoy themselves, and enjoy themselves they did, with little noticeable difference in attitude toward what they saw on the stage or in how they reacted to it. In short, Southern theater audiences reflected the customs and mores of their times, not their geographic section. And in general the same was true of the plays they liked.

CHAPTER XI

THE
PROGRAMS

1.

IT HAS LONG BEEN ACKNOWLEDGED THAT THE THEATER OF A GIVEN TIME
and place to some extent reflects the thought, the customs and values,
the "spirit" of the society it serves. Shakespeare believed that the
stage mirrored nature, and he termed the players "the abstract and
brief chronicles of the time . . ." (*Hamlet*, II, ii). Old Samuel Johnson
observed that "the Stage but echoes back the publick Voice," and
that the "Drama's Laws" are given by its patrons.[1] Dr. Johnson also
knew why this was so: "we that live to please," he wrote, "must
please to live." Clearly the theater must reflect something of its
patrons; otherwise it could communicate nothing and entertain not
at all—indeed, it could not even exist.

Since the theater does reflect society, at least to some extent, an
investigation of the type of theater most popular at a given time must
reveal something of the people of that time.[2] The difficulty ordinarily

1. Samuel Johnson, "Prologue Spoken by Mr. Garrick at the Opening of the
Theatre in Drury-Lane 1747," in David Nichol Smith and Edward L. McAdam
(eds.), *The Poems of Samuel Johnson* (Oxford: Clarendon Press, 1941), p. 53.
2. At this point a distinction must be drawn between "theater" and "drama."
"Theater" for the purposes of the present study refers to acted drama, i.e., plays
produced on stage. "Drama" refers to the entire body of dramatic literature, i.e.,
the written plays. Attention here is focused upon theater, not drama. Although
both are doubtless relevant to the culture producing them, the written drama
of the ante bellum South was almost exclusively derivative and imitative, hence
limited in value as a commentary on Southern society.

would be in trying to establish what specific plays were most popular. Fortunately, however, the stage annalists of the major ante bellum Southern towns have amassed reliable statistics on plays performed in the South. Thus, the most popular plays and play types may be determined by a process of actual count.[3]

But before attempting to establish what plays were most popular, and why, and what their popularity reflects of the society, it should be noted that that society was a complex structure comprising elements that ranged from the highly cultured to the utterly crude. And, as was noted in the preceding chapter, all these disparate elements partook of the theater experience. It is obvious that each of the different levels of intellect and sophistication viewed the theater from a different perspective and that the theater's appeal lay on widely differing strata of perception. Stated somewhat differently, the theater represented a form of "high culture" to one part of the audience and "pop culture" to another, a much larger part. To the former group, the theater was an intellectual and aesthetic experience; to the latter the playhouse was merely a source of entertainment and escape. Managers were acutely aware of the necessity of appealing to a broad spectrum of society and culture, and the programs they offered reveal this awareness. Theater programing thus represented another unique facet of the ante bellum stage.

Diversity was the keynote of programing in the period. In addition to the featured play of a given evening, theater-goers were offered music, dancing, variety acts, and an afterpiece, which was almost invariably a comic or satiric farce. These farces were legion in number and varied in quality—most of them richly deserve the extinction that has overtaken them. But the better ones were rich in broad comic appeal.

Of the scores of farces offered, both musical and otherwise, perhaps the most frequently performed were those of Prince Hoare (*Three and a Deuce; No Song, No Supper*), John Baldwin Buckstone (*The Dead Shot; The Pet of the Petticoats; A Kiss in the Dark*), James

---

3. Performance statistics for this chapter were compiled from play lists and similar data in the following: Shockley, "Richmond Theatre, 1819–1838," pp. 160–63, 171–75, and *passim*; Hoole, *Charleston Theatre*, pp. 40–42; Roppolo, "American Stage in New Orleans," *passim*; Roppolo, "Theatre in New Orleans," *passim*; Smither, "New Orleans," pp. 86–87 and *passim*; Free, "Southwestern Mississippi," *passim*; Carson, *St. Louis Stage*, pp. 313–14; Carson, *Managers in Distress*, p. 288; Weisert, *Curtain Rose, passim*; Weisert, *Large and Fashionable Audience, passim*; Crum, "Lexington Theatre," pp. 594–95; Rusk, *Middle Western Frontier*, p. 412–19.

Robinson Planché (*Loan of a Lover*; *The Dumb Belle*; *The Green Eyed Monster*), Marie Therese Kemble (*The Day After the Wedding*), Thomas Haynes Bayly (*You Can't Marry Your Grandmother*; *Perfection, or the Maid of Munster*), and James Kenney (*Raising the Wind*; *Sweethearts and Wives*; *Turn Out*). They were invariably good-natured though sometimes rather coarse, and they frequently portrayed common human failings in the form of satire or caricature. But perhaps the best way to illustrate the sort of thing one might expect in a typical farce is to quote a bit of dialogue from one of them—John Maddison Morton's *Box and Cox*—as recalled by the contemporary critic Henry Austin Clapp:

> Box: Ah, tell me, in mercy tell me; have you a strawberry mark on your left arm?
> Cox: No.
> Box: Then it is he,—my long-lost brother.[4]

Such was the sort of humor upon which the farce was based. Its function was purely and simply to entertain and amuse, and there is no doubt but that it served this function admirably.

Variety entertainment was commonly included in the programs, sometimes resulting in odd combinations of artistic and escapist fare. For example, one program at the American Theater in New Orleans featured a production of von Weber's *Der Freischütz* along with the "GRAND TRAMPOLINE FRANCAISE, OR, MATHIS'S LEAPS." Mathis, it seems, came first on the program. According to the bills, he was to "throw a Somerset over *seven horses*!!" as well as perform the "DRUNKEN SOLDIER, on stilts," during which he would "go thro' the manual of exercise and fire off his gun while standing on one Stilt." Having been thus prepared, the audience was doubtless ready for *Der Freischütz* "with all the original Music. . . ."[5] Or, more likely, the opera fans returning from the bar encountered the Mathis partisans retiring to it.

On another occasion, a Mobile audience was offered the Isaac Bickerstaff version of Molière's *Tartuffe* ("The Hypocrite") on the same program with "MR. BELMONT" the "FIRE-KING OF THE WEST," who, the patrons were informed, was to "EAT A SUPPER composed of

4. Henry Austin Clapp, *Reminiscences of a Dramatic Critic. With an Essay on the Art of Henry Irving* (Boston: Houghton, Mifflin and Company, 1902), p. 16. Clapp observed that this dialogue was "worthy of Plautus."

5. Playbill, American Theater, April 3, 1826, Harvard Theater Collection, Harvard College Library.

LIVE COALS, HEATED ROSIN, BURNING BRIMSTONE, &c."[6] One *Macbeth* production at the Camp in New Orleans shared the bill with the "Real Bedouin ARABS," who offered "extraordinary" acts of gymnastic derring-do. The Bedouins closed their show with a "Grand Eastern Drama" entitled *The Sheik of the Desert* that included "Arabian Gymnastics and surprising Feats. . . ."[7] These seemingly outrageous programs were by no means uncommon in the period. They illustrate clearly the necessity for managers to draw from as wide a spectrum of the theater-going public as possible.[8]

Music was particularly popular in the theaters of the period and was found on virtually every program in one form or another. Songs appeared as incidental music in most of the plays, especially the farces, as well as in entr'acte and specialty numbers. There were two broad categories of songs: the comic and the sentimental. Among the most popular of the sentimental songs were such standards as "Coming Thru the Rye," "Home, Sweet Home," "John Anderson, My Jo," and "The Last Rose of Summer," as well as such lesser-known numbers as "Bird in Yonder Cage Confined," "Cherry Ripe," "The Soldier's Bride," "Is There a Heart that Never Loved?" "Soldier Tired of War's Alarms," and "Scots Wha Hae Wi' Wallace Bled." The comic songs that were frequently called for included the likes of "Barney, Leave the Girls Alone," "Coal Black Rose," "The Good Old Days of Adam and Eve," "Honey and Mustard, or the Ghost of My Wife," "The Lad with the Carroty Poll," "A Man With No Head Won't Care for a Hat," "Paddy Carey," "Tippity Witchetty," "Tis Love that Bothers us All," "What is Woman Like?" "Prime Bang Up," and Sol Smith's favorite, "All in the Oyster Line." Humor and sentimentality, the qualities that formed the emotional basis of the songs, provide an important indication of what would be likely to appeal in the way of drama.

6. *Mobile Commercial Register*, Feb. 17, 1832.

7. Playbill, Camp Street Theater, March 16, 1839, Harvard Theater Collection, Harvard College Library.

8. In a perceptive recent study, David Grimsted contends that such diversity in programing began to disappear nationally about 1850, as theaters began to appear that specialized in only one type of stage entertainment. Separate playhouses came to offer legitimate drama, vaudeville, burlesque, the circus, minstrelsy, and opera, and each of these had its own audience. This tendency is noticeable in the South of the 1850's, though only in the largest towns, those that could support more than one playhouse. See David Allen Grimsted, "A Mirror for Nature: American Theater, 1800–1850" (Doctoral dissertation, University of California, Berkeley, 1963), pp. 132–33.

2.

For all the diversity of incidental entertainment provided at the playhouse, it was still fundamentally the featured play of the evening that drew the audience. Once again, there was great variety in the choice of pieces to head the bills. They were usually five-act plays, or comparable operas or ballets, or sometimes separate acts from several favorite plays. The plays were of varying quality, ranging from Shakespeare to low melodrama and spectacle, but it is possible to divide them into three general categories: legitimate drama of enduring merit, more ephemeral drama of lesser consequence, and the purely escapist "spectacular pieces" of little or no literary worth. And the plays of each category reveal something of the taste and values of the time.

Clearly heading the list of the playwrights of the first category was the name William Shakespeare, unquestionably the most popular dramatist represented on the mid-nineteenth-century stage, if estimation of his popularity may be based on the frequency of productions of his works. The most popular of the Shakespearean plays was almost certainly *Richard III*, perhaps the single play most often performed in the period. Then came, in approximate order of their popularity, *Macbeth, Hamlet, Romeo and Juliet, Othello,* and *King Lear*, all of which could be expected to appear at least once during any theater season, and many of which formed part of the repertoire of the better touring companies. Of the comedies, the most frequently produced were *Merchant of Venice* and *Taming of the Shrew*, usually performed in the David Garrick adaptation entitled *Catherine and Petruchio. Much Ado about Nothing, Comedy of Errors,* and *The Tempest* were offered only occasionally. The remainder of the Shakespearean repertoire was limited almost exclusively to the large theater centers and was only rarely performed even there.[9]

The prevalence of Shakespearean drama in the theaters of the period would seem to indicate rather highly developed dramatic taste in the playgoing public. Perhaps for a small segment of that

9. New Orleans, for example, saw but two productions each of *Winter's Tale* and *Coriolanus*, and only one *King John*, in the years between 1845 and 1860. During this same period *Macbeth* was presented seventy-three times and *Richard III* sixty-one. Roppolo, "Theatre in New Orleans," p. 109.

public it does. But there were various considerations other than
literary merit contributing to the frequent presentation of Shakespeare. And these considerations prevent the conclusion that an enlightened public demanded Shakespeare for his poetic genius.

First among these contributing factors was the star system. Shakespearean drama formed the staple of virtually every star's repertoire;
thus every star engagement was sure to include Shakespearean productions, whether or not the public demanded them. Moreover,
certain Shakespearean characters became closely identified with
particular actors, who performed them regularly. The most obvious
example was the Richard III of Junius Brutus Booth, and Booth's
identification with the part of Gloucester was certainly an important
factor in the frequency of the play's presentation. Similarly, all the
rising young tragedians had to essay the role of Hamlet, hence
numerous *Hamlet* productions. So the tendency of the stars to select
Shakespeare's plays in which to demonstrate their talents contributed
to the apparent anomaly of the great Bard's dominating an essentially frontier theater.[10]

The necessity of overcoming religious and moralistic objections to
the theater provided still another factor contributing to the prevalence of Shakespeare. Particularly in the early years of the period,
his plays were frequently offered as something of a sop to puritanical
theater-haters. His pre-eminent legitimacy and acknowledged greatness lent his works a respectability lacking in those of any other
playwright. Shakespeare served as a standard rebuttal to the vociferous critics of the theater, and his works were constantly cited by its
defenders as a major justification of the theater's existence.[11]

So there were other factors than public demand that accounted for
Shakespeare's popularity. But this is not to say there was no demand
for his works. Obviously they were patronized; otherwise they would
have been discontinued, stars or no stars. Yet on the surface it would

10. The rarity of stock Shakespearean productions is another indication that
his plays were not really in great demand. Most managers found such productions financially hazardous. Indeed, a standard joke among the managers was
the comment attributed to Robert L. Place to the effect that he would not
present another one of Shakespeare's plays, "no matter how many more he
wrote." Noah Miller Ludlow MS Diary, end-paper notation, 1857, Ludlow-
Field-Maury Collection, Missouri Historical Society.
11. See, for example, "Otway," *The Theatre Defended. A Reply To Two
Discourses of the Rev. Thomas Smyth* (Charleston: Thomas J. Eccles, 1838),
p. 31.

seem difficult to account for even such limited actual demand as there was for Elizabethan verse drama. The public was, after all, overwhelmingly uneducated. The answer lies partly in the fact that most of the plays were not presented in their original form but extensively revised, drastically cut, and frequently in the form of adaptations. *Richard III* was almost invariably given in the Colley Cibber version, which, in addition to being shorter, was simplified in structure, with Richard the sole focus of the play, all the blacker by virtue of the reduced evil of his peers. Nineteenth-century audiences liked a clear dichotomy between good and evil, black and white.[12] Hence the preference for Cibber.

Similarly, *King Lear* was generally performed in the much-altered Nahum Tate version, in which Edgar and Cordelia marry, and Lear is permitted to live and even to recover his sanity.[13] As noted above, the Garrick version of *Taming of the Shrew* was ordinarily chosen over the original. Such considerations go a long way toward explaining the public acceptance of Shakespeare.[14]

Finally, it is clear that such actual appeal as Shakespeare had for the less discriminating playgoer lay not in the subtleties of his art but in the emphasis upon the melodrama, oratory, and violence that characterized period productions. Such qualities are eminently present in Shakespearean drama and had the same appeal to the occupants of the pit in a theater on the Southern frontier as they had had to the Elizabethan groundling, toward whom they were originally directed. Indeed, in many respects the theater audiences of the Old South and of Elizabethan England were comparable, both in their social diversity and in their tendency toward unruly behavior.[15] Shakespeare could communicate with the unsophisticated at the level of action and oratory while appealing to the small refined element at the level of dramatic and poetic artistry.

12. Alice I. Perry Wood, *The Stage History of Shakespeare's King Richard The Third* (New York: Columbia University Press, 1909), pp. 165–77.
13. Tucker Brooke, "The History of the Play," Appendix B, *The Tragedy of King Lear*, in Tucker Brooke and William Lyons Phelps, *The Yale Shakespeare* (rev. ed.; New Haven: Yale University Press, 1947), p. 192.
14. Other small alterations were often made to render the plays less offensive to the sensibilities of the times. In the acting version of *Romeo and Juliet*, for example, Juliet is played as seventeen years old rather than thirteen, as in the original.
15. For an interesting development of this point, see Esther Cloudman Dunn, *Shakespeare in America* (New York: The Macmillan Company, 1939), p. 175.

In addition to the great Elizabethan, several other major dramatists found a place in the repertoires of Southern stock companies, particularly in the period preceding the mid-1840's. For example, Beaumont and Fletcher's *Rule a Wife and Have a Wife* proved a favorite comedy, largely because of the popularity of its theme, well expressed in the title. George Farquhar's *Beaux' Strategem* was produced rather frequently, as were William Wycherley's *Country Wife* (usually in the form of Garrick's adaptation, *The Country Girl*) and John Dryden's *All for Love*. Oliver Goldsmith's *She Stoops to Conquer* was even more popular, and Richard Brinsley Sheridan was a real favorite. *The Rivals*, and more especially *School For Scandal*, appeared quite frequently in the playbills of the time. In general, lusty comedies of the Restoration and the eighteenth century fared much better than did other forms of quality drama, which accounts for the greater popularity of Sheridan than, say, Webster, Marlowe, or Jonson.

3.

For all the popularity of *School For Scandal*, Sheridan was more frequently represented in period repertoires by a later work—his translation and adaptation of Auguste Von Kotzebue's *Die Spanier in Peru, oder Rollas Tod*, entitled simply *Pizarro*.[16] This play, usually described in acting editions as a "melodramatic tragedy," is representative of the second, much larger, category of popular drama: the ephemeral and transient plays of only limited dramatic merit. Most of the plays of this category were of late eighteenth- or early nineteenth-century origin; they were, then, the contemporary drama. And it is these plays rather than those of Shakespeare or Dryden or Goldsmith, that most accurately reflect the theatrical taste of the times. As such, they deserve the greatest emphasis in these pages.

The popular favorites are difficult to categorize by type. *Pizarro*, for example, may well be melodrama, but it is emphatically not tragedy, despite the contemporary description of it as such. The favorites, for the most part, dealt with similar themes; all exemplified the dramatic conventions of the time, and all were decidedly romantic. If the essence of melodrama is, as Arthur Hobson Quinn

16. William Dunlap also did a famous adaptation of *Die Spanier in Peru*, but the Sheridan version was more popular and far more frequently performed.

insists, "its freedom from the observance of the strict dramatic law of cause and effect, its intensification of sentiment and exaggeration of passion,"[17] the plays of this category were certainly a form of melodrama. And virtually all are permeated with that peculiarly Victorian variety of hypersentimentalism. Hence, despite numerous minor differences, these plays may be treated as a class, and that class termed for convenience's sake "sentimental melodrama."

Among the countless now more-or-less forgotten playwrights who contributed to this broad category were such contemporary favorites as John Tobin, whose romantic comedy *The Honey Moon* served as opening-night feature for so many playhouses of the period; William Dunlap, whose adaptations of Kotzebue as well as his more original creations were performed regularly; Isaac Pocock and the other playwrights who adapted the favorite novels and poems of Sir Walter Scott;[18] George Colman the Younger, who contributed such thrillers as *Blue Beard* (or, *Female Curiosity*), and *The Iron Chest* (or, *The Mysterious Murder*), as well as popular comedies such as *The Heir at Law*; Robert Montgomery Bird, one of very few American playwrights to gain great popular acceptance, who gave Edwin Forrest such staples of his repertoire as *The Gladiator* and *The Broker of Bogota*; John Augustus Stone, creator of another Forrest standard, *Metamora*; John Howard Payne, a third American, who contributed the successful ballad opera *Clari* (or, *The Maid of Milan*) and, with Washington Irving, the fine comedy *Charles the Second*; Matthew Gregory Lewis, the novelist-playwright of the gothic persuasion, who contributed such favorites as *Adelgitha* (or, *The Fruits of a Single Error*), *The Captive*, *The Castle Spectre*, and *Timour the Tartar*; Richard Lalor Sheil, the Irish playwright who followed Lewis with the likes of *The Apostate* (or, *The Horrors of the Inquisition*), and *Evadne* (or, *The Hall of Statues*); William Dimond, who created *Adrian and Orilla*, *The Aethiop*, *The Bride*

17. *A History of the American Drama From the Beginning to the Civil War* (2nd ed.; New York: F. S. Crofts and Company, 1946), p. 102.

18. Most of the novels and many poems were dramatized, frequently with musical scores. Pocock did *Rob Roy*, the most popular of the plays based on Scott. There were several versions of *Lady of the Lake*, and the Daniel Terry version of *Guy Mannering* gave Charlotte Cushman one of her greatest roles, Meg Merrillies. James N. Barker's *Marmion* was also popular. Of lesser significance were *The Highland Widow*, from *Chronicles of Canongate*, *Bride of Lammermoor*, *Talisman*, from *Tales of the Crusades*, *The Whistler*, from *Heart of Midlothian*, and *Ivanhoe*. See Harold F. Bogner, "Sir Walter Scott in New Orleans, 1818–1832," *Louisiana Historical Quarterly*, XXI (April, 1938), *passim*.

of Abydos, The Broken Sword, The Foundling of the Forest, and *The Lady and the Devil*; Edward Fitzball, who contributed such ephemera as *The Floating Beacon* (*or, The Norwegian Wreckers*), *The Burgomaster's Daughter, Esmeralda, The Last Days of Pompeii*, and *The Lord of the Isles*, all of which drew quite well; Henry Hart Milman, creator of the incredibly popular *Fazio* (*or, The Italian Wife*); Thomas Morton, who provided such comedies as *The Way to get Married, A Cure for the Heartache, Speed the Plough*, and *The School of Reform*; Douglas William Jerrold, who delivered indelible sermons with *Ambrose Gwinnette, The Hazard of the Die*, and *The Drunkard's Fate*; Thomas Holcroft, who preached with the likes of *The Road to Ruin* but also offered such thrillers as *The Tale of Mystery*; James Sheridan Knowles, whose verse plays, especially *The Hunchback, The Wife, William Tell*, and *Virginius*, were among those most frequently produced; and finally Edward Bulwer-Lytton, another of the great drawing cards, who contributed such favorites as *Richelieu, Money*, and *The Lady of Lyons*.

Of all the sentimental melodramas (and there were a great many more than those listed), three stand out as being both representative of the class and markedly popular individually. They are the Kotzebue-Benjamin Thompson "domestic" melodrama *The Stranger*,[19] James Sheridan Knowles's neo-Elizabethan verse "tragedy" *Virginius*,[20] and Bulwer's sentimental comedy-melodrama *Lady of Lyons, or Love and Pride*.[21] Close examination of each of these plays from the standpoint of plot, thematic emphasis, and language reveals much about the theater of the time and of the people who patronized it.

The Stranger, like most of the melodramas, has an involved and rather contrived plot. It centers on the figure of a mysterious, misanthropic stranger who, as exposition reveals, had for some two

19. Versions of Kotzebue's *Menschenhass und Reue*, from which *The Stranger* was derived, were also written by Dunlap and by Sheridan, but the Thompson adaptation was unquestionably the one most often performed. The edition utilized for the present study was Epes Sargent (ed.), *Modern Standard Drama: A Collection of the Most Popular Acting Plays, with Critical Remarks* (New York: William Taylor and Company, 1847), IX, 8–59.

20. See James Sheridan Knowles, *Virginius. A Tragedy*, in Calvin Smith Brown (ed.), *The Later English Drama* (New York: A. S. Barnes and Company, 1898), pp. 293–371.

21. See Edward Bulwer-Lytton, *The Lady of Lyons; or, Love and Pride*, in Brown, *Later English Drama*, pp. 377–436. Hereafter citations to these three plays will be made parenthetically in the text, by act and scene.

years occupied a peasant's hut on the outskirts of the estate of the wealthy German aristocrat, Count Wintersen. The Stranger's female counterpart is the equally mysterious "Mrs. Haller," a kind, charitable, and very beautiful stewardess of Wintersen Castle. She is, according to one character, "plaguy odd"; among other things she loves solitude and is given to frequent spells of quiet weeping "without any one knowing why, or wherefore" (I, i). But in a first-act soliloquy she reveals that she has a family somewhere whose absence is the cause of her chronic loneliness and grief.

Baron Steinfort, brother of Countess Wintersen, appears at the castle for a visit and immediately succumbs to the charms of Mrs. Haller. He decides he must marry her and solicits the aid of his sister in his suit. But Countess Wintersen's effort forces Mrs. Haller's revelation—she is, in reality, the notorious Countess Adelaide Waldbourg, who three years before had deserted her family in favor of a lover. In her words, "I left my children—father—husband, to follow a villain" (III, ii). She has long since repented her fall before the "serpent tongue" of her "seducer," but for all her contrition, she has committed an unforgivable act and has no hope of seeing husband or children again. But fate works to arrange just such a confrontation. The small child of the Wintersens falls into a nearby river, and is rescued by the Stranger. Count Wintersen, overwhelmed with gratitude, sends Steinfort to fetch the hero to receive proper thanks and the meeting between Steinfort and Stranger provides a dramatic recognition scene. The misanthropic Stranger is revealed to be none other than Count Waldbourg and, in addition, the long-lost friend of Baron Steinfort. As they converse, it is revealed that Waldbourg has not forgotten his misguided wife: "Oh!" he cries to his friend, "what are the chains of death compared to the tortures of a deceived, yet doting husband!" (IV, i). And Steinfort, struck by the Stranger's enduring affection for the woman who has so wronged him, determines to attempt their reconciliation. In order to effect a surprise meeting between husband and wife, he insists that the Stranger come to the castle to receive the Wintersens' thanks. In the play's climax, the ill-fated couple confront one another. According to the stage directions, Mrs. Haller is so overcome when she recognizes her husband that she *"shrieks, and swoons in the arms of the Baron"* (IV, ii). The Stranger rushes out.

But Steinfort continues to attempt to bring about the rapprochement. He follows his friend to plead with him to forgive his repentant spouse:

> STEINFORT (*to Stranger*): She has erred; she has repented; and during three years, her conduct has been so far above reproach, that even the piercing eye of calumny has not discovered a speck upon this radiant orb. (V, ii)

But the Stranger, fearing society's derision of the cuckold, refuses to hear of a reconciliation. And just as well, for Mrs. Haller has no intention of further dishonoring her husband by returning to him.—"No!" she exclaims, "Never! My husband's honor is sacred to me. I love him unutterably: but never, never can I be his wife again; even if he were generous enough to pardon me" (V, i). But they agree to meet once more so that Mrs. Haller might bid a final farewell to her children.

The final scene is particularly revealing of the values of the society that found this play so appealing. As the principals meet, the Stranger silently invokes "insulted pride" and "injured honor" to protect him from the pervasive charms of his still beloved but unforgivable wife. Throughout most of their bathetic farewell, according to the stage directions, he remains "*in silent contention between honor and affection.*" Then they speak their parting words:

> MRS. HALLER: In this world, then, we have no more to say.—(*seizing his hand.*) Forget a wretch who never will forget you.—Let me press this hand once more to my lips—this hand which once was mine. And when my penance shall have broken my heart,—when we again meet in a better world—
> STRANGER: There, Adelaide, you may be mine again.
>
> (V, ii)

In all American productions the final curtain falls on these lines. It is significant, however, that in Kotzebue's original the children rush in just as the parents are about to part, and the play ends with an emotional reunification of the family. But Epes Sargent, in his editorial introduction to the American acting edition, reflects the attitude of his countrymen in observing that "there is something repulsive in the terminating scene of this play as it exists in the original German. . . . The characters of both man and wife suffer in their reconciliation."[22] In a society that demanded the ultimate in repentance for the unforgivable sin, a happy ending for the unfaithful wife was inconceivable. And it should be noted that in the final analysis, the sin was not adultery per se, but cuckoldry. The sacrifice of the husband's status through a loss of pride and honor was the real crime—a consideration that reveals much of the place of a shallow and superficial sense of honor within the value system of the times, as well as of the relative position of woman in society. A woman's virtue was considered the summit of the value scale, but the loss of virtue in a wife represented the ultimate evil only in that it tarnished the honor of the husband.

The Stranger, then, is representative of a favorite category of popular drama—the play of seduction, atonement, and penance.[23] Its appeal quite obviously operated at two levels: The audience could vicariously experience (and enjoy) the sensuality of the seduction itself, then be purged and expiated through identification with the guilty party throughout her sorrowful penance. It is not difficult to imagine why such plays were especially popular with the women of the day, against whom the inhibitions imposed by Victorian morality operated most harshly. For all its typically stilted and overblown language, its idealized characterizations, its contrived plot, and its distance from all other Aristotelian standards, *The Stranger* no doubt produced catharsis in countless ante bellum theater-goers.

James Sheridan Knowles's *Virginius,* a five-act, neo-Elizabethan verse "tragedy" illustrates a second popular play type as well as another favorite theme: the defense of female virtue. The play, based on Livy's account of the fall of the second Roman Decemvirate, had as its setting Rome in the fifth century B.C. Exposition reveals that the newly installed First Decemvir, Appius Claudius, is in the process of assuming tyrannical powers. Among the freedom-loving Romans most disturbed by this development is the worthy Centurion, Virginius, father of the breathtakingly beauti-

22. Sargent, *Modern Standard Drama,* pp. iii–iv.

23. Nicholas Rowe utilized the theme of *The Stranger* as early as 1714, when he wrote the verse tragedy *Jane Shore; or, The Fatal Imprudence,* another favorite of ante bellum audiences. The theme was used time and time again, perhaps reaching its greatest popularity only with the tremendous success of the Clifton Tayleure version of Ellen Price Wood's *East Lynne* late in the nineteenth century.

ful and nubile Virginia. The attack of the Sabines upon Rome initiates the play's development; Virginius, along with his daughter's affianced, Icilius, takes to the field to repel the invaders.

But shortly after the departure of Virginius and Icilius, the villainous Decemvir Appius spies Virginia in the Forum and, spellbound by her beauty, vows he will have her. When normal overtures fail to attract the virtuous heroine, Appius determines to resort to extremes. He addresses his aide and panderer Claudius:

> APPIUS: I burn, my Claudius! brain and heart—there's not
> A fibre in my body but's on fire!
> With what a gait she moves! . . . Find me, Claudius,
> Some way to compass the possession of her.
>
> .   .   .   .
>
> Spare not my gold—nor stop at promises.
> I will fulfil them fast as thou canst make them.
> To purchase such a draught of ecstasy
> I'd drain a kingdom—Set about it, Claudius!
>
> (II, iv)

And Claudius is worthy of the charge. He seizes Virginia under pretext that she is one of his slaves—illegally sold to Virginius's barren wife as an infant and passed off by the wife as the Centurion's true daughter. Claudius drags the terrified Virginia before the tribunal, where, of course, Appius himself is to adjudicate the proceeding.

At the insistence of a crowd of incensed citizens, Appius agrees to delay his verdict until Virginius can be summoned to his daughter's defense. And when the Centurion is informed of the outrageous charge and of the true intent of the Decemvir, he races to Rome, where he makes an impassioned plea for Virginia. But to no avail. Appius declares in favor of Claudius and permits Virginius and his daughter only a brief farewell. As father and daughter embrace, Virginius perceives his only possible course of action:

> VIRGINIUS: My dear child! My dear Virginia!
> There is one only way to save thine honour—
> Tis this!—(*Stabs her. . . .*)
>
> (IV, ii)

And Virginia dies in his arms.

The tragic incident serves as the spark of revolution. The second Decemvirate is overthrown. But Virginius, overwhelmed by the turn of events, is driven insane. He refuses to believe his daughter is dead and seeks her out in the prison cell where Appius has been impounded. There he sees a spectral image of Virginia, whom he believes has been violated by the cruel tyrant:

> VIRGINIUS: (*to Appius*) . . . Why, there she is!
> There, at your back—her locks dishevell'd and
> Her vestment torn! Her cheeks all faded with
> Her pouring tears, as flowers with too much rain!
> Her form no longer kept and treasured up
> By her maiden-pride, like a rich casket, cast
> Aside, neglected and forgot, because
> The richer gem was shrined in it is lost!
>
> (V, iii)

Overcome with the horror of the apparition, Virginius strangles Appius, and so the play ends.

In theme and language *Virginius* was as typical of its times as *The Stranger*. The sacrosanct nature of maidenhood and the necessity of its defense at all costs was a theme that pervaded the theater of the period. In the value system of the day, maiden virtue was the touchstone by which all other values were tested. Hence the theme was never too far below the surface in popular drama and never failed to elicit the warm responses of a sympathetic public, a public that could weep for the plight of poor Virginia but at the same time fully appreciate the necessity of her father's precipitate action.

With the third of these examples, Bulwer-Lytton's *Lady of Lyons*, the central theme shifts from sex to excessive pride (though sex is by no means ignored). It was another extremely popular theme of the period, and plays about pride of social status and its ability to thwart the course of true love were legion.[24] But the significance of *Lady of Lyons* lies as much in several subthemes and in its dramatic type as in its central theme. For this incredibly popular play has virtually all of the characteristics of the kind of melodrama that was to emerge fully about the turn of the century and is still frequently performed in burlesque on showboats and in other speciality playhouses.

It would be difficult to overemphasize the vogue this play expe-

---

24. Among them Tobin's *Honey Moon* and Knowles's *The Hunchback*, certainly two of the most successful plays of the period.

rienced. *Lady of Lyons* reached New York in May of 1838, just three months after its London premiere. On June 13, 1838, it was offered as Josephine Clifton's benefit in St. Louis,[25] where it met with resounding success. By October 21 it had proceeded down-river to New Orleans, and the initial performance there was followed by an unprecedented run.[26] On April 4, 1839, it was billed at the Camp Theater "for the 49th Time, (by particular desire.). . . ."[27] And by December of 1838 it had reached Charleston.[28] Sol Smith noted in his diary in August of 1840 that "a kind of garment called 'Claude Melnottes,'" after the hero of *Lady*, were "almost universally worn at the South."[29] And in 1842 the play received the ultimate sign of acceptance. It was burlesqued, as *The Lady of Irons*.[30]

The Lady of Lyons; or, Love and Pride is set in Lyons and its environs in 1795, during the rule of the Directory. Its heroine, Pauline Deschappelles, is the beautiful, gracious, but spoiled daughter of a wealthy Lyons merchant. Her combination of attractions render her the object of many an ardent suit. But Pauline and her ambitious mother prefer that she marry nobility, and alas, there is no more of that in France. So all of the local swains are rejected out of hand, including two wealthy former nobles, Beauseant and Glavis. Each stung by his cursory rejection, the pair together seek revenge upon this prideful parvenue.

As agent for their vengeful plot, Beauseant and Glavis choose a local gardener's son by the name of Claude Melnotte. Young Melnotte, though low-born, is handsome and accomplished; indeed, through study and hard work he has acquired considerable refinement and rather noble tastes, including a highly developed taste for Pauline Deschappelles. He has, it seems, long harbored a secret love for the proud beauty and had only recently made his affection known to her by sending her a set of love poems he had

25. Carson, *St. Louis Stage*, p. 248.

26. Playbill, Camp Street Theater, Oct. 22, 1838, Harvard Theater Collection, Harvard College Library.

27. *Ibid.*, April 4, 1839.

28. Hoole, *Charleston Theatre*, p. 177.

29. Solomon Franklin Smith MS Diary, Smith Collection, Missouri Historical Society.

30. Smither, "New Orleans," p. 512. Another burlesque, *The Lady of the Lions*, featuring Clod Meddlenot, "a Boston Gardener," played St. Louis in 1846. Playbill, St. Louis Theater, June 17, 1846, Harvard Theater Collection, Harvard College Library.

composed. But Pauline had spurned the verses, and Claude, deeply offended, is only too ready to listen to the plan of the vengeful conspirators. Melnotte, whom Pauline had never seen in person, would be passed off as an Italian prince who would woo and win the lady, marry her, then take her to his mother's humble cottage and reveal the horrible truth.

The conspiracy works beautifully; Pauline falls in love with the "Prince of Como" and agrees to marry him. But in the process Melnotte, at heart an honest and fair-minded fellow, has begun to regret the deception and only his "honor" holds him to his agreement to go through with the wedding. By the time he actually marries the happy Pauline, he is nearly griefstricken with the evil thing he has done. But go through with it he must, and so he does. Naturally, Pauline is duly horrified when the truth is revealed. A gardener's son! "Sir," she informs Claude, "you have acted most treacherously" (III, ii). But the honorable and repentant hero offers to leave her virtue unsullied and to grant her an immediate divorce. He addresses her father (who had been quickly summoned):

> CLAUDE: Your daughter has been foully wronged—I grant it sir, but her own lips will tell you that, from the hour in which she crossed this threshold, I returned to my own station and respected hers. Pure and inviolate as when yestermorn you laid your hand upon head and blessed her, I yield her back to you. (IV, i)

Pauline, however, soon realizes that she actually loves Claude, gardener's son or not, and even comes to wish secretly that he would ask her forgiveness. When the evil Beauseant arrives the day after the wedding to gloat over her misfortune, she defends both Claude and his home:

> PAULINE: Sir! leave this house—it is humble; but a husband's roof, however lowly, is, in the eyes of God and man, the temple of a wife's honor! (IV, i)

And when it seems that Claude plans to go through with his decision to divorce her, she gives in completely, forgives him, and begs that he keep her as his wife:

> PAULINE:— . . . [No] law, human or divine, [should] separate the wife from her husband's sorrows. Claude— Claude—all is forgotten—forgiven—I am thine for ever! . . .

> Claude, take me; thou canst not give me wealth, titles, station—but thou canst give me a true heart. I will work for thee, tend thee, bear with thee, and never, never shall these lips reproach thee for the past. (IV, i)

But Melnotte has a blemish on his reputation that must be obliterated before he can become worthy of Pauline. So he joins the army and in two years rises through the ranks to become a colonel and, in addition, the hero of the Battle of Lodi. He also saves his money and somehow manages to amass a considerable fortune before returning to Lyons to reclaim his wife. His actions, he feels, have exonerated him.

Claude arrives in Lyons not a minute too soon. Believing him gone forever, Pauline is about to sign the divorce decree and marry Beauseant. Her father has suffered business reverses and is on the verge of going to prison for debt. And the villainous Beauseant has agreed to pay off his debts in return for Pauline's hand. Melnotte intervenes at the last possible moment, offering Deschappelles ample money for the debts and reclaiming his blissful wife, as Beauseant exits muttering, "Torments and death!" (V, ii). The play ends with Claude speaking its explicit moral: "he who seeks repentance for the Past/ Should woo the Angel Virtue in the future" (V, ii).

Lady of Lyons, then, proclaims the virtues of marriage, home, chastity, family, and virtue. As such it was totally in keeping with the requirements of contemporary public sentiment. But it also illustrates a third popular theme: the denunciation of aristocracy and the exaltation of the common man.[31] The villains here were aristocrats, or former aristocrats; the hero was a common man of talent and honor. It should be noted, however, that it is necessary for Melnotte to rise to the rank of colonel before he can possibly claim possession of Pauline. He could not do so as a gardener's son. Thus, though lip service is tendered democracy, the egalitarianism of the play is strictly qualified and limited. Perhaps it was in this respect more than in any other that *Lady of Lyons* reflected ante bellum society. In any case, the appeal of the play lay less in its message than in its felicitous combination of language, plot, and characterization. It contained humor, pathos, suspense, and

31. There are strong undercurrents of the anti-aristocratic theme in both of the other "model" plays as well.

romance, while expressing the "correct" morals and sentiments. It possessed broad appeal, and its enormous popularity is an indication that at mid-century the theater-going public was growing ever larger.[32]

To understand the most important single reason for the appeal of these plays and thus of all the successful plays of this category, one must understand the contemporary attitude toward the function of the theater. Noah Ludlow expressed it succinctly when he advertised the opening of a season in St. Louis in 1820. As noted in Chapter III, Ludlow assured his prospective patrons that he would do all in his power "to offer a source of amusement that shall be at the same time rational, moral, and entertaining."[33] The theater was expected to exercise strong didactic and moral influences; indeed, the didactic function was believed to take precedence over the entertainment function. The ability of the drama to teach and especially to inculcate morals was the strongest argument in favor of its existence and was utilized in practically every public defense of the theater. And such defenses were numerous, as numerous as the attacks upon the institution that inspired them.

As early as 1811, a defense of the theater appeared in the *Lexington Kentucky Gazette*. "The most pleasing and instructive lessons of morality," argued the defender, "are to be obtained at a well regulated Theatre; and the frailty and vices of mankind are there depicted in the strongest colours, and in too abhorrent a shape not to be detested, and perhaps shunned. It is there that instruction and amusement are so delightfully blended, as scarcely to fail producing a good effect upon the morals of society."[34] An 1838 pamphlet, written in reply to a Charleston cleric's attack upon the stage, employs the same argument.[35] In 1840, the editor of the *Jefferson City* (Missouri) *Jeffersonian Republican* welcomed a stroll-

32. Several other factors contributed to the popularity of the play. For example, virtually every romantic star performed either Claude or Pauline, and *Lady* quickly became a standard in the repertoire. Moreover, there are indications that from the outset the play was staged somewhat more realistically than was customary in the period, i.e., real furniture was employed, as well as more realistic set decorations. If this was the case, *Lady of Lyons* played a decided role in the evolution of the box set and heightened stage realism.

33. *St. Louis Enquirer*, March 8, 1820.

34. Clay, "Lexington Theater," p. 126, quoting *Lexington Kentucky Gazette*, Feb. 19, 1811.

35. "Otway," *Theatre Defended*, p. 31.

ing troupe to town, pointing out that the stage was "no inconsiderable corrective to public depravity; vices are lashed, their faults exposed, and virtue inculcated, in a way most pleasant of all that have been invented by the moralists of any age."[36] The editor of the *Richmond Whig* declared in 1845: "Of all the inventions of man to inculcate a love of goodness, and a horror of wickedness, *the stage,* when properly conducted, is the most powerful and impressive. . . ."[37] And in 1855 the *St. Joseph Commercial Cycle* offered an even stronger version of the argument, declaring: "The theatre unmasks villainy and shows up human nature in its naked creation, sifts virtue from vice and unmasks error in exhibiting truth. It is a great moraliizer [*sic*] when properly conducted, as it applies facts to a moral purpose; and it is a great Theologizer, in that it teaches the existence, the laws and attributes of the deity."[38]

So the didactic-moralistic purpose of the theater was commonly accepted, at least among the theater's public champions. Plays were supposed to sermonize, and sermonize they did, in a tacit and straightforward manner.[39] The most successful of them however, also entertained while they sermonized. And that large category of popular but largely ephemeral plays was uniquely successful in this respect. Here is the fundamental reason for their ability to hold the stage as long as they did.

36. Bowen, *Rural Missouri,* p. 122, quoting *Jefferson City Jeffersonian Republican,* May 2, 1840.
37. *Richmond Whig and Public Advertiser,* Nov. 28, 1845.
38. Bowen, *Rural Missouri,* p. 122, quoting *St. Joseph Commercial Cycle,* Sept. 28, 1855.
39. Most direct of all in its sermon was Lillo's *George Barnwell,* which traced the fall of a young man led astray by a wanton beauty. Barnwell was finally apprehended for murder, and as he was being taken off to await the gallows he spoke the terrible moral:

> Be warn'd, ye youths, who see my sad despair,
> Avoid lewd women, false as they are fair;
> By reason guided, honest joys pursue;
> The fair, to honour and to virtue true,
> Just to her self, will ne'er be false to you.
>
> .   .   .   .
> Ere innocence, and fame, and life be lost,
> Here purchase wisdom, cheaply, at my cost!

George Lillo, *The London Merchant; or, The History of George Barnwell,* ed. Adolphus William Ward (Boston: D. C. Heath and Company, 1906), IV, xiii. The play was frequently performed on Christmas or on New Year's Eve, and young men were especially encouraged by their parents to attend.

4.

But so subject was the theater to the currents of economic fluctuation that managers found all too frequently they could not attract audiences with legitimate theater of whatever quality. And when hard times arrived, the managers, willing to experiment with anything likely to draw, usually brought out the "spectacular pieces," plays that depended upon technical effects of a spectacular nature for their appeal. Among these curiosities, the most popular were the equestrian plays, so often noted in the pages above. But there were other varieties of the spectacular piece. By using transparencies, levels, ramps, treadmills, and other elaborate technical machinery, the inventive manager could stage huge fires, erupting volcanoes, rainstorms (with lightning and thunder), waterfalls, ships at sea, naval battles, even the devastation of entire cities. And such effects provided the central action of any number of thrilling spectaculars in the period.

One of the more popular of the spectacular pieces was entitled *Cherry and Fair Star; or, The Children of Cyprus.* A Mobile playbill, describing an elaborate production of this "Grand Romantic Fairy Drama,"[40] illustrates this class of popular theater. The "play" opens in " A FAIRY FOREST" in which "Birds of various plumage" are seen "feeding on the branches of the trees." Presently the Queen of the Fairies, Aviarzana, makes her entrance "in a SPLENDID CAR, drawn by a FIERY PEGASUS, riding on the bosom of a Cloud." In the second act another fairy, Papillo, enters in a "beautiful CAR, drawn by GRASSHOPPERS. . . ." The second act also featured a view of a "BURNING CAVERN—In the midst of which appears a FOUNTAIN OF REAL WATER." But the grand finale topped all that came before. It was a panorama featuring "A DRAGON, And Serpents spitting Fire!!!" who attacked the heroine Cherry. A "Grand Combat" followed, with Cherry, aided by "the Magic Waters," emerging victorious. The spectacle concluded with a "Grand Chorus" of all participants.[41]

Lexington, Kentucky, witnessed a spectacular piece as early as

40. Playbill, Mobile Theater, n.d. [early 1830's], Ludlow-Field-Maury Collection, Missouri Historical Society.
41. If this was the production advertised in the *Mobile Commercial Register,* May 9, 1832, it also included a scene in which a "full rigg'd ship appears to cross the stage—tack, and return."

1825 when Samuel Drake and company presented a production of *The Woodman's Hut; or, The Forest of Bohemia.* The *Reporter* described the special effects that Drake promised: "A view of Baron Hernhaushoffs' Castle and domains as perspective. The inside of Amelia's cottage. IN A TREMENDOUS STORM the cottage will be destroyed by a THUNDERBOLT. Through the chasm will be presented to the open view Count Conenberg and Amelia; who having escaped their pursuers will be seen RIDING on the WAVES IN AN OPEN BOAT."[42] And all of this action took place in Act I. The second act was to feature a forest fire that destroyed the cottage of the woodsman.

Perhaps the most famous of the spectaculars was the Byron-Payne *Mazeppa,* an equestrian melodrama later rendered immortal by the semi-nude performances of Adah Isaacs Menken. But there were earlier productions, such as that of Llwellen and his Arabian Horse Timour performed in St. Louis in 1840. The *Missouri Republican* described the most spectacular scene:

> In Act 1st Mazeppa is condemned to be lashed to the back of the UNTAMED STEED, who is released amidst the glare of torches, savage shouts and beacon fires, and is seen pursuing his furious course amongst the almost inaccessible rocky heights of Poland, constructed by platforms from the stage to extreme height of the Theatre. In Act 2nd, the descent of the horse, with the victim still lashed to his back, into the plains of Tartary.[43]

It is difficult to imagine, despite the claims of the advertisements, that the spectacular scenes were even slightly realistic in effect. After all, the managers had only crude oil or gas footlights separating stage and audience, and the house lights were invariably kept burning throughout the performances. But there are indications that the people were often duly impressed with the imaginative effects they were offered. Such was at least the case with a St. Louis observer of an early Ludlow production of *The Innkeeper's Daughter.* He wrote:

> Its varied scenery, of land and water, was arranged in the happiest manner, and does the greatest credit to the talent

42. Crum, "Lexington Theatre," p. 276, quoting *Lexington Kentucky Reporter*, Sept. 19, 1825.

43. *St. Louis Missouri Republican*, Sept. 15, 1840. This was, of course, the scene that Menken played wearing only flesh-colored tights.

and industry of the Manager. The old church yard was most excellently delineated; its half-ruined and half-fallen tombstones, with their half-obliterated descriptions—the gloom which was thrown around it—the waving of its trees in the night storm—the deep, solemn tones of the church bell— all gave to the beholder impressions of a secret dread which such scenes are calculated to produce. The difficulties attending the representation of sea scenes have been almost completely overcome by the ingenuity of the Manager. There where Mary springs into a boat, and dashes out onto the waves to the defense of Richard, is almost perfect. We see the perturbed waters lashing the shore, the breaking waves in the distance, the boat gliding over them with its sail spread to the wind, and as if at every instant it would be engulfed.[44]

But realistic or not, the managers could usually rely on the spectacular pieces to draw when all else failed, and throughout the period they never hesitated to resort to special effects to appeal to the public. Though none of these plays is of the slightest literary consequence, they do represent another popular element in the theater of the day. As such they are an important part of the theater history of the ante bellum period.[45]

5.

To this point, little has been said of distinctively Southern regional manifestations in the theater programing of the period. The reason for this apparent oversight is simple: there were very few regional distinctions in programing. Even in the case of the dramatizations of Sir Walter Scott there was little difference, despite the supposedly greater popularity of the Waverly novels in the Cavalier South. The Scott plays, most especially *Rob Roy*, were as successful in New York as they were in New Orleans.[46]

44. Carson, *St. Louis Stage*, pp. 128–29, quoting *St. Louis Beacon*, June 9, 1831. Carson points out that the review was probably written by Colonel Charles Keemle, a local newspaperman and printer predisposed to theatrical activity in St. Louis. His account may well have been colored by his special interest.

45. There are strong indications that as the 1850's advanced, a coalescence of the older lurid melodrama and the spectacular piece occurred, and that this "new sensational dispensation" began to dominate theater programs in the popular playhouses. Krone, "Recollections," III, 174.

46. For example, *Rob Roy* (or *Rob Roy Macgregor*) was produced thirty times in New Orleans between its premier in 1823 and 1832; in New York it was offered forty-six times between 1818 and 1832. Bogner, "Scott in New Orleans," p. 465; Odell, *Annals*, II, 504, 505, 527, 595; III, *passim*.

But in a region with the pronounced sectional distinctions present in the Old South, it is inconceivable that regional issues of moment would not occasionally be reflected on the Southern stage.

One early example of a distinctively local reaction of a theater audience occurred in Augusta, Georgia, in 1831. The contemporary actor and elocutionist James Edward Murdoch recalled that Edwin Forrest was playing *Metamora* there at a time when the question of Cherokee Indian removal was a topic of major interest to most Georgians. Forrest played the noble savage with his usual forceful histrionics and in the council scene outdid himself in swearing vengeance on the avaricious whites. At the climax of the scene, he hurled his knife into the center of the stage, where it quivered as he made his dramatic exit. The Georgians were incensed. As Murdoch observed, Forrest's exit "was followed by loud yells and a perfect storm of hisses from the excited audience, who seemed ready in their fury to tear everything to pieces."[47] It seems that the actor had been so convincing in his characterization that the audience felt it was an intentional affront to all Georgians. As a local judge was said to have insisted, "Forrest believes in that d——d Indian speech."[48] Naturally his engagement at Augusta was ruined.

The Nullification controversy was another sectional issue to crop up on the Southern stage. In 1837, for example, a minor actor attached to the company of Scott and Thorne at Vicksburg, Mississippi, told a "Jack Downing" story that the audience believed condemned the Nullifiers. The *Vicksburg Sentinel and Expositor* was outraged. The story, declared the editor, with its "fling at nullification" was "intolerable. . . ."[49] Such stories, he continued, "may suit other latitudes where people are pleased to be considered the slaves of General Jackson . . . , but here, we hope it will never be tolerated." He concluded by advising the managers to take note of the "hissing and hollowing" that greeted the story and in the future to avoid showing any lack of respect for those favoring Nullification.

As a matter of fact, period managers did attempt to avoid controversial material, and in general they succeeded. But occasionally they produced topical plays written by local citizens, and

47. *The Stage*, pp. 298–99.
48. *Ibid.*, p. 300.
49. Free, "Southwestern Mississippi," p. 370, quoting *Vicksburg Sentinel and Expositor*, Feb. 14, 1837.

these frequently dealt with timely issues, many of them sectional.[50] Such, for example, was the case of an afterpiece entitled *East and South, or Yankees and Southerners* presented in St. Louis in 1837. It was described in the "bills of the day" as "a new Comedy, written by a Gentleman of this City" and was advertised as an "Anti-Political, Anti-Tariffical, Anti-Abolitional, Anti-Pistolical, Anti-Touristical, Anti-Tragical, Anti-Sectional Commedietta, in 3 acts. . . ." The characters listed in the bills tell much of the content of the play. They included "Hairbrain Harrington," a "*redhot* Nullifier," "Madame Vulgaro," an "English Tourist," and various "Gentlemen, Sportsmen, Lynchers, and Rowdies."[51]

Of all the Southern topical questions, however, the most important ones that impinged upon the theater were naturally those concerning slavery and the Negro. Several of the more frequently performed plays dealt with these explosive matters, either implicitly or explicitly. And there seems to have been a noteworthy tendency in their handling in Southern theaters.

The most obvious case of a play imbued with a racial theme is, of course, *Othello*. And this play proved among the most popular of the Shakespearean tragedies in the South as in the North, despite its celebrated inter-racial match. This apparent anomaly may be in part resolved when it is considered that *Othello* was commonly viewed as an anti-miscegenation play.[52] In any case, Southern audiences do not seem ordinarily to have been offended by

50. Roppolo found records of 141 performances of "local and topical plays" in New Orleans in the ante bellum period. Joseph Patrick Roppolo, "Local and Topical Plays in New Orleans, 1806–1865," *Tulane Studies in English*, IV (1954), 116–24.

51. Playbill, St. Louis Theater, Sept. 30, 1837, Harvard Theater Collection, Harvard College Library. It is noteworthy that this "comedietta" was apparently anti-Southern in sentiment. According to a newspaper account, several people walked out on an earlier performance of the piece in protest against its Yankee attitudes. See Carson, *St. Louis Stage*, p. 208, quoting *Missouri Republican*, September 30, 1837.

52. The classic statement of this interpretation is that of John Quincy Adams, an amateur Shakespearean scholar. He wrote: "The great moral lesson of the tragedy of *Othello* is, that black and white blood cannot be intermingled in marriage without a gross outrage upon the law of Nature; and that, in such violations, Nature will vindicate her laws." "Upon the stage," adds Adams, ". . . [Desdemona's] fondling with Othello is disgusting." John Quincy Adams, "Misconceptions of Shakespeare, Upon the Stage," in James Henry Hackett, *Notes and Comments upon Certain Plays and Actors of Shakespeare, with Criticism and Correspondence* (New York: Carleton, Publisher, 1863), pp. 224–25.

the theme, at least not in the first decades of the nineteenth century.[53] Indeed in 1822 a Savannah critic commended Junius Brutus Booth for playing the hero as black-skinned, rather than as a mulatto, as was more conventional.[54] The plight of the Moor drew sympathetic comment from a Natchez commentator in 1839, who in a critique of a Forrest performance observed that the "passions, the love, the jealousy, and the outbursting agony of Othello was before us during the performance of the five long acts."[55]

But as the slavery controversy grew ever more heated and the Southern defense of the institution more militant, Othello became a more objectionable figure in the South. Strolling player Harry Watkins was told in Macon, Georgia, in 1852, that the play was "very displeasing to many citizens" and that they would "not permit his being played dark" under any circumstances.[56] In order "to avoid a row," Watkins wrote, "I played him nearly white." Finally, on December 24, 1860, Noah Ludlow noted in his diary that in a Mobile production of the play, star James Wallack, Jr., flatly refused to perform the lead. He was, according to Ludlow, "afraid of the negro part."[57] Wallack's refusal is understandable. The Alabama Secession Convention convened on December 24. So by the end of the ante bellum period, Othello had to be played as near-white, or not at all.

A similar trend is perceptible in the Southern stage history of Robert Montgomery Bird's *The Gladiator*. The play, which premiered in 1831, has a tacitly abolitionist theme. Moreover, it contains dialogue that it seems would have been utterly inflammatory in the South, especially when it is considered that Negro slaves at-

53. There were exceptions. In 1836 the editor of the *Natchez Free Trader* referred to Othello as a "dirty moor" and commented that had any other playwright "laid such a plot, and made such an ill-assorted match, it would have damned him. . . ." Free, "Theatre of Southwestern Mississippi," p. 253, quoting the *Natchez Free Trader*, Jan. 8, 1836.

54. Sparks, "Theatre in Savannah," p. 53, quoting *Savannah Republican*, March 15, 1822.

55. Gates, "Theatre in Natchez," p. 108, quoting the *Natchez Free Trader*, March n.d., 1839. Similarly, a review of Forrest's Othello in the *Missouri Republican* was completely sympathetic with the characterization. "In the opening scenes," observed the critic, "which exhibits his [Othello's] fond love for Desdemona, it was as tender as deep passion could portray it. . . ." *St. Louis Missouri Republican*, June 14, 1844.

56. Skinner, *The Adventures of H. Watkins*, p. 112.

57. Noah Miller Ludlow MS Diary, Dec. 24, 1860, Ludlow-Field-Maury Collection, Missouri Historical Society.

tended the theater. For example, when Spartacus initiates the slave insurrection at the close of Act II, he calls to his fellow gladiators:

> Death to the Roman fiends, that make their mirth
> Out of the groans of bleeding misery!
> Ho, slaves, arise! it is your hour to kill!
> Kill and spare not—For wrath and liberty!—
> Freedom for bondmen—freedom and revenge![58]

But the play was a standard in Forrest's repertoire, and he played Spartacus on each of his engagements in the South—at least until the mid-1840's. Then, such sentiments as were expressed in the play became an anathema. The play was not performed south of St. Louis after 1847.[59]

Unquestionably, the play that stirred the most sectional animosity was the George L. Aiken version of *Uncle Tom's Cabin*. It is entirely possible that Aiken's *Uncle Tom* provoked fully as much anti-Southern sentiment in the North as had the original novel. Its long premier run in 1852 was unprecedented in the period and in 1854 the *New York Spirit of the Times* declared that "the performance of this drama has made converts to the abolition doctrine many persons, we have no doubt, who have never examined the subject, and know nothing of its merits. . . ."[60] It is not surprising that the Aiken *Uncle Tom* was not welcomed in the playhouses of the South, save perhaps in St. Louis, where the road-show version played without incident in 1858.[61]

But *Uncle Tom's Cabin* provoked a spate of Southern plays written in rebuttal to Stowe and Aiken. In New Orleans a series of Irish burlesques led off the reaction; *Uncle Pat's Cabin* opened in 1853. Then came *Uncle Mike's Cabin; or, the Irishman's Home* in 1855.[62] In rapid succession there followed three more direct rebuttals: Jo-

58. Robert Montgomery Bird, *The Gladiator. A Tragedy*, II, iii, in Clement Edgar Foust, *The Life and Dramatic Works of Robert Montgomery Bird* (New York: The Knickerbocker Press, 1919).

59. New Orleans saw its last *Gladiator* in 1844; Charleston in 1847.

60. *New York Spirit of the Times*, March 1, 1854.

61. George P. Howard (ed.), "Memoirs of the Original Little Eva," *Educational Theatre Journal*, VIII (May, 1956), 277. On the Eastern seaboard, Baltimore was the farthest south the play was produced. A somewhat watered-down version was presented there in 1855, with manager John E. Owens playing Uncle Tom, so that he might "be on the spot should any trouble take place." None did. Owens, *Memories*, pp. 74–75.

62. Joseph Patrick Roppolo, "Uncle Tom in New Orleans: Three Lost Plays," *New England Quarterly* XXVII (June, 1954), 218.

seph M. Field's *Uncle Tom's Cabin; or Life in the South As It is,* Dr. William T. Leonard's *Uncle Tom's Cabin in Louisiana,* and George Jamieson's *The Old Plantation; or Uncle Tom As He Is.*[63] Another burlesque version of the play appeared in Charleston in October of 1853, performed by Kunkel's Nightingale Opera Troupe.[64] The Kunkel troupe brought out still another burlesque in Richmond in 1854, one written by John T. Ford, entitled *The Cloud with the Silver Lining.*[65] Lynchburg saw the S. S. Sanford "Old Established and Original New Orleans Opera Troupe" perform "HAPPY UNCLE TOM'S CABIN: *Or Real Life in Old Virginia*" in January of the same year.[66]

There are no extant copies of any of these parodies and rebuttals. But contemporary descriptions reveal what they were like. The version performed by Kunkel in Charleston was described in the *Courier* as "illustrating the real history of a fugitive, who, weary of living *free to starve* among abolition bigots, returns voluntarily to slavery."[67] The *Courier* advertisement also described vignettes from the play; scene 2, for example, was identified as "A Southern Scene," and it featured such events as "MASSA IS COMING," and "JOYOUS NEGROES." The conclusion was an ensemble number, "SOUTH-CAROLINA PLANTATION DANCE."[68] The Charleston version was probably typical of all of them. The *Happy Uncle Tom* portrayed "the happiness of the negroes of the South": "Introducing the harmony that prevails upon plantations—Their [the slaves'] holiday festivals—Marriages—Congo Dances &c."[69] The Joe Field version, as is revealed in a contemporary playbill, was a travesty purporting to have been written by "Mrs. Harriet Screecher Blow."[70] One of

63. *Ibid.,* p. 219. Leonard was a New Orleans physician and editor of the *Southern Ladies Book.* Jamieson was an actor and minor playwright whose career was largely Southern.

64. *Charleston Daily Courier,* Oct. 24, 1853. Hoole's contention that it was the Aiken *Uncle Tom* that played Charleston Oct. 24–26, 1853, is clearly in error.

65. *Richmond Enquirer,* May 26, 1854.

66. Hadley, "Lynchburg Theatre," p. 176, quoting *Lynchburg Daily Virginian,* Jan. 10, 1854.

67. *Charleston Daily Courier,* Oct. 24, 1853. The *Courier* of the following day declared that the play "was received with the most rapturous applause by a large audience."

68. *Ibid.,* Oct. 25, 1853.

69. Hadley, "Lynchburg Theatre," p. 176, quoting *Lynchburg Daily Virginian,* Jan. 10, 1854.

70. Playbill, Varieties Theater (St. Louis), April 24, 1854, Playbill Collection, Missouri Historical Society.

the routines was a dialogue between "Mrs. Blow and Brother Crow"; another was the "World's convention of the Friends of everyone, opposed to every thing"; a third, "The Nigger EDEN in Canada!"[71] It takes but little imagination to visualize what such productions must have been like.

But the *Uncle Tom* vogue was short-lived. The rebuttals were popular for a while and then all but disappeared from the stage. They were rarely performed after 1855. The most significant thing about them was that they appeared at all, so rare was any theatrical expression of regional animosity, or indeed, of any distinctive regional characteristics. Programing, like most other aspects of theatrical production, was nearly identical North, South, East, and West. A patron of the theater in Boston would usually have found himself quite at home in a theater in Charleston, or St. Louis, or even Mobile. Once again, most of the plays that were popular in the South reflect not sectional or regional distinctions, but rather the values and conventions of the times, the era.

71. *Ibid.*

CHAPTER XII

EPILOGUE

————— ◆•◆• ◆ —————

THE SOUTH

AND THE

THEATER

IN THE SUMMER OF THE EVENTFUL YEAR 1860, THE *Spirit of the Times,* long a close observer of Southern theatrical affairs, noted that the "Southern and Western managers are in town [New York] making arrangements for their next seasons." Ben De Bar was on hand, recruiting for his New Orleans-St. Louis circuit. George Kunkle of Richmond was also there, as were Samuel Duffield of Mobile, W. H. Fleming of "the Georgia circuit," Cowell of St. Louis, Waldren of Louisville, Thompson "of the Tennessee theatres," and others.[1] They were in New York City to fill the depleted ranks of their companies at the marketplace of American theatrical talent. They were, in effect, "provincial" managers in the nation's theatrical metropolis. For within the American theatrical establishment of the pre-Civil War period, the South was a vast theatrical province, the most important in the country.

The provinces have always served vital functions in the theater history of any nation. They provide legitimate drama for the

1. *Wilkes' Spirit of the Times,* July 21, 1860.

people of the hinterlands. They provide training grounds on which young actors and actresses may acquire stage experience. They provide outlets for the exhibition of star talent, and by reducing the concentration of stars in any one area, they enlarge the pantheon of stage luminaries. In short, the provinces provide for the expansion of the theatrical structure beyond the metropolis, rendering it larger both at its base and its peak. In the remarkable theatrical structure of the ante bellum United States, the South served all of these functions. It might even be said that the South was vital to the existence of that structure. For the New York of the nineteenth century, unlike that of the twentieth, was inadequate to support more than a purely local repertory theater. Without the provinces, the stage could not have flourished as it did.

Throughout the colonial period, England supplied America's theatrical personnel. In a sense, the American colonies served as a distinct province of the British stage. But as theatrical development continued to follow in the wake of the receding frontiers to the Mississippi River and beyond, there was an ever increasing demand for actors, actresses, managers, and technicians. The capacity of England to fill this demand was soon surpassed. An American acting profession was born, and as new frontiers produced new theaters, that profession grew ever larger. Moreover, the new theaters led to the establishment of new circuits available for the tours of the stars, foreign and domestic. The extraordinary theatrical growth that marked the mid-nineteenth-century United States could not have taken place without the development of the Southern province.

But more specifically, what were the contributions of the South to the theater history of the period? In part, they may be detailed in the names of theater people whose careers were in large measure identified with the South. The Placide family would head such a list. Alexander, the father of the clan, was one of the key figures of the early Charleston stage and of Richmond's as well. During her brief, brilliant career, his daughter Jane attained repute throughout the country while leading James H. Caldwell's New Orleans stock. Thomas Placide was a prominent comedian-manager of the period, and he remained for the most part in the South until the mid-1850's when he gained star status on the stages of New York and Philadelphia. Henry, most famous of the offspring of Alexander Placide, was known to the South only as a visiting star, but he received his early training under his father in the Charleston stock company. Without a doubt, he was one of the truly great comedians of American stage history.

Several talented actresses of the period, romantic heroines who ultimately gained national reputations, spent the greater portion of their careers in the South. Frances Ann Drake, the "Siddons of the West," was unquestionably first among these talented ladies. She even earned the good graces of (and an actual compliment from) the acidulous Mrs. Trollope.[2] Julia Dean, niece of Fanny Drake and granddaughter of pioneer manager Samuel Drake, served her acting apprenticeship in the South and in the 1850's became one of the favorite stars of Southern audiences. She ultimately gained fame in the theaters of the Northeast and in California.[3] Her career was closely paralleled by that of the Logan sisters, Eliza and Olive, more especially by Eliza, who achieved far the greater success. And there were many more: Mary Vos Stuart, Eliza Petrie, Eliza Riddle, Priscilla Cooper, Charlotte Barnes—these and others deserve mention in this list of successful "Southern" heroines.

The South also figured prominently in the careers of some of the greatest theatrical luminaries of the day. Junius Brutus Booth made his American debut in Richmond, Virginia, returned frequently to the South on tour, and gave his final performance in New Orleans. Edwin Forrest, as noted above, served his apprenticeship in the Southwest and made his rapid ascent to stardom immediately after leaving the tutelage of James H. Caldwell. Caldwell was also a powerful influence on the career of perhaps the greatest actress of the period—the brilliant Charlotte Cushman. It was in New Orleans in 1835 that Cushman, at the advice of manager Caldwell, gave up her proposed operatic career to concentrate on the drama. On April 23, 1836, at the St. Charles Theater, she played her first Lady Macbeth.[4]

2. Trollope, *Domestic Manners*, p. 129. Odell refers to Mrs. Drake as "the recognized leader of tragedy in America" prior to the advent of Charlotte Cushman. Odell, *Annals*, III, 370.

3. George D. Ford, *These Were Actors. A Story of the Chapmans and the Drakes* (New York: Library Publishers, 1955), p. 192.

4. Nelle Kroger Smither, "Charlotte Cushman's Apprenticeship in New Orleans," *Louisiana Historical Quarterly*, XXXI (Oct., 1948), 979–80. The *New Orleans Bee* of April 25, 1836, suggested that Cushman "should confine her at-

Still another renowned period actor to serve a Southern apprenticeship was comedian Joseph Jefferson, III. Following the death of his father in 1842, young Jefferson toured with his mother, Cornelia Burke Jefferson, throughout the Mississippi Valley. One biographer credits his early experience at the St. Charles in New Orleans with bringing the great character actor into contact with the reigning talents of the 1840's, thus priming him for his long career as a star. Apparently Jefferson had a certain affection for the South. At the close of the Civil War he purchased a plantation in the Teche Country of Louisiana where he spent parts of each winter and where he eventually retired to write his valuable autobiography.[5]

At a somewhat less exalted scale there were countless notable players who were either products of the South or influenced to some extent by their provincial apprenticeships. Adah Isaacs Menken was apparently born just outside of New Orleans, and her early career was spent touring with the James S. Charles troupe in the Red River Valley. Her rise to fame was launched in New Orleans in 1858, though her great notoriety was the product of postwar activities, commencing with her *Mazeppa* performances in 1863. Strangely enough, at least three of the great stage "Yankees" gained provincial success before attaining stardom in the Northeast. George Handel "Yankee" Hill, though Boston-born, made his stage debut in Charleston. He then toured widely in the South, perfecting his characterization of the shrewd, laconic New Englander before making his successful New York debut in 1832.[6] Danforth Marble toured the South with John S. Potter's troupe as a general utility man before attempting the Northeastern cities. His biographer declared that Ludlow and Smith frequently featured Marble as a star in their theaters and that in ten years time paid him some $40,000. Little wonder that he had "strong regard" for "that particular section of the country," the Southwest.[7] Joshua S. Silsbee, the third of the stage Yankees with strong Southern con-

tention" to such roles "if she means to excel on the stage. . . ." The actress personally credited Caldwell with guiding her into her career as a tragedienne. See Emma Stebbins (ed.), *Charlotte Cushman: Her Letters and Memories of Her Life* (Boston: Houghton, Osgood, and Company, 1878), p. 22.

5. Jefferson, *Autobiography*, pp. 467–68.
6. Northall, *Yankee Hill*, pp. 18–19.
7. "Falconbridge," *Dan. Marble*, pp. 47, 114.

tacts, made his debut in Natchez under Caldwell in 1838, then toured the South extensively before his 1843 debut in the Northern metropolis. But the following year he returned to the South, this time as a star.[8] All three Yankees long remained favorites of Southern audiences.

Another notable comedian, George Holland, spent many years with Southern companies, especially that of James H. Caldwell, before achieving star status in the Northeast. Lester Wallack recalled that he played his first starring engagement in Charleston prior to launching his New York career.[9] William Warren served his theatrical apprenticeship in the Southwest.[10] The great Edwin Booth chose to tour widely in the South before commencing his brilliant career in New York.[11] The list could be extended indefinitely if players of lesser renown were to be mentioned. Typical was the letter written by fledging player Andrew Jackson Neafie to Ludlow and Smith in 1841. Neafie, a minor New York actor, decided he needed provincial experience before making his bid for stardom. "I am desirous of visiting the South and West professionally," he informed the co-managers, "to remain a year, and . . . [possibly] longer. I should be happy to treat with you, for your winter and summer season, to play Seconds to stars, and the leading heavy business. It is under the advice of Edwin Forrest Esqr. that I address *you thus*. . . ."[12] Neafie was perfectly aware that a period of "seasoning" in the provinces would enhance his career immeasurably. This was the way it was done.

In addition to serving as a training ground for actors and actresses, however, the South also provided a vast arena for the stars to exhibit their talents outside the theatrical metropolis. Thus, for better or worse, the South helped to initiate and perpetuate the star system in the United States. Following Thomas Abthorpe Cooper's visit to Charleston in April of 1805,[13] virtually every star

8. Coad and Mims, *American Stage*, p. 174.

9. [John] Lester Wallack, *Memories of Fifty Years*, ed. Laurence Hutton (New York: Charles Scribner's Sons, 1889), p. 187.

10. Anon., *Life and Memoirs of William Warren, Boston's Favorite Comedian. Fifty Years of an Actor's Life* (Boston: James Daly, 1882), p. 8.

11. Coad and Mims, *American Stage*, p. 216.

12. Andrew Jackson Neafie to Ludlow and Smith, April 21, 1841, Smith Collection, Missouri Historical Society. Forrest held the co-managers in high esteem. Significantly, Ludlow's *Dramatic Life* is dedicated to the great American actor.

13. Hoole, *Charleston Theatre*, p. 71.

of the English-speaking stage toured the Southern circuit at one time or another.[14] In the case of British stars, no visit to the United States was complete without a Southern tour.[15] The close-knit nature of the Southern circuit and the relative accessibility of the theater towns permitted them to tour without unbearable inconvenience (though they frequently complained of inconvenience, especially when en route to engagements in interior Georgia and Alabama). In any case, the star system was dependent upon lucrative starring tours for its very existence, and the Southern circuit provided the stars ample opportunity and ample economic incentive to tour.

So much for the contributions of the South to the theater. What of the contributions of the theater to the South? They are not easily determined; the importance of any social institution is a difficult thing to measure. But such limited evidence as bears directly on the matter does indicate that the theater had an established place in the society, particularly the nascent urban society, of the region.

14. A limited and highly selective list of period stars who made Southern tours would include:

Edwin Thomas Booth	William Charles Macready
Junius Brutus Booth	Danforth Marble
Dion Boucicault	Charles Kemble Mason
William Evans Burton	Lola Montez
Céline Céleste	Anna Cora Mowatt
Frank S. Chanfrau	James Edward Murdoch
Edmon S. Conner	Henry Placide
William Augustus Conway	Jane Placide
Thomas Abthorpe Cooper	Thomas Placide
Charlotte Cushman	Tyrone Power
Fanny Elssler	Ravel family
Clara Fisher	Thomas Dartmouth Rice
Fanny Fitzwilliam	Agnes Robertson
Edwin Forrest	John Sefton
James Henry Hackett	Joshua S. Silsbee
Thomas Sowerby Hamblin	Barry Sullivan
George Handel Hill	George Vandenhoff
George Holland	James William Wallack
Joseph Jefferson, III	Lester Wallack
Charles and Ellen Kean	William Warren

15. As Charles Kean wrote Sol Smith from London just prior to a proposed visit in 1860, "I quite agree with you that New York & New Orleans are sufficient to have settled before we [Charles and his actress wife Ellen] leave England. . . ." Charles Kean to Solomon Franklin Smith, April 5, 1860, Smith Collection, Missouri Historical Society. It should be understood that a visit to New Orleans meant a Southern tour, for no star would journey so far without prospects of several profitable engagements.

Theater and drama, plays and players, were things that people, or at least many people, enjoyed, thought about, talked about. Of course, many others reviled the institution and fought it with fervor. The important thing is, they were concerned, and that popular concern is the best general indication that the theater was an institution of real social significance. There are other indications. In the first place, in addition to fanatical religious attack, the theater prevailed over periodic economic distress, frequent epidemics of a variety of diseases, recurrent fires, and an unfavorable climate. In spite of awesome disadvantages, the institution grew. This in itself denotes its basic strength.

There were other less patently obvious signs of the theater's appeal to a large segment of the population. The widespread existence of amateur theatrical companies, even in isolated rural communities, points to a people who believed the theater to be a normal, desirable form of entertainment and recreation. Another sure sign of the appeal of the theater was the common phenomenon of local citizens' attempting to join the ranks of the professional actors or undertaking to write performable plays. Ludlow and Smith found it necessary to establish a "Committee on Authors and Amateurs" to handle the requests of the aspiring players and playwrights with which the managers were plagued.[16] Typical was the letter they received from one John F. Osborn, a discontented clerk from Columbia, South Carolina, that began: "Gentlemen, having Some Idea of trying a theatrical life, I have taken the liberty to address a few lines to you on the Subject of an Engagement. . . ."[17] The "authors" also deluged period managers with their laboriously handwritten manuscripts, some few of which were even produced. As early as 1827 the *Lynchburg Virginian* advertised a performance of *Virginia, or Love and Bravery* "written by a Gentleman of Lynchburg."[18] Such productions were not uncommon. Playwriting was apparently a favorite endeavor of the literate and creative element in the South, and the writing of plays certainly indicates an interest, even an involvement, in the theater.

16. Smith, *Theatrical Management*, pp. 251–52.
17. John F. Osborn to Ludlow and Smith, July 14, 1835, Smith Collection, Missouri Historical Society. For other such applications, see Smith, *Theatrical Management*, pp. 252–55.
18. Hadley, "Lynchburg Theatre," p. 259, quoting *Lynchburg Virginian*, Nov. 19, 1827.

So the theater was important to at least some, and probably many, ante bellum Southerners. They accepted it, supported it. And the institution served certain functions in Southern society, some sharply defined, others more vague but no less certain. One need only turn to the public defenses of the theater to find the purposes that the contemporaries believed it served. In 1820, the *Charleston Courier* published a letter to the editor unequivocally stating the benefits of the theater: "In the first place," it began, "the Theatre is [a] source of public revenue," paying annually "a tax equal to that of the owner of 500 negroes, or of one hundred thousand dollars in real estate." But in addition, the theater "imparts information . . . quickens thought . . . corrects taste . . . tends to introduce a proper pronunciation . . . inculcates politeness, ease and grace, and teaches society how to mingle together without jarring and collision."[19] In addition it contributed to the aesthetic, moral, and recreational life of the people.

With only minor variations, these were the claims made for the theater by all its public supporters. Although the writers doubtless claimed too much in the defense of their cause, there is no reason to doubt the sincerity of the arguments. Indeed, much of their case was founded in reality. For example, the public did derive considerable benefit from entertainment taxes and from the constant support of local charities by theater managers, ever in quest of good public relations. Charity benefits were common. Moreover, virtually every catastrophe was met with a theater benefit for the sufferers, and devastating fires and floods were frequent occurrences in the South.

But clearly a more important contribution of the theater to Southern society lay in the area of what might be called "accultural" factors. Noah Ludlow was thinking of the theater's role in acculturation of frontier society when he wrote: "Like milestones, that serve to mark the progress of the traveller, so the pioneers of the Drama serve to mark the progress of civilization and refinement."[20] In a similar vein, when a new "thespian society" was organized in Boonville, Missouri, in 1841, the *Dramatic Mirror* observed: "Verily, the march of improvement progresses west rapidly."[21] There can be no doubt but that the theater influenced the society of the urban South by providing a source of rational amusement for the people of the towns. Although elegance and decorum were not always conspicu-

19. *Charleston Courier*, Feb. 2, 1820.
20. Ludlow, *Dramatic Life*, p. 2.
21. *Dramatic Mirror and Literary Companion*, Aug. 14, 1841.

ously in evidence in the Southern playhouses, the existence of the playhouses reveals a certain desire for refinement and culture, and the institution surely must have helped to realize that desire. Such urbanity as Southern society could claim was surely heightened by the presence of the theater.[22]

But, in the final analysis, the ultimate significance of the theater lay not in its economic contributions nor its potential for intellectual and spiritual uplift, but in its unique ability to entertain. In a period when life was often arduous and sources of amusement limited, the theater provided escape, diversion, and recreation. For numberless bored, or disenchanted, or discouraged people, the theater was a rich source of pleasure. And that, it must be admitted, is no small thing.

22. Significantly, a notable study of the first decade of the San Francisco stage credits the prevalence of Southerners in the Bay area (given as 30 to 40 per cent of the population) with the ready acceptance of the legitimate theater there. Frank Fenton, "San Francisco Theater, 1849–1859" (Doctoral dissertation, Stanford University, 1942), pp. 17–18.

SELECTED BIBLIOGRAPHY

I. *Primary Sources*

A. UNPUBLISHED MATERIAL

Caldwell, James Henry. Handbill, "To the Masters, Pilots, Engineers, and Boatmen of the West," December, 1836. Harvard Theater Collection, Harvard College Library.

James Henry Caldwell File. Harvard Theater Collection, Harvard College Library. Seven autograph letters.

Benedict De Bar File. Harvard Theater Collection, Harvard College Library. Thirteen autograph letters, playbills, and other De Bar memorabilia.

Holmes, Emma. "A Charleston Lady Sees the Civil War," typescript of MS diary. Southern Historical Collection, The University of North Carolina.

Noah Miller Ludlow File. Harvard Theater Collection, Harvard College Library. Uncatalogued collection of Ludlow materials, including approximately two hundred autograph letters, scrapbooks, and memorabilia.

Noah Miller Ludlow MS diaries, 1840–1870. Missouri Historical Society.

Ludlow-Field-Maury Collection, *ca.* 1820–1940. Missouri Historical Society. 1,500 items, including correspondence, scrapbooks, memorandum daybooks, clippings, and other printed material relating to three families connected by marriage.

[291]

Playbill Collection. Harvard Theater Collection, Harvard College Library. Files of bills from various Southern cities.

Playbill Collection. Missouri Historical Society. Files of bills relating largely to St. Louis theater history.

"Rules and Regulations of The Marshall and The Avon Theatres, Virginia, and all others under the management of George Jones, or His Deputy." Theater Collection, Valentine Museum, Richmond, Virginia.

"Rules and Regulations of the Theatres under the Direction of Ludlow and Smith." Missouri Historical Society.

Russell, Richard. Handbill, "To the Masters, Pilots, Engineers, and Boatmen of the West," December 10, 1836. Harvard Theater Collection, Harvard College Library.

Solomon Franklin Smith Collection, *ca.* 1832–1868. Missouri Historical Society. 1,058 items, including correspondence, playbills, account books of the firm of Ludlow and Smith, and other business records.

Solomon Franklin Smith File. Harvard Theater Collection, Harvard College Library. Nineteen autograph letters, playbills, and memorabilia.

Solomon Franklin Smith MS diaries, 1842–1860 (intermittent). Missouri Historical Society.

Theatre Collection. Valentine Museum, Richmond, Virginia. Miscellaneous playbills, prompt books, clippings, and autograph letters of managers and actors related to the theater in Richmond. Includes notes on the Richmond Theater by Edward Virginius Valentine, compiled from newspaper files.

B. NEWSPAPERS AND PERIODICALS

Charleston Courier, 1803–1861.

Columbus (Georgia) *Enquirer,* 1832–1861.

Commercial Review of the South and West, The, 1846.

Dramatic Mirror and Literary Companion, The, 1841–1842.

Mobile Commercial Register, 1823–1832.

Mobile Commercial Register and Patriot, 1834–1841.

Mobile Daily Register, 1853–1860.

Mobile Register and Journal, 1845–1846.

Nashville Whig and Tennessee Advertiser, 1818.

New Orleans Argus, 1828.

New Orleans Bee, 1832–1861.

New Orleans Louisiana Courier, 1830–1831.

New Orleans Louisiana Gazette, 1818–1823.

New Orleans Picayune, 1837–1860.

New York Spirit of the Times, 1836–1860.

Niles' Weekly Register. 76 vols. Baltimore, 1811–1849.
Petersburg Intelligencer, 1811.
Porter's Spirit of the Times. 9 vols. New York, 1856–1861.
Raleigh (North Carolina) *Minerva,* 1820.
Raleigh (North Carolina) *Register,* 1835.
Richmond Compiler, 1818–1844 (incomplete file).
Richmond Enquirer, 1811–1860 (incomplete file).
Richmond Whig, 1827–1836 (incomplete file).
Richmond Whig and Public Advertiser, 1845–1851 (incomplete file).
St. Louis Enquirer, 1820.
St. Louis Missouri Gazette, 1814–1821 (incomplete file).
St. Louis Missouri Republican, 1825–1850.
Tallis's Dramatic Magazine and General Theatrical and Musical Review. 1 vol. New York, 1850–1851.
Theatrical Times, The, 1846–1849. 3 vols. London, 1846–1849.
Wilkes' Spirit of the Times. 3 vols. New York, 1859–1860.

C. GOVERNMENT PUBLICATIONS

DeBow, James Dunwoody Brownson. *Statistical View of the United States, Embracing its Territory, Population—White, Free Colored, and Slave—Moral and Social Conditions, Industry, Property, and Revenue; The Detailed Statistics of Cities, Towns and Counties; Being a Compendium of the Seventh Census.* Washington: A. O. P. Nicholson, Public Printer, 1854.

Ford, Worthington Chauncey, *et al.* (eds.) *Journals of the Continental Congress, 1774–1789.* 34 vols. Washington: Government Printing Office, 1904–1934.

U.S. Bureau of the Census. *Statistical Abstract of the United States.* 1941. Washington: Government Printing Office, 1942.

U.S. Department of the Interior, Census Office. *Report on the Social Statistics of Cities,* Part II, *The Southern and the Western States.* Washington: Government Printing Office, 1887.

U.S. Department of State. *Compendium of the Inhabitants and Statistics of the United States, as obtained at the Department of State from the Returns of the Sixth Census.* Washington: Printed by Blair and Rives, 1841.

———. *Fifth Census, or, Enumeration of the Inhabitants of the United States. 1830.* Washington: Printed by Duff Green, 1832.

———. *The Seventh Census of the United States: 1850.* Washington: Robert Armstrong, Public Printer, 1853.

D. PUBLISHED MEMOIRS, DIARIES, TRAVEL ACCOUNTS

Asbury, Francis. *The Journal of the Rev. Francis Asbury, Bishop of the Methodist Episcopal Church, From August 7, 1771 to De-*

cember 7, 1815. New York: N. Bangs and T. Mason, 1821.

Carson, William Glascow Bruce (ed.). "The Diary of Mat Field. St. Louis, April 2–May 16, 1839," *Bulletin of the Missouri Historical Society,* V (January, 1949), 91–108; (April, 1949), 157–84.

Clapp, Henry Austin. *Reminiscences of a Dramatic Critic. With an Essay on the Art of Henry Irving.* Boston: Houghton, Mifflin and Company, 1902.

Cowell, Joseph Leathley. *Thirty Years Passed Among the Players in England and America.* 2 vols. New York: Harper and Brothers, 1844.

Drew, Mrs. John [Louisa Lane Drew]. *Autobiographical Sketch of Mrs. John Drew with an Introduction by her son John Drew with Biographical Notes by Douglas Taylor.* New York: Charles Scribner's Sons, 1899.

[Hamilton, Thomas]. *Men and Manners in America.* 2 vols. London: T. Cadell, Strand, 1833.

Hammack, J. Alan (ed.). "An American Actor's Diary—1858" [Diary of Charles Roehr Pope), *Educational Theatre Journal,* VII (December, 1955), 324–37.

Hogan, William Ransom, and Edwin Adams Davis (eds.). *William Johnson's Natchez. The Ante-Bellum Diary of a Free Negro.* Baton Rouge: Louisiana State University Press, 1951.

Howard, George P. (ed.). "Memoirs of the Original Little Eva," *Educational Theatre Journal,* VIII May, 1956), 267–282.

Jefferson, Joseph. *The Autobiography of Joseph Jefferson.* New York: The Century Company, 1889.

Krone, Charles A. "Recollections of an Old Actor," *Missouri Historical Society Collections,* II (October, 1906), 25–43; III (January, 1908), 53–70; (April, 1908), 170–82; (1911), 275–306; IV (1911), 423–36.

Leman, Walter M. *Memories of an Old Actor.* San Francisco: A. Roman and Company, 1886.

Ludlow, Noah Miller. *Dramatic Life as I Found it: A Record of Personal Experiences.* St. Louis: G. I. Jones and Company, 1880.

McDermott, John Francis (ed.). *Travels in Search of the Elephant: The Wanderings of Alfred S. Waugh, Artist, In Louisiana, Missouri, and Santa Fe, in 1845–1846.* St. Louis: Missouri Historical Society, 1951.

Marshall, Thomas Maitland (ed.). "The Journal of Henry B. Miller," *Missouri Historical Society Collections,* III (1931), 213–87.

Martin, Charlotte M. (ed.). *The Stage Reminiscences of Mrs.* [Anne Hartley] *Gilbert.* New York: Charles Scribner's Sons, 1901.

Melish, John. *Travels Through the United States of America in the*

Years 1806 & 1807, and 1809, 1810, & 1811. 2 vols. Philadelphia: privately published by the author, 1815.

Mowatt, Anna Cora. *Autobiography of an Actress; or, Eight Years on the Stage.* Boston: Ticknor, Reed, and Fields, 1853.

Murdoch, James Edward. *The Stage, or Recollections of Actors and Acting from an Experience of Fifty Years.* Philadelphia: J. M. Stoddart and Company, 1880.

Owens, Mrs. John E. [Mary C. Owens]. *Memories of the Professional and Social Life of John E. Owens, By His Wife.* Baltimore: John Murphy and Company, 1892.

Pollack, Frederick (ed.). *Macready's Reminiscences, and Selections from His Diaries and Letters.* New York: Harper and Brothers, 1875.

Power, Tyrone. *Impressions of America during the Years 1833, 1834, and 1835.* 2 vols. Philadelphia: Carey, Lea, and Blanchard, 1836.

Robinson, Emmett (ed.). "Dr. [John Beaufain] Irving's Reminiscences of the Charleston Stage," *South Carolina Historical and Genealogical Magazine,* LI (July, 1950), 125–31; (October, 1950), 195–215; LII (January, 1951), 26–33; (April, 1951), 93–106; (July, 1951), 166–79; (October, 1951), 225–32; LIII (January, 1952), 37–47.

Rodenbough, Theophilus Francis (ed.). *From Everglade to Cañon with the Second Dragoons, (Second United States Cavalry.) An Authentic Account of Service in Florida, Mexico, Virginia, and the Indian Country, Including the Personal Recollections of Prominent Officers.* New York: D. Van Nostrand, 1875.

Royall, Anne. *Mrs. Royall's Southern Tour, or Second Series of the Black Book.* 3 vols. Washington: privately published, 1830.

Saxe-Weimar Eisenach, Bernhard, Duke of. *Travels Through North America, During the Years 1825 and 1826.* 2 vols. Philadelphia: Carey, Lea, and Carey, 1828.

Skinner, Maud, and Otis Skinner (eds.). *One Man in His Time. The Adventures of H. [Harry] Watkins, Strolling Player, 1845–1863 from His Journal.* Philadelphia: University of Pennsylvania Press, 1938.

Smith, Solomon Franklin. *The Theatrical Journey-Work and Anecdotal Recollections of Sol. Smith, Comedian, Attorney at Law, Etc. Etc.* Philadelphia: B. Peterson, 1854.

———. *Theatrical Management in the West and South for Thirty Years. Interspersed with Anecdotical Sketches: Autobiographically Given.* New York: Harper and Brothers, 1868.

Stoddart, James Henry. *Recollections of a Player.* New York: The Century Company, 1902.

Stone, Henry Dickinson. *Personal Recollections of the Drama or Theatrical Reminiscences, Embracing Sketches of Prominent Actors and Actresses, their Chief Characteristics, original Anecdotes of them, and incidents Connected therewith.* Albany: Charles Van Benthuysen and Sons, 1873.

Tasistro, Louis Fitzgerald. *Random Shots and Southern Breezes, containing Critical Remarks on the Southern States and Southern Institutions, with Semi-Serious Observations on Men and Manners.* 2 vols. New York: Harper and Brothers, 1842.

Taylor, Douglas (ed.). *Autobiography of Clara Fisher Maeder.* New York: The Dunlap Society, 1897.

Toynbee, William (ed.). *The Diaries of William Charles Macready 1833–1851.* 2 vols. New York: G. P. Putnam's Sons, 1912.

Trollope, Frances. *Domestic Manners of the Americans,* ed. Donald Smalley. New York: Vintage Books, 1960.

Vandenhoff, George. *Leaves from an Actor's Note-Book; with Reminiscences and Chit-Chat of the Green-Room and the Stage, In England and America.* New York: D. Appleton and Company, 1860.

Wallack, [John] Lester. *Memories of Fifty Years,* ed. Laurence Hutton. New York: Charles Scribner's Sons, 1889.

Wemyss, Francis Courtney. *Twenty-Six Years of the Life of An Actor and Manager. Interspersed with Sketches, Anecdotes and Opinions of the most Celebrated Actors and Actresses of our Day.* 2 vols. New York: Burgess, Stringer, and Company, 1847.

Wood, William Burk. *Personal Recollections of the Stage, Embracing Notices of Actors, Authors, and Auditors, During a Period of Forty Years.* Philadelphia: Henry Carey Baird, 1855.

E. MISCELLANEOUS CONTEMPORARY WORKS

Anon. *The Actor; or, a Peep Behind the Curtain. Being Passages in the Lives of Booth and Some of his Contemporaries.* New York: William H. Graham, 1846.

Anon. *Life and Memoirs of William Warren, Boston's Favorite Comedian. Fifty Years of an Actor's Life.* Boston: James Daly, 1882.

Aston, Anthony. *The Fool's Opera; or, The Taste of the Age.* London: Printed for T. Payne at the Crown in Paternoster-Row, n.d. [ca. 1731].

Brown, Calvin Smith (ed.). *The Later English Drama.* New York: A. S. Barnes and Company, 1898.

Carson, William Glascow Bruce (ed.). *Letters of Mr. and Mrs. Charles Kean Relating to Their American Tours.* St. Louis: Washington University Publications in Language and Literature, 1945.

Foust, Clement Edgar. *The Life and Dramatic Works of Robert Montgomery Bird.* New York: The Knickerbocker Press, 1919.

Gaisford, John. *The Drama in New Orleans.* New Orleans: J. B. Steel, 1849.

Hamilton, William T. *A Sermon on Theatrical Entertainments.* Mobile: Dade and Thompson, 1841.

Hutton, Laurence (ed.), *Opening Addresses.* New York: The Dunlap Society, 1887.

Hutton, Laurence, and William Carey (eds.). *Occasional Addresses.* New York: The Dunlap Society, 1890.

"Letters of Rev. James Madison, President of the College of William and Mary, To Thomas Jefferson," *William and Mary Quarterly,* 2nd ser. V (April, 1925), 77–95.

Lillo, George. *The London Merchant; or, The History of George Barnwell,* ed. Adolphus William Ward. Boston: D. C. Heath and Company, 1906.

"Otway." *The Theatre Defended. A Reply to Two Discourses of the Rev. Thomas Smyth.* Charleston: Thomas J. Eccles, 1838.

[Parsons, Charles Booth.] *The Pulpit and the Stage; or, The Two Itinerancies. An Historic, Biographic, Philosophic Miscellany. By One Who Knows.* Nashville: Southern Methodist Publishing House, 1860.

[Rees, James]. "The Southern Stage, Actors and Authors," *Dramatic Mirror and Literary Companion,* I–II (December 11, 1841–May 7, 1842). (Sequential issues.)

Sargent, Epes (ed.). *Modern Standard Drama: A Collection of the Most Popular Acting Plays, with Critical Remarks.* 12 vols. New York: Berford, 1847.

Smyth, Thomas. *The Theatre, A School of Religion, Manners and Morals! Two Discourses Delivered on the Opening of the New Theatre in Charleston.* Charleston: Jenkins and Hussey, 1838.

Stebbins, Emma (ed.). *Charlotte Cushman: Her Letters and Memories of Her Life.* Boston: Houghton, Osgood, and Company, 1878.

"Thespis." *A Review of the Rev. Thomas Smyth's Two Sermons Against Theatres.* Charleston: E. C. Councell, 1838.

Wikoff, Henry. "Fanny Ellsler in the United States," *New York Spirit of the Times,* May 25, 1844.

II. *Secondary Sources*

A. BIBLIOGRAPHICAL AIDS

Baker, Blanche M. *Dramatic Bibliography. An Annotated List of Books on the History and Criticism of the Drama and Stage and on the Allied Arts of the Theatre.* New York: The H. W. Wilson Company, 1933.

———. *Theater and Allied Arts. A Guide to Books Dealing With the History, Criticism, and Technique of the Drama and Theater and Related Arts and Crafts.* New York: The H. W. Wilson Company, 1952.

Brockett, O. G. "The Theatre of the Southern United States from the Beginnings through 1865. A Bibliographical Essay," *Theatre Research*, II (1960), 163–74.

Cantrell, Clyde H., and Walton R. Patrick. *Southern Literary Culture. A Bibliography of Masters' and Doctors' Theses.* Tuscaloosa: University of Alabama Press, 1955.

Carson, William Glascow Bruce. "The Theatre of the American Frontier. A Bibliographical Essay," *Theatre Research*, I (March, 1958), 14–23.

Catalogue of the Allen A. Brown Collection of Books Relating to the Stage in the Public Library of the City of Boston. Boston: Published by the Trustees, 1919.

Clark, Thomas D. (ed.). *Travels in the Old South. A Bibliography.* 4 vols. Norman, Okla.: University of Oklahoma Press, 1959.

Firkins, Ina Ten Eyck. *Index to Plays 1800–1926.* New York: H. W. Wilson Company, 1927.

———. *Index to Plays Supplement.* New York: H. W. Wilson Company, 1935.

Gilder, Rosamond, and George Freedley. *Theatre Collections in Libraries and Museums. An International Handbook.* London: B. F. Stevens and Brown, Ltd., 1936.

Hamar, Clifford E. "American Theatre History: A Geographical Index," *Educational Theatre Journal*, I (December 1949), 164–94.

Hamer, Philip M. (ed.). *A Guide to Archives and Manuscripts in the United States Compiled for the National Historical Publications Commission.* New Haven: Yale University Press, 1961.

Leary, Lewis. *Articles on American Literature, 1900–1950.* Durham: Duke University Press, 1954.

McDowell, John H. "A Bibliography on Theatre and Drama in American Colleges and Universities 1937–1947," *Speech Monographs*, XVI (November, 1949), 2–124.

Marshall, Thomas F. "Beyond New York: A Bibliography of the 19th-Century American Stage from the Atlantic to the Mississippi," *Theatre Research*, III (1961), 208–17.

Matthews, William (ed.). *American Diaries; An Annotated Bibliography of American Diaries Written Prior to the Year 1861.* Berkeley: University of California Press, 1945.

Mauk, Ernest P. "Addenda to AETA Monograph No. 1: Theatre
Arts Publications in The United States, 1947–1952," *Educational
Theatre Journal*, XIV (December, 1962), 324–31.
Melnitz, William W. *Theatre Arts Publications in the United States
1947–1952. A Five Year Bibliography. American Educational The-
atre Association Monograph Number 1.* Dubuque, Iowa: William
C. Brown Company, 1959.
Santaniello, A. E. *Theatre Books in Print.* New York: The Drama
Book Shop, 1963.

B. UNPUBLISHED THESES AND DISSERTATIONS

Arnold, Wayne William. "Sol Smith: Chapters for a Biography." Un-
published Master's thesis, Washington University, 1939.
Bailey, Frances Margaret. "A History of the Stage in Mobile, Alabama from 1824–1850." Unpublished Master's thesis, State University of Iowa, 1934.
Blackburn, Margaret. "The Stage in St. Louis, Missouri, After 1850."
Unpublished Master's thesis, State University of Iowa, 1927.
Blesi, Marius. "The Life and Letters of Anna Cora Mowatt." Unpublished Doctoral dissertation, University of Virginia, 1938.
Bradford, Clinton William. "The Non-Professional Theater in Loui-
siana. A Survey of Organized and Miscellaneous Theatrical Activ-
ities from the Beginnings to 1900." Unpublished Doctoral disserta-
tion, Louisiana State University, 1951.
Clay, Lucile Naff. "The Lexington Theater from 1800–1840." Un-
published Master's thesis, University of Kentucky, 1930.
Craig, William Scott. "The Theatrical Management of Sol Smith:
Organization, Operation, Methods and Techniques." Unpublished
Doctoral dissertation, University of Illinois, 1963.
Crum, Mabel Tyree. "The History of the Lexington Theatre From
the Beginning To 1860." Unpublished Doctoral dissertation, Uni-
versity of Kentucky, 1956.
Dietz, Mary Martha. "A History of the Theatre in Louisville." Un-
published Master's thesis, University of Louisville, 1921.
Duggar, Mary Morgan. "The Theatre in Mobile 1822–1860." Unpub-
lished Master's thesis, University of Alabama, 1941.
Fenton, Frank. "San Francisco Theater, 1849–1859." Unpublished
Doctoral dissertation, Stanford University, 1942.
Fife, Iline. "The Theatre During the Confederacy." Unpublished
Doctoral dissertation, Louisiana State University, 1949.
Free, Joseph Miller. "Studies in American Theatre History: The
Theatre of Southwestern Mississippi To 1850." Unpublished Doc-
toral dissertation, State University of Iowa, 1941.

Gafford, Lucile. "A History of the St. Charles Theatre in New Orleans, 1835–43." Unpublished Doctoral dissertation, University of Chicago, 1930.

Gray, Wallace Allison. "An Historical Study of Professional Dramatic Activities in Alexandria, Louisiana, From the Beginning to 1920." Unpublished Master's thesis, Louisiana State University, 1948.

Grimsted, David Allen. "A Mirror for Nature: American Theater, 1800–1850." Unpublished Doctoral dissertation, University of California, Berkeley, 1963.

Hadley, Richard Hanna. "The Theatre in Lynchburg, Virginia From Its Beginnings in 1822 to the Outbreak of the Civil War." Unpublished Doctoral dissertation, University of Michigan, 1942.

Hanley, Kathryn Tierney. "The Amateur Theatre in New Orleans Before 1835." Unpublished Master's thesis, Tulane University, 1940.

Hester, Wyoline. "The Savannah Stage." Unpublished Master's thesis, Alabama Polytechnic Institute, 1930.

Hostetler, Paul Smith. "James H. Caldwell: Theatre Manager." Unpublished Doctoral dissertation, Louisiana State University, 1964.

Jones, Jane Elinor. "A History of the Stage in Louisville, Kentucky, From Its Beginnings To 1855." Unpublished Master's thesis, State University of Iowa, 1932.

Kling, Esther Louise. "The New Orleans Academy of Music Theatre, 1853–1861." Unpublished Master's thesis, Louisiana State University, 1960.

Langley, William Osler. "The Theatre in Columbus, Georgia, From 1828 to 1878." Unpublished Master's thesis, Alabama Polytechnic Institute, 1937.

Lindsey, Henry Carlton. "The History of the Theatre in Shreveport, Louisiana, to 1900." Unpublished Master's thesis, Louisiana State University, 1951.

Luttrell, Wanda. "The Theatre of Memphis, Tennessee, From 1829 to 1860." Unpublished Master's thesis, Louisiana State University, 1951.

McKee, Edna H. "History of Theatrical Entertainment in Jackson, Mississippi, From August 1839 to April 1860." Unpublished Master's thesis, Florida State University, 1959.

Meek, Beryl. "A Record of the Theatre in Lexington, Kentucky, From 1799–1850." Unpublished Master's thesis, State University of Iowa, 1930.

Parrott, Frederick James. "The Mid-Nineteenth Century American Theatre 1840–1860. A Survey of Theatre Production, Comment, and Opinion." Unpublished Doctoral dissertation, Cornell University, 1948.

Rietz, Louise Jean. "History of the Theatre of Kansas City, Missouri, From the Beginnings Until 1900." Unpublished Doctoral dissertation, State University of Iowa, 1939.

Ritter, Charles Clifford. "The Theatre in Memphis, Tennessee, From Its Beginning to 1859." Unpublished Doctoral dissertation, State University of Iowa, 1956.

Roppolo, Joseph Patrick. "A History of the American Stage in New Orleans, 1842 to 1845." Unpublished Master's thesis, Tulane University, 1948.

———. "A History of the English Language Theatre in New Orleans, 1845 to 1861." Unpublished Doctoral dissertation, Tulane University, 1950.

Sherman, Susanne Ketchum. "Post-Revolutionary Theatre in Virginia, 1784–1810." Unpublished Master's thesis, William and Mary College, 1950.

Shockley, Martin Staples. "A History of the Theatre in Richmond, Virginia, 1819–1838." Unpublished Doctoral dissertation, University of North Carolina, 1938.

Sparks, Andrew. "A History of the Theatre in Savannah, 1800–1836." Unpublished Master's thesis, University of Georgia, 1940.

Teague, Oran. "The Professional Theater in Rural Louisiana." Unpublished Master's thesis, Louisiana State University, 1949.

Varnado, Alban Fordesh. "A History of Theatrical Activity in Baton Rouge, Louisiana, 1819–1900." Unpublished Master's thesis, Louisiana State University, 1947.

Wooten, Denham Lee. "Annals of the Stage in Little Rock, Arkansas, 1834–1890." Unpublished Master's thesis, Columbia University, 1935.

C. GENERAL WORKS

Brown, Thomas Allston. *History of the American Stage. Containing Biographical Sketches of Nearly every Member of the Profession that has Appeared On the American Stage, from 1733 to 1870.* New York: Dick and Fitzgerald, 1870.

Coad, Oral Sumner and Edwin Mims, *The American Stage.* Vol. XIV of Ralph Henry Gabriel, *et al* (eds.), *The Pageant of America. A Pictorial History of the United States.* New Haven: Yale University Press, 1929.

Crawford, Mary Caroline. *The Romance of the American Theatre.* Boston: Little, Brown, and Company, 1913.

Dunlap, William. *A History of the American Theatre and Anecdotes of the Principal Actors.* 2nd ed. 3 vols. in 1. New York: Burt Franklin, 1963.

Hewitt, Barnard. *Theatre U. S. A. 1668 to 1957.* New York: McGraw-

Hill Book Company, 1959.

Hornblow, Arthur. *A History of the Theatre in America From Its Beginnings to the Present Time.* 2 vols. Philadelphia: J. B. Lippincott Company, 1919.

Hughes, Glenn. *A History of the American Theatre, 1700–1950.* New York: Samuel French, 1951.

Mayorga, Margaret G. *A Short History of the American Drama. Commentaries on Plays Prior to 1920.* New York: Dodd, Mead and Company, 1932.

Morris, Lloyd. *Curtain Time. The Story of the American Theater.* New York: Random House, 1953.

Quinn, Arthur Hobson. *A History of the American Drama From the Beginning to the Civil War.* 2nd ed. New York: F. S. Crofts and Company, 1946.

Rankin, Hugh Frank. *The Theater in Colonial America.* Chapel Hill: University of North Carolina Press, 1965.

Seilhamer, George Overcash. *History of the American Theatre.* 3 vols. Philadelphia: Globe Printing House, 1888–1891.

Wemyss, Francis Courtney. *Wemyss' Chronology of the American Stage, from 1752 to 1852.* New York: William Taylor and Company, 1852.

D. MONOGRAPHS AND BIOGRAPHIES

Adams, Henry W. *The Montgomery Theatre, 1822–1835.* Tuscaloosa: University of Alabama Press, 1955.

Alger, William Rounseville. *Life of Edwin Forrest, the American Tragedian.* 2 vols. Philadelphia: J. B. Lippincott and Company, 1877.

Ambler, Charles H. (ed.). *The Life and Diary of John Floyd, Governor of Virginia, An Apostle of Secession, and the Father of the Oregon Country.* Richmond: Richmond Press, Inc., 1918.

Barnes, Eric Wollencott. *The Lady of Fashion. The Life and the Theatre of Anna Cora Mowatt.* New York: Charles Scribner's Sons, 1954.

Baroncelli, Joseph Gabrièl de. *Le Théatre Français à la Nouvelle Orleans.* New Orleans: Muller, 1906.

Bondurant, Agnes M. *Poe's Richmond.* Richmond: Garrett and Massie, 1942.

Bowen, Elbert R. *Theatrical Entertainments in Rural Missouri Before the Civil War.* ("University of Missouri Studies," Vol. XXXII.) Columbia: University of Missouri Press, 1959.

Brown, Thomas Allston. *A History of the New York Stage From the First Performance in 1732 to 1901.* 3 vols. New York: Dodd, Mead and Company, 1903.

Capers, Gerald Mortimer. *The Biography of a River Town; Memphis: Its Heroic Age.* Chapel Hill: University of North Carolina Press, 1939.

Carson, William Glascow Bruce. *Managers in Distress. The St. Louis Stage, 1840–1844.* St. Louis: St. Louis Historical Documents Foundation, 1949.

———. *The Theater on the Frontier. The Early Years of the St. Louis Stage.* Chicago: University of Chicago Press, 1932.

Casseday, Benjamin. *The History of Louisville, From its Earliest Settlement Till the Year 1852.* Louisville: Hull and Brother, 1852.

Clark, Asia Booth. *The Elder and the Younger Booth.* Boston: James R. Osgood and Company, 1882.

Coleman, Elizabeth Tyler. *Priscilla Cooper Tyler and the American Scene, 1816–1889.* Tuscaloosa: University of Alabama Press, 1955.

Davenport, Francis Garvin. *Ante-Bellum Kentucky. A Social History, 1800–1860.* Oxford, Ohio: The Mississippi Valley Press, 1943.

———. *Cultural Life in Nashville on the Eve of the Civil War.* Chapel Hill: University of North Carolina Press, 1941.

Dick, Everett. *The Dixie Frontier. A Social History of the Southern Frontier from the First Transmontane Beginnings to the Civil War.* New York: Alfred A. Knopf, 1948.

Dunn, Esther Cloudman. *Shakespeare in America.* New York. The Macmillan Company, 1939.

"Falconbridge" [Jonathan Falconbridge Kelly]. *Dan. Marble; A Biographical Sketch of that Famous and Diverting Humorist, with Reminiscences, Comicalities, Anecdotes, etc., etc.* New York: Dewitt and Davenport, 1851.

Fletcher, Edward Garland. *The Beginnings of the Professional Theatre in Texas.* ("The University of Texas Bulletin," No. 3621.) Austin: University of Texas Press, 1936.

Ford, George D. *These Were Actors. A Story of the Chapmans and the Drakes.* New York: Library Publishers, 1955.

Gallegly, Joseph. *Footlights on the Border. The Galveston and Houston Stage Before 1900.* The Hague, Netherlands: Mouton and Company, 1962.

Graham, Philip. *Showboats. The History of an American Institution.* Austin: University of Texas Press, 1951.

Hackett, James Henry. *Notes and Comments upon Certain Plays and Actors of Shakespeare, with Criticism and Correspondence.* New York: Carleton, Publisher, 1863.

Hodge, Francis. *Yankee Theatre. The Image of America on the Stage, 1825–1850.* Austin: University of Texas Press, 1964.

Holland Memorial [William Brown Maclay?]. *Sketch of the Life of George Holland, The Veteran Comedian, with Dramatic Reminis-*

cences, Anecdotes, &c. New York: T. H. Morrell, 1871.

Hoole, William Stanley. *The Ante-Bellum Charleston Theatre.* Tuscaloosa: University of Alabama Press, 1946.

Hunter, Alexander. *New National Theater, Washington, D. C. A Record of Fifty Years.* Washington: R. O. Polkinham and Son, 1885.

Ireland, Joseph Norton. *A Memoir of the Professional Life of Thomas Abthorpe Cooper.* New York: The Dunlap Society, 1888.

———. *Mrs. Duff* [Mary Ann Duff]. Boston: James R. Osgood and Company, 1882.

James, Reese Davis. *Old Drury of Philadelphia. A History of the Philadelphia Stage 1800–1835. Including the Diary or Daily Account Book of William Burke Wood, Co-Manager with William Warren of the Chesnut Street Theatre, familiarly known as Old Drury.* Philadelphia: University of Pennsylvania Press, 1932.

Johnson, Guion Griffis. *Ante-Bellum North Carolina. A Social History.* Chapel Hill: University of North Carolina Press, 1937.

Kendall, John Smith. *The Golden Age of the New Orleans Theater.* Baton Rouge: Louisiana State University Press, 1952.

Kimmel, Stanley. *The Mad Booths of Maryland.* New York: The Bobbs-Merrill Company, 1940.

Le Gardeur, René J. *The First New Orleans Theatre 1792–1803.* New Orleans: Leeward Books, 1963.

Mayo, Bernard. "Lexington: Frontier Metropolis," *Historiography and Urbanization. Essays in American History in Honor of W. Stull Holt,* ed. Eric F. Goldman. Baltimore: The Johns Hopkins Press, 1941.

Moody, Richard. *America Takes the Stage. Romanticism in American Drama and Theatre, 1750–1900.* Bloomington: Indiana University Press, 1955.

———. *Edwin Forrest. First Star of the American Stage.* New York: Alfred A. Knopf, 1960.

Moses, Montrose Jonas. *The Fabulous Forrest. The Record of an American Actor.* Boston: Little, Brown, and Company, 1929.

———. *Famous Actor-Families in America.* New York: Thomas Y. Crowell and Company, 1906.

Nolle, Alfred Henry. *The German Drama on the St. Louis Stage.* Philadelphia: University of Pennsylvania Press, 1917.

Northall, William Knight (ed.). *Life and Recollections of Yankee Hill: Together With Anecdotes and Incidents of His Travels.* New York: W. F. Burgess, 1850.

Odell, George Clinton Densmore. *Annals of the New York Stage.* 15 vols. New York: Columbia University Press, 1927–1949.

Patrick, John Max. *Savannah's Pioneer Theater from Its Origins to 1810.* Athens: University of Georgia Press, 1953.

Rees, James. *The Dramatic Authors of America.* Philadelphia: G. B. Zeiber and Company, 1845.

———. *The Life of Edwin Forrest with Reminiscences and Personal Recollections.* Philadelphia: T. B. Peterson and Brothers, 1874.

Rourke, Constance. *American Humor. A Study of the National Character.* New York: Harcourt, Brace and Company, 1931.

———. *The Roots of American Culture and Other Essays.* New York: Harcourt, Brace and Company, 1942.

Rusk, Ralph Leslie. *The Literature of the Middle Western Frontier.* 2 vols. New York: Columbia University Press, 1825.

Sonneck, Oscar George. *Early Opera in America.* New York: G. Schirmer, 1915.

Strang, Lewis Clinton. *Players and Plays of the Last Quarter Century.* 2 vols. Boston: L. C. Page and Company, 1902.

Wade, Richard C. *The Urban Frontier. The Rise of Western Cities, 1790–1830.* Cambridge: Harvard University Press, 1959.

Weisert, John Jacob. *The Curtain Rose: A Checklist of Performances at Samuel Drake's City Theatre and Other Theatres at Louisville from the Beginning to 1843.* Louisville: University of Louisville Press, 1958.

———. *A Large and Fashionable Audience: A Checklist of Performances at the Louisville Theatre 1846 to 1866.* Louisville: University of Louisville Press, 1955.

———. *Mozart Hall: 1851 to 1866. A Checklist of Attractions at a Minor Theatre of Louisville, Kentucky, Known Variously as Mozart Hall, Wood's Theatre, or The Academy of Music.* Louisville: University of Louisville Press, 1962.

Willis, Eola. *The Charleston Stage in the XVIII Century. With Social Settings of the Time.* Columbia, S.C.: The State Company, 1924.

Wilson, Arthur Herman. *A History of the Philadelphia Theatre 1835 to 1855.* Philadelphia: University of Pennsylvania Press, 1935.

Winter, William. *Brief Chronicles.* 3 vols. New York: The Dunlap Society, 1889.

Wood, Alice I. Perry. *The Stage History of Shakespeare's King Richard the Third.* New York: Columbia University Press, 1909.

Wright, Richardson Little. *Revels in Jamaica, 1682–1838.* New York: Dodd, Mead, and Company, 1937.

E. PERIODICAL ARTICLES

Armistead, Margaret Beauchamp. "The Savannah Theater—Oldest in America," *Georgia Review*, VII (Spring, 1953), 50–54.

Barker, Meta. "Some Highlights of the Old Atlanta Stage," *Atlanta Historical Bulletin*, I (January, 1929), 33–50.

Bernard, Bayle. "Early Days of the American Stage, Being a Selection from the Papers of One of its Managers [John Bernard]," *Tallis's Dramatic Magazine and General Theatrical and Musical Review*, I (December, 1850), 45–48.

Bogner, Harold F. "Sir Walter Scott in New Orleans, 1818–1832," *Louisiana Historical Quarterly*, XXI (April, 1938), 420–517.

Bowen, Elbert R. "The German Theatre of Early Rural Missouri," *Missouri Historical Review*, XLVI (January, 1952), 157–61.

———. "Thespian Societies in Rural Missouri," *Bulletin of the Missouri Historical Society*, XIV (July, 1958), 331–56.

"Colly Cibber" [James Rees]. "Biography of the Late Miss Jane Placide," *Dramatic Mirror and Literary Companion*, I (October 16, 1841), 73–74; (October 23, 1841), 87–88; (November 6, 1841), 104.

Cleaton, Edward Allen. "Placide Players and Puritanism" *The Reviewer*, V (July, 1925), 94–97.

Davenport, Francis Garvin, "Culture Versus Frontier in Tennessee, 1825–1850," *Journal of Southern History*, V (February, 1939), 18–33.

Dodd, William G. "Theatrical Entertainment in Early Florida," *Florida Historical Quarterly*, XXV (October, 1946), 121–74.

Free, Joseph Miller. "The Ante-Bellum Theatre of the Old Natchez Region," *Journal of Mississippi History*, V (January, 1943), 14–27.

Gates, William Bryan. "Performances of Shakespeare in Ante-Bellum Mississippi," *Journal of Mississippi History*, V (January, 1943), 28–37.

———. "The Theatre in Natchez," *Journal of Mississippi History*, III (April, 1941), 71–129.

Hamilton, William B. "The Theater in the Old Southwest: The First Decade at Natchez," *American Literature*, XII (January, 1941), 471–85.

Harrison, Fairfax. "Stage Plays Prohibited," *Virginia Magazine of History and Biography*, XXXI (July, 1923), 270–71.

Henderson, Archibald. "Early Drama and Amateur Entertainment in North Carolina," *The Reviewer*, V (October, 1925), 68–77.

———. "Early Drama and Professional Entertainment in North Carolina," *The Reviewer*, V (July, 1925), 47–57.

———. "Strolling Players in Eighteenth Century North Carolina," *Carolina Playbook*, XV (March, 1942), 24–26; (June, 1942), 43–46.

Hill, Raymond S. "Memphis Theatre, 1836–1846," *West Tennessee Historical Society Papers*, IX (1955), 48–58.

Hogan, William Ransom. "The Theater in the Republic of Texas," *Southwest Review*, XIX (July, 1934), 374–401.

Hoole, William Stanley. "Charleston Theatres," *Southwest Review*, XXV (January, 1940), 193–204.

————. "Charleston Theatricals During the Tragic Decade, 1860–1869," *Journal of Southern History*, XI (November, 1945), 538–47.

————. "Shakespeare on the Ante-Bellum Charleston Stage," *Shakespeare Association Bulletin*, XXI (January, 1946), 37–45.

————. "Two Famous Theatres of the Old South," *South Atlantic Quarterly*, XXXVI (July, 1937), 273–77.

Hostetler, Paul Smith. "Studies in Southern Theatre History: I. The Influence of New Orleans on Early Nineteenth Century Theatre," *Southern Speech Journal*, XXIX (Fall, 1963), 12–19.

Hunt, Douglas Lucas. "The Nashville Theatre, 1830–1840," *Birmingham-Southern College Bulletin*, XXVIII (May, 1935).

Johnston, Winifred. "Early Theatre in the Spanish Borderlands," *Mid-America*, XIII, n.s. II (October, 1930), 121–31.

Land, Robert Hunt. "The First Williamsburg Theatre," *William and Mary Quarterly*, 3rd ser. V (July, 1948), 359–74.

Law, Robert Adger. "News for Bibliophiles," *The Nation*, XCVI (February 27, 1913), 201.

Lippman, Monroe. "Uncle Tom and His Poor Relations: American Slavery Plays," *Southern Speech Journal*, XXVIII (Spring, 1963), 183–97.

Lyle, Beverly, and Claude L. Shaver. "Early English Drama in New Orleans," *Quarterly Journal of Speech*, XXV (April, 1939), 305–9.

McCutcheon, Roger P. "The First English Plays in New Orleans," *American Literature*, XI (May, 1939), 183–99.

Moehlenbrock, Arthur Henry. "The German Drama on the New Orleans Stage," *Louisiana Historical Quarterly*, XXVI (April, 1943), 361–627.

Moffatt, Walter. "First Theatrical Activities in Arkansas," *Arkansas Historical Quarterly*, XII (Winter, 1953), 327–32.

O'Brien, Frank P. "Passing of the Old Montgomery Theatre," *Alabama Historical Quarterly*, III (Spring, 1941), 8–14.

Price, Nellie Warner. "Le Spectacle de la Rue St. Pierre," *Louisiana Historical Quarterly*, I (January, 1918), 215–23.

Ritter, Charles C. " 'The Drama in Our Midst' The Early History of the Theater in Memphis," *West Tennessee Historical Society Papers*, XI (1957), 5–35.

Roppolo, Joseph Patrick. "Audiences in New Orleans Theatres, 1845–1861," *Tulane Studies in English*, II (1950), 121–35.

————. "Local and Topical Plays in New Orleans, 1806–1865," *Tulane*

Studies in English, IV (1954), 91–124.

———. "Uncle Tom in New Orleans: Three Lost Plays," *New England Quarterly*, XXVII (June, 1954), 213–26.

Rowland, Thomas B. "Norfolk Theatres of the Olden Time," *Lower Norfolk County Virginia Antiquary*, II (1898), 102.

Rulfs, Donald J. "The Ante-Bellum Professional Theater in Fayette-ville," *North Carolina Historical Review*, XXXI (April, 1954), 125–33.

———. "The Ante-Bellum Professional Theater in Raleigh," *North Carolina Historical Review*, XXIX (July, 1952), 344–58.

———. "The Professional Theater in Wilmington, 1858–1930," *North Carolina Historical Review*, XXVIII (April, 1951), 119–36.

Sherman, Susanne Ketchum. "Thomas Wade West, Theatrical Impressario, 1790–1799," *William and Mary Quarterly*, 3rd ser. IX (January, 1952), 10–28.

Shockley, Martin Staples. "American Plays in the Richmond Theatre, 1819–1838," *Studies in Philology*, XXXVII (January, 1940), 100–19.

———. "First American Performances of English Plays in Richmond Before 1819," *Journal of Southern History*, XIII (February, 1947), 91–105.

———. "The Proprietors of Richmond's New Theatre of 1819," *William and Mary Quarterly Historical Magazine*, 2nd ser. XIX (July, 1939), 302–8.

———. "The Richmond Theatre, 1780–1790," *Virginia Magazine of History and Biography*, LX (July, 1952), 421–36.

———. "Shakespeare's Plays in the Richmond Theatre, 1819–1838," *Shakespeare Association Bulletin*, XV (April, 1940), 88–94.

Smither, Nelle Kroger. "Charlotte Cushman's Apprenticeship in New Orleans," *Louisiana Historical Quarterly*, XXXI (October, 1948), 973–80.

———. "A History of the English Theatre at New Orleans, 1806–1842," *Louisiana Historical Quarterly*, XXVIII (January, 1945), 85–276; (April, 1945), 361–572.

Spell, Lota M. "The Theatre in Texas Before the Civil War," *The Texas Monthly*, V (April, 1930), 291–301.

Stokes, D. Allen. "The First Theatrical Season in Arkansas: Little Rock, 1838–1839," *Arkansas Historical Quarterly*, XXIII (Summer, 1964), 166–83.

Tregle, Joseph G. "Early New Orleans Society: A Reappraisal," *Journal of Southern History*, XVIII (February, 1952), 20–36.

Warren, Harris Gaylord. "Vignettes of Culture in Old Claiborne," *Journal of Mississippi History*, XX (July, 1958), 125–46.

Weisert, John Jacob. "Beginnings of German Theatricals in Louisville," *Filson Club History Quarterly*, XXVI (October, 1952), 347–59.

———. "Beginnings of the Kentucky Theatre Circuit," *Filson Club Historical Quarterly*, XXXIV (July, 1960), 264–85.

Wyatt, Edward A. "Three Petersburg Theatres," *William and Mary College Quarterly Historical Magazine*, XXI (April, 1941), 83–110.

INDEX

[311]

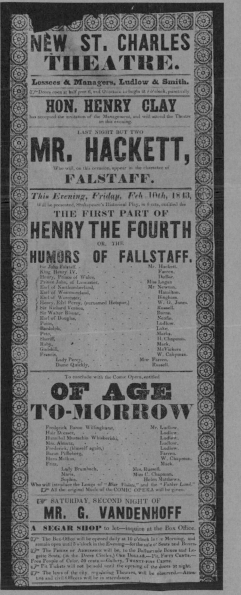